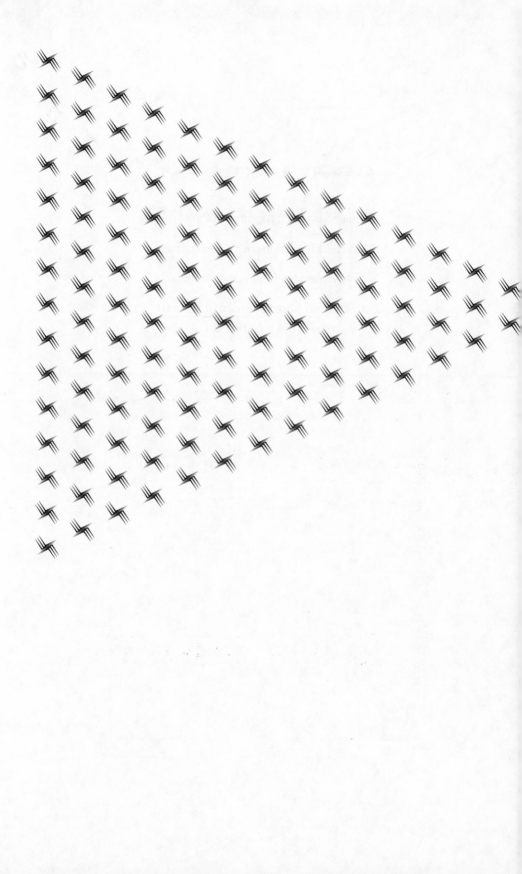

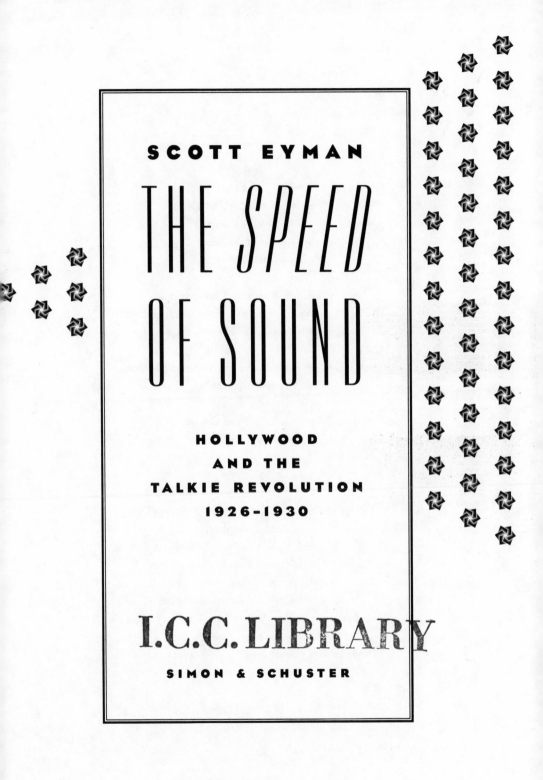

SCOTT EYMAN

THE *SPEED* OF SOUND

HOLLYWOOD AND THE TALKIE REVOLUTION 1926-1930

SIMON & SCHUSTER

SIMON & SCHUSTER

Rockefeller Center

1230 Avenue of the Americas

New York, NY 10020

Simon & Schuster and colophon are registered trademarks

of Simon & Schuster Inc.

Designed by Jeanette Olender

Manufactured in the United States of America

1   3   5   7   9   10   8   6   4   2

Library of Congress Cataloging-in-Publication Data

Eyman, Scott, date.

The speed of sound: Hollywood and the talkie revolution,

1926–1930 / Scott Eyman.

p.   cm.

Includes bibliographical references and index.

1. Sound motion pictures—United States—History.   I. Title.

PN1995.7.E96   1997

791.43'0973—dc20   96-45941   CIP

ISBN 0-684-81162-6

For

Kevin Brownlow

David Gill

and

Patrick Stanbury

You see, the film studio...is really the palace of the sixteenth century. There one sees what Shakespeare saw: the absolute power of the tyrant, the courtiers, the flatterers, the jesters, the cunningly ambitious intriguers. There are fantastically beautiful women, there are incompetent favorites. There are great men who are suddenly disgraced. There is the most insane extravagance, and unexpected parsimony over a few pence. There is enormous splendour which is a sham; and also horrible squalor hidden behind the scenery. There are vast schemes, abandoned because of some caprice. There are secrets which everybody knows and no one speaks of. There are even two or three honest advisers. These are the court fools, who speak the deepest wisdom in puns, lest they should be taken seriously. They grimace, and tear their hair privately, and weep.

Christopher Isherwood
Prater Violet

The scene that began to close the door on silent movies:
Al Jolson and Eugénie Besserer in *The Jazz Singer.*
AUTHOR'S COLLECTION

Prologue

It is the muggy afternoon of August 30, 1927. On the newly constructed soundstage of the Warner Bros. Studio on Sunset Boulevard, Al Jolson is industriously, unwittingly, engaged in the destruction of one great art and the creation of another.

The scene: a son's homecoming. The man universally recognized as the greatest entertainer of his day is singing Irving Berlin's "Blue Skies" to Eugénie Besserer, playing his mother. After an initial chorus sung with Jolson's usual nervy bravura, he suddenly stops. He asks his mother if she likes the song, tells her he'd rather please her than anybody. The floodgates open and the hilarious babbling begins:

"Mama, darlin', if I'm a success in this show, well, we're gonna move from here. Oh yes, we're gonna move up in the Bronx. A lot of nice green grass up there and a whole lot of people you know. There's the Ginsbergs, the Guttenbergs, and the Goldbergs. Oh, a whole lotta Bergs, I don't know 'em all.

"And I'm gonna buy you a nice black silk dress, Mama. You see Mrs. Friedman, the butcher's wife, she'll be jealous of you . . . Yes, she will. You see if she isn't. And I'm gonna get you a nice pink dress that'll go with your brown eyes . . ."

While the crew stands transfixed, Jolson keeps talking, a torrent of unaccustomed words in the midst of a predominantly silent film, a medium that has proudly subsisted on pantomime or, at the most, synchronized underscoring, sound effects, and a laconic word or two. But now every word that Jolson says is being recorded by a single large, black, cylindrical microphone a foot above his head, which transmits the sound to a 16-inch wax disc spinning at $33\frac{1}{3}$ revolutions a minute.

Singing has never been a trial for Al Jolson; it is life that is difficult, and carrying a picture, a family drama mixed with a rough approximation of a backstage musical before backstage musicals are invented, has been causing him enormous anxiety. Only four years before, he walked out on a silent film for D. W. Griffith because of nerves, and the desperate volubility with which Jolson is haranguing Besserer may well be the result of an adrenaline rush of pure fear.

Certainly, costar May McAvoy has observed a much quieter, needier man than will ever be on public view in later years. "Act like he knew it all?" asked McAvoy. "Oh no. Never! He was the most cooperative person, and just darling." Jolson leans on McAvoy, an experienced actress who has worked for leading directors such as Ernst Lubitsch. After most scenes, he asks "How'd I do? Was I all right? Please tell me. Let me know. Let's do it over again if it wasn't good."

Production of *The Jazz Singer* had actually begun two months earlier. While Jolson is out of town fulfilling a nightclub engagement, Warners begins production with location scenes in New York that don't require his presence. Meanwhile, the Warner studio on Sunset Boulevard gears up for sound with difficulty, for the studio is stretched thin financially.

"I ordered $40 worth of parts to build a sound-mixing panel," Warner Bros. technician William Mueller will remember years later, "but the man wouldn't leave [the parts] until he got his money. I paid him out of my own pocket only to be told by the studio purchasing agent, Jack Warner's brother-in-law, that I probably wouldn't get my money back. They also demanded that I return what I had left from a $500 cash advance so they could meet the payroll that week."

Likewise, Mueller and Nathan Levinson, Western Electric's man in Hollywood, knew they needed $10,000 to build proper sound facilities and had taken an entire morning to convince Jack Warner to spend the money. He finally agreed, then left for lunch. Knowing their man, Levinson and Mueller got the studio superintendent to clear the necessary area and began construction. "When Jack came back two hours later, he told us he'd changed his mind, but by that time it was too late."

The "Blue Skies" sequence is business as usual for *The Jazz Singer*.

All the sound scenes are being made as separate little films, after the surrounding silent footage has been shot. With one exception, the sound sequences are shot within nine consecutive days beginning August 17, and each of them is given its own production code number on the schedule sheets. (Warners might be thinking about eventually releasing them separately as short subjects should Sam Warner's crazy advocacy of feature-length sound films not work out. It is also possible that this is simply because Vitaphone, the name of their sound system, is a separate production entity.)

The sound scenes are usually shot in the afternoon, from 1 to 5 P.M., with three cameras. Work throughout the rest of the studio is suspended while the production staff gathers to listen to Jolson give what amounts to free concerts.

Shooting of the sound sequences begins with "It All Depends on You," completed in seven takes; "Mother of Mine," shot on August 18, in only two; "Mammy," shot that same day in three takes; and so on. The last number is "Blue Skies," which replaces "It All Depends on You." It is the only scene with any meaningful dialogue beyond Jolson's catchphrase "You ain't heard nothin' yet!" Aside from its comfortable position in the arsenal of Jolson hits, "Blue Skies" is a favorite of the Warners; it has already been performed twice in their Vitaphone sound shorts within the last year.

In later years, sound engineer George Groves asserts that Jolson's cheerful speech to his movie mother is *purely* ad-lib . . . without any rehearsal. Everybody just held their breath." Likewise, head engineer Stanley Watkins says that "Jolson was to sing, but there was to be no dialogue . . . when the picture was being made he insisted on ad-libbing in a couple of places. Sam Warner managed to persuade his brothers to leave the scenes in. 'It won't do any harm,' [Sam said.] In my opinion it was a put-up job between Sam Warner and Jolson."

Yet, technician William Mueller will have a diametrically opposed recollection and spins a remarkably involved conspiratorial tale: "When the songs went well, someone—I don't remember who— decided to have a talking sequence as well. Jolson absolutely would not do it. He said he was a singer and not an actor. He thought it would ruin his career and even offered to pay Warners the money they had already spent to get out of it.

"Finally, they got him to make a test. Then they framed him. While the director and assistant director went to his house to tell him how wonderful it was, they had the prop man view the dailies ... He rushed out to Jolson's house, burst in, and raved about the films. Then he said that [George] Jessel had sneaked in to watch and was very excited about it. He said that Jessel, knowing that Jolson wanted out, also had gone to Jack Warner and offered to do the film for nothing. That did it. Jolson couldn't stand that, so he agreed to do [the scene] himself."

Certainly, no such scene and no such dialogue exist in the script ["*224. Full Shot Room.* Sara walks over to the piano as Jack sits down and starts to play a jazzy tune. He gets through several bars when the front door opens and the cantor appears. He hesitates at the unwonted sounds coming from his cherished piano."]. The game but dazed look of Eugénie Besserer indicates a performer without the vaguest idea of where the scene is going.

But, realistically, the moment can't be completely ad-libbed. Jolson is not actually playing the piano—the daily production report reveals that a studio musician named Bert Fiske is actually playing off camera, while Jolson mimes at the keyboard. During Jolson's monologue, Fiske drops the volume and vamps, making room for Jolson's speech, a process that demands at least some rehearsal to check sound balances.

The truth behind this scene that did so much to change the world in spite of its giddy banality lies in an article for the *Motion Picture News* of July 8. Director Alan Crosland is just finishing up location work in New York, and Jolson has not yet arrived in Hollywood. Journalist Edwin Schallert writes that Warner Bros. is "planning to use dialogue in certain scenes of this production—dialogue with musical accompaniment ... the scenes in which [talking] will be used will probably be those between Jolson and his father."

Warners, then, has simply switched the dialogue to a scene between Jolson and his mother, indulging their nervous star to the extent of not giving him specific dialogue to memorize. If the scene doesn't work, it can always be cut.

With the "Blue Skies" sequence, production is completed. The background musical score for the silent footage is recorded in only three days (September 12–14). The studio quickly prepares a trailer for the film, hosted by actor John Miljan, who introduces clips from key dramatic passages in the film with a hilariously feigned enthusiasm ("Oh, Mammy, how that bird can warble! . . . "). Sam and Jack Warner withhold any footage of Jolson actually singing, the essential reason for the film's existence. By the end of September, *The Jazz Singer* is almost ready for release.

Jolson singing "Blue Skies" and extemporizing about the Goldbergs, the Ginsbergs, and the Guttenbergs would not be cut; indeed, the scene will be the centerpiece of the film. After his soliloquy, Jolson again launches into "Blue Skies" only to be interrupted by the arrival of Warner Oland, playing his cantor father. As Oland yells "Stop!" the synchronized dialogue ends, and the droning background score begins again. The immediacy of sound, the illusion of life, vanishes, and *The Jazz Singer* once again becomes a silent film with music and sound effects — sagaesque, remote.

By producing a film that slides from sound to silence and back again, the Warner brothers will negatively emphasize silence. This sudden reversion to an abruptly passé convention is far more damaging to the traditions and values of silent cinema than any all-talkie could have been.

The Jazz Singer offers not just music but an effervescent personality projecting itself in words, bursting through the screen to wrap the audience in an exuberant embrace. The picture is a gamble, of course — the brothers have spent $500,000 on a film that can be shown in precisely two theaters in the United States — but, as Sam, Jack, and Harry Warner look at it for the first time, it must seem like the gamble has paid off: the first feature starring the world's most popular entertainer — and in synchronized sound. Surely, triumph is only a month away.

Within three weeks, Sam Warner, who has ramrodded sound past his obstinate brothers, will be suddenly, incomprehensibly dead. *The Jazz Singer,* his best testament, will be acclaimed and settle in for long, successful runs everywhere in the world. Warner Bros. will begin a sudden ascent from a position in the lower third of the industry to highly competitive jostling with MGM and Paramount.

Because of this single scene, made as a flier on a hot summer afternoon, a modest story about a cantor's son who would rather sing Irving Berlin than "Kol Nidre" fires the starting pistol for an unparalleled industrial and aesthetic revolution.

❏ ❏ ❏

Hollywood, 1927.

Silent films — an art impassioned by music, focused by darkness, pure emotion transmitted through light — were at the height of their aesthetic and commercial success.

In the late summer of that last tranquil year, *Beau Geste* and *Seventh Heaven* were finishing up their successful roadshow engagements. *Wings*, William Wellman's World War I epic, was opening, as was Josef von Sternberg's *Underworld*. Paramount announced that they were going to take the mass of footage Erich von Stroheim had shot for *The Wedding March* and make two separate movies out of it. *Variety*'s headline for Dorothy Arzner's new assignment was GIRL DIRECTING CLARA BOW. Mary Pickford was thinking of playing Joan of Arc, and 2,000 girls were vying for the part of Lorelei Lee in *Gentlemen Prefer Blondes*. New York's Cameo Theater was advertising "Emil Jannings in *Passion*. Cooled by Refrigeration."

On La Brea Avenue, the Chaplin studio was just days away from resuming production on *The Circus*, a tortured film that had been on hiatus since December 1926, when Chaplin's wife served him with divorce papers and attached the studio. In Culver City, Ramon Novarro announced that he was quitting movies and entering a monastery. MGM didn't renew Lillian Gish's contract; but, in a not entirely unrelated event, the studio signed Louis B. Mayer to a new five-year deal that could bring him as much as $800,000 annually, making him the highest-paid production head in Hollywood.

And, in a small item, *Variety* reported that Warner Bros. might have as many as eleven theaters equipped to show Vitaphone in another month.

Eight hundred feature films a year were being turned out for an audience of 100 million people who attended 25,000 movie theaters every week. Three-quarters of those theaters were located in small towns, but they took in less than a quarter of the box-office receipts, which amounted to between $1 billion and $1.2 billion a year.

Some 42,000 people were employed in Hollywood. The American

film industry accounted for 82 percent of the world's movies, while the foreign market accounted for 40 percent of Hollywood's total business. The American studios, exclusive of their attached theater chains, were valued at about $65 million.

Despite the presence of big money, Hollywood had retained its alfresco, bucolic atmosphere. Sets for silent films were constructed next to each other, and the photographing of a scene would be punctuated by hammering and sawing going on just out of camera range. The atmosphere tended strongly toward the informal. "When I first came out to Hollywood in 1919," said the cameraman Karl Struss, "I was walking down Hollywood Boulevard and here come Doug [Fairbanks] and Charlie Chaplin, one riding a donkey, the other a horse. They stopped near Highland Avenue — this is around eleven at night — got off the horses and went in. They were having a good time; nothing alcoholic, just fooling around."

Stars and directors were well-paid and well-treated, but otherwise the men who ran the studios could do what they pleased with their employees. While the American Federation of Labor had tried to unionize the studio crafts as early as 1916, and there had been a labor strike in 1918, Hollywood would remain a nonunion town until the Depression.

Within the studios, there was an element of personal pride in making pictures that relied on the visuals rather than the titles. SAY IT WITH PROPS — SAY IT WITH ACTION were signs that hung over scenario writers' desks. Speech was indicated by printed titles that interrupted the picture itself, always an irritant to creative directors. The ideal, of course, was the picture without titles, which was accomplished a few times, once by a director named Joseph De Grasse in a film called *The Old Swimming Hole,* and once by the great F. W. Murnau in his fabled *The Last Laugh*. Further than that, they could not go. Or so they thought.

Even though there were no microphones, actors were not free to mouth any clownish thing that came to mind. "In the silent days, you did learn the lines that you were supposed to speak," said the actor William Bakewell. "But technique-wise, before you spoke an important line, it was important that you register the expression, the thought . . . because the cutter then could have a clean cut there in which to inject the subtitle. In other words, you had to time it, to register enough ahead before you spoke, so that [the title] would fit."

Some actors were less painstaking than others. The child star Frank "Junior" Coghlan remembered making a silent film called *Rubber Tires,* which had a scene where the leading man [Harrison Ford, emphatically not the Harrison Ford of the present day] stops his car and runs across the road to see if he can be of any help to a car that's broken down. Ford walked up to the other actors and said, "Geef geef geef. Geef geef geef. Geef geef geef." Since it was a long shot, not even the director, let alone the audience, could tell the difference, but Ford's lack of participatory spirit startled the other actors.

Even modestly budgeted films provided musical ensembles of two or three pieces on the set — a typical grouping would be organ, violin, and cello. The mood music helped the actors express the emotion of a given scene . . . and helped them block out the construction sounds from nearby sets. For heavily emotional moments, actors would request their favorite lachrymose ballads or tragic arias from opera; for comedies, sprightly, up-tempo jazz numbers.

"I used to have the little orchestra play from *Samson and Delilah,*" remembered the MGM star Anita Page. "The music was one of the reasons that I loved silent pictures much better than talkies. You acted better in silents — talkies had so many more things to worry about. But in silents, you could just float. You moved to the music and you lived the part. You just did it!"

How the director talked the actors through the scene varied with the personality. Madge Bellamy, the star of John Ford's *The Iron Horse,* recalled that "[Allan] Dwan used sarcasm. He would say, for instance, 'To the left, you see your love approaching. You believe that he doesn't love you anymore. He comes up and kisses you tenderly. You burst into tears of happiness and relief — if you can manage it.'

"[Thomas] Ince would have yelled, 'You see him coming. You love him. God, how you love him! What pain you feel — you are in an agony of suspense! He kisses you! What happiness! Cut! Let's do it again!'

"[Frank] Borzage was just as emotional, but quieter. He would weep as he directed. He would say, 'You see him. He means everything to you. He may not love you anymore! He is your whole life! Doesn't he care for you now?' By this time, Borzage would be in tears. 'He kisses you! Oh, what joy!' Frank would be too choked up to go on."

On Tuesday nights around town, the place to be seen was The Coconut Grove, the nightclub at the Ambassador Hotel. The promenading of the stars was the main attraction, despite the ostensible presence of Gus Arnheim's orchestra. Another popular nightspot was The Biltmore Hotel in downtown Los Angeles, where the second Saturday of the month was the occasion for The Mayfair Club. It was a dinner dance, with speakers. "Jack Warner would get up and make his usual wisecracks," recalled Evelyn Brent. "It was a small industry . . . (and) everybody in the business was at those Mayfair dances."

For kicks, people would pile into their cars and head down to Venice to ride the roller coaster. The entertainment at parties was usually a buffet supper, unless it was at Pickfair, in which case it was a formal sit-down dinner. For after-dinner, there was often a screening of a movie, or a new game called charades that swept through the community. Paramount's leading lady Esther Ralston traditionally gave a New Year's Eve party for about 100 people. One year, there was a prize for whoever dressed the youngest. Director Frank Tuttle won the prize when he arrived dressed as an unborn child, complete with umbilical cord.

In Hollywood itself, the Montmartre was the favorite place for lunch, while Musso & Frank's was already in place on Hollywood Boulevard, one door north of where it is now (it would relocate in 1936). Musso's had stiff competition from Henry's, also on Hollywood Boulevard, five doors east of Vine Street. Although the restaurant was named after and run by Henry Bergman, a rotund member of Charlie Chaplin's repertory company, it was common knowledge that Chaplin had financed the establishment. The great comedian would eat there at least one night a week. In keeping with his own culinary tastes, the bill of fare was basic, steaks and chops, immaculately prepared. And, Henry's delivered.

Although the factory town that turned out the movies was largely unpretentious in matters of style, the theaters in which the movies were shown were palaces, baroque fantasies on Moorish/Byzantine/

Oriental themes. The carpeting was plush, the orchestra in the pit superb. The audience walked to their seats through air scented with incense to worship at the cathedral of light, part of a congregation composed of all members of society, in all parts of the world. Silent movies were more than an accomplished popular art; as Lillian Gish often insisted, they were a universal language.

Because of the immensely seductive atmospherics of the overall experience, the silent film had an unparalleled capacity to draw an audience inside it, probably because it demanded the audience use its imagination. Viewers had to supply the voices and sound effects; in so doing, they made the final creative contribution to the film-making process. Silent film was about more than a movie; it was about an experience.

The joining together of a movie with live music and the audience's participation created something that was more than the sum of its parts; in Kevin Brownlow's metaphor, the effect was that of cultural carbons joined in an arc lamp, creating light of extraordinary intensity.

Sound changed *everything*.

It changed how movies were made, of course, but more importantly, it changed what movies *were*.

To take just one example, sound permanently altered the nature of screen comedy: the fizzy surrealism of Mack Sennett, the incredibly expressive pantomime of Chaplin, gave way to the racy cross-talk of Ben Hecht and his confreres. The primarily visual was supplanted by the primarily verbal.

Sound standardized movies, made them less malleable, less open to individual interpretation. Allusion and metaphor were the bedrocks of the silent medium, but dialogue literalized every moment, converted it from subjective to objective.

Sound also changed the character of the men and women who made the movies. Sound demanded writers of dialogue, and it seemed as if anyone with the most modest theatrical or journalistic credentials was imported to Hollywood. Paramount went in so heavily for journalists that their hiring strategy was informally but widely known as the Paramount Fresh Air Fund for New York Newspapermen. Lightweight New York literati became West Coast wage slaves and hated themselves for abandoning what they imagined would have been glorious literary careers. While $50-a-week journalists became grudgingly affluent, veteran actors, writers, and directors used to making $100,000 a year suddenly had their credentials called into question.

And, sound brought the unions to Hollywood, for, along with New York journalists, it brought a mass importation of New York actors and playwrights, all of them members of one union or another who saw no reason why Hollywood should be exempt from the same nominal bargaining agents as New York.

And all of it happened within four short years.

There is no aspect of film history that has been so slighted. After noting the extermination of an art form at the height of its power — something unprecedented in history — the conventional volume gives us a nudge of Jolson, a touch of Lubitsch and Mamoulian, a mention of *All Quiet on the Western Front,* a sorrowing comment on Chaplin's Luddite tendencies, and suddenly it's 1935 and Victor McLaglen is staggering through the fog-shrouded streets of *The Informer.* As a result, most people assume the delightful, if broadly exaggerated, satire of *Singin' in the Rain* is more or less the whole story.

To examine this period of unparalleled industrial change, it is necessary to reverse the perspective, to give a fair, detailed idea of what silents were like to the people who made and watched them, and how talkies permanently changed the creative and personal equations.

As if the art form had an independent consciousness and was determined to flaunt its attributes in the face of imminent extinction, in 1927 and 1928 silent movies exploded in a riot of style, dramatic intensity, and thematic complexity. There were accomplished works of art such as King Vidor's *The Crowd* and von Sternberg's *The Last Command,* eye-popping entertainments like *The Beloved Rogue* and *The Gaucho,* the intense lyrical romanticism of Borzage's *Seventh Heaven* and *Street Angel.*

In most respects, late silent pictures seem more complete than early talkies, so painfully landlocked, so eerily styleless. With few exceptions, we see early talkies as grotesque curios; beginning in 1926, with the first Vitaphone films, audiences saw them as miracles. It is impossible to re-create the sense of wonder that made the public eager to abandon the visual and gestural dynamism of silent film, made them so eager to overlook the crudity of the technology and the stiffness of the first wave of sound films. For audiences of 1926–1930, talkies were what the Lumière films had been for audiences of 1895 — the recording function was paramount; that what was being recorded was of no real dramatic interest was irrelevant.

The conventional wisdom has always been that talkies evolved out of silent films, but sound actually grew up alongside silents. The initially half-witted hybrid thrived in spite of itself, expanding voraciously and choking off the more fragile strain. Talkies were not an evolution, but a mutation, a different art form entirely; as a result, an art form was eliminated and hundreds of careers were extinguished. Major directors were ruined, great stars plummeted.

It is an epic story, full of bewildered losers who exceeded the abilities of their primitive technology and ran out of capital, counterpointed by the triumph of the flamboyant Warner Bros. and of William Fox, whose tremendous commercial success was purchased with full shares of the hubris that eventually destroyed him.

This, then, is the story of a few years in which the way movies were created and watched was totally reinvented. If a conventional biography involves the solving of the mystery of character, then this is a biography of a time — why talkies happened when they did; how they affected Hollywood creatively, socially, and politically; and how the coming of sound led inexorably to the modern movie industry.

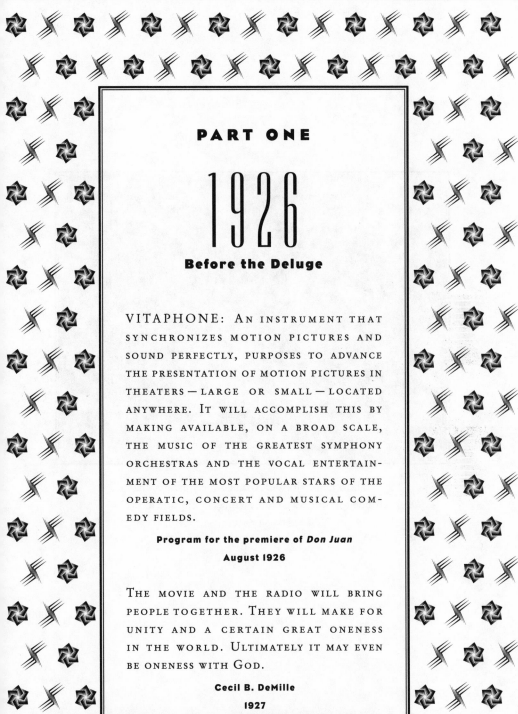

PART ONE

1926

Before the Deluge

VITAPHONE: AN INSTRUMENT THAT SYNCHRONIZES MOTION PICTURES AND SOUND PERFECTLY, PURPOSES TO ADVANCE THE PRESENTATION OF MOTION PICTURES IN THEATERS — LARGE OR SMALL — LOCATED ANYWHERE. IT WILL ACCOMPLISH THIS BY MAKING AVAILABLE, ON A BROAD SCALE, THE MUSIC OF THE GREATEST SYMPHONY ORCHESTRAS AND THE VOCAL ENTERTAIN- MENT OF THE MOST POPULAR STARS OF THE OPERATIC, CONCERT AND MUSICAL COM- EDY FIELDS.

Program for the premiere of *Don Juan*
August 1926

THE MOVIE AND THE RADIO WILL BRING PEOPLE TOGETHER. THEY WILL MAKE FOR UNITY AND A CERTAIN GREAT ONENESS IN THE WORLD. ULTIMATELY IT MAY EVEN BE ONENESS WITH GOD.

Cecil B. DeMille
1927

Talkies before Jolson: Arthur Kingston directing
Grindell-Matthews talking pictures in England in 1922.

CHAPTER I

In New York, in the year of our Lord 1907, the horse-drawn cars on West Street, Chambers Street, and Canal Street and even the cable cars on Broadway were slowly being replaced by electric streetcars. After the trolley passed, pedestrians would walk over, kneel down, and feel the heat coursing silently through the tracks. For those theaters and stores that wanted to be in style, electricity, in the form of the arc light, was *de rigueur*.

It had been only a few years since nickelodeons started showing movies, and some audiences still believed that the actors on the screen were real people behind gauze. On Clinton Street, a theater was actually advertising talking pictures, which turned out to be nothing more or less than two actors in back of the screen improvising dialogue to accompany the action on the translucent screen in front of them. One night a western was on the bill, and an actor moonlighting from the Yiddish theater got excited and began speaking Yiddish. "There was," remembered a reporter who was there, "nearly a riot in the . . . audience."

In 1907, movies were new, but not that new. Likewise, sound movies. Talking pictures existed for years before *The Jazz Singer*. The desire for synchronized sound arose simultaneously with the possibility of projecting images. From the beginning, the cinema abhorred silence; the cinema *needed* some sort of sound, if only to cover up the distracting noises of the projector and the shuffling of the audience. That sound was music; by the mid-1920s, movie theaters were the foremost employers of musicians in the country.

The most obvious method for achieving sound movies was to harness the projector with Edison's phonograph, but this was not as easy as it appeared. Uniform speed was difficult to maintain, and achieving decent amplification was deeply problematic. Not only that, but a reel of film lasted about ten minutes whereas a phonograph record couldn't last more than three or four, so the discs or cylinders had to be specially machined. In addition, as one technician wrote in 1914, "The sound must proceed from the stage . . . at the front of the house while the projector must of necessity be located at the rear. This great distance between the mechanisms . . . makes a positive mechanical connection impossible . . ."

Thomas Edison's obsession with sound had produced the phonograph in 1877, and he was even more determined to take the next logical step: extend his invention into movies. As early as 1891, he had announced that "I hope to be able . . . to throw upon a canvas a perfect picture of anybody, and reproduce his words . . . Should Patti be singing somewhere, this invention will put her full-length picture upon the canvas so perfectly as to enable one to distinguish every feature and expression on her face, see all her actions, and listen to the entrancing melody of her peerless voice. I have already perfected the invention so far as to be able to picture a prize fight—the two men, the ring, the intensely interested faces of those surrounding it —and you can hear the sounds of the blows."

Despite his self-confidence, Edison got nowhere with synchronization at this point. By 1895, he seems to have abandoned work on authentic synchronization and settled for dabbling with what he called the Kinetophone: a Kinetoscope with a built-in phonograph and an earphone. A belt drive connected the two machines, and provided a nonsynchronous musical background to Edison's brief visual vignettes. The Kinetophone never took off, selling only 45 units compared with over a thousand units for the Kinetoscope.

Across the Atlantic, other corporate and creative minds were toying with the problem. Among the most interesting experiments was Léon Gaumont's Chronophone, little one-reel performance films made during 1905–06, most of them directed by Alice Guy Blaché. The Chronophone usually featured headliners from the French music hall. The performers would emerge from behind a curtain and advance toward the camera until they were in a medium shot, cut off at the waist or knees, startlingly close for the period.

They would then launch into their routine, while a sound horn behind the camera recorded the routine at the same time it was being photographed. Because of the essential insensitivity of the apparatus, the actors had to SPEAK THEIR LINES VERY LOUDLY! The projectionist had a motor to control the differential; move the lever in one direction, the projector would speed up and the phonograph slow down; moving the lever in the other direction would slow the picture and speed up the record.

The Chronophone was successfully exhibited in theaters, some holding as many as three thousand people. The necessary amplification was achieved via pneumatic sound boxes powered by a one-horsepower compressor that blew air through the speakers and the sound out into the auditorium. Synchronization would always be an inherent problem for any film/disc system, so the Chronophone's jerry-built system for producing a sufficient volume of sound for a large auditorium would seem to have been another obstacle. Yet, "the sound amplification was terrific," inventor and cameraman Arthur Kingston told film historian Kevin Brownlow. "It was marvelous."

With the marginal differences of electrical recording replacing acoustic recording, and the presence of that crude but workable rheostat, the Chronophone was virtually identical to the Vitaphone that would sweep the world in twenty years: a large disc in supposed sync with a movie projector. Some of the Chronophones survive, notably a reel of a scene from *Cyrano de Bergerac* starring the great French actor Coquelin, who is passionate and quite intelligible.

Concurrently with the Chronophone, but back in America, an invention called the Cameraphone was marketed, with a studio and laboratory on the top of Daly's Theater, on Broadway near Thirtieth Street. The records were made first, at the plant of Columbia Records. At the movie studio, the actors would memorize the prerecorded lines until they could play in perfect synchronization with the record.

John Arnold, who later became head cameraman at Metro-Goldwyn-Mayer, was one of those who made films using the Cameraphone. "We made them by selecting a good phonograph record," he remembered in 1929, "rehearsing the artist . . . in unison with the record until his synchronization was passable, then photographing him." According to William Haddock, a director for the Edison company, the first Cameraphone pictures were exhibited at Sevin Rock, Rhode Island, in 1907.

The Cameraphone used two Edison phonographs with very large horns that alternated for the length of the film. It achieved a fair amount of success in markets as large as Baltimore and Washington, and as small as Johnston and Elkins, West Virginia. "All the operator had to do," wrote projectionist Gustav Petersen, "was to match the two things by listening to the record, reading the lips and watching the motions of the players and keeping the speed of the projector adjusted to the sounds. But that was easier said than done, and if he got a second or so behind or ahead he was in trouble, sometimes till the end of that reel."

Using already existing records such as "Silver Threads Among the Gold" and "Harrigan, That's Me" soon gave way to Cameraphone producing their own records, "record[ing] the sound on records in the old mechanical way," said John Arnold, "then photographing the cast on a set as a moving picture, they singing and playing their roles in time to the phonograph offstage." These films were up to two and three reels long. Cameraphone made films of *The Mikado, The Corsican Brothers, H.M.S. Pinafore,* and personality shorts with people like Eva Tanguay, Blanche Ring, and George M. Cohan.

The system needed two men, one to man the twin phonographs behind the stage, another in the booth, with a buzzer system enabling them to communicate. Gustav Petersen was working the phonograph one night when they started off with an Eva Tanguay short. It began in perfect synchronization but soon the record began moving ahead of the projector. "Speed up!" buzzed Petersen, to no avail. "The record finished," he remembered, "but Miss Tanguay was still on the screen, hopping back and forth, waving her hands, opening and shutting her mouth without a sound coming forth."

The longer the film, the more opportunities for disaster; if the actors were in long shot for a while, chaos was imminent, because they were too far away to allow for lipreading. "By the time we got familiar with all of the cues . . . we had another show come in," groused Petersen. Cameraphone cost exhibitors about $200 a week, not counting the operator's salary. It went out of business in 1910, the victim of what Haddock in 1938 called "friction among the backers of the company."

As early as 1908, Carl Laemmle, then headquartered in Chicago, had imported a machine called the Synchroscope, invented by a German named Jules Greenbaum, that he had seen on one of his frequent trips to Europe. As might be inferred from its name, the Synchroscope attempted to synchronize records with specially made films (". . . It is still the only device which makes the moving picture machine and the phonograph work in perfect unison," read Laemmle's advertising). Initially showing only German-language shorts, Laemmle hired Greenbaum's son to personally install every Synchroscope that he sold.

Although the invention was pretty much limited to towns with either a large German-speaking audience or a taste for classical music — the programs were strictly musical in nature — Laemmle managed to place one in Omaha. Greenbaum's son spoke no English, which, recalled the theater manager, "permitted me to say to him with impunity and delightful safety many very caustic things when the first Synchroscope tests in Omaha did not work out as smoothly as was desired."

The initial Synchroscope price was a hefty $750, but Laemmle managed to get it down to $395 on the low end and $550 on the high end. The business reacted with alarm. "Is the moving picture business about to be revolutionized?" asked *Billboard*. "Has the time arrived when vaudeville houses can put on a whole bill by machinery? . . . I was fairly stunned the other day, when I witnessed a performance that was so startlingly realistic that I don't hesitate to say the questions already are answered in the affirmative."

Yet, cooler heads understood that inventions like the Synchroscope were for novelty only. Silent films were still groping toward a syntax, let alone a comprehensive vocabulary, so sound must have seemed a classic example of putting the cart before the horse. The Synchroscope petered out because, Will Hays claimed, "there were not enough sound films to meet the market's demand. The supply was exhausted. Another reason for failure was that the phonograph records which were used were capable of holding material for only two reels, while the theaters were demanding four and five reels."

What was the caliber of sound that audiences were hearing? William Hornbeck, later to become the editor of *Shane* and *Giant,* recalled a talking picture he saw as a boy in Los Angeles in 1913. "The picture was always out of sync," he remembered. "The sound did not match the photography at all. The screechy sound was pretty bad; you could hardly understand what was being said. [The audience wasn't] pleased with it; they kind of laughed at it because it was so crude that the voices didn't match what the lips were saying."

While the Cameraphone, the Chronophone, the Synchroscope, and various and sundry imitations approached their predestined doom, an unheralded, amazing man named Eugene Augustine Lauste was busily forging the matrix for a revolution that wouldn't happen for another twenty years. The semifamous Lee De Forest would be the nominal Edison of film sound, appropriating, borrowing, doing little real inventing of his own; Lauste would be sound movies' Augustin Le Prince, the man who, in 1890, may very well have been the first to invent the movie projector.

Born in Montmartre in 1856, Lauste had filed fifty-three patents in France before he was twenty-three. By trade he was an electrical engineer who worked for Edison for six years beginning in 1886, and, in 1896, Biograph. The impetus for Lauste's inventions was an article about Alexander Graham Bell's telephone. It occurred to Lauste that sound waves could be photographed and reproduced using a variation on Bell's technology.

In 1904, Lauste built his first complete sound-on-film apparatus. It was primitive but clearly the product of a man who was on the right path. Because there was no amplification system, Lauste's invention utilized earphones rather than speakers, and a selenium cell rather than one of the photoelectric variety. In addition, it was a double system, that is, the sound was on a different piece of film from the picture, and occupied almost the entire strip of 35mm film. In 1907, Lauste was issued an English patent (number 18,057) for what he called the Photocinematophone.

It was, in every way, a master patent, but under English law a patent lasted only sixteen years; by the time sound pictures became commercially viable, Lauste's ideas were in the public domain. In essence, the sound was captured by a microphone and translated into light waves via a light valve, a thin ribbon of sensitive metal over a tiny slit. The sound reaching this ribbon would be converted into light by the shivering of the diaphragm, focusing the resulting light waves through the slit, where it would be photographed on the side of the film, on a strip about a tenth of an inch wide.

"I visited Mr. Lauste every week," remembered George Jones, whose company, London Cinematograph, was financing the inventor, "and saw and heard of his progress, and he got as far so that we could hear the sound through a telephone receiver but could not get the loudspeaker. We went to Paris and tried to get something in that line but failed . . . We paid Mr. Lauste a weekly wage, also all of his expenses and the rent of his shop and house."

Despite the failure of London Cinematograph in 1910, Lauste continued working at his studio at Brixton, outside of London. That year, he was visited by an engineer named Egrot, who recalled in 1930 that "the results [Lauste] obtained were very promising. Listening to the music . . . was as good as listening through [the] telephone . . . He had already records on both principles, variable density and variable area . . . Mr. Lauste was doing everything himself — designs, patterns for casting, all the delicate engineering and precision work, all electrical fitments, coils, transformers, etc. . . . ."

Lauste's work was interrupted by the war and his own poverty, difficulties that were heightened by the traditional indifference of English capital to the economic possibilities of inventions. Lauste did partially demonstrate his invention in 1913 in London: "The machine was set at work, like an ordinary cinematograph," said one contemporary account. "No pictures, however, appeared, but from a great megaphone there came voice sounds, and later the strains of a band. The rays of light pouring from the cinema projector were cut off suddenly. The sounds as suddenly ceased. A moment later the light began to play again, and the speech was resumed at the exact syllable where it was cut off."

According to the *Daily Chronicle* of August 27, 1913, the selections Lauste demonstrated included the sound of a match being struck, a duet on flute and piano, a military band playing "El Capitan," and a little speech by the inventor's son: "Gentlemen, I have great pleasure in giving you a demonstration of this wonderful invention called the Photocinematophone, invented by my father, Mr.

Eugene Lauste, by means of which sound waves are photographed and reproduced on a film by a new process."

In 1914, it seemed that Lauste's run of bad luck was about to end; two wealthy Englishmen agreed to spend $100,000 to equip a modern laboratory, hire some assistants, and give Lauste a full year to perfect his sound-on-film process. The contracts were drawn, but the outbreak of World War I put an end to that particular deal. In truth, Lauste's run of bad luck was just beginning.

"My capital was too limited to make great progress on my invention," he wrote in 1930. "Also, it was very difficult for me to interest anybody in it as at the time nobody would believe such a revolutionary invention was possible. Therefore I had to do the best I could with the means at my command. I knew that it would take considerable money to experiment on the vacuum tube [for amplification] and as I could not then afford to spend any great sum, I decided to turn my attention to work on a loud-speaking telephone . . ." Although he never really got out of the lab with his invention, except for the problem of amplification Lauste had devised the essentials of the talking picture.

Lauste ended up in Bloomfield, New Jersey, philosophically resigned to his fate but insistent about his theoretical accomplishments (his stationery was headed SOUND-FILM ENGINEERING). Almost penniless by the late 1920s, Lauste was given a sinecure by the Bell Laboratories that enabled him to live comfortably in a small cottage. "I think the wine will be good this year," he wrote in 1932 to a friend and supporter, ". . . so when you come out, which we hope will be soon, we will make a very good test of them." This remarkable, unsung man died in 1935.

❑ ❑ ❑

Thomas Edison had his old interest in sound movies reawakened by the Cameraphone experiments. In 1909, Edison staff director William Haddock was told to make no more standard silent pictures but to put himself and his staff at the disposal of Daniel Higham, from the Edison Laboratory at Orange. Their task, wrote Haddock in 1938, was "to do the experimental work on what was to revolutionize the industry, an Edison machine to combine the motion picture and the phonograph."

Actually, it appears that Edison had begun his research a year earlier, in 1908, at his studio on Decatur Avenue in the Bronx. The partial basis for Edison's efforts was an invention by the Frenchman Auguste Baron, who received a French patent in April 1896 for a machine very similar to what Edison would call the Kinetophone, and an American patent in August 1900. How did Edison utilize somebody else's technology and get away with it? "He was Edison," says Robert Gitt, film archivist at UCLA. "He had an awful lot of clout."

As with the Cameraphone, the initial records and pictures for Edison's first system were made separately. Haddock spent weeks convincing his boss that the "only way to get perfect synchronization was to make the picture and the record at the same time." According to Haddock, after successful tests with an actor named Thomas Fortune singing "My Wife's Gone to the Country" on February 1, 1910, the Edison Talking Picture Company opened for business on West Forty-third Street. "The Forty-third Street studio was used for several months and then production was moved to the Bronx studio," wrote Haddock. "But they did not make many pictures there, as Mr. Edison found something more interesting to work on and dropped the 'talkies.' "

A few years later, the mercurial Edison reactivated the project and called it the Kinetophone. After four years and what Edison said was nearly a million dollars in research-and-development costs, he was ready to bring his invention to market. In essence, the Kinetophone was Edison's phonograph hooked up to a projector by means of a silk cord or belt. The spring-driven recording unit with a large recording horn was placed alongside the set and was connected by a belt to the camera. To mark the start of synchronization, two halves of a coconut shell were knocked together in a primitive form of a clapper board.

The Kinetophone was hampered by Edison's odd but chronic habit of misjudging some of his best ideas. When a record was made in those days, the artist usually stood within a foot of the recording horn. When orchestras made records, horns were directly attached to certain instruments in order to direct the sound waves into the recorder. It was nearly impossible to make a record of anybody standing any distance from the horn, yet Edison was trying to reproduce opera and stage drama with a technology that made movement impossible.

The films were shot at about sixteen frames per second on 35mm film, with the sound being captured on soft wax cylinders rather than discs. The films for this second incarnation of the Kinetophone ran about five minutes and fifty-five seconds because that was the length of time it took to photograph 400 feet of film.

Edison worked hard to make the phonograph horn sensitive enough to pick up actors' voices from a distance, but that meant it also picked up noise from the street. Another complication was that the heat from the lights softened the wax used for the phonograph cylinders.

In order to show the films, a large phonograph was placed by the screen, connected by a looping cord that ran over a system of pulleys to the projector in the back of the theater. The projectionist's assistant would line up the filmed striking of the coconut shells with the sound of the knock on the disc. The projectionist would start to crank, and the resulting synchronization was totally controlled by how smoothly the projectionist cranked his machine. Many of the first Kinetophone shorts were dramas and musical numbers deriving from the stage, including scenes from *Faust, Julius Caesar,* and *Il Trovatore.*

On Monday, February 17, 1913, four theaters in New York and seven others from Chicago to St. Louis simultaneously premiered the Kinetophone. The evening began with a man on-screen explaining Edison's latest invention. He ended his introduction by breaking a plate and blowing a whistle. "The distinctive sound of each was heard," reported the *St. Louis Post-Dispatch* the next day. Other performers appeared in the same stage setting, playing "The Last Rose of Summer" and "Way Down Upon the Swanee River."

"The voice reproduction was astonishingly good," reported the *Post-Dispatch,* "and, most convincing of all, the notes of the song seemed to come actually from the singer's own throat . . . The big . . . audience sat literally spellbound before this exhibition . . . when the screen became black for a moment, the Columbia [theater] rang again and again with applause." *The New York Times* reported that the musicians were listened to "with fascinated attention." At one theater, "at the close of the pictures the audience applauded for fifteen minutes . . . New York applauds the talking picture."

Introduced to vaudeville by the powerful United Booking Company, the Kinetophone quickly became quite popular, or at least Edison labored mightily to give that impression. It even inspired knockoff inventions, such as the "Real Life Talking Motion Picture" based on West Thirty-first Street in New York. Kinetophone studios were established in Vienna and St. Petersburg, and among those who appeared in the films were Andrew Carnegie, Thomas Watson, and New York's Mayor Gaynor. In spite of the initial success, Edison realized the system was too primitive. "The talking pictures are very crude as yet," he told the *New York Tribune* in September 1913. "It will take a year to perfect them and my new invention." But Edison didn't have that long.

Variety reported of a Kinetophone show at the Palace Music Hall on May 7 in Chicago that "from the very beginning the house was in an uproar. Persons in the audience mocked the voices, shouted, catcalled and applauded so it was impossible to hear the voices. During the speech some shouted 'Louder' and 'Sit down.' Others clamored for the show to go on." By March, *Variety* was calling the Kinetophone THE SENSATION THAT FAILED. By that time, Edison's only hope was the foreign market, but the outbreak of World War I put an end to that possibility.

The tide had turned, and quickly; *Variety* wrote that "The talking, instead of enhancing the picture, simply annoys . . . The general verdict was that the Edison Pictures are an out-and-out flop." The Kinetophone studio was dismantled and sold. Years later, after Vitaphone had taken the world of show business by storm, surviving technicians who had worked on the Kinetophone would claim that "the Kinetophone was the equal of any sound picture system existing today."

What had happened becomes clear when the Kinetophone recordings preserved at the Library of Congress are examined. The sound is that of a static-filled radio broadcast—the performers are intelligible, but you have to concentrate. What finally makes the invention insupportable is the fact that they're all virtually screaming their lines. Initially funny, it's wearing after five minutes; an entire program of it would be maddening.

The mere fact that Edison had to resort to vaudeville as a means of getting some of his money back, rather than far more lucrative bookings in either nickelodeons or legitimate theaters, is indicative of trouble behind the scenes. Certainly, the sound volume would have been inadequate — the amplifier that had been devised by Daniel Higham increased surface noise as well as volume — and synchronization would have been very difficult to maintain. Just because something works moderately well under the controlled conditions of the lab is no guarantee it will work in the field.

The great Edison had slammed into the same barrier that would stymie all inventors seeking to perfect a film/disc system: the phonograph and the motion picture worked on two separate principles. The phonograph involved a continuous record of vibrations etched onto a wax-coated cylinder; the motion picture involved a discrete series of individual frames that created the illusion of continuous motion by the phenomenon of persistence of vision. Trying to synchronize one unit moving continuously with another unit engaged in stopping and starting some sixteen times a second was a virtual impossibility. Fewer than fifty of the Kinetophone units were sold.

It seems clear that the Patents Company — a trust formed in 1908 that pooled competing motion-picture patent claims and assigned them to Edison — was none too thrilled about one of their own introducing an invention that just might render the rest of the company's product obsolete. There were also rumors of powerful enemies bribing projectionists to throw off synchronization purposely, not that the projectionists would have needed much encouragement — they weren't paid anything extra for what they regarded as additional work.

In short, the Kinetophone — indeed, the entire confluence of sound and cinema — was an idea without a constituency. The abrupt failure of the Kinetophone — it was extinct by 1915, after having been used for the production of about 260 films — meant that the idea of adding sound to movies was regarded as a fool's errand. It had been tried in the marketplace, found wanting, and that was that.

By the mid-1920s, the resistance of exhibitors to spending money on anything technical or experimental was ubiquitous within the industry. "We owned a lot of theaters," said J. J. (Joe) Cohn, production manager at Metro-Goldwyn-Mayer, "and a lot of the theater [managers] said if we made [pictures with] sound, they wouldn't run 'em."

Even Edison was chastened by the failure, and decided that if he couldn't beat them, he would join them. "Americans require a restful quiet in the moving picture theater," he said in May 1926, "and for them talking from the lips of the figures on the screen destroys the illusion ... the idea is not practical. The stage is the place for the spoken word."

Clearly, if sound was going to reappear, it would have to come from outside the industry for which it was intended. Only technicians and theoreticians continued to believe in movies with words. Among the undiscouraged partisans was a man named Austin Lescarboura, who fearlessly ventured an outrageous opinion in 1921: "The talking picture ... is gathering strength in the laboratory. When the proper time comes, it will soon live down its unfortunate past."

CHAPTER 2

In those days, in that time, the largest downtown movie palaces carried symphony orchestras of fifty or more to accompany the films, and a medium-sized neighborhood theater might carry between five and ten musicians. Even the meanest fleapit in the sticks had a piano player.

Take, for instance, one specific fleapit: the Eagle Theater, in the Borough Park section of Brooklyn. It was a small, boxlike place, and about all Abraham Lass, the relief piano player, could hear when the film started was the cracking of nuts. Audiences in the neighborhood theaters were noisy, and children would usually read the subtitles aloud to their mothers or to themselves.

Because air-conditioning hadn't been invented yet, and ventilation was poor, periodically the owner would walk up and down the aisles with a Flit gun that sprayed a sickeningly sweet deodorant. At about 5 P.M., parents would begin wandering through the theater, calling out for their children, who were watching the feature for the third time.

At theaters like this, the musical accompaniment could be as ragged as the architecture. Max Winkler, who ran a cue-sheet business, remembered seeing *War Brides*, a 1916 Alla Nazimova vehicle. For the climactic scene wherein Nazimova committed suicide as a war protest, the pianist played "You Made Me What I Am Today."

In larger theaters, the orchestra conductor had the responsibility of compiling the musical score for a film from large libraries of sheet music: light classics or source music composed especially for stock situations, agitatos for action scenes, and so on. (Prior to Joseph Carl Breil's score for *The Birth of a Nation,* all American film scores seem to have been compiled rather than composed; the practice of composing original scores didn't really take hold until the early 1930s.) Sometimes the conductor followed the cue sheets sent out by the studios; other times, if he thought he could do better, he compiled his own.

Very early, the showcase theaters provided music of considerable sophistication. Accompanying the premiere engagement of Cecil B. DeMille's *Chimmie Fadden* at the Strand Theater in 1915, audiences heard the overture from *Cavelleria Rusticana,* a duet from *La Forza del Destino,* and the sextet from *Lucia di Lammermoor.*

At a showcase theater like the Capitol Theater in New York, the orchestra had two rehearsals a week lasting three and a half hours each, under the direction of musical director William Mendoza. Mendoza would conduct all day Sunday, logging over nine hours on the podium, and each evening show during the week, while his assistant led the matinees. "Every one of the 28 [weekly] performances at the theater is given the same serious attention as would be given in the case of preparation for a symphonic concert," asserted a critic in 1926.

At the Capitol, the orchestra numbered up to eighty-five pieces, and the concertmaster was a young man named Eugene Ormandy.* Soloists included a young Jan Peerce. Erno Rapee, one of the conductors, might give a Sunday-morning Mahler concert for a dollar a ticket.

The impact of the music was enormous. As Robert Sherwood wrote, "I once saw *The Cabinet of Dr. Caligari* in a projection room, with no musical accompaniment, and, while it excited and impressed me profoundly, it didn't quite scare me out of my skin.

"I later saw it in a crowded and substantial theater. At the moment when the heroine woke up suddenly and gazed into the fiendish

---

* Commenting years later on his debut conducting the Philadelphia Orchestra on very short notice, Ormandy said that it had been easy. "Of course," he said, "I knew *Till Eulenspiegel* very well. We played it at the Capitol."

countenance of the maniacal somnambulist, the clarinet player in the theater orchestra emitted a wild, piercing shriek.

"Fear came through my ear then, all right. In fact, the gruesome sound of that clarinet terrifies me to this day . . ."

The largest theaters also offered stage shows in addition to the movie. In a typical presentation, the program would open with an overture — Rossini or Tchaikovsky — followed by a live presentation of about twenty minutes — a revue, one or two vaudeville acts — followed by some shorts, including a cartoon, a two-reel comedy, and some newsreels. Then came the feature. Since all this could add up to a two-and-a-half- or three-hour show, the feature itself was often projected as quickly as possible; records indicate that features such as *The General* were actually projected slightly faster than the twenty-four frames a second that would be considered top speed for silent — or soon, sound — movies.

In second-run or neighborhood houses, the pairings of features could sometimes be ridiculously inappropriate. Josef von Sternberg's *Underworld,* which, in all meaningful essentials created the gangster picture, might be paired with a comedy of marital infidelity like *One Woman to Another.* The Capitol Theater in Allston, Massachusetts, seemed to specialize in bizarre double features consisting of one "art" movie accompanied by a grindingly commercial feature, a system evidently devised as a means of offering something for everyone: Mauritz Stiller's *Hotel Imperial* was accompanied by *Blonde or Brunette* ("Which do men really prefer?"); King Vidor's majestic *The Crowd* was accompanied by a terminally innocuous comedy called *Finder's Keepers,* and von Sternberg's *The Last Command* was preceded by *The Cohens and Kellys in Paris.* Still, you got an awful lot for your admission price: 30 to 75 cents in the nabes, $1 or $2 at the prestige movie palaces.

The technicians at Western Electric didn't mean to upset this highly evolved web of commerce. All they were trying to do was improve their primary franchise operation, the telephone. Western Electric's primary problem was the limited distance over which telephone conversation could be transmitted. Service had been established between New York and as far west as Denver, but that was the absolute limit under the current technology.

What was missing was an amplification system, and that was

solved by Dr. Lee De Forest in 1906. De Forest had electrified the 1904 St. Louis World's Fair with his De Forest Wireless Telegraph Tower, which stood several hundred feet high and could transmit radio messages fifteen hundred miles. De Forest's invention was a three-filament, gas-filled tube he called the Audion. While the Audion tube was too weak to be practical, it did amplify electrical signals, which was all Western Electric needed.

In 1913, Western Electric purchased the rights to De Forest's invention; one of Western Electric's scientists, Dr. Harold Arnold, discovered that by pumping out the gas with which De Forest had filled the Audion tube and creating a near vacuum, the tube could amplify sound up to 130 times its original volume without distortion. By the end of 1914, Arnold's improved amplifiers had worked successfully in tests on lines running from New York to San Francisco. Commercial application soon followed.

Born in Council Bluffs, Iowa, in 1873, Lee De Forest had more than one hundred patents issued in his name by 1915. As early as 1900 he had prophesied that talking pictures could be produced simply, not by synchronizing a record with a film, as most people thought, but by photographing a voice record simultaneously with the image on the same piece of celluloid. "The phonograph," he once said, "is a miracle of technical skill, and might be called a triumph over a bad principle. The needle traveling over a disc is not the ideal kind of phonograph." After inventing the Audion tube, De Forest began playing around with talking pictures.

Dr. Elman Meyers, De Forest's assistant engineer, said in a 1970 speech that De Forest was conducting successful sound tests as early as 1913. "The star of this first test was a mongrel dog. In front of our cameras, the dog barked and did a complete flipover stunt. We developed the exposed motion picture (with sound and picture on a single film), reached a decision on the proper light exposure for a reproduction from our negative to a composite positive, and the first 'daily' was born. Projecting the film with its sound on a De Forest–invented projector sound device marked this experiment as the first sound ever to be heard loud and clear, and coming directly from a motion picture film."

Following on the heels of Lauste, De Forest utilized not a needle in the groove of a record but a needle of light, with voice vibrations converted to light focused and photographically printed in various densities on a strip alongside the picture. De Forest reasoned that if he could perfect that process, it would be comparatively simple to reverse the process for projection and amplification of the sound track.

De Forest's main problem was in development; if the sound record was developed sufficiently, the picture was overdeveloped; proper development of the picture part left the sound too faint. In his note-book, De Forest wrote, "Too faint! Had to develop this film for six minutes to get at all the heavy track. This completely fogged it so that the picture would have been ruined."

De Forest tried other labs besides his own. On April 6, 1919, he wrote in his notebook, "Second half of film developed by Eastman. In appearance, it is clearer (and cleaner) than my half. These records reproduced quite noticeably better than those I developed . . ." But even Eastman's finer labwork left the picture area overdeveloped. De Forest had to mimic Lauste yet again and use a double system, that is, recording the sound on one strip of film, the picture on another, marrying them in the printing process.

Another man working on a system very similar to De Forest's, one Joseph Tykocinski-Tykociner, was a research professor in electrical engineering at the University of Illinois. On June 9, 1922, he showed a demonstration film in which a woman in a long white dress stood in front of a phonograph horn holding a bell. She said "I will ring," and then did. The woman (Tykociner's wife) then asked, "Did you hear the bell ring?" The demonstration made *The New York World* on Sunday, July 30, under the headline TALKING, LAUGHING, SINGING SCREEN TO RIVAL THE SILENT DRAMA FILMS.

Tykociner's early experiments involved a sound track without vi-suals; the track was directly in the center of the 35mm film; later experiments involved film of a violinist playing, and the sound track was placed on the opposite side from what would become standard practice, and in a different width. In addition, Tykociner was re-cording at camera speeds that ranged from 102 feet of film a minute —for voices—and 162 feet a minute—for music—compared to the 90 feet a minute that would become industry standard.

The system was workable, but Tykociner's invention foundered; he asked for $10,000 a year for himself in addition to having his costs underwritten, and the university couldn't see their way clear to finance him unless he assigned his patents to the college. Tykociner made a counterproposal, giving the college 5 percent of the profits for every $10,000 they invested, but the college refused to finance further research unless they controlled the basic patents.

The two parties agreed to disagree; Tykociner unsuccessfully foraged for outside financing, then ended up selling his patent in August 1927 for $50,000. It was a very profitable deal; Tykociner's original system had cost him less than $1,000 to construct, most of which was footed by the university. Tykociner proceeded to forget about sound on film and worked at the college until he retired in 1946.

Both the corporate Western Electric and independents like De Forest and Tykociner were working outside the film industry, and the latter two were struggling for financing. George Eastman, one of the technical leaders of the film business, synopsized the feelings of the profession: "I wouldn't give a dime for all the possibilities of that invention. The public will never accept it."

□ □ □

D. W. Griffith, always interested in the latest wrinkle, dabbled with sound in 1921, when he added some dialogue scenes to a picture called *Dream Street*. No fool, Griffith realized that *Dream Street* needed all the help it could get (it's easily his worst movie). The picture had been shot and released as a silent feature in April of 1921. Shortly after its fast fade, Griffith was approached by Orlando Kellum, who suggested adding a dash of sound so Griffith might recoup some of his losses, using an old sound-on-78-rpm-disc system invented by Kellum about the time of Edison's experiments.

On April 27, Ralph Graves went to the Kellum studios at 203 West Fortieth Street and recorded a love song that was dubbed into a scene already filmed silent by Griffith. (Presumably Griffith recorded his introduction the same day.) The revised film premiered at Town Hall on May 1, and the response must have convinced Griffith that the film was salvageable, for on May 15, more sound was dubbed in. On Sunday, May 29, *Dream Street* and a program of Kellum shorts opened at the Shubert-Crescent Theater in Brooklyn.

Kellum's system depended on a complicated commutator, looking a lot like an auto engine, that regulated the speed of the projector.

The program of Kellum shorts along with *Dream Street* closed quickly, one more failure in the long history of sound synchronized with the movies. Kellum attempted to sign up top performing talent from the William Morris Agency, but his efforts would be short-circuited by the superior system Western Electric was perfecting.

A fragment of Griffith's introduction to *Dream Street* survives; it is purple in content, outrageously hammy in delivery (*"Dream Street!* I wonder if there isn't a Dream Street running through the heart and soul of every man and woman in the world . . ."), and the sound is analogous to a worn 78 rpm record.

□ □ □

The pressure of De Forest's work on radio deferred further research into sound motion-pictures until 1918. By 1920, De Forest had devised a method of taking sound waves, amplifying them, and transmitting them to an oxide-coated vacuum tube that dimmed or brightened according to the fluctuations of the electric signal. The wavering light from the tube passed through a narrow slit and was recorded in a special area near the edge of a strip of movie film. Sound was turned into light. When the process was reversed, the original sound was reproduced.

De Forest filed for his patent by July 16, 1921. Seven days earlier he had written in his diary, "Today I made my first 'talking movie' picture — of myself, very hot and somewhat flurried; talked too loud, and the photography was poor, due to white 'back drop' and bad placing of the light. But it was at last made, despite all the jinxes and hoodoos — two months behind schedule, and after two years of hard work in preparation — a definite promise of great things to come."

A year later, De Forest took $200,000 he had received for the De Forest Radio Company and incorporated as De Forest Phonofilms for the purpose of producing synchronized, sound-on-film talking pictures.

While Lee De Forest was making slow progress, Western Electric was working on their own sound movie project, splitting their efforts into two groups, one working on sound on film, the other sound on disc. Initially, sound films had been far down the company's list of priorities, but their primary area of research had spawned a number of breakthroughs — the perfection of the Audion tube in 1914; the public-address system in 1916; the condenser microphone that same year. The company had incrementally amassed most of the necessary component parts.

In a choice between the two possible technologies, Western Electric made the decision to emphasize sound on disc for the simple reason that disc technology was forty years old, familiar, and could be harnessed much more quickly. Sound on film was still in the experimental stage. As an initial sound-on-disc demonstration film, an animated movie called *The Audion* was produced, explaining the workings of the vacuum tube.

To maintain synchronization, two revolution counters were mounted side by side, one connected to the turntable, one to the projector. The operator kept the counters reading alike to within a second by controlling the rheostat on the projector, so synchronization was close enough for a loosely synchronized project like *The Audion.*

The Audion was exhibited in New Haven on October 27, 1922. As a backup, engineer Stanley Watkins, who had spoken the narration for the film, was installed in the organ loft with a microphone. Unfortunately, the view from the organ loft meant that Watkins couldn't see the screen, but the sound-on-disc system worked sufficiently well so that Watkins' improvisational abilities remained untested.

Encouraged, Western Electric decided to produce an experimental series of shorts in room 1109 of their headquarters. Room 1109 was not large enough for all the necessary gear, but there was a roof outside the window that was. With the camera located in a shed on the roof, there was just enough space in the room for lights, director, performer, and sound gear.

Despite the reasonably successful presentation of *The Audion* at Woolsey Hall at Yale University, within Western Electric there was a good deal of internal debate over the ultimate point of their efforts, for the failure of the Kinetophone continued to discourage even the industry that was developing sound.

In October 1923, chief engineer E. B. Craft wrote to Western Electric vice president Frank Jewett proposing a concerted effort to develop a commercial system for sound motion pictures. As Craft explained it to Jewett, "It seems obvious that we are in the best position of anyone to develop and manufacture the best apparatus and systems for use in this field."

Jewett grudgingly agreed, as did management. But, as Jewett wrote in 1946, "When we at West Street in our early excitement staged a first crude demonstration for the then 'brass hats' of the Bell System . . . the result was universal ice water—a complete lack of imagination. As a consequence for a time we had to go ahead practically in defiance of orders."

❏ ❏ ❏

Lee De Forest and his wife spent a year in Germany continuing his research. There, he demonstrated his system, now combining sound and image on one piece of film, in September 1922. The German press, he remembered, was "polite, if not enthusiastically laudatory." Upon returning to America, he enlisted the support—and, apparently, the money—of Hugo Riesenfeld, the musical director of the Rivoli and Rialto theaters in New York. Through Riesenfeld's efforts, De Forest outfitted a studio and hired a cameraman and some musicians.

De Forest exhibited his system publicly in America for the first time on April 23, 1923. The show-business journalist Karl Kitchen reported, "The invention which is called the Phonofilm and which has been perfected by Dr. Lee De Forest does all that is claimed for it. The action and the sound synchronize perfectly."

What hardly anybody was aware of at this point was that De Forest's invention was not really his. Much of what was being brought to market under the name Phonofilm had been "ghosted" by two other men.

❏ ❏ ❏

The competing claims of Lee De Forest and Theodore Case for the honor of the invention of a workable system of motion picture sound on film have long inflamed the passions of a subset of motion picture historians with all the fervor of the squabbles between Mensheviks and Bolsheviks.

In the early 1920s, at least five different sound systems were being worked on in America alone: Western Electric had their dual research project, there was De Forest, there was Case, and there was a group at General Electric playing with a system that had been invented at their laboratories in 1921.* Out of this welter of claims and cross-claims that tended to take minutely varied paths to the same destination, sound movies emerged.

It is clear that De Forest worked in loose collaboration with Case and his assistant Earl Sponable. (Case and De Forest began corresponding in 1916, and De Forest was using Case's photoelectric cell as early as August 1920.)

De Forest's system would not have worked as well as it did without Case's contributions. (It might not have worked at all.) While De Forest was using Case's photoelectric cell, Case was engaged in work on his own camera; when Case and Sponable split from De Forest, they began working on improvements by themselves, while De Forest soldiered on alone. When finally perfected, the Case/Sponable system was superior to De Forest's, and they were quickly able to sell it to William Fox. De Forest eventually sued Fox for patent infringement and, after many years of litigation, received a small sum for his work.

While De Forest would get the lion's share of the credit — and, in 1960, a special Academy Award — for his contributions to the development of sound motion pictures, the truth is that his primary contribution to talking pictures was that of solving the essential problem of amplification via the Audion tube — which was actually perfected by Western Electric.

Theodore Case had been mulling over the problem of sound on film since 1911, when he was a student at Yale. In a letter to his mother written in January 1911, Case wrote, "Most of my time now is taken up in experimenting with my selenium cell with the idea in mind of photographing sound waves and using the positives as records for a new kind of phonograph..." A month later he was reporting that he had succeeded in transmitting sound by light: "The eye could not detect the variation of the light at all, but it was

---

* The Western Electric system would be called "variable density"; that is, it translated sound into different levels of gray. The General Electric/RCA system was called "variable area," and turned sound into a continuous line resembling a bar graph. By changing a single projector part, the same machine could reproduce either type of sound track.

registered perfectly in the varying of the resistance of the selenium. The reproduction of the voice was perfect. Next I have to set up an apparatus for very delicate photographing of the light variations . . ."

Case continued playing with the idea for years after his graduation. In 1916, Earl Sponable, a chemistry student from Case's alma mater, joined forces with Case. Case's breakthrough invention was what he called the AEO light, a light source that varied in intensity with an electrical current that had been stimulated by sounds, thus providing the light for a variable-density sound track.

The first movement toward collaboration came from De Forest: "Professor R. W. Wood has informed me that you are producing a very sensitive photoelectric cell," De Forest wrote on August 13, 1920. "I am much interested in this subject and would be pleased to have details . . ." The two men began a cautious dance. On September 22, 1922, De Forest wrote Case that his letter of the eighteenth was "very interesting," and that he hoped to try one of his new photoelectric cells "just as soon as you can send it to me . . . I should like to meet you in regard to discussing what arrangements might be made for the use of your light cells in fairly large numbers in connection with my speaking film equipment."

De Forest leased the Case/Sponable cell. By March 1923, De Forest had completed eight sound-on-film shorts using Case's AEO light, a Western Electric amp, and a Case Thalofide cell to reproduce the sound tracks. De Forest wrote Case on March 17 that "I admire the . . . cell and certainly want to use it very much in my work. It looks now as though I can make a contract before long with the Keith Vaudeville Circuit which alone will call for the eventual equipment of over a thousand theaters . . . Each of these theaters should have, at least, two . . . cells. At $50 a piece, this runs into $100,000 . . . and the Moving Picture Theatre field has not even been touched . . . It is certainly only good business on your part to cooperate with me . . ."

De Forest even tried to interest Case in investing in the firm, but Case demurred. De Forest then tried to convince Case to make an agreement with him without the intercession of attorneys "until the papers are actually ready to be drawn up." Case evidently considered rounding up some capital for De Forest's concern, but as one prospective investor wrote him, "The proposition is too jug-handled . . . Dr. De Forest will get the lion's share of whatever profits the company may make. Under the circumstances, I think you are wise in having decided upon royalty rather than a stock basis."

De Forest's Phonofilms were publicly launched on April 15, 1923, at the Rivoli Theater in New York, an added fillip on a bill headlined by *Bella Donna*, Pola Negri's first American picture. That August, De Forest and Case finally signed a contract, Case granting De Forest a license to use the AEO light and the Thalofide cells in his work. De Forest was worried about Western Electric's disc system — "it is highly important that we do not disclose to any of their force just what we are doing . . ." — but the relationship between the two men began to sour rather quickly. In December 1923, De Forest gave an interview to some New York papers in which he took credit for the design and construction of the original cell, which had actually been entirely the work of Case and Sponable.

De Forest attempted to soothe Case's ego, but cracks began appearing. A chastened De Forest admitted the primary role Case had played in making the invention possible. "I cheerfully agree," he wrote Case on February 11, 1924, "in consideration of the fact that *so many of the devices and methods we are using in the Phonofilm are of your design or improvement* [italics added], to use the terms De Forest–Case System or De Forest–Case on all our literature or advertising . . ."

Even before that private admission of dependence, De Forest had publicly acknowledged Case's work; in a *Scientific American* article of August 1923, he had outlined his sound-on-film system and noted that "[the sound] attachment includes a small incandescent lamp and a highly sensitive photoelectric cell, the latter being the invention of T. W. Case."

De Forest's Phonofilms were shorts featuring vaudeville stars such as Eddie Cantor, George Jessel, Chic Sale, Weber and Fields, Sissle and Blake, and Ben Bernie. He photographed operas, minstrel shows, concerts, and speeches by politicians — Al Smith, Senator Robert La Follette, and President Calvin Coolidge.

De Forest's trade-paper ads initially suggested that he thought of his shorts ("films that actually talk and reproduce music without the use of a phonograph") as comprising "a sensational two-hour show," but that hope soon dwindled, and De Forest concentrated on creating a market that would accept shorts as appetizers before the main course of the feature.

A good many of these shorts have survived, such as a May 1924 film in which Harvard president Charles William Eliot reads a speech. Eliot—a stiff, proper Henry James-ish personality—is sitting down and has to place his legs awkwardly around the legs of the tripod holding the microphone while he reads a speech commemorating a colleague. Eliot's nervous cough interrupts his reading, but De Forest didn't bother with retakes. The recording is faint but clear.

The De Forest system worked, but was of variable quality; the Phonofilm of DeWolf Hopper fervently reciting "Casey at the Bat" has heavy background noise, and no perceptible high end. Others are better, notably a film of Eddie Cantor made in 1922, wherein Cantor announces that he's really Thomas Meighan, sings, dances, and tells Jewish jokes. According to tests conducted by Maurice Zouary, the De Forest films were shot at twenty-one frames per second.

The competition was keeping a wary eye on De Forest's activities. A March 20, 1924, Western Electric memo outlined how a De Forest film called *The Harlequin's Serenade* looked and—more important —sounded to Bell engineers: "It was difficult to tell whether the music was furnished by a small orchestra or only three or four musicians . . . The reproduction . . . was very far from satisfactory both as regards overloading and frequency characteristics. All of the heavy piano notes showed marked signs of overloading. This effect would have rendered the reproduction very disagreeable had not the volume been held much lower than we would consider necessary for filling a theater of [the] size [of the Rivoli] . . ."

In spite of the fact that the costs to convert a theater to the De Forest system were modest—about $1,500—his production efforts would be firmly marginalized by his inability to interest any major studios or theater chains in investing in sound. Woefully undercapitalized though they were, De Forest and Riesenfeld managed to wire thirty-four theaters for sound, all on the East Coast, including the Capitol and Rivoli theaters, and the Tivoli in London.

Audiences accepted the Phonofilms as a pleasant novelty, nothing more. James Quirk, the editor of *Photoplay,* put it simply: "Talking pictures are perfected, says Dr. Lee De Forest. So is castor oil." Nobody cared.

By September 1924, relations between Case and De Forest were beginning to break down. Among other things, De Forest was habitually late with money. That month, Case demanded a special credit ("Taken by Case Studios") for the Phonofilm pictures of Calvin Coolidge and Robert La Follette that had been taken by the camera Case had designed. De Forest resisted, but Case made grumbling noises about getting his royalty payments on time, and De Forest capitulated.*

De Forest's perennial cash-flow problems began to affect Case's confidence seriously. De Forest asked Case to take $2,500 in partial payment, with the rest to be promised in a thirty-day note. In October 1925, he offered Case a new contract that would have given him 10 to 15 percent of De Forest's own stock in Phonofilms. That offer was changed to one paying Case $2,000 a month, in addition to 4 percent of the gross, for a thirteen-year license. Case stalled.

In addition to running short of funds, De Forest was arousing enmity on the part of the people who worked with him. A De Forest cameraman named Freeman Owens would tell the historian Miles Kreuger that "De Forest was interested in selling phony stock to his company. He had no interest in developing sound; he had a great interest in going backstage and telling chorus girls he could make them famous." As a possible corroboration, it should be noted that De Forest failed to copyright a single one of his films.

Likewise, Earl Sponable would remember that De Forest had an unending stream of PR people at a time when hardly anybody had PR people. De Forest's adherents claim that Case took a good look at what De Forest was doing and promptly returned to his lab in Auburn, New York, flagrantly ripped off De Forest's inventions, adding some minor improvements of his own. Freeman Owens and others would assert that Case simply realized De Forest was a phony and withdrew his patents.

* The Case film of that irrepressible madcap Calvin Coolidge features the president going off on a very modern, hectoring tirade about low taxes equaling freedom and high taxes equaling slavery. It was the first sound-film appearance of an American president, and it proved that Case's camera gave better results than De Forest's.

Certainly, De Forest would never have gotten as far as he had without Case's inventions, and it was obvious to Case that De Forest's ragged financing and catch-as-catch-can methods were never going to be the spark of an industrial revolution. Why not just take back the AEO light, without which sound on film was very problematic, and try to do it himself?

In December of 1925, the arrangement between Case and De Forest was brusquely terminated ("We are now forced to cease all negotiations and withdraw all offers made by us and reject all offers submitted by you," wrote Case), and Case and Sponable began working on their own. De Forest quickly acquired a slightly different set of patents to continue production of the Phonofilms.

For a good part of 1925, Case had been producing a series of his own test films that featured the inventor himself in extreme close-up blowing at the microphone and saying "Can you feel the air?", then muttering "Gee whillikers, these lights are awfully bright, E.I. [Sponable]."

Case tried other things: a bird singing and, most memorably, a vaudeville act of a man holding a duck that squawks on cue when the performer holding him squeezes the duck's rear end while singing, "Ma, He's Making Eyes at Me." (It's the only case on record of a duck being goosed.) In all of these tests, Case's sound system is amazingly clean, a considerable improvement on the fuzzy De Forest system, and far superior to any sound-on-disc system.

Two months before Case took his invention and went home, De Forest had approached Western Electric for help with an amplifying system, but Western Electric, after about two seconds of thoughtful consideration, decided against altruistically sharing the developments they were about to bring to market. "In view of the fact that we do not ordinarily undertake research and development work except on our own problems," wrote President Frank Jewett, "and because of the large amount of such work now in hand, I find that it will not be possible for us to do the thing which you have in mind."

Studios and exhibitors were ignoring the Phonofilms because the public didn't seem to care. The technique of synchronizing sound with motion pictures was essentially irrelevant, as far as the public was concerned. They needed to be primed for sound; the idea needed to be sold, with publicity and with the kind of stars that De Forest couldn't afford.*

De Forest continued to nibble around the edges of the industry. Early in 1926, Allan Dwan was shooting a picture in New York called *Tin Gods,* with the popular leading man Thomas Meighan. Meighan was the shepherd of the Lamb's Club, which produced a fund-raising benefit every year. Meighan asked Dwan if he had any ideas to make the show more exciting.

Dwan was living in the Algonquin Hotel and knew De Forest, whose office was two blocks away, through their mutual interests in electronics. Dwan dreamed up the idea of making a sound short with Meighan and Gloria Swanson, a friend of long standing who was also in New York. During the benefit, the film was switched on. Meighan, on film, was addressing the audience, when he was interrupted by Swanson, also on film.

"What are you doing here?" he said.

"I came here to sing a song," said Swanson.

"We don't allow women in here, so get out, you're not wanted."

"I came to sing and I'm going to sing."

"What are you going to sing? Sing it and get out."

"I'm going to sing the club song." Whereupon Swanson launched into the club song of the Players, not the Lambs, prompting a groundswell of boos and hisses. "People were figuring, 'Ah, I know, they're both in back of the screen and talking to each other and coming through to us with microphones or something,' " remembered Allan Dwan. "So, to avoid that, I had spotlights on the two

---

* Scientists were no more enthusiastic than the lay public. An editorial note in the *Scientific American* in January 1923 rather brutally undercut De Forest's enthusiasm by doubting that talking pictures would ever supplant silents: "The bald truth is that the present screen play is based on the silent drama technique; it tells the story by action and suggestion rather than by dialogue, now given in the form of titles. It has a wonderful appeal to its audience — an appeal entirely distinct from that of the spoken play. It is in no wise an imitation of the spoken play; it is a thing by itself. Why, therefore, replace it with a more or less realistic imitation? Our belief is that the talking picture has great possibilities in many directions, but as a factor in the motion picture field it must not be taken too seriously."

sides of the proscenium, and on one side was Meighan himself, in the flesh, and Gloria, the same way, mouths closed, saying nothing, but talking to each other on the screen."

When the film ended, Meighan — the real Meighan — stepped forward and assured the audience that they had not seen a magic trick, but a scientific miracle, a film made several weeks before. The applause was tumultuous.

Despite his own wayward path, Lee De Forest had a fairly clear idea of what kind of changes would be wrought by sound, if and when it arrived. In 1923 he said, "If you ask whether the ordinary silent drama to which we are all so familiarized can in general be improved by the addition of the voice, the answer is unquestionably 'no.' Many, and in fact most of the moving picture artists are not trained on the legitimate stage; they have no adequate speaking voices — many in fact are incapable of speaking good English . . ." (This insistence that the actors who made silent films were a veritable circus tent of clownish illiterates would gain momentum with the years. By the time of the 1952 musical *Singin' in the Rain*, it had become a commonly accepted bromide.)

If silent films themselves were to be rendered obsolete, what exactly did De Forest foresee replacing them? "I claim that an entirely new form of screen drama can be worked out, taking advantage of the possibilities of introducing music and voice and appropriate acoustic effects, not necessarily through the entire action, but here and there, where the effects can be made much more startling or theatrical . . . or significant than is possible by pantomime alone, no matter how cleverly it may be worked out."

Not an elaboration, then, or even an addition, but an entirely new hybrid altogether.

❑ ❑ ❑

While Case and De Forest were squabbling, Western Electric's research began to gather momentum and converge. Once the vacuum tube had established the possibility of long-distance phone conversations, the Western Electric engineers turned their attentions toward public-address systems. In November 1921, Warren Harding dedicated the Tomb of the Unknown Soldier, and the simultaneous broadcast of his speech to thousands in the audience at Arlington, as well as loudspeaker systems in New York and San Francisco, galvanized those lucky enough to hear it.

By 1922, Western Electric PA systems were standard issue, with directors like Cecil B. DeMille using them for instructing thousands of extras in crowd scenes. By 1924, Western Electric condenser microphones had been adopted by both the Victor and Columbia record companies, replacing the old acoustic horns.

At the same time, the sound experiments being carried on in room 1109 began to approach fruition. Under the system devised by Western Electric, sound was recorded on a circular, two-inch-thick wax blank made of metallic soap resting on a turntable. The blank had to be kept at a constant temperature, and in a dust-free environment, which made filming outdoors very difficult. The sounds were amplified, causing the sapphire stylus to vibrate from side to side, cutting modulated grooves in the blank. If anything went wrong during the shoot, technicians would shave the top layer off the wax blank and start over again.

After a satisfactory recording was made, the wax blank was dusted with graphite and dipped into an electroplating bath where copper would form on the surface. When the copper was peeled off, it formed an exact negative impression of the original wax blank. This was then electroplated again to produce a master positive called the "mother," which, Western Electric theorized, could produce as many negative "stampers" as would be needed to produce the final batch of records for release.

In May 1924, the sales department felt sufficient confidence in their system to begin demonstrating it. Among those who were invited to witness it was Thomas Edison. "Two things I remember about him," wrote engineer Stanley Watkins. "He said that our sound was very good; and he was extremely deaf."

It was time to lay siege to Paramount, MGM, First National, and several second-tier companies. By the end of 1924, all of them had seen the system demonstrated, and all of them had expressed an overwhelming apathy. Stanley Watkins characterized their collective response as being identical to a sophisticated adult being shown a mildly amusing toy. Sound, they brusquely explained, had been tried several times. It didn't work. Besides, the audience wasn't interested. Everybody knew that. Everybody but Sam Warner and William Fox.

CHAPTER 3

The family name was not Warner, but there is some question as to just what it was originally. "On Ellis Island," Sam Warner explained to his wife, "nobody could figure out the name on the documents so somebody writes down Warner an' it stuck." Even Jack Warner Jr. was unsure about the real family name.

They came from Poland. Ben Warner was born there and married his wife, Pearl (Eichelbaum), in 1876. Children began arriving the following year, and would continue to come until there were twelve in all. Ben arrived in America in 1888, settling at first in Baltimore. Wife Pearl, son Harry (born 1881), and daughter Anna came later. Nine-year-old Harry Warner went to work selling newspapers and shining shoes. Ben tried stores in Bluefield, West Virginia; Louisville; Detroit; and London, Ontario, where he lost his nest egg in furs. It was back to West Virginia, and a shoe repair shop where Harry worked the bench alongside his father.*

In 1894, the family settled in Youngstown, Ohio, where Ben Warner first opened a shoe repair shop on Spring Common and later a

---

* Harry had a checkered but useful employment history. In later years, he would enjoy taking off his shirt and expertly cutting up a calf. "He was an accomplished butcher," remembered his nephew, Jack Warner Jr., "which helps you in the movies." As for Sam (born 1885, in Baltimore), one of his first jobs was as a brakeman on the Erie railroad.

grocery store and butcher shop on East Federal Street. As they remembered it, the word "mine" was never heard in the house, the plural "ours" being preferred. Any brotherly squabbles were soon ended by Ben and Pearl Warner, who demanded an attitude of "One for all and all for one." Ben practiced what he preached; his one quality possession, a watch and chain brought from Poland, was pawned for a family bicycle.

The only one of the brothers to graduate from high school was the ill-fated David, who in any case eschewed show business. Albert "Abe" Warner (born 1884) would enroll at Youngstown's Rayen High School for three months in the fall, just to work off his aggressions playing football. Harry had no interest in athletics, but did enjoy dancing; he and his sister Rose won most of the town's dance contests. Myron Penner, a family friend who lived with them for a time, remembered how the brothers would come home to the house and hug their mother, telling her, "Mom, we're gonna be millionaires some day." Pearl Warner, a homely *yiddishe momma*, would take a raspberry pie from the oven and give Jack, her favorite (born 1892), the largest piece. "Did you hear that, now?" she would say. "Did you hear what my boy said?"

It was the family custom for the brothers to turn over the money they earned to their mother, keeping only fifty cents a week for themselves. The other boys were always broke in a day or two, but Harry could stretch his measly allowance for a full week, even having enough left for a Saturday-night dance. When Harry was running a poolroom on South Champion Street, he wouldn't allow customers to sink the last ball in the rack, as that took up time on the table. Even as a young man, Harry knew the value of a quick turnover.

Finding a home big enough for a family the size of the Warners was never easy. At various times, the family lived over their butcher shop, at 315 North Walnut, and on Belmont Avenue, near Youngstown's St. Elizabeth Hospital. Eventually, as the boys began bringing home more money, Ben Warner could afford to build some apartments at the corner of Elm and Bissell, where the couple would live until they left for California in 1924.

For a time, Jack and a man named Pike Rickard had a comedy song-and-dance vaudeville act on the Gus Sun circuit in the Midwest. The act consisted entirely of bits lifted from other acts, courtesy of Jack's magpie brain and a book of vaudeville routines called *Madison's Budget,* which sold for one dollar. Jack continued with his show-business career, until one day he and his partner played Youngstown, where Sam caught the act.

"You were OK, Jack," Sam said, "but let me give you some advice. Get out in front of the theater where you pay the actors instead of the other way around."

Soon, Jack joined with his brothers in managing what was becoming a small chain of nickelodeons. Sam found they could clear $300 a week in one theater, more than Ben Warner could make in a month at his Federal Street market. By this time, the division of labor was clear: Sam — nobody ever called him Samuel — got the ideas, Harry financed them, Jack and Abe implemented them.

The theaters were in Ohio towns like Niles and Hubbard, Pennsylvania towns like Newcastle. Harry Warner was fond of telling a story about one they opened in 1903, in Newcastle. "When the theater was all finished," he reminisced, "we found we had no chairs. My brothers and I got together and tried to decide where we were going to get them. One said, 'What's the matter with the undertaker?' So we went over and engaged ninety-six chairs from a neighboring undertaker. The consequence was that whenever there was a funeral we had to ask the audience to stand up." The number of chairs varied in the telling — sometimes it was ninety-nine — but the punchline was always the same, for the number of seats had to be below one hundred in order to comply with local fire laws.

It was Harry who proposed the idea of forming film exchanges, that is, a consortium of exhibitors buying prints and circulating them among each other, rather than each exhibitor amassing his own film library. Harry built up one exchange in Baltimore, another in Pittsburgh, then in 1912 sold them for $100,000 to the General Film Company.

The Warner boys took their money and went to California, renting a studio on Sunset Boulevard. Sam and Jack made the movies, Albert distributed them, Harry ran the overall operation. The studio was so small that Joe Marks, a Youngstown chum who accompanied them to Los Angeles, remembered that if the brothers needed someplace for a confidential conversation, they had to go outside on the lot.

In 1922, after twenty years of scuffling, Sam decided they needed a studio of their own. He spotted a likely piece of property at Sunset and Van Ness in Hollywood. Harry and Jack weren't crazy about the idea — it was tough enough to meet the payroll, let alone mortgage payments — but they were convinced when Sam put up $200 of his own money for the option. The price was $36,000; while they were conferring as to whether or not they could afford it, the price went up to $40,000. They elected to buy it before the price went up again.

By this time their personalities were fully formed: Harry was both the flinty businessman and the company's conscience; Sam was the man's man, the woman's man, the organizer. And there was Jack. Then, and for the rest of his life, Jack Warner would display — no, cultivate — the glib, cheap demeanor of the cliché vaudevillian. The rest of the Jewish moguls — Zukor, Lasky, Laemmle, Mayer — were dignified, conservative in their demeanor; Jack, along with Harry Cohn, was cocky, brash, vulgar, and proud of it.

At a party, a woman would wave to Jack across the room, and he would respond with a thundering "Hiya, honey! Didja bring your douche bag?" Although he would proudly proclaim his name to be Jack L. Warner, in reality he had no middle name. He appropriated the initial from the head minstrel of a show that once passed through Youngstown. The minstrel had the letter *L* as a middle initial, and Jack thought that added a music that plain "Jack Warner" didn't have.

Soon after the brothers arrived in Hollywood, Jack was regarded as the loose cannon. "Paramount was the best-liked studio in town, as a place to work," remembered Joe Youngerman, who began work at the studio as a laborer in 1926 and rose to the rank of studio manager. "It was better than Metro, better than Warners. The trouble with Metro was always that they had too many bosses. And the trouble with Warners was always Jack. The big shot."

Despite Jack's surface geniality, money was tight. Irving Asher went to work at Warners when they were making two-reel comedies with Al St. John on Washington Boulevard in Culver City and stayed with them through the 1930s. "I remember very well that Jack paid everyone on payday," he told Kevin Brownlow. "He had a big accordion-type wallet and he had the checks in it alphabetically. He would go around to everybody and hand them their checks, and he'd always hand me my check and say, 'I want to see you in my office.'

"Later that evening I'd go to his office and he'd take the check back and say, 'That's not any good, I didn't have enough to quite make it this week.'" Since Asher was impressed with Jack's flashy car, Jack magnanimously would let him drive whenever he was there to supervise. This went on for some time until Asher realized that Jack was using him as an unpaid chauffeur. "It's a gospel fact that he never got off at the front door of the studio," recalled Asher of this period. "I let him off around the back because the sheriff was possibly waiting at the front door to either attach the studio or take the car."

Henry Blanke, who came to the studio in 1924 as personal assistant to Ernst Lubitsch and stayed for the next thirty-five years, would take the Bell and Howell cameras home at night so they couldn't be attached by creditors. When money was short, Blanke took coupons instead of cash, and made up any financial shortfall by free-lancing for German movie magazines.

By 1924, the Warner product was well-defined. Apart from Lubitsch's magnificent, utterly original comedies of marital deceit, Warners' big pictures were films like *Beau Brummel,* costume dramas deadened by a surfeit of respect for their star—John Barrymore—or their source. This, the brothers seemed to be saying, is classy, so it doesn't have to be interesting. Lubitsch aside, Warners' best pictures were programmers like *Brass, The Little Church Around the Corner,* and some of the Rin Tin Tin pictures, little stories of small-town life that were cheap but unpretentious pieces of Americana.

The Warners staff was hardworking and unerringly competent, partly because Harry, Jack, and Sam had an eye for talent and partly because the atmosphere on the lot was too demanding for anyone who wasn't absolutely at the top of their game. By the mid-1920s, Warners had assembled a talented team. Frank Murphy ran the electrical department, Whitey Wilson ran props, and Art Klein ran the transportation department. Klein was believed to have raced cars at Indianapolis and was well known for his amazing ability to take apart any truck—or truckdriver—and put it back together again. Sam and Art Klein were both immense racing fans, which is why Warners produced a picture with the great race-car driver Barney

Oldfield. The bright young man of the studio was Darryl Zanuck, a strenuously ambitious writer who had been hired in 1924. Zanuck proved so prolific he had to adopt multiple pseudonyms such as Melville Crossman, Mark Canfield, and Gregory Rogers.

The studio was ruled by the uneasy partnership of Jack and Harry. "Harry, being president, was prone to jump on Jack for any film that did not come out well," remembered Darryl Zanuck. "There was a time, I think, when they did not see each other. Sam was the bridge between them. What a boring guy Harry was," concluded Zanuck. "Jack was unreliable, but never boring." Lina Basquette, Sam Warner's wife, said that all Harry and Abe Warner cared about was money, and all Jack Warner cared about was women. "He was a heller . . . very devious. I don't think he ever drew a truthful breath."

❑ ❑ ❑

The most avaricious individual in the history of the motion picture industry, a man who was singularly shrewd, devious, demonically energetic, and incapable of trusting anyone but his family, was born in Tulchva, Hungary, probably under the name of Fuchs, although some have speculated the family name was actually Fried. Coming to America at the age of nine months, William Fox grew up on the Lower East Side of New York, the eldest of thirteen children — six of whom died in infancy.

One day, the young Fox fell off a truck and broke his arm; an unskilled surgeon took out the elbow joint, freezing Fox's left arm in a locked position. Although Fox learned how to play a good game of golf in spite of the arm, the injury seems to have been the beginning of a series of grievances and grudges that Fox would nurse for the rest of his life.

Initially, Fox followed in his father's trade, manufacturing shoe polish and selling newspapers. He then was employed in a cleaning and pressing establishment, making $17 a week. One day in 1904 he asked for a raise and was told that he was really worth only $15 a week, whereupon he took $1,600 he had laboriously saved and, along with two partners, bought a nickelodeon in Brooklyn. He was twenty-five.

By 1910, Fox's hard work and showmanship had paid off; he had built a chain of twelve vaudeville/movie theaters. He was already distributing pictures, in spite of the best efforts of the Patents Company to drive him out of business. Fox sued the Patents monopoly under the newly enacted Sherman Anti-Trust Act and won.

Although the victory restored Fox's access to films for his theaters, he quickly figured out that the windfall profits were in production, rather than the steady sure thing of distribution. In 1914, William Fox began production of his own films in New Jersey; in 1916, he leased a studio in the Los Angeles suburb of Edendale, then opened his own on the corner of Sunset and Western Avenue.

In the first two decades of the century, Fox was Marcus Loew's main competitor in the theater business, but he could never quite catch up. Loew, as historian Douglas Gomery put it, "always seemed to get the best corners." By 1920, all Fox had was twenty-five theaters, all within New York City. It was at this point that he redirected most of his energies into film production.

Always observant, nose forever to the wind, in the early 1920s Fox noticed that the pattern of his trade had altered. Traditionally, the theater business was stronger in bad weather than in good, but now Fox realized that rainy nights consistently brought dismal business. People were staying inside; people were listening to something called radio.

Needing more *lebensraum*, Fox bought a hundred acres in West Los Angeles and opened what he called the Fox Hills studio in August of 1926. Fox stayed on the East Coast, maintaining his headquarters in a Manhattan office building at Tenth Avenue and Forty-fifth Street. The top floor, initially used as a studio, was converted to a gym for employees. The lab, later called Deluxe, was owned by Fox and located in the same building.

In the early years, Fox did a lot of the production work himself, and kept the studio on a very tight rein; cameraman Joseph Ruttenberg recalled coming back from the Fort Lee studios about eight or nine o'clock to find Fox and his wife "reviewing the dailies, and after reviewing the dailies, they were reviewing the feature pictures that were completed. Fox would sort of write the titles; he'd make up the titles or correct the titles with the director. Mrs. Fox used to help out. But nobody ever got out of the studio until three or four o'clock in the morning."

Ruttenberg and his fellow employees would have to wait to be paid until the dimes were hauled in from the theaters, but they didn't mind, for Fox was an appreciative employer. "Every time he'd see something nice on the screen, he'd come up on the stage. He used to smoke a huge cigar and I'd smell him coming. One day I was grinding away at the camera, standing on an apple box, and I looked down, and he's got a butt, smoking. And after I stopped, he says, 'I just saw the film.' 'Yeah? Was it good?' 'A little something in your envelope.' So I got a little increase in salary every now and then."

Fox never played and seldom rested. If his wife, Eve, dragged him away to Atlantic City for the weekend, Fox would spend his mornings in a rented theater watching the rushes of the Fox films in production. He didn't carry a watch because he didn't want to know what time it was. The day would end when the day's work was done. "He was a slave," his wife told Upton Sinclair. "The only way I could have a husband was to go and be a slave with him."

The Los Angeles studio was left to the ministrations of Winfield Sheehan, formerly private secretary to New York Police Commissioner Rhinelander Waldo. Sheehan had already had several close calls over charges of graft and general malfeasance when, in April of 1914, he was forced to resign when a madam testified she was paying protection money to a bagman for Sheehan. A man who understood the uses of power and money and had few scruples about applying what he knew could do very well in Hollywood. Sheehan had found his true métier.

Fox was a canny, street-smart, relatively modest man, at least in the early stages of his career. Like his confreres Zukor, Mayer, Goldwyn et al., Fox had spent his youth in an accessory business, where meeting and pleasing the public were essential to survival, let alone success. Fox's ego was displaced into the expansion of his business, not in personal celebrity. "This mug of mine will never sell any tickets," he once told a publicity man, "so just concentrate on getting the stars into magazines and newspapers and forget about me." (He was right; he strongly resembled the character actor Porter Hall.)

Fox was unprepossessing, a bit paunchy, and quite bald; he managed to keep clean-shaven only because he used a razor twice a day. He pronounced "film" as "fillum," and said things like "I done it" and "I seen it," even though he knew better. Mostly, his speech was described as "good, average New Yorkese."

Success, unfortunately, did not agree with him; as his empire expanded, as he approached a position of dominance in the world of cinema, he developed a tendency to refer to himself in the third person. Within the industry, Fox was a slightly shadowy figure, unloved and, more remarkably, unfeared.

Although he could be even-tempered around the office—the publicist Glendon Allvine worked for him for five years and never saw him in a bad mood—with other people, he felt free to explode. "Once to have seen him roused to wrath is a thing never forgotten," wrote the trade-paper reporter Merritt Crawford. "When most angry, at first he often appears to be embarrassed . . . Once Fox begins to stutter, get ready for the riot call. Or make your exit by the shortest route. It is an unerring storm signal. Normally, Fox is nervous in manner and habitually clips his speech in short staccato sentences. He can, however, be most suave when it pleases him and among his intimates is said to be a pleasing and entertaining companion. It might be well to add that Fox is devoted to his wife and family. No backstage or studio gossip has ever been attached to his name."

At home he was a tyrant. Fox supported his entire family, but expected strict obedience in return. "I watched my mother labor for a week over a 'thank you' note," remembered Angela Fox Dunn, the daughter of Fox's youngest sister. "The note should have just the right tone. It should be appropriately grateful, but it shouldn't be too groveling. One word might turn the king off. You could fall out of favor with the king, and you could be in a lot of trouble . . . My mother wasn't a business person; she was an actress. She used to keep shoeboxes of receipts and she could never find anything . . . The sweat would be running down her face. 'Brother Bill is coming! Go through that box!' . . . It was a horrible way to live."

Fox was a driven man, with all the feral belligerence one might expect to find in a success who begins in lowly circumstances. Reporters who interviewed Fox knew that the first part of the session would invariably involve a disquisition on his Horatio Alger–like rise, offered as much for his own benefit as the public's, for Fox constantly needed to reassure himself that he had indeed done what he had done. Should this monologue be brushed aside, the interview would be indignantly terminated.

By 1925, William Fox's company was somewhere in the middle of the Hollywood pecking order. Certainly, he was a distant third in terms of capital; MGM had resources of $38 million, Paramount $20 million, Fox $13 million. Likewise, Fox's films were predominantly bread-and-butter pictures, melodramas and westerns. (Universal, the most reliably low-brow of the studios, devoted a full 44 percent of its efforts to westerns, which constituted about a quarter of Fox's output.)

During the mid-1920s, William Fox set out to build or own the primary movie palace in every major city in America. He very nearly succeeded. "[Fox] told me," said A. C. Blumenthal, his lawyer, in July 1924, " 'If you can find any real estate in Los Angeles below market, wire me, and I will send you at once a check. I'm looking for such bargains.' "

To finance his expansion, Fox issued common stock for the first time, bringing in $6.6 million. In July 1925 he acquired West Coast Theaters, which had the dominant position in California and a few other western states. By 1927, he had grand palaces in Philadelphia; Washington, D.C.; Brooklyn; St. Louis; Detroit; and Milwaukee. The Fox flagship was the grandest theater of them all, New York's Roxy. What Fox now had to do was devise something glorious enough to play on the screens of all those theaters, something that would draw millions eager to see something they had never seen before.

To do that, he determined to make a preemptive strike on sound film. He bought the German sound-film system known as Tri-Ergon ("Work of the Three"). The Tri-Ergon system was similar, but inferior in design, to what would become known as the Fox-Case system. Essentially, the system used the principle of the oscilloscope and converted sound into light beams, recording the beams onto the side of the filmstrip next to the image.

Fox paid $60,000 for 90 percent of the Western Hemisphere rights to Tri-Ergon. In May 1926, Theodore Case demonstrated his sound system to Fox. Two short months later, on July 23, Fox bought the

Case system. Between the Case and Tri-Ergon systems, Fox had a stranglehold on sound on film, which he believed to be inevitable. Now he was prepared for any eventuality.

❑ ❑ ❑

The Warner boys had been very busy. Although their financial ledgers indicated the studio lost $279,000 for the five months ending August 28, 1926, coming on top of a $1.3-million loss for the year ending March 27, 1926, any sense of impending doom was largely an illusion. Harry had tied up with a man with the Perelmanesque name of Waddill Catchings, a man who would prove as vital to the future of the company as Sam, Harry, or Jack.

Catchings had joined Goldman, Sachs in 1918 as an investment banker, where he found time to write two books on economic theory. Catchings' ideas centered around bold, buccaneering action and an adequate money supply, and he was in the process of helping Woolworth's and Sears grow from regional businesses to nationwide chains.

Catchings first noticed Warner Bros. in December 1924, when a friend at another investment house mentioned that the movie company was looking to expand and needed the help of a large Wall Street firm. Although traditional banking interests had only been involved with the movie industry on a nodding basis — mostly in relation to Famous Players–Lasky — and Catchings had never even heard of Warner Bros., he gave the firm a once-over.

He liked what he saw. Harry and Jack kept tight control of their budgets, and Harry had implemented rigid accounting procedures, including daily audits. Because of Harry and Jack's care, Warner Bros. was about to show a profit of $1.1 million for the year ending March 31, 1925. Harry seemed to be a man of his word, and Catchings liked the idea of helping young, first-generation businessmen make it. Catchings agreed to help finance Warners' expansion if they would follow his master plan. Catchings and Harry commenced negotiations in January 1925.

Things went smoothly; that March, Harry bought the debt-ridden Vitagraph Company, which had been losing large amounts of money for the past five years. Harry paid off $980,000 in debts and gave Vitagraph founder Albert E. Smith and his partner's estate $800,000 for the company. Harry got a film library, a studio in Brooklyn, a studio in Hollywood, some real estate, some story rights, and, most important, a film-distribution system* — 26 exchanges in America, 10 in England, and 10 on the Continent.

That same month, Goldman, Sachs and another firm agreed to underwrite new shares of Warner Bros. stock. In May, Catchings joined the Warner board of directors and, appropriately, was named chairman of the finance committee. By the fall of 1925, Waddill Catchings had arranged a $4-million, 6½-percent debenture spread over three years. By a fortuitous coincidence, Catchings's son soon went to work at the studio; under the name Cedric Francis, he eventually became head of the shorts department.

With the influx of cash, Harry bought first-run theaters in Seattle, Baltimore, and Cleveland, among other places, and put Sam in charge. In New York, Harry purchased the 1,500-seat Piccadilly Theater for $800,000 and renamed it the Warner. Warners opened eight new exchanges to go with the outlets they bought from Vitagraph, and made $250,000 in improvements to the Vitagraph studio in Hollywood.

Almost as an afterthought, Warners also started a radio station, probably because Sam and Frank Murphy, head of the studio electrical department, were openly fascinated by the paraphernalia being manufactured by Western Electric. It might, they thought, come in handy for publicity. Their model was undoubtedly S. L. Rothafel, better known as "Roxy," who began his long-running radio show over station WEAF in New York in 1922. Roxy would stand in the wings of the Capitol Theater describing the dancers, the costumes, the lighting, the glistening delicacy of Maria Gambarelli, the Capitol's prima ballerina. Along the way he would prominently mention the name of the film playing at the Capitol, and wasn't it a shame all the listeners couldn't see such a wonderful picture?

---

* Previously, Warners sold their films via the franchise method, in which a major exhibitor from a given geographical area would pay an advance for a group of films and be given exclusive distribution rights to those films in his area as well as a fixed percentage of the profits. It was a clumsy, top-heavy system that could never return enough money to the Warners for them to advance much beyond where they were.

Before long, Roxy's two hours every Sunday night were heard over half the United States. With his farewell tag line of "Good night . . . pleasant dreams . . . God bless you," he became a symbol of the movies just as surely as Charlie Chaplin or Doug Fairbanks, and all because of access to a microphone and a studio.

Buying equipment secondhand from a bankrupt station, Warners called their operation KFWB. By the spring of 1925, Warner Bros. was the only movie company in Hollywood with their own radio station; indeed, they were only the third station in the entire Los Angeles area.*

The brothers weren't exactly sure how to fill up all of KFWB's airtime, so Jack, under the delightfully baroque name of Leon Zuardo, began making appearances as a singer. Since Jack wasn't much of a singer and knew it, he would interrupt himself by telling corny jokes. "Whenever any of Jack's old vaudeville friends were in town," remembered Mervyn LeRoy with a perceptible sense of wonderment, "they would drop around and join Leon Zuardo on the air. They would tell their rotten jokes, swap stories, kill time."

It was while setting up KFWB that Sam once again encountered Nathan Levinson, the West Coast representative of Western Electric. Levinson had been Western Electric's point man in Hollywood since 1922, when he rented a public-address system to Universal for use in the crowd scenes of *The Hunchback of Notre Dame*. Levinson showed Sam a demonstration film of something the company had been playing with for a few years. The demonstration took place at Bell Labs, 463 West Street, in New York, in April 1925.

Louis B. Mayer had called it "a toy." Adolph Zukor said it was "just a gimmick." Sam Warner was immediately entranced.

"[Sam] thought it was a wonderful thing," remembered George Groves, a young Bell engineer who would soon be transferred to

---

* The brothers quickly caught on to what a later generation would call synergy. By November 1926, Warners was using KFWB to broadcast the arrival of stars and dignitaries at the Los Angeles premiere of their second Vitaphone program, Syd Chaplin's *The Better 'Ole,* at Grauman's Egyptian.

Warner Bros. "It was a very simple demonstration of synchronized sound and picture—somebody dropping something on a table and making a noise so that you could see distinctly that the sound and picture were synchronized."

Levinson told Sam that with the facilities and technique of the Warner Bros. organization, and the expertise of the Bell engineers, there was no reason that they couldn't produce such record-breaking hits as Friml's *Rose Marie*. In early May 1925, Sam sat Harry down to watch the same films. Sam was careful not to tell his brother the exact nature of the demonstration, for Harry was adamantly uninterested in talking pictures.

Sam told Harry that he needed him at a banker's meeting, and afterward they had to stop at a reception—"for social purposes"—with some people at the Bell Labs. On the way, Harry stopped at the bank to sign some papers and ran into Waddill Catchings. When Harry told Catchings that he and his brother were on their way to the Bell Labs, the reserved, formal Catchings grasped his lapels and said, "My dear Mr. Warner, you can have all the money you want from this bank, but if you don't mind, I would like to have one of my partners accompany you to the Bell Laboratories ... Left to your own devices, you'd wind up buying the whole of Bell Telephone and Western Electric Company."

"If I said 'talking pictures' to Harry he would [have] thrown me out of the window," said Sam. Harry concurred. "If [they] had said talking pictures," he said later, "I never would have gone, because [talking pictures] had been made up to that time several times, and each was a failure. I am positive if [they] had said talking pictures I would not [have] gone."

As it happened, the Warners were all fond of music, so Sam told Harry that he had stumbled over "an instrument that would bring the best music, the best voices and the best instrumentation to all the small places of the world. He gave me a half-promise that he would take a look ... It took a week of tactful work to get Harry to see Vitaphone and he fell harder than I ever did."

Harry would later report that when he first saw the invention that would be named the Vitaphone, all he could think of was that first nickelodeon in Newcastle with ninety-six — or ninety-nine — chairs borrowed from the funeral parlor, a parallel case of a humble beginning fraught with titanic possibilities.

"Get this," Harry Warner told his brother.*

❑ ❑ ❑

Western Electric had evidently added a few films to the ones Sam had seen; Harry remembered watching a film of a man talking, followed by a jazz band. "When I heard a twelve-piece orchestra on that screen at the Bell Telephone Laboratories, I could not believe my own ears," Harry reported to a class at Harvard eighteen months later. "I walked in back of the screen to see if they did not have an orchestra there synchronizing with the picture. They laughed at me. The whole affair was in a ten-by-twelve room. There were a lot of bulbs working and things I knew nothing about, but there was not any concealed orchestra."

Sitting with Harry was Waddill Catchings's assistant. Talking to Catchings about the demonstration later, Harry said, "If it can talk, it can sing." Harry quickly envisioned a whole new ancillary market; this invention could bring the great vaudeville and theatrical headliners to small and medium-sized theaters that could never have been able to afford them in person. As the brothers talked it over, Sam enthusiastically broke in with "But don't forget you can have actors talk too."

"Who the hell wants to hear actors talk?" Harry snorted. "The music — that's the big plus about this."

Harry's reasoning was simple: "If I myself would not have gone across the street to see or hear a talking picture, I surely could not expect the public to do it. But music! That is another story." And, from a purely business standpoint, they felt the addition of sound might be the wedge that could give the Warners a way to break the monopoly of the bigger film companies.

In spite of their conservatively managed company, neither Harry

* Although Jack would try to grab some of the credit for Vitaphone in later years, Irving Asher — as well as many others who were there — flatly asserted, "He was of no importance at all in the beginning of it. Sam Warner discovered the whole thing and forced the company to take it. It was Sam Warner who did it."

nor Sam was thinking conservatively. "I finally decided to do the thing on a liberal scale," said Harry, "because if it was worth doing at all it was worth doing well . . . Let's get the greatest artists and the best orchestras in the country. Let's have confidence in this and put all our muscle behind it."

Beyond commercial considerations, Harry was already thinking millennial thoughts of sociology and brotherhood. "The time is not far distant when you will be able to see and hear the inauguration of the next president . . . we all know that if you and I can talk to one another, we can understand one another. If Lincoln's Gettysburg Address could be repeated all over the world, maybe the world at large would understand what America stands for . . . if we have a message of friendship or enlightenment that can be broadcast throughout the world, maybe the nations will be led to understand one another better. The Vitaphone can do all that."

It was, in every sense, a fateful trip East. While in New York to see the demonstration at the Bell Labs, Sam had gone to see a musical comedy called *Louie the Fourteenth*. Sam fell hard for the *première danseuse*, an eighteen-year-old veteran of the Ziegfeld Follies named Lina Basquette. As with the Bell system, when Sam saw something he wanted, he went after it. On July 4, 1925, Sam married Lina Basquette. The family was appalled — Basquette was not Jewish — but Sam was blithely unconcerned. He *knew* that he was right about pictures with sound; he knew he was right about Lina.

On April 26, under a *New York Times* headline, PERFECT AUTOMATIC MUSIC FOR MOVIES, Warner Bros. and Western Electric announced their partnership. The article then quickly lurched into complete fabrication: "The apparatus by which combined films and sound records will be reproduced in motion picture theatres is no more complicated from the standpoint of operation than an ordinary motion picture projector . . . if the film breaks, there is no interference with the accuracy of synchronization." Yet, the article achieved an accuracy rare in journalism when it prophesied that the as-yet unnamed invention would "revolutionize the presentation of motion pictures in the largest metropolitan theaters as well as the smallest theaters in the little towns."

Western Electric was unenthusiastic about who they were going into business with, but there were no better offers. An unsigned internal memo of February 4, 1926, notes that "the state of the art is such that it now seems feasible to enter into arrangements for the commercial exploitation of the methods, systems and equipments involved," and outlines their lukewarm view of their new partners: "Warner Bros. Pictures, Incorporated . . . is a corporation composed of four Warner Brothers individually, who [have] had long experience in the motion picture business, Harry Warner, the eldest, having been engaged in that business for twenty-five years. They have recently produced several high grade pictures which have been successful and which are apparently good revenue producers . . ."

Western Electric took a look at Warners' books and liked what they saw: $4 million of three-year, 6½-percent notes sold privately by Goldman, Sachs on October 15, 1925; in July 1925, cash on hand was about $830,000; construction of a new $2-million theater in Los Angeles was to begin in January 1926; no other funded debt. On July 16, 1925, notes payable were nominal and accounts payable very reasonable, about $271,000. The memo noted the comforting presence on the board of directors of the eminent Waddill Catchings, who was also on the boards of B. F. Goodrich; Sears, Roebuck; and Studebaker.

From the contract that Harry, Sam, and Jack finally signed with a Western Electric obviously represented by a crew of Philadelphia lawyers, you might have thought that the entire movie industry was in hot pursuit of sound motion pictures. Warners put down earnest money of $100,000 and agreed to pay Western Electric 8 percent of the Vitaphone gross, in addition to committing to minimum royalties of $40,000 in 1927, $60,000 in 1928, and $75,000 in 1929. They agreed to purchase 160 Vitaphone units in 1927 and double that the following year. If Vitaphone subleased the invention to other producers, Western Electric received half the proceeds. Should Vitaphone fail to maintain the necessary sales levels, the contract would be void.

About the only sop offered by Western Electric was the agreement to defend at its own cost any lawsuits based on patent infringements, a very real threat at the time because of the similarity between Vitaphone and a half-dozen other sound-on-disc systems from the distant or recent past.

Since Warner Bros. had to bear all production and advertising costs, and Western Electric's investment was limited to what they had already spent on research and development, the financial risk was largely on the shoulders of the Warners. Yet, to a great extent, Harry was banking on Western Electric's corporate ego as much as he was on their engineering expertise. While the Warners might go broke, Western Electric's name and prestige were intimately connected with the invention. For the phone company, humiliation and failure would be only marginally less damaging than bankruptcy. "The stake," Harry wisely observed, "was there for both of us."

From a strictly business point of view, Western Electric would undoubtedly have preferred to tie in with Loew's, Inc., or Paramount, but there were other considerations involved. According to Jack Warner Jr., family folklore had it that John Otterson, the general manager of Western Electric, was anti-Semitic and was opposed to his company being in business with "those Jews." * But doing busi-

---

* Otterson graduated from Annapolis and spent fifteen years in the Navy, retiring as a lieutenant. He was president of Winchester Arms before becoming president of Western Electric, a 98-percent-owned subsidiary of AT&T. "He is as cold as ice," said William Fox, who would become his blood enemy, "and feels that because he represents the Telephone Company he is privileged to break his word at will."

Otterson's business correspondence, as preserved in the files of the AT&T archives, fails to substantiate the charge of anti-Semitism, but he clearly didn't trust the Warner brothers and felt that they, and all of show business, were beneath him and his company. "The rather extravagant language of these telegrams is characteristic of the profession," he snidely observed about some telegrams between the brothers, and he defined Grauman's Chinese Theater as "a big show theater patronized by the profession."

At the same time, Otterson genuinely believed in sound movies, approving massive cost overruns (Western Electric spent $250,000 on Vitaphone in 1926, as opposed to the $104,300 that had been budgeted) and was not above nudging E. B. Craft, Bell's executive vice president, about them even after Vitaphone was successfully launched; "I do not want you to lose your interest in this matter," Otterson wrote him.

Whether or not Otterson and, by extension, Western Electric were anti-Semitic, Harry Warner genuinely believed they were, and racial intolerance was anathema to Harry. Years later, when the two companies were locked in an ongoing legal dispute, the president of Bell invited Harry to air his grievances in a private meeting. (cont.)

ness with Sam Warner, a fine young man whose wife wore a cross, was another matter entirely. So it was that Western Electric became partners with Warner Bros.: because Sam Warner, with his broken nose and showgirl *shiksa* wife, looked like an Irishman.

"Mr. Gray, this can be a very short meeting," said Harry. "I will give you all rights to our patents. I will withdraw all our suits . . . I'll do it immediately and at no cost to you, if you'll do only one thing. If you'll give me the name of one Jew who works for your company."

After much sputtering and backtracking, the Bell president said that he couldn't give Harry that one name.

"It's a policy of your company not to employ Jews," charged Harry. "It's a policy of my company not to do business with you." He walked out of the room.

CHAPTER 4

The uneducated, gifted man who would overturn an industry was "a natural salesman," according to his wife, Lina Basquette. She characterized Sam as "a square, box-car man," solid, verging on the portly. He had gray-green eyes with amber flecks in them, and his sandy hair had a reddish-gold tint. Of the other brothers, Sam's favorite was Abe. "He ain't bright," he told his wife, "in fact he's a real dumb bunny, but he's the easiest to get along with."

"Sam had been selling third-rate Warner products for years, all over the world," remembered Basquette. "He could charm most people, men or women. He was closest to Frank Murphy, who ran the electrical department, the crews. He was very well-liked by the performers as well, and women, especially women. I was insanely jealous because so many women were throwing themselves at him. I have nothing to say against Sam Warner; actually, it is hard for me to think he came from the same family [as his brothers]."

"Sam," recalled his nephew Jack Warner Jr., "was the kind of guy who would go to a movie theater, and there would be a breakdown. He'd go up into the booth, fix it, show the projectionist how to run the show so it wouldn't happen again, and go back down to his seat. He had a great feeling for equipment and human relations. My father had a feel for story and for casting, but none whatsoever for human relations. And Harry was removed from them both, first by geography—he spent most of his time in New York in those days—later by a temperamental remoteness. He was a more reserved man."

"Harry was a great financier," said Lina Basquette. "He bombarded Wall Street and was a genius as a money man. He also had the filthiest mouth that ever was; when he ran out of American filth, he'd use Yiddish filth. As a matter of fact, they talked Yiddish a lot of the time. Jack had a certain amount of creativity, but he was always careful to surround himself with good people: Zanuck, LeRoy, Lubitsch."

By this time, the one-for-all-and-all-for-one spirit of the Youngstown days had been obliterated. The Warner family was now a maze of competing egos and ideas. Jack was an impetuous conniver who needed a new woman every week and was jealous of Harry's *gravitas,* while Sam had to devote himself to preserving the equilibrium between the two men. Father Ben, remembered his daughter-in-law, was "a nice old guy, very Orthodox Jewish." He also had the lecherous streak prominently displayed by his son Jack, for he would occasionally sneak over to visit Lina's mother, eat some of her good home cooking, and conclude his visit by pinching her on the ass.

As for Sam, he had one primary insecurity, that of his Jewish identity. "He *never* presented himself as a Jew," remembered his wife. "Most people thought he was a big Irishman."

When Sam came to his brothers with the Vitaphone deal, his wife remembered that "they thought he'd lost his head. They called it his 'toy phonograph.'" While it was meant as a slur, the name had an element of truth; by 1920, the phonograph had even made its appearance in fiction, in the home of Sinclair Lewis's George Babbitt, to play the jazz records that made him feel "wealthy and cultured."

Six years later, a phonograph was as essential a part of a middle-class living room as a sofa. The explosion of radio had only increased the public's appetite for recorded music. Moreover, the microphone had permanently altered the nature of popular song and how it was presented. Heavy, formal renditions of "Ah, Sweet Mystery of Life" had given way to light-voiced crooners ambling their way through "Sweet Georgia Brown" or "Tea for Two." Sound, by whatever means, was an increasing component of American lives.

❑ ❑ ❑

The records for the new sound system that had so impressed Sam and Harry were sixteen inches in diameter, and functioned more or less as a normal record did, except that the needle moved from the center out, and the turntable speed was 33⅓, chosen primarily to extend the playing time of the record to equal that of a reel of film —nine or ten minutes. The projectionist would carefully thread the projector so that a frame marked START was centered in the projection gate. The record for that reel would be placed on the turntable and the needle placed at the tip of the first groove, a spot that was marked with an arrow etched into the disc. As the projector and record player were operated by the same driveshaft, they would remain in interlock as they started up and reached the proper speed.

So far, so good. But the Vitaphone system had inherent instabilities, lots of them. Because of the extreme amplification, a quiet record surface was of maximum importance. Victor, who handled the initial batch of Vitaphone pressings, left out the abrasives that were normally present in 78 rpm records to prolong record life. The lack of abrasives meant that a Vitaphone disc wore out very quickly. Each Vitaphone record carried a series of numbers running from 1 to 24, and after a showing, the projectionist would check off one of the numbers. By the time a disc had been played a mere twenty-four times, it had picked up a sufficient number of pops and clicks as to render it unplayable.

This meant that each set of discs for a given print had to be replaced on the average of once a week; in fact, Warners had to formulate an entire delivery system for the discs in addition to the one they already had for the films. An extra set of discs would be delivered with each print, in case the primary set was defective.

Soon after the contract with Western Electric was signed, Harry, Sam, and Jack decided to maintain Vitaphone headquarters in New York. In July, the old Vitagraph studios in Flatbush were being inspected for their suitability for the production of sound films.*

---

* There were several reasons for centering the production of sound films on the East Coast: the technology was already there, and moving it across Manhattan was a considerably easier task than moving it across the country. Also, the musicians that Sam and Harry were counting on to put Vitaphone over were all in and around New York.

"Two things impressed me vividly," wrote engineer C. R. Sawyer, who reconnoitered the property for Western Electric: "One was that the studio was immediately adjacent to the B.M.T. subway/Brighton line; secondly, the roof of the large studio was entirely of glass (similar to a florist's hothouse). These two factors did not appear attractive from the standpoint of recording sound . . ."

The engineers chose one of the glass-roofed stages ("It was like working in a miniature Crystal Palace," remembered Stanley Watkins) and lined it with sound-absorbing material — old carpets from the prop room. In a nearby room, amplifiers, recording machines, monitoring loudspeakers, and staff were installed.

Of the technicians working on the nascent Vitaphone, it was Stanley Watkins who would prove the most important to the future of sound. Watkins was born in London in May 1888 and had been working for Bell since 1911, mostly on research on hearing aids and loudspeakers. A quiet, dapper, diplomatic man, Watkins was given a year's leave to get Vitaphone up and running. Soon, his native technical abilities and innate gift for navigating the dangerous, competing shoals of Jack, Harry, and Sam meant that Watkins was made chief engineer.

By August 1925, all of the Western Electric equipment from room 1109 was relocated to the old Vitagraph studio. Interspersed with the roar of the trains at the Avenue M station, tests began on the Vitaphone process. Cameraman Edwin DuPar found that the microphones were so sensitive "that we can detect if anybody on the set makes the least noise, such as walking, whispering or even the flickering of a light . . . A flicker of a light sounds out like a pistol shot."

Draperies were hung in the rafters to deaden the sound, and Stanley Watkins went around the floor of the stage clapping his hands, listening for echoes. Sam Warner, a scamp in spite of the pressures, would occasionally hide in a corner and clap simultaneously with Watkins, causing the worried soundman to hang still more draperies, convinced that the echoes were, against all natural laws, getting worse. The only other major problem derived from pigeons, who had grown used to roosting in the roof girders. Someone was designated to be in charge of a long pole used to discourage them from lighting. Carpenters, cameramen, and soundmen began to be hired. Actual production began in late September/early October.

Although it was Jack's nature to interfere in anything he thought he understood, since he understood almost nothing about sound he left Sam blessedly alone. Sam and Stan Watkins worked hard at training the instrumentalists hired to play music for the shorts in the necessary technique. In his traditional manner, Mischa Elman chinned his violin, leaned back, and focused on a spot in the top balcony. The technicians explained that he didn't have to do that anymore, that if he looked directly at the camera it would put his face in front of every member of the audience no matter where they were sitting. Elman couldn't grasp the concept. "But I always look at someone in the top balcony when I give a concert," he complained. He agreed to look at the camera, and as soon as the cameras began rolling, he reverted to looking at the balcony. "We had to give in," wrote Watkins, "and of course when the pictures came through, Elman [looked] as though he was playing to the moon."

While the production of the first series of sound shorts inched forward, the Warner brothers noodled around with the idea of adding music to the John Barrymore swashbuckler *Don Juan*. They also opened their second radio station, WBPI, in New York City. While all this was going on, Sam was giving the matter of sound some deep thought.

"In my opinion," Sam told a reporter on the lot in Brooklyn, "we shall have to draw our actors and actresses for leading parts chiefly from the speaking stage. I believe the most popular film star in the world would become a laughingstock in this form of drama if his voice were uncultivated. Some of the great stars talk broken English . . .

"We were dismayed when we looked over the field and found how limited we are in the selection of actors and actresses who can play their parts well both for the camera and for the phonograph. John Barrymore naturally comes to the mind as a star with a great voice and a fine film presence, but there are very few others . . .

"The most probable development is that scenarios with dialogue will be written solely for the film and phonograph drama. If this form of entertainment becomes popular, it will create a new specialty — dialogue writers. There will be no titles. Dialogue writing will not be exactly the same art that it is in the legitimate drama . . ."

When the reporter inquired as to the possibility of dubbing other voices onto old favorites ("the enthralling voice of Nance O'Neill ... could be grafted onto the pictures of imported sirens like Pola Negri and Greta Nissen..."), Sam understood that it wouldn't work, and foretold the scenario of *Singin' in the Rain:* "The audience would soon discover what was happening and resent the imposition ... Suppose the thing could be faked ... What a battle there would be between the face and the voice for the money! The voice might start at a nominal figure. Later on, after the combination had become a great popular favorite, the voice could hold up the face for fifty percent. If the voice went on strike, the face would be ruined. A great motion picture star might have a deep bass voice in one picture and a mellow baritone in another."

❑ ❑ ❑

On January 2, 1926, William Fox placed an ad in *Moving Picture World* that set the tone for the next several tumultuous years of his studio. "For release in the new season, starting September 1926, Fox takes another great step forward through the production of the world's best stage plays and popular novels of high screen value." Among the planned pictures were *What Price Glory,* the smash Maxwell Anderson–Laurence Stallings play that Fox bought for $100,000; *The Cradle Snatchers,* a hit comedy play of the previous season; and four David Belasco plays. In all, fifteen prestige pictures were planned, nine of them adaptations of plays, two more spun off from novels.

Simultaneously, Fox was cutting back his reliance on westerns, the number of which would be reduced by half between 1924 and 1928. Fox's plans were clear; he would compete with MGM and Paramount, not with stars, but with prestige—famous plays and novels, and a famous director, a jewel in the crown of staff talent.

That same *Moving Picture World* announced Fox's signing of F. W. Murnau, and clearly implied that the relationship between the two men was not that of employer and employee, but patron and artist. Murnau, the director of *Nosferatu* and *The Last Laugh,* the film Fox believed to be the greatest of all time, was coming to America "to put ... subjective thought on the screen, to open up the mind, the heart, the soul." (As will be seen, it is no accident that *The*

Last Laugh, a drama of humiliation and fairy-tale revenge through prosperity, struck such a responsive chord in Fox.)

Fox certainly needed somebody to bulk up his level of talent. John Ford, Raoul Walsh, and Frank Borzage, Fox's top directorial names, were three of the best in the business, but they couldn't make enough pictures to carry the studio. Beneath them was a vast wasteland. Lavish Fox specials like 1926's *The Johnstown Flood* played as if they were produced in 1919 or 1920: indifferently shot and edited, arrhythmic, with mediocre, presentational camerawork, they lacked in mood despite expensive location shooting. Compared to the systematic level of production polish and style that MGM and Paramount had established by 1926 on even their second-tier product, Fox was an also-ran.

Fox clearly knew he had a problem, and he also clearly had a strong eye for talent. He had actually signed Murnau to a contract in January 1925, just weeks after the Berlin premiere of *The Last Laugh*, long before the film arrived in America and caused a revolutionary reappraisal of the value of a moving camera. Murnau's contract was nothing if not lavish. It covered four years and four films and mandated a salary of $125,000 for the first year, $150,000 for the second, $170,000 for the third, and $200,000 for the fourth. If he made more than one film a year, he was to get an additional $125,000 per film.

Murnau was a very different breed of cat from the hardworking Hollywood pros Fox was used to. "He was a great poet, a wonderful man, and a great artist," remembered William Dieterle, who acted for Murnau in his film of *Faust*. "He was very serious. The films he did were all exquisite material. You could not buy him for anything ... He would have starved rather than do something he didn't like ... He was the finest German director."

"[Murnau] was an incredible man," recalled Peter Viertel, the son of Salka Viertel, one of Murnau's best friends. "Very handsome, rather Germanic. Homosexual. Great charm. Like all directors, a bit of a dictator."

He was also incredibly painstaking. "When we came in and saw the rushes at night," remembered Edgar G. Ulmer, Murnau's assistant art director, "Murnau used to get up when the light went on again and say, 'Now we know how *not* to do it.'" By the time Murnau came to make *The Last Laugh*, he had arrived at the idea that each set had to be built for one specific shot, one single perspective; otherwise, the sloping floors and skewed furniture that had been built for one angle would become obvious. If there were ten varying shots of a set, ten sets of slightly varying perspective had to be built. "It gave you," said Ulmer, "a completely controlled style. When you look at the old UFA pictures today, you're startled how precise each and every shot is."

Thin, nearly six and a half feet tall, with hair somewhere between ginger and red, Murnau was reserved, a watcher, the sort of man who missed nothing. He found New York even better than Berlin for people watching. To Murnau, crowds implied stories, and he enjoyed walking in the Broadway district, gazing into faces, noticing eyes. He even looked at feet. In Manhattan, Murnau went to a restaurant that was three steps down from the sidewalk. Inside the restaurant, he looked up and saw hundreds of anonymous legs moving past. He filed the image away for future use.

After too much of the city's congestion, he would need to escape, and escape, for Murnau, meant the sea, its ceaseless movement, its subtly shifting colors. "I like the sea whenever I meet it," he would say.

Murnau and Carl Mayer began to write the script and outline the production of his first American film in Berlin, shaping the material to their own ends. The film that was eventually called *Sunrise* was an adaptation of Hermann Sudermann's *A Trip to Tilsit*. In Sudermann's original, the third leg of the romantic triangle is merely a new maid at the farm, but, in keeping with Murnau's pantheistic bent, she was changed to make her an urban intruder in the idyllic country environment. Throughout, the city was to be treated as a strange, alien environment capable of both destruction and redemption. It was the city that would supply the woman that threatened the happy marriage, and it would be the city, massive, intimidatingly bizarre, that would provide a healing balm to the wounded relationship.

Murnau and Mayer used points from Sudermann's story as islands, set pieces—the seduction, the woman's suggestion that the man murder his wife, the boat trip and the amusement park—and constructed new narrative incidents as bridges. Murnau and Rochus Gliese, his art director, made two hundred sketches, which were then converted into plaster models for the cameramen to determine the best possible lighting methods before the sets were actually constructed.

As construction of the city set began on the back lot, newspaper reports said that the main set was a mile and a half wide and needed two thousand extras to dress the set and run the taxicabs and street-cars. Both figures are exaggerations, even allowing for the streetcar spur that Murnau and Gliese appended to the set. On the other hand, a reported set cost of $200,000 probably isn't too far off the mark.

For a profoundly visual artist like Murnau, his choice of camera-men was all-important. "To me," Murnau said, "the camera repre-sents the eye of a person through whose mind one is watching the events on the screen. It must follow the characters at times into different places . . . it must whirl and peep and move from place to place as swiftly as thought itself when it is necessary to exaggerate for the audience the idea or emotion that is uppermost in the mind of a character . . . [In this way it] photographs thought."

He chose well. Even by then, the blue-collar, workaday mentality of Hollywood crews was well-established, and Murnau consciously chose two men who weren't ashamed to think of themselves as artists. "Charlie Rosher would occasionally call me in to help him," remembered Karl Struss in 1972. "While I was in Italy doing Ben-Hur, Charlie had made connections with Murnau in Berlin and was preparing to shoot Sunrise. When I got back, Charlie called me, and that's how we got together on the film."

Murnau was no less demanding of his actors than he was of his technicians. "I try to make the actors understand the minds of the characters they are asked to portray so that they will know their very thoughts. I talk to an actor of what he should be thinking rather than what he should be doing."

Murnau's initial choice for the part of the loyal wife had been Lois Moran, but Fox production head Winfield Sheehan suggested a rising young actress named Janet Gaynor. Murnau tested her in the restau-rant scene, where the husband tries to convince his wife he loves her after he has been unable to carry through his plan to kill her. Gaynor got the part.

"He was very tall," remembered Gaynor, "six feet four or some-thing, and very handsome, and he had red hair, and he wore a blue jumpsuit, the kind that Mr. Churchill made famous during the war, and a blue beret. He wore around his neck a blue glass, and he would twirl it. He did not wear a monocle, but somehow the blue glass sort of took the place of that. He had a German assistant director, and I was told by people who could understand German that he was very, very cruel to him in his language, but he was absolutely marvelous to me."

For his leading man, Murnau cast George O'Brien, a handsome, gregarious Fox contract player who had risen to stardom in John Ford's *The Iron Horse.* "Murnau liked him for that peculiar quality of innocence he had," said Darcy O'Brien, the actor's son. "Plus Murnau had the hots for him."

O'Brien was devoutly heterosexual, and secure enough to be amused and not threatened. His father, formerly the chief of police and police commissioner of San Francisco, shared his son's outlook. "If George becomes a fairy, he'll be the best fairy there is," he joked with paternal pride. Yet, as *Sunrise* entered production, all smiles stopped. "This was a different experience and a different picture," said Darcy O'Brien. "It would be [O'Brien's] favorite of all his movies. He felt he was doing something significant; he felt he was doing art."

William Fox was acquiring theater chains, expensive plays, and expensive directors; the movie mogul was transforming himself into a Medici prince.

Because of the massive outlay of capital, Warner Bros. began to show a loss. But the company had more than doubled its asset base, and, as Douglas Gomery wrote, it now "possessed an international distribution network, owned a growing chain of theaters, and was producing higher-priced films. Moreover, it had the support of the nation's best banks in its climb towards the top of the industry."

The Warner boys determined that they would not introduce their new process hesitantly, in the piecemeal fashion of De Forest. No, they would present an all-Vitaphone program, a series of talking and musical shorts followed by a feature with a synchronized score. They committed themselves to this course of action in spite of the fact that Western Electric hadn't yet developed the necessary speakers.

At the Brooklyn Vitaphone studios, lighting turned out to be a serious problem. The arc lights used for silent pictures gave off a slight but perceptible hiss. For the production of the shorts, cameraman Edwin DuPar decided to try to modify an arc light in conjunction with more traditional Cooper-Hewitts, but first he had to work with engineers to create lights that would work for at least eleven minutes and be absolutely noiseless.

Even after the lights were quiet and the building had been soundproofed, the technicians had a problem with the elevated trains that ran close to the studio. An alternative location was needed, and fast.

In May 1926, Warners leased Oscar Hammerstein's old Manhattan Opera House on West Thirty-fourth Street and Seventh Avenue.

Again, improvements were necessary. The stage was extended out over the auditorium and seats were removed; amplifiers and recording machines were installed in the boxes; dressing rooms were turned into equipment rooms; and a multitude of draperies were hung to deaden the acoustics. The only location in the building that was suitable for a control room was a Masonic Shrine meeting room on the sixth floor, so lines were run from the amplifiers, up the ventilating shafts, through a metal grill in the wall, and then were hooked up to a primitive mixing panel. Each night, all the equipment had to be removed to make way for the Masonic meetings.

If George Groves had to modify the recording setup for any reason, he had to take the elevator down six floors, run to the stage, then take the elevator back. In the midst of all this, a new subway line was under construction, and the blasting underneath Manhattan occasionally caused the needle to jump out of the wax master recording disc.

Because the cameras now had to be motor driven, and the microphones picked up the sound, the cameras were placed in newly constructed booths, about seven feet high, four feet deep, and three feet wide, mounted on rubber swivel wheels, with a door in the back for the cameraman and his equipment.

At least the Opera House was devoid of pigeons, but other problems arose. When an opera singer was to be recorded in a woodland setting, a crew member brought in a box of field crickets for atmosphere and a few escaped. As Stanley Watkins dryly put it, "Crickets are difficult to locate and sing loudest when the director says 'Quiet.' " There were more baroque interruptions; once, a janitress ruined a take when she began screaming that she had seen the ghost of Oscar Hammerstein walking across the balcony of the Opera House.*

---

* Sam and Harry quickly realized that the Opera House would be yet another short-term installation. Vitaphone production had been centered at the Brooklyn Vitagraph studio from September 1925 to May 1926; Warners would close down the Manhattan Opera House production after little more than a year, in July 1927, to relocate to Hollywood.

Through all this agony, Sam persisted with what had become, according to his wife, "his Holy Grail. He was determined to change the business to sound. He was thinking of transposing operas and concerts and vaudeville, singers and musicians. He really didn't give too much thought to anything else." Sam even talked Harry into paying $52,000 to the Metropolitan Opera for the right to negotiate with its individual stars.

On May 24, Sam put the first Vitaphone short, *The Volga Boatman,* into production. The production style quickly became codified. The performers would do their act as if they were onstage, in a presentational style; the booths the performers faced usually held three cameras — long shot, medium shot, close-up — and each act ran eight to ten minutes, that is, enough to fill up a Vitaphone disc.

The close-up camera had four lenses, ranging from 40mm to a 6-inch, all focused in advance. Since there was no room in the camera booths for the director, he sat outside, where the cameramen could see him signaling, resulting in a quick swivel of the camera and a change of lens. "I often wish for an extra set of hands," said Vitaphone cameraman Edwin DuPar, "as I am as busy as a one-armed paper hanger, and the booth is too small to permit my assistant to come in with me." As there was no way of editing the sound, the performers would do their act until they did it without flubs.

Although one would think that the Warners would have quickly standardized fees for the shorts, in fact everything was negotiable. The low end was represented by the banjo-playing Roy Smeck, who shot his Vitaphone short on July 12 at 9:30 in the morning for $350. The high end was Al Jolson, who got $25,000 for one short, the same price as Giovanni Martinelli. George Jessel got $2,500, Van and Schenck $10,000, Marion Talley $6,000. The violinist Efrem Zimbalist got $3,000, but he had to provide his own accompanist. Ernestine Schumann-Heink got $3,500 for her appearances if they ran more than seven minutes, $2,000 each if they ran less.

DeWolf Hopper had made a living for years in vaudeville doing his famous rendition of "Casey at the Bat," but his market value must have dropped by 1926, for the most Sam would pay him was $1,000, and that for three days' work (one for testing, two for recording). Sam might have been low-balling him because Hopper had already done "Casey" for a De Forest Phonofilm. If anything went wrong, second-line performers like Hopper had to do retakes for free.

While they were recording the shorts, Jack, Harry, and Sam were also working on adding an orchestral sound track to *Don Juan*. Bess Meredyth's script for the Barrymore vehicle makes no mention of any sound track or musical accompaniment of any kind, but does suggest shooting the prologue and the finale in Technicolor, a temptation the Warner brothers successfully resisted.

Don Juan was shaping up as lavish, exuberant fun. It shouldn't have been; the script had nothing to do with Lord Byron's poem, Lubitsch had wisely declined to direct it, and a tired Barrymore was drinking heavily throughout production. His performance was a humorless parody of Douglas Fairbanks, but director Alan Crosland —a Dartmouth man who began as an actor, fell to the lowly status of journalist, then redeemed himself when he began directing shortly before World War I—had given the film great visual style, complete with a flamboyant climactic duel scene.* *Don Juan* was tailor-made for Vitaphone; good but not great, it would showcase the new invention without overwhelming it.

The money kept pouring out, but the brothers persisted. William Axt and David Mendoza were paid $3,500 to write the score for *Don Juan;* Axt chafed at his lowly fee and tried to hold on to the publishing rights to the music as compensation. Conductor Henry Hadley earned $1,000 a week, and the New York Philharmonic signed on to record the score for $1,550 per session, each session to last three hours. Recording work began at 9 A.M. on June 15, 1926, and between June 23 and June 29 the orchestra recorded two 10-minute reels per day. Oddly enough, the film was recorded in apparently random order, perhaps to accommodate the editing process. According to Harry, "It cost us exactly $110,000 to add music to *Don Juan*" (a figure that probably includes the accompanying shorts). A

---

* According to costar Mary Astor, Barrymore followed in Fairbanks' bounding footsteps and did the most dangerous stunt, an impressive leap down a staircase, without benefit of a stuntman; according to Kevin Brownlow, Paul Malvern did the leap for Barrymore.

month before the premiere, Western Electric still didn't have speakers, but they assured Sam they were very close.

Sam's commitment to Vitaphone was unswerving; he met many of the performers at the Opera House, supervised their performances, and tended to the business side as well. His correspondence from this period is detailed and incisive, although the occasional ungrammatical sentence ("I dislike to bother you with matters of this kind . . .") betrays the lack of formal schooling that was never an obstacle for this remarkable man.

Sam was not a man to be pushed around. When the novelty group The Yacht Club Boys contracted for one number for $2,000, they agreed to do a second for an additional $1,000. When they tried to squeeze an extra $1,000 out of Warners, Sam shot off a letter to their agent saying that "if they have received $3,000, that is all they are entitled to, and at that price, they got away with murder."

For the premiere program, the first short to be photographed was, appropriately, the opening of the program, Will Hays' welcoming address, shot on June 17. Production sped up in July, as all but one of the initial shorts were photographed during the first three weeks of the month. Toward the end of July, E. C. Wente finally arrived with the speakers for Vitaphone. Since the brothers had set August 6, 1926, as the date for the premiere, they had only two weeks to install and test the equipment at the Warner Theater.

Inside the theater, days moved seamlessly into nights; Stanley Watkins and his crew began pulling twenty-four-hour shifts. In later years, Watkins would pay heartfelt tribute to the attentions of an osteopath, one Dr. John Beuhler, who came on a daily basis to give treatments to the entire Vitaphone engineering crew.

The brothers stepped up the publicity drumbeat. Posters were slathered over New York buildings. The July 24 issue of *Brass Tacks*, the exhibitors' newsletter published by Warner Bros., let loose with a stentorian open letter on the front page worthy of an Egyptian pharaoh:

"A new era in motion picture presentation has arrived. It will thrill and startle the world. The marvelous Vitaphone process, which will have its first public presentation at the Warner Theater on August 6, will revolutionize the industry. It will make it possible for small town theaters to have the same musical accompaniment as that enjoyed in the biggest theaters the world over. Small town exhibitors will become big time showmen. They can rent music and they can rent film . . .

"The greatest artists of the operatic and musical field can be heard in the smallest of theaters as well as the largest. Millions of people will be educated to a finer appreciation of the best music that has ever been written by the foremost composers.

"Imagine! The wonderful New York Philharmonic Orchestra . . . 107 pieces . . . Henry Hadley, the great musical director, directing . . . In a small town! The synchronization of music and motion pictures is an established fact, and on August 6 the great invention will be heard by the public . . .

"Spread the great message, and deliver it to the exhibitors of the world!"

The ad was signed "Harry Warner."

❑ ❑ ❑

At the Warner Theater, the engineers placed the speakers in the orchestra pit and, possibly, at the sides of the screen. As the film was readied for its premiere, Sam had the idea of inserting a long shot of Henry Hadley and the orchestra taking a bow after the end title of *Don Juan* flashed on the screen, "thereby bringing home to the audience that the music they have been hearing is the Philharmonic Orchestra on the VITAPHONE."

The pressure—and the expense—were beginning to get to Sam. The year before, his nose had been broken by a sucker punch thrown by a disgruntled stuntman named Slim Cole. Ever since, he had been troubled by sinus headaches. Lina now noticed that he was eating aspirin tablets by the dozen, gulping milk of magnesia after every meal. As if he didn't have enough on his mind, Lina was expecting a baby in October.

❑ ❑ ❑

The August 3 issue of *The Film Daily*, just a few days before the premiere of *Don Juan*, is full of chatty news—*Ben-Hur* was being road-shown in fifteen cities, and so on. There was not a word about the nearness of sound.

Because of the modest size of the Warner Theater (1,360 seats), the press preview was held on Thursday, August 5, but the reviewers were requested to hold their notices until Saturday morning, as if they had actually been there the night of the premiere rather than two nights before. Nine shorts were previewed, but only eight were actually shown the night of the premiere. Sam, tinkering obsessively, dropped *The Song of the Volga Boatmen,* and then altered the running order of the eight remaining shorts, switching the positions of Roy Smeck and Marion Talley, and doing likewise with Efrem Zimbalist and Giovanni Martinelli.

Don Juan opened on schedule on Friday, August 6, 1926, at the Warner Theater, on Broadway and Fifty-second Street, at prices that topped out at $3.30. Will Hays recalled, "It was more than a usual first-night gathering. It was an occasion." As an onlooker named Fitzhugh Green observed, "It was a curious, speculative audience, there on unfamiliar grounds, uncertain what it was about to see, or how it should be received. It was prepared more to see a scientific marvel than to be entertained . . .

"Eight-thirty arrived. The lights dimmed . . . a white beam shot overhead and splashed upon the screen . . . but it fell first on the draped curtains on the stage, revealing a subtitle . . . The title gave way, familiarly, to . . . Will Hays. He advanced to the foreground and there was a little sound. It penetrated through people's minds that they had 'heard' him clear his throat.

"The audience hung on his every word, half expecting something to happen . . . that the machinery would break down . . . The phenomenon was like watching a man flying without wings . . . As the picture disappeared a buzz of talk ran through the theater.

"Then silence again as the second number appeared: the Philharmonic Orchestra playing the 'Tannhäuser' overture . . . As the movie image of [conductor] Henry Hadley turned to his auditors after the last note, he 'faced' a theater full of people applauding spontaneously —yet he wasn't there!

"Throughout the rest of the first half of the program the audience sat breathlessly drinking the novelty in. It found that it liked films that talked. It found it impossible to judge such a film . . . it found itself fascinated by the intimacy with which the artist was revealed . . . found itself brought closer to those artists than ever before . . .

91

"When the lights went up for intermission the audience cheered, then gave way to a concentrated buzz of excitement. History was being made and they were there to see the event . . ."

Will Hays, a rat-faced politician from the Harding administration who had been recruited to lend a patina of respectability to an industry reeling from the "Fatty" Arbuckle/Wallace Reid/William Desmond Taylor scandals, gave his little speech with the stock gestures of a small-town orator on the Fourth of July. Watching himself, he was so thunderstruck he didn't even realize how absurd he looked. "In the darkness," he wrote three years later, "I said to myself, 'A new miracle has been wrought and I have had a part in it.' " As for Harry Warner, he wiped his mouth nervously and muttered, "Maybe we'll win."

After the intermission came the feature. *Don Juan* gave a separate credit panel to its accompaniment:

Musical Accompaniment to
DON JUAN
Played on
VITAPHONE
by
The New York
Philharmonic Orchestra

The film was and is an enjoyably baroque concoction featuring first-rate art direction (Ben Carré) and photography (Byron Haskin), sexual perversity, malevolent hunchbacks, torture on the rack, walled-up adulterers, flooded dungeons, and bad wigs. The titles featured a full measure of nudge-nudge-wink-wink, as in the title "Don Juan's home — where innocence might enter — but never depart."

The recording of the Philharmonic was noticeably tubby, as if there was too much sound for the microphone's capabilities; the smaller ensembles used in the accompanying shorts featured far superior recording quality. (This need to keep aural clutter to a minimum is perhaps why Sam and Jack managed to avoid the temptation of having too many sound effects in the feature, limiting them to heraldric trumpets, tolling bells, the thump of hands knocking on doors.)

But, to an audience in 1926, when electrical recording had only been in use for a year, and with those records being played in small living rooms, the theatrical amplification of Vitaphone, its clarity and range, were a revelation. One woman from the audience hovered outside the stage door waiting for Giovanni Martinelli to emerge; she was sure that he had been hidden behind the screen. "He had a big voice," commented Stanley Watkins, "but he never could have come within a mile of the volume of sound that we pumped into that auditorium. And in any case, he was in the audience."

The critical response was all that the Warner brothers could have wished. Most of the attention was devoted to the music heard on the shorts, and properly so; the score Axt and Mendoza composed for *Don Juan* was a bland, characterless hodgepodge, rather like mediocre ballet music. Nobody even noticed that they had cribbed from Strauss's *Till Eulenspiegel.*

The New York Times review gushed that "no single word, however compounded, is quite adequate to suggest the amazing triumph which man has at last achieved in making pictures talk naturally, sing enthrallingly and play all manner of instruments as skillfully as if the living beings were present instead of their shadows . . . marvelous— Uncanny!"

Moving Picture World reported that "the effect of the *Tannhäuser* overture . . . and the singing of 'Vesti la Giubba' . . . by Giovanni Martinelli, was so compelling that the 'professional' audience began to applaud almost before the last note died away . . . As [Mischa] Elman swayed to right or left and touched the bow against the strings, sound and movement touched it off in perfect accord." After noting the muffled sound of the orchestra's film accompaniment, the trade paper concluded, "It is a gigantic stride forward, but not yet a perfect step."

Even the musical journals were bowled over. *Musical Courier* acknowledged that "the reproduction of the music [is] by far the best yet produced. The reproduction of tone colors is perfect. With closed eyes one could easily believe that the actual orchestra was playing . . . One got exactly the same esthetic pleasure and emotion from the Vitaphone performance as if the artists had been playing."

The New York Times movie critic Mordaunt Hall had obviously been talking to Harry and Sam: "The Warner Brothers are to be commended for the high class entertainment they are giving with the Vitaphone. They sought world-renowned musicians and singers, instead of presenting subjects with low comedians. Was it not far better to hear the strident tones of Giovanni Martinelli, singing the 'Vesta la Giubba' aria . . . than to hear a dubious entertainer rendering to the full of his ability that well-known classic, 'Yes, We Have No Bananas'? Was it not infinitely more edifying to listen to Mischa Elman's rendition of Dvořák's 'Humoresque' than to have to sit through a squeaky fiddling of 'Yes, Sir, That's My Baby'?"

Only the upper-crust intellectuals remained unimpressed, but they didn't go to the movies much anyway. *The Literary Digest* said that the Vitaphone reminded them of Dr. Johnson's reaction to a dog dancing on his hind legs: "Wonderful, wonderful. I wish it wasn't possible!" And George Jean Nathan, the eminent drama critic, wrote in the *Morning Telegraph* that "it will bring to the motion picture exactly the thing that the motion picture should have no use for, to wit, the human voice, and that, further, once it brings it, the motion picture will have a tough time holding its own even among the boobs who now make it the profitable institution it is."

Nathan went off into a Mencken-like rant that predicted a wholesale reordering of the star firmament and a mass migration of the movie audience. "To expect a pantomimist, talented though he may be, to be the possessor of a vocal organ capable of expressing all the shadings of dramatic speech is surely expecting a lot. The theater, . . . in all its history, owned [no] more than one or two pantomimists . . . who were simultaneously gifted with the requirements of such dramatic speech . . . The regular . . . movie patron is a person upon whom a strain may be placed only at the risk of losing him. When he is asked to use his eyes, that is enough. To bid him use his ears as well, and, coincidentally, his intelligence . . . is to ask the impossible."

The only silence to be found in the press was in *Variety*, where Sime Silverman gave the film a rave review without ever once mentioning its sound accompaniment or the talking/singing/musical shorts that preceded it.

A week after the premiere, Ben and Pearl Warner wrote Jack a letter: ". . . Mere words cannot express how happy and proud we were of our boys the night of the opening . . . We never dreamed that we would live to the day to witness such a performance, and above all we would be the parents of such wonderful boys. I don't have to tell you that we always were proud of our boys, but this instance gave us the opportunity to realize it more and more . . . When four marvelous boys like you stick together through thick and thin, there is no question but that you will attain all the success you hope for.

"Jack dear, we want to tell you that the only thing that marred our happiness the night of the opening was that you weren't there . . ."

The notably unsentimental Jack Warner pasted the letter in his scrapbook, one of the few intimate family communications he preserved.

❏ ❏ ❏

Among the films playing in New York the week *Don Juan* premiered were Rex Ingram's *Mare Nostrum*, Valentino's *The Son of the Sheik*, Vidor's *The Big Parade*, Seastrom's *The Scarlet Letter*, MGM's *Ben-Hur*, Dupont's *Variety*, and a series of Emil Jannings films in repertory — movies as both entertainment and art.

The films were alike in several characteristics only: they shared a sophisticated outlook and style of storytelling; they lacked speech yet were intelligible in any language; they were the material of everyday entertainment, attended by all classes; and within a year and a half both their style and their essence would be obliterated by a man in blackface singing about his mammy.

CHAPTER 6

ack at the Warner lot on Sunset Boulevard, Patsy Ruth Miller and Douglas Fairbanks Jr. were shooting late at night on an execrable picture called *Broken Hearts of Hollywood* when Jack Warner stormed onto the set yelling "Hold it! Hold it! Harry just called from New York. We're in!" When the shouts and cheers had died down, Jack, overcome by emotion, said, "OK, boys and girls, you can all go home . . . and to hell with expense."

Sam and Jack must have felt *Don Juan* could use some tightening. To accommodate editing changes in the film, a week after the premiere the New York Philharmonic was called back yet again to rerecord reels 2, 3, and 4. At that point, the picture was finally locked in.

Stanley Watkins stayed close to the theater. He estimated that he saw the entire program upward of ninety times from his special seat about halfway back in the auditorium, which was equipped with a telephone to the projection booth and buttons to signal the volume up or down. Watkins said that the main thing he learned from the experience was "how to sleep in a cinema without snoring."

Don Juan remained in place at the Warner Theater well into April of 1927, a notable run of nine months at prices ranging from 50 cents to $2. In each week's advertising, Warners would note the number of weeks the film had played and the total number of people that had attended ("649,683 people have seen *Don Juan* in 32 weeks at the Warner Theater . . .").

Clearly, Sam's instincts had been right. Warner Bros. made an abrupt decision to add music to all the features they would be releasing thereafter. Vitaphone made its next appearance in *The Better 'Ole,* with Syd Chaplin. Although Warners had only bought Bruce Bairnsfather's 1918 play *The Better 'Ole* ("A Fragment for France in two explosions, seven splinters and a short gas attack") that March — and for the very modest stipend of $5,000 — Bairnsfather's agents wanted to make sure that Warners' newfangled invention wouldn't preclude a revival of the play. The contract expressly stated that "rights hereby granted do not include the right to use any spoken words in connection with said motion picture or photoplay . . . all such rights being hereby expressly reserved by the authors . . ." *

As part of the accompanying program for *The Better 'Ole,* Warners paid the incredible sum of $25,000 — $10,000 in advance — to Al Jolson to make a Vitaphone short. Although Warners told Jolson "we anticipate that it will require the whole or part of four different days," and reserved the right to use him for two additional days' worth of retakes, the short was successfully filmed on Tuesday, September 7, at the Manhattan Opera House.

"They started to work," remembered Frances Cowles, the wife of recording engineer Stanley Watkins, "and Jolson began to make such a fuss he got everybody upset. He was a nervous wreck himself . . . When they ran it through, he [had] got everybody so upset that it didn't work; he opened his mouth and nothing came out. He blew up and Stannie went up to him in his calm, quiet way and said, 'Mr. Jolson, you are making everybody miserable and upset and you are behaving very badly. If you would just go out in the lobby and smoke a cigarette or something for five minutes until I get this thing [sorted out] and then come back and do it again, I assure you it will

---

* Jack and Sam couldn't resist chiseling just a little bit; after a painstaking restoration by UCLA's Robert Gitt, *The Better 'Ole* has been preserved, proving that the word "coffee" was whispered in excellent sync, apparently during the orchestra recording sessions, rather than live on the set. It was a small but definite progression from the sound effects and music of *Don Juan,* and it was apparently unnoticed by both contemporary critics and Bairnsfather's agents. Warners continued their coy displays into 1927, and a movie called *The First Auto,* where actor Russell Simpson clearly says one word ("Bob"), four full months before *The Jazz Singer.*

be all right.' And Jolson went off muttering and he came back and he did it, and it was all right."

A few days after the short was filmed, Jolson had to go back to work in the stage show *Big Boy,* but he went grudgingly, for, as he exulted to a columnist: "The Vitaphone has given me the biggest thrill I've ever had, and after this year *I'm going to play with it*" (italics added).

The Better 'Ole, along with Al Jolson in *A Plantation Act* and four other shorts, premiered in New York on October 7. Three days later, Sam and Lina Basquette Warner welcomed their daughter, Lita, named after Lita Grey Chaplin.

Syd Chaplin was a gifted farceur who had the considerable misfortune to be brother to a genius; the feature went over well, but it was Al Jolson who stole the show. In superb voice, Jolson sang three numbers in blackface—"When the Red, Red Robin Comes Bob-Bob-Bobbin' Along," "April Showers," and "Rock-a-Bye Your Baby"—with some high notes he was never heard to hit anytime thereafter. He even talked to the audience ("You ain't heard nothin' yet, folks! You ain't heard nothin'!") and his short was widely regarded as the highlight of the entire program, especially by Jolson, who takes three curtain calls at the end of the film. In the final one, he's blowing kisses to the audience.

Jolson's turn even eclipsed George Jessel's short, with its infra dig kidding. (Jessel is about to sing, when the telephone rings. "Isn't that disgusting?" he says to the camera. "When Martinelli was here, there wasn't one sound, and when I come out, they ring a bell!") The success of the Jolson short, and the singer's positive feelings about Vitaphone, would have shattering consequences in less than a year.*

Syd Chaplin had been working at Warners for a year; his previous pictures had each grossed less than $500,000. While Vitaphone cost more, it also brought in more. Sound boosted the worldwide gross of *The Better 'Ole* to $1.2 million.

---

* The Jolson short would be considered lost by 1933; the film itself existed, but the sound disc had been lost, and it would stay lost until 1995, when the Herculean efforts of a group called The Vitaphone Project resulted in the discovery and restoration of the long-lost sound half of the film.

❑ ❑ ❑

The production of *Sunrise* began on September 15, 1926. In return for complete creative control, Murnau had agreed to work a seven-day week, to bring the expensive film in as quickly as possible. Yet, there were some petty economies: Rosher and Struss had only four days of active preparation to shoot one of the most technically innovative films in cinema.

All of Rochus Gliese's sets were built in forced perspective. The first time Karl Struss walked onto the vast city set, Janet Gaynor was standing in a doorway that was only slightly higher than her head. Across the hall, Struss noticed that the door behind her was precisely three feet tall. Interestingly, even shots that would be glimpsed only for a few seconds, or as part of a montage, weren't fobbed off on a second unit, but were handled by Rosher and Struss. Fox obviously knew what he was letting himself in for, for the production schedule set aside entire days for retakes of water scenes that were being shot with insufficient preparation.

"It was nothing to have twenty, thirty, forty takes," recalled Janet Gaynor. "And it was usually not because of the actors, it was because of . . . light. In *Sunrise* we had all those scenes in the bullrushes, and that was out in the sun. We were out on location, and the light either hit one bullrush, or didn't hit the bullrush."

Murnau's Teutonic quest for perfection produced an ambience far from the happy-go-lucky environment usually found on sets in the silent era. One day, Gaynor and O'Brien were waiting for the light, when one of the crew said something that prompted Gaynor to laugh. "Do not make jokes with Janet!" snapped Murnau.

The American crew quickly grew to resent what Janet Gaynor called "his high and mighty attitude." It became apparent that only one person could lighten his mood. "Sometimes I wouldn't be on the set until ten o'clock if I was not in the first scene," said Gaynor. "[I'd arrive on the set and] I could just feel the tension. I could tell the assistant director was upset, and Murnau would be there too, so stiff, twirling his glass, and everybody was just tense and shy.

"Then the property man would come over and he'd put another stool right next to Mr. Murnau's. I'd come in very quietly and I'd just get up and sit on the stool and never say good morning or anything like that, just sit there very quietly. Finally, a great big arm would come around and go round my shoulders and literally you could almost hear the set go 'Ahhhhhh.' At least I got him in a good mood."

During the weeks spent on location at Lake Arrowhead, Murnau and company would watch the rushes at night, in an open-air theater. Murnau would stand in the back. Gaynor would groggily watch several dozen takes that all looked alike to her. But during the twentieth or the thirty-first take, she would feel a gentle little scratch on her head, Murnau's way of telling her *that* was the one.

Because of the false perspectives of the sets for the city, some of the skyscrapers were only twenty-five feet tall. "In the scene inside the restaurant," said Karl Struss, "we shot out a window looking out across the street, which was downhill on the set. The people that you see across the street are all midgets dressed like normal people!"

Hollywood hadn't seen a production this lavish since *Intolerance.* For the trolley ride into the city, the studio laid track, got a real trolley car, and piped in the electricity so the trolley car could operate. All this for a scene in which the background would almost imperceptibly change from a rural landscape to the outskirts of a city.

"The film almost closed the studio down," said Karl Struss. "Oh, the other people on the Fox lot hated *Sunrise.* They looked on us as trespassers. I guess you could say we were a rental company. We didn't even do our developing at the Fox lab, but sent it out to the Auer lab."

The most difficult shot in a film full of difficult shots was the tracking shot that followed George O'Brien through the woods on his way to a rendezvous with his lover. "We were suspended from an overhead dolly," remembered Karl Struss. "The set used the north, west, and south walls of the studio. It was filled up with trees, open country, etc. The camera picks up George and pans over to where we can see the low moon. Then, we follow him as he slowly turns to the right, finally going out of the shot. The camera, however, keeps going on through all this foliage, tree trunks, everything. We had a wedge-shaped thing in front of the dolly that spread all this as we moved. Finally, as we come through the trees, Margaret Livingston's standing there powdering her nose . . .

"All during the shot the camera was between my legs. It was a son of a gun; all I had to work off was a tiny image on a ground-glass to keep it framed properly. And no viewfinder!" For all of his endless capacity for taking pains, Murnau could be oddly careless about certain things; Karl Struss chafed for the rest of his life about the slightly phony wig Murnau had OK'd for Janet Gaynor, for which he never bothered to shoot tests.

Murnau felt free to invent sequences that weren't in the script. The entire barbershop sequence seems to have been improvised, as was the scene of the runaway pig and the peasant dance. Likewise, some scenes that were in the script failed to make it to the film, notably a rather nice sequence in the city, placed just before the scene in the photographer's studio, in which a clerk helps the wife try on a shawl and tells her that she looks like a Madonna.

"Murnau was marvelous," said Struss. "Very open. I made a number of suggestions that he listened to." In particular, Struss remembered that the slow dissolve to water at the bottom of the frame as the husband lies thinking about killing his wife was his idea. "[One day], we were fighting daylight and wanted to get this one last shot," said Karl Struss. "We only had fifteen minutes before the sun was going to set, so, in order to get the effect of light coming through a window, we put white powder on the ground underneath the window to give the illusion of streaming light . . . It was all studio, all artificial, but it had the atmosphere of reality."

"Murnau [was] the first director I ever worked with who really knew what was going on when he started to move that camera. He knew that you move until you come to a climax, the end of your scene. That's the ultimate, that's what it's all leading up to."

Month succeeded month; as 1926 moved toward 1927, Murnau just kept shooting.

❑ ❑ ❑

For public consumption, Warner Bros. were coy about just what Vitaphone was and how it was achieved. The program for *Don Juan* said only that "a specially designed system registers electrical vibrations — music, singing, etc. The music so registered is reproduced by another device, operated from the projection booth."

In terms of the industry, they were considerably more forthcoming. Warners prepared a three-reel explanatory short called *The Voice From the Screen,* which was shown to the New York Electrical Society on October 27, 1926. The short is divided into six parts: an introduction by Edward B. Craft, executive vice president of the Bell Labs; an inside look at the Vitaphone studio at the old Opera House, including views of the camera and recording gear; a long shot of the studio in operation during an actual recording session for one of the Vitaphone shorts, this one featuring a mid-range guitar-and-ukulele act called "Witt and Berg, Premier Entertainers"; a look inside the projection booth of a Vitaphone theater, complete with the playback equipment; a screening of the completed Witt and Berg short; and closing words by Craft.

Amusingly, when the film cuts from Craft speaking at a podium in controlled conditions to Craft at the Opera House talking about the equipment, the quality of the sound deteriorates, suddenly descending into the bass register. Because of the impossibility of editing sound in the early days of Vitaphone, the studio in production is revealed only in one extreme long-shot, without the close-ups that are needed to reveal the details of the recording process. After Witt and Berg finish their number, a bell rings, the lights are shut off, and everybody goes home.

Craft's oration, very much in the stilted style of the day, foresees a time when "the Faraday of the future, the Pasteur, the Galileo" may use the Vitaphone for educational and scientific purposes: "Our entire educational process may undergo changes beyond our present imagination." This was to be Craft's last bow in regard to the invention he had done so much to promote. As Frank Jewett would remember, because of internecine political warfare, "the commercial people in the Western [Electric] practically eliminated him from the picture. As a result, he alone of those who had had most to do with the whole affair was absent from the initial performance [of *Don Juan*]. It was a slight he never fully got over."

❑ ❑ ❑

As *Don Juan* moved across the country, the audience reaction of stunned enthusiasm was repeated in city after city. Sam, Harry, and Jack now knew that the main attraction was not *Don Juan*, not John Barrymore. In Chicago, where the bill opened at the McVickers

Theater, the ads proclaimed, "Combining a season of concerts with a great motion picture. Warner Bros. present Vitaphone, the wonder of the age! *and* John Barrymore in *Don Juan.*"

Ashton Stevens, the drama critic for the Hearst Chicago paper, wrote that "it sounded great, Vitaphone did, like super-radio when the one hundred and four Philharmonic bandsmen . . . cut loose with the *Tannhäuser* overture. [But] it sounded like a phonograph that needed a new needle when Marion Talley warbled *Rigoletto*'s 'Caro Nome.' I think something slipped here."

Although Stevens thought it most curious that his friend John Barrymore wasn't given an opportunity to speak even a single line, the house as a whole reserved its highest applause for Giovanni Martinelli. "Hand-claps were not enough now. The old house rocked with boot-thunder."

On October 27, *Don Juan* and friends opened at Grauman's Egyptian Theater in Los Angeles to an equally tumultuous response. The film had actually been running at the theater since August 20, but in the conventional silent version, without Vitaphone, possibly because there weren't enough trustworthy technicians to keep Vitaphone on screens in three different cities. Seats were $5.50 apiece, but the show was sold out before the doors opened to an industry crowd curious to see for themselves what had taken New York by storm.

Crowds gathered in the forecourt by 7:45; the audience included John Barrymore, Mary Astor, Charlie Chaplin, Sam Goldwyn, Cecil B. DeMille, Tom Mix, Buster Keaton, Harry Carey, Hoot Gibson, Fay Wray, King Vidor, Harold Lloyd, Jack Holt, Pola Negri, Greta Garbo, Roscoe "Fatty" Arbuckle, Wallace Beery, Allan Dwan, Victor Fleming, Henry King, and 1,780 others.

The show began at 8:30 and, as *Variety* noted, "the audience had not expected such perfect synchronization, and the applause at the conclusion of Mr. Hays' address was deafening." The highlight of the shorts seems to have been Giovanni Martinelli: "The house applauded, cheered and stamped with its feet."

The presentation of shorts and feature went off without a hitch. "Every claim made by its promoters was substantiated," editorialized *Variety*, which had finally tumbled to the fact that something remarkable was happening. In stark contrast to their stony silence for the New York premiere, for the Los Angeles opening the journal published an exhaustive special edition, including the fact that there were 191 kisses in *Don Juan:* "Note: a lady reporter was there with notebook and pencil and counted 'em."

Edwin Schallert, in the *Los Angeles Times,* equaled *Variety*'s sudden burst of enthusiasm: "[Vitaphone's] advent has proven to be as far-reaching and undoubtedly as momentous as anything that has ever transpired in the history of the theater . . . If encores could have been given there would undoubtedly have been a number last night . . . The orchestral accompaniment to the feature was a revelation of what can be done with the Vitaphone in perfectly matching the performance of a large body of musicians with the scenes of a picture . . . The peculiar part is that as soon as one has heard the first program there is a desire to hear a second . . ."

An exultant Jack sent a beguiling wire to Harry in New York:

> WE ARE SPELLBOUND — ALL OTHER OPENINGS LIKE KINDERGARTEN IN COMPARISON WITH TO-NIGHT. NO USE TRYING TO TELL YOU HOW IT WENT OVER; MULTIPLY YOUR WILDEST IMAGINATION BY ONE THOUSAND — THAT'S IT. EVERYONE IN MOTION PICTURES FROM THE DOORMAN TO EXECUTIVES OF ALL STUDIOS WHO HAD TO BE SHOWN, ARE ALL FIGURING HOW TO BECOME PART OF THE VITAPHONE . . . SHOW RAN AS THOUGH IT HAD BEEN HERE FOR TWO YEARS . . . ONLY SENDING THIS ONE WIRE. PLEASE READ TO EVERYONE. HAPPY DAYS. MOTHER AND FATHER AT OPENING ALL SMILED. REGARDS TO BROADWAY.

Sid Grauman seconded Jack in a wire he sent to Harry that same night:

> ANOTHER VITAPHONE TRIUMPH. IT WOULD HAVE DONE YOUR HEARTS GOOD TO SEE AN AUDIENCE TONIGHT APPLAUD AND SOME OF THEM CHEERING . . . CONSIDERING THAT THIS WAS FIVE DOLLAR AND FIFTY CENT AUDIENCE MEANS THAT THE ACID TEST ON THE PACIFIC COAST HAS BEEN GIVEN TO THIS WONDER OF WONDERS . . . IN THE

MIDDLE OF DON JUAN JOHN BARRYMORE LEFT HIS
SEAT, RUSHED TO MY OFFICE SPEECHLESS. CHAR-
LIE CHAPLIN, DOUGLAS FAIRBANKS, MARY PICK-
FORD, MAE MURRAY, HAROLD LLOYD, ERNST
LUBITSCH, . . . AND HUNDREDS OF OTHER PROMI-
NENT CELEBRITIES CLAIM VITAPHONE TO BE A
NOTABLE ACCOMPLISHMENT AND WISH ME TO
CONVEY TO YOU THEIR HEARTIEST CONGRATULA-
TIONS AND WELL WISHES . . ."

Although the reviews and response were immensely favorable, the Vitaphone version of *Don Juan* ran for only three weeks at the Egyptian, where it was replaced by *The Better 'Ole*. Clearly, talking pictures had a longer way to go to convince Los Angeles than they did in New York.

Finally, the industry could see firsthand what had been causing the uproar in New York. Were they impressed? Mightily. Were they scared? Definitely.

Harry Carr, an old Hollywood hand as both journalist and screenwriter *(The Wedding March)*, knew trouble when he saw it and wrote a prescient column: "It is quite possible that some new kind of talking picture might be developed. But the present [style of filmmaking] will never become talkative. Instead of making the movies more real, it makes them less real. The voice accentuates a fact that we sometimes forget—that movie characters are flat shadows on a wall . . . Another reason why the present pictures will never successfully talk is the danger of disillusion.

"The public has seen many lovely girls on the screen; and handsome sheiks. To each one they have given an imaginary voice. In real life, some of them talk like sick peacocks. Many fires of movie fame would be doused forever were they suddenly to talk. The cards would have to be reshuffled . . ."

Carr predicted that the standards for staging opera would have to be radically improved, that vaudeville would be seriously damaged, and that politicians would be able to use the new invention to promulgate their message with a dangerous immediacy.

"The question is not," he wrote, "what are we going to do with it; but what is it going to do to us?"

□ □ □

By the time *Don Juan* opened in Los Angeles, Jack and Sam had made enough shorts to feel confident about the technique; they decided to move the production of some of the shorts from New York to the Coast, and put Bryan Foy in charge. Foy was the oldest of the Seven Little Foys (he wrote the song "Mr. Gallagher and Mr. Shean") and, up to this point, had been a gagman for Sennett, Keaton, and Syd Chaplin. "I had been in vaudeville as a kid," recalled Foy just a few months before he died in 1977. "They figured I knew all the vaudeville acts and could hire them."

Foy was an unapologetic second-rater who had risen to the top of the gagman pile by assiduous plagiarism. "In those days I'd go out at seven o'clock to a theater and see the short subjects. There'd be like a two-reeler and a one-reeler. Then I'd leave that theater and go to another theater to catch the first nine-o'clock show [to see] all the gags they were doing. Then we'd switch them, or they'd give us some ideas. But every night for years I'd go to two theaters, not to see the feature picture — the hell with that — just to see the comedies."

As he began grinding out Vitaphone shorts, Bryan Foy idly suggested to his boss the possibility of making a feature talking picture. Sam Warner waved him away. "Brynie, it's five years away; forget it."

□ □ □

By the end of the year, Vitaphone had been successfully launched, but the technicians at Fox remained unimpressed. "The gossip about town this morning," wrote one Fox executive to Theodore Case on December 10, "[is that] last night at the VITAPHONE show, when Martinelli came out and opened his mouth to start singing, the audience was greeted with the delightful strains of Roy Smeck's banjo. It apparently ruined their show, but was amusing to all of us . . ."

Industry opinions about the future of sound remained deeply divided. *The Film Daily* cautiously mentioned the debut of the Vitaphone as being on the same level of importance as the opening of the Paramount Theater and Carl Laemmle's twentieth anniversary in movies. "[The Vitaphone] definitely marked that long anticipated new era in motion picture entertainment — the science of synchronizing pictures with sound ... [It] seems destined to make history ..."

Yet, in a section of the same annual headlined FIVE YEARS FROM NOW, devoted to predictions, industry luminaries such as Zukor, Fox, and Winfield Sheehan failed to foresee that sound would be the industry norm by 1931. Only the quiet Albert Warner mentioned sound, and then only in passing: "... The public will demand ... proper musical accompaniment, suitable for their particular production." With considerable naïveté, Earl Sponable could say of the invention in which he had a considerable part that "the novelty of 'talking pictures' is past."

It was as if, having discovered North America, the Warner brothers, Fox, Theodore Case, and the rest of the industry imagined that the charting and exploration of the vast new continent was irrelevant.

The truth was something else entirely.

PART TWO

1927

Now that love has made us wise,
Darling, let us synchronize!

Contract for a happy doom
In a churchly mixing room—

Speak our lines in solemn tone,
To some reverend microphone . . .

Thus, 'in sink' we two shall be
One sound-track through eternity!

Leonard Hall
Photoplay
September 1929

Making the silent sequences of The Jazz Singer. Cameraman
Hal N. Mohr is sitting by camera at left, director Alan
Crosland is standing holding megaphone and Al Jolson is
next to Crosland, with his arm around May McAvoy.

The new year began with demonstrations of new inventions, refinements of old inventions, and ceaseless corporate maneuvering.

On January 5, William Fox projected his newly christened Movietone sound-on-film system at the Fox studio at Tenth Avenue and Fifty-third Street. Several shorts were shown to an invited audience. The first was of a baby crying, and Mordaunt Hall of *The New York Times* noticed "a modulated broad hissing sound before the weeping of the baby was heard." A screaming child was an exceedingly odd choice to demonstrate sound on film, but it made at least as much sense as the next film, a singing canary. "This again was not a subject to determine whether the synchronization of the sound and the singing was perfect," dryly noted Hall.

After a presentation of Frieda Hempel singing "The Last Rose of Summer," the popular singer Raquel Meller was presented. "The tones of her voice were as clear as a bell, but, as in other cases, on the quick, short beats, there seemed to be a lack of coordination between the sound and Miss Meller's lips ... One of Miss Meller's most impressive subjects was 'The Wife of the Toreador' which was rendered with fidelity to tone and action ... Not only were her clear tones quite stirring but her movements and expressions added to the interest. In periods of silence no undue scratching was heard."

After such screenings, producers would stand around with worried looks on their faces. Performers like Mary Astor, who was married to the director Kenneth Hawks, contented themselves with smug gibes about how all the noise would do nothing except drive audiences out of the theaters.

The speed of the film bearing the sound track had been standardized at 90 feet a minute, 24 frames a second. Although tradition has had it that 90 feet a minute was the optimum speed for the quality of sound reproduction, the fact of the matter was that, originally, Earl Sponable and Theodore Case had been experimenting with a speed of 85 feet a minute, which appears to have worked satisfactorily. As Sponable said, "After our affiliation with the [Fox company] this was changed to ninety feet a minute in order to use the controlled motors already worked out and used in the Vitaphone system."* The standardization, then, was not made for purposes of sound quality, but for maximum profit for Western Electric.

The first public showing of Fox's sound-on-film process was *What*

---

* Western Electric engineer Stanley Watkins averred that 24 frames per second for Vitaphone was not part of a capitalist plot, but a purely arbitrary decision. "According to strict laboratory procedures, we should have made exhaustive tests and calculations and six months later come up with the correct answer," he related in 1961. "What happened was that we got together with Warners' chief projectionist and asked him how fast they ran the [silent] film in theaters. He told us it went at eighty to ninety feet per minute in the best first-run houses and in the small ones anything from one hundred feet up, according to how many shows they wanted to get in during the day. After a little thought, we settled on ninety feet a minute as a reasonable compromise."

Likewise, the decision about the size and speed of the sound discs revolved around manufacturing expedience. "We had our discs processed by the commercial record companies," said Watkins, "and the largest diameter they could handle was about seventeen inches. With a record of that size, the optimum speed to get the ten minutes of recording time we needed was somewhere around 35 revolutions a minute. We standardized at 33⅓ because that happened to fit best with the gearing arrangement our engineers were working out for coupling the turntable to the picture machine."

Since silent film was shot at speeds ranging from 60 to 80 feet a minute, and projectors became standardized at 90 feet a minute, silent films projected for sound-era audiences would move at a hyper pace that was only occasionally the way they were run for contemporary audiences.

Price Glory on January 21 — the silent version had opened the previous November — preceded by the Raquel Meller short. The last week of February saw a demonstration arranged for about fifty representatives of the press at the Harris Theater before the regular matinee of *What Price Glory*. The demonstration was in two parts: experimental shorts — Hawaiian music on the steel guitar, banjo and piano numbers, a canary singing — and the Meller short, along with one or two newer Movietone shorts. Fox was moving ahead with all deliberate speed, but he wasn't moving fast enough for Earl Sponable, who thought the appropriate mode was a rapid lunge, not a steady stroll.

"Fox with his Movietone could have been ahead of Vitaphone if Fox had let us go ahead," Sponable remembered in 1969. "But he kept me doing tests . . . I made tests of Gertrude Lawrence, Beatrice Lillie, Ben Bernie, Chic Sale, and others. While I was testing Harry Lauder, who did not trust Fox, the singer stopped in the middle of a refrain of 'Roamin' in the Gloamin' ' to announce in his delightful brogue, 'This is a tist.' "

The response to the public showing of Movietone was sufficiently enthusiastic that the *Motion Picture Herald* devoted two pages to it, along with a coherent explanation of the process and the AEO light ("so called because of an alkaline earth oxide deposit on the filament . . ."). By May 25, Fox had an all-Movietone program ready: *Seventh Heaven* — possibly with a synchronized score, probably without* — and a series of shorts — Meller again, Chic Sale in a comedy short, Ben Bernie's orchestra, Gertrude Lawrence singing, and so on.

On May 21 Fox pulled off his greatest coup to date, with a Movietone newsreel of Charles Lindbergh taking off for Paris that was on theater screens one day after the event. The dim, misty morning

---

* *Seventh Heaven* was an enormous hit, playing twenty-two weeks in Los Angeles, nineteen weeks in New York, but as late as October there is no mention of a synchronized sound track in any reviews, while the *Variety* review specifically says the film is silent. Ads for *Sunrise* always made prominent mention of Movietone, but the initial ads for *Seventh Heaven* are silent on the subject. Previous writers have assumed that *Seventh Heaven* was always accompanied by the score that included the hit song "Diane," but it is highly probable that the score was actually completed and added after the film had been successfully launched.

and the thin, ratchety buzz of Lindbergh's fragile single-engine plane thrilled audiences and made the muddy half-tone newspaper photographs of the day seem passé. Sound made things more immediate, made it seem as if it was happening *now*. Fox geared up for a weekly newsreel operation by fall, and exhibitors who invested in new Western Electric equipment would be able to advertise Fox newsreels playing on the same bill with Vitaphone features.*

In May, *Seventh Heaven* premiered at the Carthay Circle Theater in Los Angeles, replacing *What Price Glory*, which had been running since November. The film had cost $1.3 million, and its immediate success proved that the favorable response to *What Price Glory* hadn't been a fluke. Fox was becoming a major force, and not just in terms of PR.

Fox began production on a series of one-reel shorts featuring eminent personalities of the period, such as George Bernard Shaw and Arthur Conan Doyle. The Fox reel with Shaw is a particularly charming example of the art of personality projection. "WILLIAM FOX HAS THE HONOR TO PRESENT THE WORLD'S OUTSTANDING LITERARY GENIUS" is the opening title, followed by Shaw jauntily striding down a gravel path toward the camera, only to feign surprise, complete with double-take, when he gets close enough to notice it.

Shaw was a delightful ham, completely unburdened by false dignity. He could easily have had a career as an actor, and obviously thought the whole thing was an easy way of earning some money. He

---

* Lee De Forest still couldn't catch a break, even though he tried. When Lindbergh returned for his triumphal reception in Washington, D.C., De Forest had his newsreel on the screen (at the Capitol Theater) on the same day as the Fox Movietone version (at the Roxy), less than twenty-two hours after the events. "The result," said *The New York Times* of De Forest's efforts, "gave the audience a vivid idea of the scenes, for not only were the words of the President and Colonel Lindbergh remarkably clear, but there was also an excellent conception of the atmosphere of the occasion, with the band playing, the cheers of the throng and the asides . . . Unusual enthusiasm was aroused by this presentation."

But because of Fox's widespread distribution system, his newsreel, not De Forest's, was the one the public saw. The trade press, as well as the movie industry on which it depended, seemed to have made a unilateral decision that Phonofilms were not to be mentioned in the same breath with Movietone and Vitaphone.

does an imitation of Mussolini, and gives the impression of effortless ad-libbing for seven minutes of screen time. At the end, he excuses himself by saying, "I'm always an extremely busy man, or at least I pretend to be." *

The critics, unused to such displays of personality from fellow writers — who have always tended toward the awkwardly truculent when lured out from behind their desks — were enraptured. Even the flinty Robert Sherwood, who had a good eye for the phony, wrote that "George Bernard Shaw (on the screen, at any rate) is just the sweetest, kindliest, most lovable old Santa Claus that ever was. He positively beams on the assembled multitude."

If not animated by such singular personalities, the early Fox newsreels seem exceedingly dull, for the cameramen would often concentrate on little besides capturing natural sounds: traffic noise, people crossing the street. The Fox-Movietone newsreel crews had to lug more than three hundred pounds of equipment around with them, so they were understandably loath to move any further than they had to; once the camera and microphone were in place, they tended to stay there.

Nevertheless, the foresight Fox demonstrated in sending his new sound cameras out to capture the famous personalities of the literary and political world quickly made Fox-Movietone the undisputed leader of the field, with more theaters showing Fox newsreels (3,000) than all the others combined.

While Vitaphone's and Fox's experiments were getting attention, there was no impression on the part of the public that the studios were stampeding toward sound. Behind the scenes, however, the movie studios began hedging their bets. On February 17, 1927, Paramount, MGM, First National, Universal, and Producer's Distributing Corporation signed an agreement to take a year to study the competing sound systems, then jointly to select a single system that would avoid the disastrous consequences of incompatibility.

The agreement froze the situation while the moguls got their bearings. They were undoubtedly hoping that, by referring the situation to a committee — headed by Paramount's special effects expert Roy

---

* Shaw is reputed to have "directed" the short, which probably means that the Movietone crew was browbeaten into letting him do exactly as he wished.

Pomeroy — the sound fad would fade away long before they ever had to make a decision.

❑ ❑ ❑

Murnau finally finished shooting *Sunrise* one day at noon in February 1927. Janet Gaynor went to her dressing room, took off her wig, put on another dress, and walked onto the set of *Seventh Heaven* that afternoon. After the forbidding Murnau, the warm, emotional Frank Borzage was a sunbath on a spring afternoon. "Frank loved to rehearse a scene up to a point," recalled Gaynor, "but when we'd actually [start photographing] it, he would keep on talking, and so instead of finishing, you'd keep going. He'd say, 'Turn around' or, 'You hear a knock at the door,' and it was very exciting to be able to do that, with something coming into your ear and coming out in motion."

"If you could get the intellect of Murnau," William Fox told Janet Gaynor, "and the heart of Frank Borzage, why, you'd have the perfect director."

The arrival of Murnau on the lot in 1926 signaled the beginning of a radical alteration in the house style of the Fox product. His fellow Fox directors were obviously looking at his rushes, smacking their foreheads, and rushing out to emulate the masterful German. Movies like Raoul Walsh's *The Red Dance,* John Ford's *Hangman's House,* or even a B movie like *Captain Lash,* the work of the bland second-stringer John Blystone, plunged into a dark, glowing, seductive house style that replicates the work of Karl Struss and Charles Rosher on *Sunrise. Captain Lash,* thematically an unremarkable gloss on von Sternberg's *Docks of New York,* features far more camera movement than had been seen on the Fox lot before *Sunrise,* and ventures fearlessly into arty overhead shots and even the perverse: a kinky, lingering sequence in which Claire Windsor is searched while in her slip, the hands of a matron seen pointedly massaging her hips and legs in close-up.

❑ ❑ ❑

Although the clan loyalty of the Warners was in the process of being irrevocably Balkanized, it was still a component of their personalities, as is evidenced by the fact that the third city in the country to be wired for sound was Youngstown, Ohio, where the Dome Theater premiered Vitaphone on January 15. Aside from the fact that Youngstown was their adopted hometown, a Warner brother-in-law ran the theater.

The third Vitaphone program to open in New York was *When a Man Loves,* another Barrymore romance, which premiered on February 3. The response continued to be favorable — the film grossed more than a million on a cost of $528,000 — and Sam continued schmoozing with reporters, leading *The New York Times'* Mordaunt Hall to say that "S. L. Warner is enjoying an enviable success with his Vitaphone concerts ... Each successive presentation gains in points over its predecessor. The results are pleasing and occasionally inspiring."

As before, Sam mixed a few popular numbers in with the classics. On the bill with the Barrymore film, besides a rendition of "La Donna e Mobile" and a quartet from *Rigoletto,* was a short titled *She Knows Her Onions,* which sounds like something Jack would have sung with glass-shattering gusto. "Mr. [Sam] Warner is one of those showmen who is endeavoring to please all of the people all of the time," observed Hall.

Yet, there were some ominous indications that the novelty was wearing off, at least as far as the critics were concerned. *Variety* wrote that "an hour of mechanical sound production ... is a pretty severe experience. There is something of colorless quality about the mechanical device that wears after so long a stretch ..." Other critics remarked that the presentation was uninventive.

Such veiled snideness aside, Sam, Harry, and Jack were accomplishing something remarkable. All three of their Vitaphone films were playing in Manhattan: *Don Juan,* bearing down on four hundred performances, *The Better 'Ole,* going past two hundred fifty, and now *When a Man Loves.* In the short subjects, the brothers were presenting Gigli, Van and Schenck, Fred Waring, Al Jolson, Elsie Janis, George Jessel, Willie and Eugene Howard, Giovanni Martinelli, Mischa Elman, and the New York Philharmonic. For MGM or Paramount, three feature spectaculars in simultaneously successful release would have been a notable achievement, but for

Warners, it was a coming of age, a promise as well as an accomplishment.

In the *Motion Picture News* for February 25, the Warners issued a story that claimed that by the end of the year there would be three hundred theaters equipped for Vitaphone, bringing in weekly rentals of $45,000. Since the contracts the Warners were signing with exhibitors were for five years, the three hundred installations could gross the company more than $11 million. The figures were very pie-in-the-sky, for the reality was that the brothers were having trouble filling the contracts they had. Yet Jack, Harry, and Sam knew that in show business, perception is reality, and they were strenuously attempting to create the perception of success.

Part of the bottleneck was manpower. Western Electric set up a training program that was churning out installation engineers in two and a half weeks, and there still weren't enough to keep up. The other part of the bottleneck was cost. Harry estimated that the cheapest possible cost for a Vitaphone installation in a nine-hundred-seat theater was $16,000, a figure that headed north until it hit the $25,000 needed to outfit a mammoth theater like the Roxy. It was a great deal of money to spend on something most people regarded as a speculative fad. To make the investment more palatable, Warners and ERPI (Electrical Research Products, Inc., a new subsidiary of Western Electric) offered to finance the investment if the theater put 25 percent down, with the balance to be paid over the next year, in addition to a 10-cents-a-seat tax each and every week.

There were other problems out in the field, mainly with the projectionists. One letter from Vitaphone executive J. Louis Reynolds to an employee compiling the Vitaphone instruction manual is instructive: "Our presentations to them must not appear at all formidable. When I read your introduction on page one, after looking at the index, I feel that some of these fellows are going to be scared to death, and so I am now going to dictate an introduction for you which I believe will be more in keeping with the mentality and state of mind of the average motion picture operator . . .

"I am trying to create the impression that I am talking about this thing as one regular fellow to another and not as a lecture from a specialist. I have also tried to inspire confidence in the functioning of the machine, and at the same time make it appear as a simple device, rather than the God-Almightish complicated piece of junk it looks like ... It is very important for all of us that you remember we are dealing not with the intelligentsia, but in the main with a body of middle-aged men, most of whom are scared to death to learn anything new."

Vitaphone may not have been a piece of junk, but it truly was "God-Almightish complicated," as is proven by this June 1, 1927, memo to projectionists about proper splicing procedures for Vitaphone:

> Each foot of synchronized film is numbered. There are 16 frames to the foot. The starting mark is numbered 'o.' The 16th frame after the starting mark is marked #1. The 16th frame after #1 is marked #2 and so on thruout the print. There are, therefore, 15 unnumbered frames between each number.
>
> In case of a break, be sure to insert the exact number of frames of black leader, as the number of frames you take out of the film, plus the frames used for patches. After you have replaced the black leader, be sure to check up and see that the numbers follow in sequence and that there are exactly 15 unnumbered frames between each number. For example: suppose there are two frames destroyed; when replacing these two frames, you necessarily destroy two more frames in making the two patches; you will therefore use four frames of black leader, two of these to make up for the two frames damaged and two to make up for the two frames lost in making the patch.
>
> If you are missing frames which are numbered, or the missing portion is more than one foot, you will have to check both sides of the break to the next number, and after making the splice, see that you do not forget the numbered frame which is the 16th frame of the foot. For example: if the NUMBERED FRAME 100 is damaged, you will see that

after inserting black leader you have 31 unnumbered frames between frame marked 99 and frame marked 101.

Exceptions to this rule to date are:

Prod. #423 *Margaret McKee* (The start mark instead of being at 0 is two frames earlier. In other words, count back 18 unnumbered frames instead of 15 from footage mark #1 and locate start mark at the 18th frame.)

Prod. #482 *The Revelers* (Between footage marks 6 and 7 there are 16 unnumbered frames instead of 15 on all copies up to #30. The copies numbered higher than 30 conform to the rule.)

Prod. #383 *Mary Lewis* (In this subject the start mark is not at 0 but 8 frames later. Or, in other words, count back 8 unnumbered frames from footage mark #1. The 8th frame is the start mark for this subject.)

In Synchronized Feature, but NOT in Vitaphone Presentation Acts, there are scene numbers on the margin of the film in addition to the footage numbers. These numbers can be easily distinguished from each other as the SCENE NUMBERS have a dash just ahead of and behind the number, thus: — 286 —, and the footage numbers are written without the dashes, thus: 286.

In cases where the scene and footage numbers conflict, the footage number is omitted, but is counted and reference will have to be made to the next footage number in sequence.

If a number cannot be found at the requisite 16th frame, continue counting until you reach the next number when you should then have 31 frames between each number. The 31 frames represent the two 15 frame intervals and the frame which would normally have been number . . .

Is that *perfectly* clear?

Vitaphone had inherent breakdowns built into all phases of the system, as the variations in the shorts made obvious, and projection-booth fiascos were only part of the behind-the-scenes struggle, as this 1927 letter from an enraged manager at the Stanley-Mark Strand Corporation to Vitaphone makes clear:

Gentlemen: Here it is seven o'clock Friday night and our next week's show not in, notwithstanding the fact that it was promised on Wednesday and again on Thursday . . . If you think you are going to get away with it, you are vastly mistaken and if you want to make an issue of it, we'll go to the bat with you [*sic*] and we'll see if there isn't someone in our organization that has influence enough with somebody in authority in your organization to get our shows here each week in time for a rehearsal and proper precautionary measures taken to give a decent performance at the advertised time . . .

Sam, Harry, and Jack redoubled their efforts; their financial future and their family name were at stake.

CHAPTER 2

Western Electric's new subsidiary had been formed to deal with all its sound picture and nontelephone business. ERPI was an acronym that would soon become all too common at the studios.

ERPI's general manager was John Otterson. Now that Warners had proved that the system worked, after a fashion, it was up to Western Electric to maximize the profit potential of their invention. Otterson told the Warners that they were taking far too long to get up to speed with Vitaphone. He began applying pressure to renegotiate the contract so Warners would have to cede theater installations and relations with other producers interested in sound to ERPI.

Sam, Harry, and Jack naturally thought this was a very bad idea. Otterson saw ERPI's alliance with the Warners as a crucial problem in dealing with the rest of the movie companies, simply because other firms would be reluctant to deal with a company controlled by a competitor. Otterson began harassing Warners by raising the cost of the equipment by a factor of four, and demanding a greater share of the revenues. Then he played his trump card, threatening to declare Vitaphone in default of its contract.

It wasn't true, but Warners feared losing credibility with the banks that were making expansion possible. Although Warners contractually controlled the exploitation of Vitaphone, they were powerless to resist ERPI's control of the technology. In April 1927, the brothers capitulated, taking a paltry $1.3 million in consideration of their giving up exclusivity and a share of the profits. On May 18, Warner Bros. became a nonexclusive licensee for sound-picture technology. It was one of the last times Harry, Sam, and Jack would be on the losing end of a power play.

Western Electric thus easily accomplished what had obviously been their overarching goal: since the Fox-Case system had no license to use vacuum tube amplifiers or a satisfactory public-address system, they had little choice except to negotiate with Western Electric, whose engineers easily devised a combination disc/film projection unit that would play through standard amps and loudspeakers. That same month, ERPI began installing combination sound-on-film and sound-on-disc units. By mid-1927, Western Electric had smoothly achieved a virtual monopoly on the manufacture and installation of talking-picture equipment.

❑ ❑ ❑

The Big Parade was the film that put Metro-Goldwyn-Mayer on the map of the great studios both creatively and financially. Originally budgeted at $205,000, the production expanded until the final cost reached $382,000. The film amassed a worldwide gross of $6 million and made King Vidor one of Hollywood's premier directors. It also would have made him one of Hollywood's richest directors, for he had a 25-percent share in the profits until Louis B. Mayer talked him out of it. (Vidor's actual salary for 1925 amounted to $141,124.89.)

After *The Big Parade,* Vidor directed *La Bohème,* with Lillian Gish and John Gilbert. A silent-movie version of an opera struck Vidor as something of an inherent absurdity, but he approached it with his usual picturesque intensity and made a distinguished, if not brilliant, picture.

Vidor was a fascinating combination of ascetic and pagan, passion and pragmatism, given to much contemplation of life's deeper meanings, but always pausing for invariably successful pursuits of the pleasure principle. He was, all his long life, a lethal lady's man, with the inevitable result that he was far more successful as a lover than as a husband. Along those lines, although he was fascinated by the spiritual, he was not above cheating on his income tax, which would lead to his being successfully prosecuted for fraud a few years later.*

Vidor was sufficiently self-conscious to be aware of his own quirks, and would always be fascinated by the human inability to be truly objective. He would refer to this as "the solipsistic idea that nothing exists outside of one's own consciousness. I had more of a feeling for this than any other director." As a result, he tended to focus on one primary individual in his pictures, sometimes to the extent of having them appear in virtually every scene. That made his movies, he believed, "subjective viewpoints of the lives [the characters were] leading."

And what kind of a life does an average man lead? Quiet, dutiful, falling into accepted, well-worn grooves. There are fewer villains in life than in the movies, for the things that mar most lives — divorce, death, sadness — are not dependent on villains. *The Big Parade* had been designed as the story of an ordinary man placed in extraordinary circumstances; now Vidor began to contemplate the drama of an ordinary man in ordinary circumstances.

"It takes daring, initiative and courage to get out of step with the crowd. It takes responsibility. Making your own world is a big responsibility. A lot of people try it, but fail. Most people just go along with it," Vidor said. Could he find the pathos and humor of a man who never really tried to get out of step, who was content to go along with the prevailing winds? Could he, in his words, "observe it enough" to make the ordinary interesting? In his Beverly Hills house, Vidor began making notes for his new film while playing a record of Tchaikovsky's Sixth Symphony, the *Pathétique,* an accompaniment that he would carry through to the actual shooting and ever afterward in his mind when he thought of the picture.

The initial story was completed as early as May 1926, and is credited to John V. A. Weaver. The twenty-odd pages contain the basic plot of the film that would be known as *The Crowd,* although in this version, the wife leaves at the end and doesn't come back. The vagueness that would plague the film's production is in evidence

---

* One deduction in particular caught the eye of the IRS; it seemed that Vidor had bet Sam Goldwyn $1,200 that his wife would bear him a son. Vidor lost the bet and tried to deduct the $1,200 as a business expense.

here, specifically about the title. Several are suggested: *40 Million Strong, Just One of Us, All That Matters,* and *The March of Life.* Weaver notes that "I've been racking my brains every day [for a title] . . . last one suggested by Mr. [John?] Gilbert."

Vidor completed another treatment by September. Here, the protagonist's suicide attempt is followed by his achieving great success as a real-estate salesman; the script ends with an odd little coda, with him dying in a contented old age. Vidor then began work in earnest with Harry Behn, who had also worked on *The Big Parade.* By December 21, a continuity script, now provisionally titled *The Mob,* was complete, and Irving Thalberg okayed it for production.*

One day on the lot during preproduction, Vidor was engaged in a conversation when a group of extras walked by, one of them brushing next to Vidor. The director caught a glimpse of the man's profile, and it clicked into place with his mental picture of the main character in his story: likable, agreeable, handsome in a bland, boy-next-door manner, and slightly weak.

Vidor chased the man to a bus on Washington Boulevard. "What's your name? Would you like to come out tomorrow and see me? My name is Vidor . . ." But the young extra didn't come back the next day, and Vidor had to resort to checking on all the extras on the lot until he could match the right name to the face: James Murray. Vidor called him and agreed to pay him to take a screen test. When Vidor asked why he hadn't shown up before, Murray replied, "Oh, I didn't believe you back there on the street. I thought it was a gag or something." Murray took the test and got the part.

This has the ring of something deriving from any of the versions of *A Star Is Born,* but it is true; moreover, such felicitous accidents

---

* *The Crowd,* as it was finally called, was an overtly uncommercial project for the most commercial of studios, and much has been made of Thalberg's altruism in spending a half million dollars of his corporation's money in the pursuit of culture. But Hollywood had been highly conscious of prestige ever since the importation of "artistic" German directors such as Lubitsch in the early 1920s. Each studio made one or two movies a year that were calculated to win prestige and awards, and *The Crowd* was to be MGM's yearly nod toward the critics. In addition to all that, it's highly probable that *The Crowd* was Thalberg's way of making amends to Vidor for getting jobbed out of his percentage of *The Big Parade.*

were necessary for Vidor, for he worked in a vague, intuitive way. "You never got a great deal of direction from Vidor," remembered his wife and leading lady, Eleanor Boardman. "Vidor was a Christan Scientist and he felt that people had cast themselves, and that everything would turn out all right."

Given the amorphous nature of Vidor's concept, and the essential uncommerciality of the material, MGM would undoubtedly have been happier if Vidor had used a well-known actor in the lead, but the director was adamant. "I thought that if I put a star into that part, [the audience] would never believe that he was the common, unknown man who was losing his identity in the crowd. He had to be a man who was constantly trying, but never quite 'making it.'"

Thalberg gave Vidor his head, letting him cast an unknown in the lead, letting him cast Eleanor Boardman as the long-suffering wife, even letting him leave Hollywood to go on location after the studio scenes were shot in early 1927. The studio did not stint on the production. For an office set, five hundred desks were specially built, and six actual elevators covering two floors were installed for a comparatively brief scene.

Eleanor Boardman went dutifully along with her husband's desires, but was none too thrilled about the story. An unregenerate snob ("I didn't care about ordinary people," she told Kevin Brownlow), Boardman much preferred starring in films of glamour and romance in which she could wear "lovely clothes [and men would be] madly in love with me. [*The Crowd*] was a job I had to do. I didn't like to be so drab and unattractive, the hair hanging down, no makeup on. I didn't object to it — inwardly I did — but . . . I had confidence in Vidor; I knew he knew what he was doing."

As the company arrived in New York for the location footage, Vidor and his cameraman worked out a system to get documentary shots of their actors on the busy streets. The camera was placed inside several packing cases on a sidewalk pushcart, shooting through a hole in one of the boxes. Between shots, Vidor would nonchalantly lean against the pushcart and talk to the cameraman crouching inside. Since the stars weren't well-known, and were wearing only the lightest of makeup, Vidor was able to steal the shots he needed.

Vidor's film was not one of plot, but of character, and how it determines fate. The director was not overtly shaping the film, but rather letting it accrete. "We are building this picture as they build plays," he told a reporter. "This is not any film that is ordered and turned out and delivered. It's growing and changing in details." This unorthodox method was driving the MGM unit production manager slowly frantic. "VIDOR UNCERTAIN WHAT TO SHOOT STOP CANNOT GET DEFINITE DECISION FROM HIM . . . ," reads one desperate telegram back to Culver City.

On May 27, 1927, while on location in New York, the production manager sent a telegram to MGM's J. J. Cohn: "1ST CLEAR DAY IN WEEKS — GOT FUNERAL SEQ — THINK IT'S GOOD IDEA YOU SUGGEST TO THALBERG URGE VIDOR TO SPEED UP." This litany of frustration was to be repeated for the next three weeks:

> TOM'W DECORATION DAY — PROBABLY INSUFFI-
> CIENT CROWDS FOR SHOOTING. [*May 29*]

> ONLY SHOOTING TODAY BRIDGE SEQUENCE DUE
> TO NO TRAFFIC — VIDOR NOT SATISFIED . . . LEAVE
> FOR NIAGARA SUNDAY. [*May 30*]

> V. TO SHOOT SEQUENCE SHOWING HOLD-UP OF
> CIGAR STORE BY BANDITS — DOUBT IF IT WOULD
> GET PAST THE CENSOR. [*June 3*]

> MAY DO BRIDGE SEQUENCE IN BUFFALO — THIS
> WILL SAVE TIME AND MONEY — ONE HOUR FROM
> NIAGARA — CAN BE DONE IN POOR LIGHT. [*June 8*]*

> V. WIRED THALBERG THAT HE WILL ONLY DO
> SHOTS OF MURRAY AND KID APPROACHING
> BRIDGE. [*June 12*]

> AFTER PHONE CALL WITH IRVING, V. DECIDED TO
> FINISH BRIDGE SEQUENCE IN BUFFALO. [*June 13*]

---

* The bridge sequence, in which Murray's character contemplates suicide, could not be shot in New York because there were too many structures surrounding the available bridges. Buffalo provided its own set of problems, for Vidor was trying to "steal" the scene, *sans* permission from the authorities, and the company was constantly being stopped by guards. The scene was finally shot in Los Angeles.

V. ILL—NO WORK—SPENT DAY FINDING LOCA-
TION AND GETTING PERMISSION FROM CARNEGIE
STEEL AND THE TOWN OF DUQUESNE. [*June 14*]

V. STILL ILL—SHOT TRAINS PASSING UNDER
BRIDGE AND TRAFFIC FOR FUNERAL. [*June 15*]

MADE PICK-UPS—LEAVE FOR COAST TONIGHT.
[*June 17*]

The sigh of relief is still audible after seventy years. Vidor and company entrained for Hollywood, where he would cut together his film.

□ □ □

As *Seventh Heaven* played around the country that summer, anticipation began building for *Sunrise*, the next prestige Fox production. "Reports and photographs filtering through from Hollywood indicate that the distinguished German director has created an unusual picture," wrote *Moving Picture World*. John Ford was quoted as saying that, on the basis of some footage he had seen, *Sunrise* was the greatest picture ever produced.

Yet, word was not uniformly positive, for in August, one month before the film premiered, William Fox issued a statement denying rumors that *Sunrise* was bizarre, or that Murnau had been unnecessarily extravagant in making it. This demurral was necessary, said Fox, "because of the exotic and sometimes freakish character of the majority of foreign films which have been shown in this country," a reference to Sam Goldwyn's importation, some years before, of the grotesque *The Cabinet of Dr. Caligari*, which had traumatized critics and audiences, as well as arousing a fair amount of xenophobia left over from World War I.

While Murnau was engaged in his mighty struggle to birth art, a Warner Bros. picture called *Old San Francisco* appeared, the sort of lurid, giddy melodrama that the unknowing think typical of the silent film. It involves Warner Oland as Chris Blackwell, cruel ruler of San Francisco's Tenderloin district, who ruthlessly persecutes the Chinese as his vendetta for being half-Chinese himself. He keeps his demented dwarf brother chained in the basement while nursing a major lech for the dewily beautiful Dolores Costello. Ultimately, evil is punished and virtue triumphs by dint of the superb timing of the earthquake of 1906.

Written by Darryl Zanuck with tongue firmly planted in cheek, the picture is beautifully photographed by Hal Mohr. While the story — with Yellow Peril, imperiled virgins, and a *deus ex machina* from deep left field — is redolent of 1906 in more ways than one, the Vitaphone sound track is amazingly clear, the technical equal of 1936. The sound track loses clarity only during the earthquake sequence, because this was probably the first time Warners had attempted to overdub different sounds — rumbles, screams, explosions — onto Vitaphone discs.

Despite the lack of any romantic leading man to speak of, and with a leading lady not known for her ability to carry a picture on her own, Vitaphone carried *Old San Francisco* to a gross of $638,000, more than double its cost. As a picture, it wasn't much, but Vitaphone made a very marginal picture profitable. By the time *Old San Francisco* opened in the latter part of June 1927, Sam, Harry, and Jack had already embarked on the production of the movie that would change not only their lives, but the lives of everybody in show business.

❑ ❑ ❑

Samson Raphaelson was always very specific about the beginnings of his most famous brainchild: the place was Champaign, Illinois, the name of the show was *Robinson Crusoe Jr.*, the star was Al Jolson, the date was April 25, 1917. In the audience was Raphaelson, a native of the Lower East Side of New York, an undergraduate at the University of Illinois.

"I shall never forget the first five minutes of Jolson," Raphaelson wrote in 1927, "his velocity, the amazing fluidity with which he shifted from a tremendous absorption in his audience to a tremendous absorption in his song." Raphaelson was thunderstruck by Jolson's fervor, his energy. He would tell people that he had only seen a comparable spirit and intensity in cantors in a synagogue.

The experience — and the simile — began percolating, and five years later, in January 1922, Raphaelson published "The Day of Atonement," a short story about a young Jew named Jakie Rabinowitz who ignores the wishes of his cantor father to pursue a career as a singer under the name of Jack Robin.

It was all obviously based on Jolson, but Raphaelson had not written a shallow roman à clef. Besides anticipating a primary literary genre — the Jewish novel of assimilation — Raphaelson was mining the idea of the eternal conflict between the demands of a father and the dreams of a son, between the mores of the old and the values of the young. He had unwittingly hit on a theme that could never be outdated, that would have a hard nugget of reality so long as the siren call of freedom lures children to embrace values their immigrant parents find objectionable.

Two years after the story was published, Raphaelson was working as a reporter for *The New York Times* when he ran into a college chum, Peewee Byers, who was playing the saxophone with Paul Whiteman's band at the Palais Royale. Raphaelson mentioned that he was working on turning his story into a play, and Byers said that he would tell Jolson, who often dropped in at the club.

Soon afterward, Raphaelson stopped at the Royale to see his friend; Byers promptly introduced him to Jolson, who wanted to star in the play. The singer described the show Raphaelson should write, a typical Shubert musical, with the story little more than a thin pretext for a series of Jolson songs.

Raphaelson said that while he loved Jolson and was indebted to him for inspiring the story, he believed the script needed to be played as a straight drama, with perhaps just one song at a dramatic moment. The men parted with no hard feelings. "Son," Jolson told Raphaelson, "you go ahead and write that play. And if you have any trouble getting it produced, you come to me."

Raphaelson wrote his play, and found his producer in Sam Harris, who cast the vaudeville headliner George Jessel in the part. *The Jazz Singer* tried out in Stamford, Asbury Park, and Long Branch before a smooth opening at the Fulton Theater on West Forty-sixth Street in Manhattan on September 14, 1925. Raphaelson told film historian Audrey Kupferberg that Jolson attended the opening night in Stamford. When Jessel came out to take his bows, he thanked the audience for its response to "my little play." The ferociously competitive Jolson immediately stood up and yelled "Author, author!" forcing Jessel to acknowledge Raphaelson.

"I was twenty-eight or twenty-nine years old," remembered Raphaelson, "and I was getting around $2,500 a week in royalties. The reviews were good, but they weren't what I expected. I thought I was going to be hailed as a theatrical genius, and I wasn't."

Actually, the reviews were what might delicately be called "mixed." *Variety* reviewed the tryout in Asbury Park and called it "a sure-fire hit . . . though, on analysis, it is all hokum, yet it never seems so." When the show opened in New York, the *Times* called it "a shrewd and well-planned excursion into the theater . . . so written that even the slowest of wits can understand it,"; the *Post* said that it was "literate and interesting, its buncombe obscured by careful construction and sympathetic treatment, its acting genuine." That was as good as it got. The *American* called it a "garish and tawdry Hebrew play," and the *Telegram* referred to "an illiterate comedy drama, steeped in woe and sentiment."

Whatever the critics thought, *The Jazz Singer* received great word of mouth, for business picked up steadily after the Jewish holidays and held even after the play moved to the Cort Theater in early November. On June 4, 1926, the day before *The Jazz Singer* closed so Jessel could honor a movie commitment, Raphaelson sold the movie rights to Warner Bros. for $50,000. It was a very good price but not, considering that the film would be remade twice (in 1953 and 1981), and Raphaelson would never receive any additional money. To protect the road company tour of the play, the contract stipulated that the film of *The Jazz Singer* could not be released until May 1, 1927.

There is no question that Jessel was supposed to re-create his Broadway success on film. Harry Warner had told him, "I don't think it will make any money, but it would be a good picture to do for the sake of religious tolerance, if nothing else." This sounds like Harry, who had a streak of idealism.

The picture Jessel went out to the Coast to make — *Private Izzy Murphy*, a variation on *Abie's Irish Rose* — was for Warners and proved a modest success. Jessel was paid $30,000 for the picture, and Warners had an option for two more pictures at the same price. The June 10, 1926, issue of *Brass Tacks*, an in-house Warners newsletter, announced that *The Jazz Singer* would star George Jessel, and the program for *Don Juan*, released two months later, reiterated that Jessel would be playing "in a screen adaptation of *The Jazz Singer*."

Those plans, however, were in the future; for an eight-month tour that commenced on Labor Day 1926, George Jessel made a tidy living by appearing in *The Jazz Singer*. While he was on the road with Raphaelson's play, Harry, Jack, and Sam Warner were making plans.

❑ ❑ ❑

Early in 1927, Harry, Jack, and Sam began construction on new stages for the Warners studio that were to be exclusively for sound production. On February 19, 1927, *Moving Picture World* reported that Jessel would begin work on *The Jazz Singer* on May 1. And that was the way it stayed until three months later, when, with shooting about to start, Jessel was replaced by Al Jolson.

This is where things get complicated, for the evidence ceases to be resolutely documentary and becomes vaguely anecdotal. The primary rub seems to have been that Jessel's contract was for a silent picture, and Warners wanted to make *The Jazz Singer* with Vitaphone. Jessel, who thought he had found a meal ticket à la James O'Neill's perennially touring *The Count of Monte Cristo*, believed that a sound version would render any theatrical revivals impossible.

"I pleaded with H. M. Warner that the least the company could do was to change my contract [to specify talking pictures] or give me a bonus," wrote Jessel some sixteen years after the event. "As far as I was concerned, I wanted a new deal. He talked about taking care of me if the picture was a success. I did not feel that was enough. We had very heated words, and he closed the argument by saying that I would do no pictures, to which he took an oath on his family's life."

Jack Warner's version of the clash was that the film was due to go into production when Jack phoned Jessel in New York to tell him to report to the studio. Jessel, whose salary was still a nominal $30,000, asked for more money for the musical sequences. Jack offered $10,000 but Jessel wanted it in writing. (Jessel claimed that he had once gotten five bad checks in a row from Warners.) Jack, insulted, told him he was off the picture. These stories, of course, are not mutually exclusive, but, rather, complementary.

While all this maneuvering was going on, Warner Bros. was having Bryan Foy test other possible candidates for the part of Jack Robin, including William "Buster" Collier Jr. Warners had policemen surround the block-long studio on Sunset Boulevard, and, at a given signal, they all blew their whistles, stopping traffic, so Collier could sing in the non-soundproofed studio. If the Warners had been intending to make *The Jazz Singer* as a silent, Collier might have been a fine choice, but, as the tests conclusively proved, he couldn't sing at all, rendering his services of dubious value in a semimusical.

"Jessel would walk on," remembered Foy, "[and] he'd see me working, and [he'd hear] the lines he was used to saying. What they were doing was stalling, while Sam Warner was over there in Denver signing up Jolson." Foy's specific claim that Jolson was signed while in Denver is a distinct possibility; the performer was working there from May 16 to 21 that year.

While this game of point-counterpoint went on, Warners announced that *The Jazz Singer* would be "An Extended Run Production," that is, a prestige item for which top dollar would be charged from both exhibitors and public. As plans for the film continued to be upgraded, George Jessel's screen future got dimmer and dimmer; he was a well-known vaudevillian with one successful play and one (modestly) successful movie under his belt. Al Jolson was a superstar.

Jessel remembered that he had dinner at the Biltmore in downtown L.A. with Jolson the night of Wednesday, May 25, still under the impression he would be starting the film in a week or so. Jolson said nothing about the film, and, as the evening lengthened, invited Jessel to sleep in his suite. "When I got up, early, the next morning," Jessel told Jolson's biographer Herbert Goldman, "Al was dressing. 'Go back to sleep, Georgie,' he told me, 'I'm going to play golf.'" The next day, Jessel read in the *Los Angeles Times* that Jolson had signed to do *The Jazz Singer*. "Al and I didn't talk to each other for quite some time after that," Jessel noted dryly.

Jessel's chronology seems correct. The May 28 issue of *Moving Picture World* announced *The Jazz Singer* as "the first Vitaphone production to be made by Warners on the Coast." It went on to say that "Warner Bros. announce the acquisition of Al Jolson, who will make his debut on the screen in the title role of *The Jazz Singer* . . . Jolson is now in Hollywood and starts making *The Jazz Singer* immediately."

Around the Warner lot, the presumption of guilt on the part of Jack, Sam, and Harry was overwhelming: "Jessel was [double-] crossed," asserted cameraman Byron Haskin. A month after Jolson signed his contract, *Variety* ran Jessel's first, self-justifying explanation of how he got shafted, which revolved around his supposed desire to retain the play's ethnic integrity. He asserted that he had demanded a Jewish director, and Jewish actors to play the parents' parts as well. When Warners told him that Alan Crosland was directing, and that the Swedish Warner Oland and the French Eugénie Besserer were playing his parents, he walked. Besserer may have been French, but she bore a striking resemblance to Pearl Warner, the family matriarch, which might explain why Sam and Jack had no intention of firing her.*

Jessel spent the next fifty-four years of his life — he died in 1981 — brooding over the injustice of it all. His friends at the Comedians Round Table at the Hillcrest Country Club in Los Angeles heard the story so many times they grew to feel they had been shafted as well. "Georgie wanted his salary in cash," said tablemate George Burns, "and Jack Warner wouldn't give it to him. Probably because the company didn't have it."

Jolson signed his contract on May 26, 1927.† He was to perform no more than six songs: "Mammie" [sic], "When I Lost You," "Yes, Sir, That's My Baby," "Kol Nidre," "Mighty Lak a Rose," and

---

* Jessel would attempt revenge eighteen months later when he starred in *Lucky Boy*, a low-budget, part-talkie paraphrase of *The Jazz Singer*. As with the hero of *The Jazz Singer*, Jessel (playing "Georgie Jessel") is the assimilated son of a Jewish immigrant; his father is a jeweler who thinks his son's dream of show-business stardom is absurd. "Georgie Jessel" pawns his mother's diamond earrings and makes his stage debut, but things go wrong, until they go right. Jessel sings "My Mother's Eyes" four times, twice partially, twice completely, and definitively answers the question of what would have happened had he starred in *The Jazz Singer*: Warner Bros. would have gone bankrupt and talkies would have taken another ten years to arrive.

† "Jolson and Jessel were similar types," remembered Jack Warner Jr. "They were both similar physically, they were both extroverts, and they both liked to get up and sing. But Jessel never had the force that Jolson did. Live, Jolson was overwhelming. I saw him in the theater, and, after the show ended, he came out onstage and did two more hours. Well, maybe an hour. And nobody left!

"Jessel was a harder man to get along with. He wanted everything his way. He wanted checks that wouldn't bounce. Warners wanted to give him stock in the company, and in his eyes, at that time, the stock was worthless. Jolson took a chance."

"An' Everything." The repertoire changed; only two of these songs would end up making the final cut of the film; indeed, in the final script, there are no listings of specific songs to be used. Work would begin on July 11 and continue for eight weeks. Jolson was being paid $75,000, with any additional time prorated at $9,375 per week.

And now, Jack and Sam had what they had wanted all along. Jessel's first (silent) Warners film had made a profit of about $40,000, all right but nothing special. Jolson had been a reigning theatrical and recording star since 1912, and his 1926 Vitaphone short had been a sensation; in Minneapolis, for example, the name "Jolson" took up most of the advertising space, while "Vitaphone" and the name of the feature were in much smaller type. Lending credence to the idea that the real coup was in making and releasing Al Jolson's first feature is the fact that in the film's souvenir program, Jolson is mentioned or pictured on every page; Vitaphone is mentioned on only four pages.

Jack and Sam had assigned Alan Crosland to direct *The Jazz Singer*; he was a good director who had made the Barrymore vehicles *Don Juan* and the superb *The Beloved Rogue*. "They figured if he could handle Barrymore, he could handle Jolson," remembered Jack Warner Jr. "Also, he worked well with my father. He would take direction, follow orders, make the picture my father wanted. He was a surrogate director for my father."

Evocative exteriors of Orchard Street, on the Lower East Side, and the Winter Garden Theater on Forty-ninth and Broadway, scene of so many Jolson triumphs, were shot by Crosland in the latter part of June and early July. For the ghetto scenes, Crosland set up his cameras in the window of a second-story restaurant. On cue, actor Otto Lederer, playing the neighborhood *kibitzer*, began moving through the throngs—just another patriarchal Jew. For tracking

---

Although surviving contracts indicate that Jolson worked for straight salary, there is the possibility that Jolson officially signed for a lump sum, but took part of his salary in stock under the table. Jack Warner always insisted that there was no stock involved: "I can't imagine why Jolie spread that talk unless there was a tax angle involved," he said. Yet, Harry Warner told family members that the company didn't have the kind of money needed to pay Jolson until after *The Jazz Singer*.

shots, Crosland put his cameras in the back of an old moving van, with the lens peeking through a burlap drop.

Although the Warners were rolling the dice and risking $500,000 of their money, they were not above economizing whenever possible; the set for the film's first sound sequence, Coffee Dan's café, had actually been used for a Vitaphone short only two months before. The first sound scene to be shot, "It All Depends on You," which was intended for the homecoming sequence (later replaced by "Blue Skies") was scheduled to be directed by Bryan Foy, who was in charge of the Vitaphone shorts. Foy's name was scratched out on the production sheets and Crosland's penciled in. It is probable that Jolson or Crosland or both, having already established a satisfactory working relationship on the silent footage, wanted no interlopers for the all-important sound scenes.

Jack Warner Jr. was a frequent visitor to the set and recalled going into one of the iceboxes with windows that held the camera during the shooting of Jolson's "Kol Nidre" sequence. "I wanted to be close to the action . . . One of the cameramen invited me to share the booth with him while the scene was shot and recorded.

"The door was sealed shut on us to keep the camera noise inside and the air outside. After many minutes of Jolson cantilating, then several retakes, our meager supply of air was slowly being used up and we both were getting faint and dizzy. Finally, when the end of the . . . scene came, the camera booth door was unlatched and we staggered out of the nearly airless box."

Aside from the problems caused by the sound equipment, another, much less obvious problem arose because arc lights, long the staple of silent film lighting, couldn't be used for the sound sequences — the microphones picked up their constant low buzz. The silent scenes had been shot first, and were made with conventional orthochromatic film. Cinematographer Hal Mohr had to use much quieter incandescent lights for the talking scenes, which had a sensitivity toward a different end of the spectrum, necessitating the use of the comparatively new panchromatic film.

Jolson's manically gabby monologue during the "Blue Skies" number was allowed to run uninterrupted. Jolson may have had the soul of a racetrack tout, but he was immensely charming and funny, and his vitality was blatantly sexual. Besides, the engagingly matter-of-fact, almost defiant ethnicity of the scene must have served as a powerful validation for Jolson and the Warner boys; the exuberance with which Jolson punches over the dialogue makes the social point far more expressively than a few titles would have.

Interestingly, the script for the film ends with the death of the cantor, and Jack, now a cantor replacing his father, singing "Kol Nidre." But showmanship and creative energy, always two primary attributes of the Warner lot, seemed to demand something more, and the famous ending with Jolson singing "Mammy" was added. With this ending, the explicit message of the film — that choices are difficult and unavoidable, and a commitment to one's deepest needs involves painful sacrifice — is turned into gibberish. Still, the film was overflowing with schmaltz, spirit, and showmanship. It was a good movie, and it had to be — Sam, Harry, and Jack were staking their careers on *The Jazz Singer*.

❑ ❑ ❑

Sam Warner's habitual sinus trouble was being complicated by some abscessed teeth that he had put off dealing with. There were more important things to worry about — such as completing *The Jazz Singer*. By the end of September, Sam's headaches were monstrously amplified; he complained that his head felt as if it was about to explode, and he was becoming unsteady on his feet. The doctor advised having the teeth removed at a hospital. But, once he was admitted to California Lutheran in Los Angeles, the doctors discovered Sam had a mastoid infection that was drifting into his brain. Doctors operated and tried to clean out the infection, but in that pre-antibiotic era, infection usually proved lethal. Sam sank into a coma.

In New York, Harry abandoned preparations for *The Jazz Singer* and left for California on the train, a couple of specialists in tow. Stanley Watkins was left to supervise the rehearsals at the Warner Theater. At the final run-through, Watkins sat on the aisle, in a special seat outfitted with buzzers that ran to the projection booth. One buzz raised the sound, two lowered it. Jolson sat next to Watkins, while Louis Silvers, who had supervised the musical score, squatted in the aisle. Throughout the rehearsal, Jolson and Silvers jockeyed for what they regarded as the most advantageous setting for their respective contributions.

Jolson: "The hell with your music, I want to hear my voice."

Silvers: "Your voice is OK, Al. Pipe down."

The diplomatic Watkins responded by frantically pushing buttons that would keep both men happy. What neither Jolson nor Silvers knew was that the buttons were dummies, unconnected to the projection booth.

After four operations, on Wednesday, October 5, 1927, at 3:22 A.M., Sam Warner died. The cause of death was listed as pneumonia caused by sinusitis, astromyelitis, and epidural and subdural abscesses. He was forty-two years old. His brother Abe and his wife, Lina, were at his bedside; Harry arrived three hours later. The funeral wasn't held until October 9, to allow the rest of the family to get to California. Sam was buried at the Home of Peace Cemetery.

Sam's death was a devastating blow to the Warners, both practically and psychologically.* "Among other things," said Jack Warner Jr., "I think Jack would have shared power willingly with Sam. He respected him. Sam and he were more alike. And, Sam would have been able to mediate between Jack and Harry. Sam was a free soul. He wanted to marry Lina Basquette? He married her. The family was upset? He handled it, and everybody managed to live with it. My father handled situations like that in a way that created schisms."

The day after Sam Warner died, *The Jazz Singer* premiered at the Warner Theater on Broadway and Fifty-second Street. It proved to be the theatrical equivalent of the moon landing: a long dreamed-of rite of passage that arrived with stunning suddenness.

The Warner brothers had spent a half-million dollars on a movie

---

* Five years later, the family would again be stunned by another unaccountably sudden death. Lewis Warner, Harry's son, who had already shown considerable aptitude for the business and was clearly being groomed to lead the second generation of Warners, had an infected wisdom tooth removed. Although the dentist told him to stay in town and take it easy, Lewis left for a vacation in Cuba. His gums became infected and he fell ill. Brought back to New York, Lewis seemed to rally, then came down with pneumonia. On April 5, 1931, Lewis Warner died at the age of twenty-two.

that could be shown in about a dozen theaters in the world. For that matter, the Warner Theater was the only one they were absolutely sure that the film would play in, because it was the only one they owned. Some measure of the rewards they reaped as a result of their gamble can be extrapolated from one single statistic: precisely three years later, Harry, Jack, and Al would own not one theater but seven hundred.

Although, technically speaking, Warners had sufficient corporate capital, there was still an enormous aura of sacrifice, not to mention tension, about the picture. When one of the young men at the studio asked Harry for a raise, Harry replied that he would like to give it to him, would even be willing to take it out of his own salary, but he wasn't getting one at the moment. Doris Warner, Harry's daughter, distinctly recalled that Harry had pawned his wife's jewelry and moved the family into a small apartment at the time *The Jazz Singer* was in production.

The night of the premiere, and every night thereafter, *The Jazz Singer* hovered on the edge of disaster. Each of Jolson's musical numbers was mounted on a separate reel with a separate accompanying sound disc. Even though the film was only eighty-nine minutes long, counting the overture and exit music there were fifteen reels and fifteen discs to manage, and the projectionist had to be able to thread the film and cue up the Vitaphone records very quickly. The least stumble, hesitation, or human error would result in public and financial humiliation for the company.

Doris Warner remembered that when the picture started she was still crying over the loss of her beloved Uncle Sam, but halfway through she began to be overtaken by a sense that something remarkable was happening. Jolson's "Wait a minute, wait a minute, you ain't heard nothin' yet..." provoked shouts of pleasure and applause. After each Jolson song, the audience applauded. Excitement mounted as the film progressed, and when Jolson began his scene with Eugénie Besserer, midwifing talkies into the world, the audience became hysterical.

By the film's end, the Warner brothers had shown an audience something they had never known, moved them in a way they hadn't expected. The tumultuous ovation at curtain proved that Jolson was not merely the right man for the part of Jackie Rabinowitz, alias Jack

Robin; he was the right man for the entire transition from silent fantasy to talking realism. The audience, transformed into what one critic called "a milling, battling mob," stood, stamped, and cheered "Jolson, Jolson, Jolson!"

Jolson rose from his seat and ran down to the stage. "God, I think you're really on the level about it. I feel good," he cried to the audience. Stanley Watkins would always remember Jolson signing autographs after the show, tears streaming down his face.

"There were crowds of people standing around on the street," remembered May McAvoy, Jolson's costar. "And the police were there [to control the crowds]. It was a very big thing, like *The Birth of a Nation* would have been." Alone among 1,380 people, Samson Raphaelson wasn't cheering. "I had a simple, corny, well-felt little melodrama, and they made an ill-felt, silly, maudlin, badly timed thing of it. There was absolutely no talent in the production at all, except the basic talent of the floating camera . . . It was embarrassing. A dreadful picture. I've seen few worse."

Despite the usual authorial feelings about the death of his love child, even Raphaelson had to admit that "I could see tremendous possibilities, once I heard sound on film. You heard background noises; as you went through the Lower East Side, you heard the street sounds, and so on. I could see a whole new era had come into the theater. But from this particular picture, you wouldn't have much hope for the possibilities of that era."

Variety clearly had no doubts about the picture, saying it was "undoubtedly the best thing Vitaphone has ever put on the screen," commenting that the recording quality of Jolson's songs was "about the best recording Vitaphone has turned out to date." Richard Watts Jr. probably put it best when he wrote that "the picture itself was a pleasantly sentimental orgy dealing with a struggle between religion and art, but as a photoplay it was inherently far from sensational. The important thing was that this device for synchronizing sound with cinema proved capable of catching all of that distinctive quality of voice and method, all of that unparalleled control over the emotions of his audience that is Al Jolson . . . this is not essentially a motion picture, but rather a chance to capture for comparative immortality the sight and sound of a great performer."

The most prescient review came from Robert Sherwood in *Life* magazine, who described in detail the scene between Jolson and Besserer, describing it as "fraught with tremendous significance . . . I for one suddenly realized that the end of the silent drama is in sight . . ."

Photoplay and its traditionalist editor, James Quirk, resisted. "Al Jolson with Vitaphone noises," snarled the magazine. "Jolson is no movie actor. Without his Broadway reputation he wouldn't rate as a minor player. The only interest in the picture is his six songs."

The young English writer Aldous Huxley also found the film's charms eminently resistible: "The film concludes with a scene in the theatre, with Mammy of Mine in the stalls . . . and the son . . . warbling down at her the most penetratingly vulgar mammy song that it has ever been my lot to hear. My flesh crept as the loud speaker poured out those sodden words, that greasy, sagging melody. I felt ashamed of myself for listening to such things, for even being a member of the species to which such things are addressed."

This was, to say the least, unduly harsh. *The Jazz Singer* is one of those films that does just what it says it will do. The film's second title ("THE NEW YORK GHETTO — THROBBING TO THAT RHYTHM OF MUSIC THAT IS OLDER THAN CIVILIZATION") is the prelude to a very evocative montage of the Lower East Side; the backstage atmosphere has the same hard-bitten brio that would animate *42nd Street* a few years later; there is a stunning close-up of an unbilled young actress named Myrna Loy, and that future talkie standby Roscoe Karns is prominently featured.

Most importantly, Vitaphone delivers. The unwieldy system proved amenable to various gambits that Warners had never used before: silent reaction shots interpolated into the middle of sound footage, and, most creative, a sound overlap — when Jack Robin, banished because of his show-business inclinations, says goodbye to his mother, we hear his father singing at the synogogue blocks away.

The Jazz Singer is enlivened by Jolson's skittering, waterbug movements while singing — with his swiveling hips, he was a 1920s' version of Elvis Presley. His infectious enjoyment of his own performance was transmitted in everything he did, and especially by his use of his familiar catchphrase, "You ain't heard nothin' yet," in the film's first talking scene, a sharp jab in the ribs from Jolson to the audience that something spectacular was happening.

Creatively and industrially, *The Jazz Singer* marks the beginning of the convergence of the parallel lines along which sound had been developing: features in which the voice was little more than an occasional sound effect, and shorts in which the voice itself was the focal point. Socially, it marks one of the few times Hollywood Jews allowed themselves to contemplate their own central cultural myth, and the conundrums that go with it.*

The Jazz Singer implicitly celebrates the ambition and drive needed to escape the *shtetls* of Europe and the ghettos of New York, and the attendant hunger for recognition. Jack, Sam, and Harry let Jack Robin have it all: the satisfaction of taking his father's place *and* of conquering the Winter Garden. They were, perhaps unwittingly, dramatizing some of their own ambivalence about the debt first-generation Americans owed their parents. (Sam ignored his parents' wishes and married a *shiksa*. Although Jack's first wife was Jewish, he was perennially unfaithful, usually with gentile actresses, angering both his parents and Harry.)

Jack and Sam might have ignored the integrity of their story, but they were being true to what they, and the rest of the world, wanted from the movies. The willful distension of reality was about to give them a success and a fortune they had never dreamed of.

Scanning the laudatory reviews, watching the lines form outside the Warner Theater, Jack and Harry felt it was a Pyrrhic victory. Jack would remember that "the Jolson debut was . . . empty . . . This was a *man* who had gone away. Shy, gentle, and humble, Sam was all men to all those he met . . . When Sam died — and there is no doubt that *The Jazz Singer* killed him — something wonderful went out of our lives."

---

* Warners obviously had some complaints about the Yiddish slang in the titles; in later bookings, the program would helpfully include a glossary of Yiddish phrases to help the *goys* in the audience navigate: "*kibitzer:* a busybody . . . *shiksa:* a non-Jewess . . ."

CHAPTER 3

As far as most factions of the industry were concerned, Vitaphone was still too ephemeral to notice. When *The Film Daily* ran an obituary for Sam, they made no reference to the sensational success of his brainchild, nor did they review the film—not the day after the premiere, not in the month of August, not for the rest of the year. It was a breach of basic newsgathering egregious even by the limited standards of show-business journalism at that time, a breach that could only have been intentional. Clearly, there were people who thought Vitaphone and the Warner brothers would go away if they were only ignored, especially now that Sam would no longer be around to cajole and seduce nonbelievers.

Now, in the best tribal fashion, the Warner brothers began to close ranks in order to expel Sam's widow, the dangerous *shiksa*. In 1926, the brothers had formed a holding company/joint bank account called Renraw (Warner spelled backward). It paid out salaries (a modest total of $100,000 a year). If any of the brothers needed any extra money, they took it, no questions asked; when the company needed extra money to buy something, Renraw would liquidate some stock, then lend the money at current banking rates, but without security.

Sam's will left Lina the proceeds from a $100,000 trust fund and a $40,000 insurance policy. But his all-important 62,500 shares of Warner Bros. stock were left to his three brothers. Sure, Sam's death was tragic, but now the family had a job to do: get rid of his widow and keep it—the stock, the money, even, if possible, Sam's daughter—all in the family.

"I think some of it was a question of Lina's personality," said Jack Warner Jr. "She was a chorus girl, a dancer. Mainly though, she wore a cross, and Grandma [Warner] never understood or forgave. It was a Central European thing. You see, all things being equal, Harry was an honorable man. But if things weren't equal, or if family was involved, then Harry would do what he had to do."

□ □ □

By late September, a rough cut of *The Crowd* had been prepared and was provoking disturbed reactions at MGM. A note of September 28, 1927, from the young producer Hunt Stromberg that was almost certainly solicited by Thalberg is a clear indication of the studio's discomfort with such a downbeat film. Stromberg suggests that the entire beach sequence is cute but unnecessary, and the scene where a hysterical James Murray tries to quiet people in the street after the death of his child is too depressing.

Another letter, from Laurence Stallings to Thalberg, also singled out the same scene, and suggested lightening the second half, as well as altering the ending to make John more sympathetic. As late as December 1927, both the ending and the title itself were still in question. Perhaps, suggests a studio memo of December 3, *White Collar Man* would be a good title?

□ □ □

Although *The Jazz Singer* was setting box-office records in New York, there was no line of ardent exhibitors outside the Warner Bros. studio on Sunset Boulevard. As *Fortune* magazine put it, "On October 7, the big producers . . . said *The Jazz Singer* merely proved that songs by Jolson could carry one whole picture; they ignored that one true talkie sentence."

Jesse Lasky would write that "many of us were skeptical that it would amount to anything . . . The idea of sound in pictures wasn't new . . . It had been kicking around for over thirty years. We saw no reason to think it would catch on at this late date. I thought I had flattened the arguments for sound with irrefutable logic when I pointed to [his wife] Bessie's oil painting of trees blowing in the wind that hung back of my desk in the Paramount Building and observed patronizingly, 'Do you have to hear the wind to appreciate the artist's intention?' "

Nobody realized what had been set in motion. Well, almost nobody. A few days after the premiere, Jack Warner and Darryl Zanuck charged onto the set of a costume film entitled *Glorious Betsy* and told everybody that they were going to add dialogue scenes to the film. Just like that. *Glorious Betsy*, a cheap ($198,000) picture of no particular distinction, grossed nearly a million dollars with its Vitaphone sound track. And *The Jazz Singer* would end up grossing $2.6 million on a cost of $422,000, strongly indicating to Jack and Harry that they were on the right track.

After much hustling, Jack finally reined in a well-known San Francisco exhibitor named William Wagnon for the northern California premiere of Vitaphone. San Francisco was a good test case, for it had a long history with movies with sound. The city had seen the Kinetophone as early as March 10, 1913. Edison's device was met by the *Examiner* with a story headlined TALKING MOVIES ARE ORPHEUM SENSATION, but the program, consisting of an on-screen lecture by Edison himself, followed by the great man conducting the "Edison Minstrels" in song, came and went quickly.

Wagnon's theater was called the Embassy, but under any name, it was a shoddy old house that had been shuttered for years. "He suggested to [Alexander] Pantages that he go partners with him on the new talking picture venture," remembered Wagnon's son William Junior, "but neither Pantages nor any of the other major chains or exhibitors were interested. Nobody would gamble on talking pictures then."

The problem, as Pantages and many others saw it, was that Vitaphone offered an exhibitor no fall-back position; to tear out pieces of the stage and install immobile speaker horns put them beyond the point of no return should sound prove to be a fad. Besides, Pantages told Wagnon, there weren't enough pictures in the pipeline to keep the theaters going; downtown movie palaces changed bills weekly, neighborhood theaters twice-weekly and even daily. Warners, Pantages pointed out, barely had a month's worth of movies on the shelf.

Despite all this, Wagnon committed to Vitaphone. Three days before the opening—November 3, 1927—the engineers tested the system. "It was Nick Lucas singing 'Tiptoe Through the Tulips,'" remembered William Wagnon Jr. "When the engineers yelled down they were going to run this test . . . there were painters, and carpet layers, and installers working in the theater. Everybody just stopped and looked at the screen with their mouths open . . . The whole crew just stopped."

Jack was playing his cards close to his vest. Rather than leading off with the surefire Jolson picture, he teased San Francisco with Barrymore's *When a Man Loves*, while the shorts included Giovanni Martinelli, and Vincent Lopez and his orchestra.

With Vitaphone production being sped up, Harry realized the company had to do something about its manufacturing capabilities. He heard that the Brunswick Record company was in financial trouble and quickly closed a deal to get their record presses. The presses were shipped to the Sunset Boulevard studio, where they were mounted in a long row and reconfigured to manufacture the 16-inch Vitaphone discs.

Harry's only problem derived from the fact that he was now the owner of a division that made bowling alleys and billiard tables. That aspect of Brunswick had been in a slump and Harry had no desire to enter the bowling business. He promptly sold off the bowling and billiard operations to a new company that also called itself Brunswick.

In just a few years, as the industry switched to sound on film, Harry would be stuck with an expensive collection of white-elephant record presses. Seventy years later, the Brunswick company still makes money in the bowling and billiard business. "They weren't always geniuses," wryly observed Jack Warner Jr.

❑ ❑ ❑

To title *Sunrise*, Winfield Sheehan at Fox called on the recently signed team of Katherine Hilliker and Captain H. H. Caldwell. The "Captain" stemmed from Caldwell's service as an aide to Admiral Dewey at the battle of Manila Bay. The two became close friends, and Caldwell was best man at Dewey's wedding in 1899.

In 1921, Caldwell married Katherine Hilliker, who had been a journalist until, in 1915, she went to work in the story department at Universal. In 1920, she joined the staff at the Capitol Theater in New York, titling Ernst Lubitsch's *Madame Du Barry* (a German production) for American audiences. After their marriage, Caldwell and Hilliker began hiring out as a team. They worked for Goldwyn, where Hilliker prepared *The Cabinet of Dr. Caligari* for American release, and then, in 1925, they went to MGM, where they edited and titled many important pictures, *Ben-Hur* among them.

Hilliker seems to have done the lion's share of communicating with their bosses, and she was a spiky individualist who refused to truckle. Lured to Fox in July 1926 by a starting salary of $800 a week, Hilliker and Caldwell sent a letter to their ex-boss Irving Thalberg, thanking him for the opportunities he had given them, and for allowing them to take their names off Victor Seastrom's film of *The Scarlet Letter.* They then proceeded to chastise the film's existing titles for the "bad grammar" that was "open to misconstruction" and other failings they classified as "blunders . . . which you have been too busy to catch."

Some of their bile might have been occasioned by the facts of life of working at MGM. "There is no such thing as being given a picture to work on," she complained. "You're told to write a set of titles for a picture, then instead of having them made up even in temps and fitting them into the picture, you have to take your title list into Mr. Rapf or Mr. Thalberg as the case may be; then the cutter, the continuity writer, a stray author or two, possibly Mr. Wid Gunning, sometimes another title writer and the chief reader are invited in and hullaballoo begins, everyone of the assembled guests trying to outdo each of your titles as it is read out. How much of that do you think you could stand?"

Hilliker and Caldwell approached their work on *Sunrise* with agonizing thoroughness, subjecting each title to multiple drafts, working on the film in sequences. The opening titles were written and rewritten dozens of times, in order to strike just the right note of universality. Even minor titles were approached with painstaking care.*

---

* Perhaps too much so. Cameraman Karl Struss was chagrined to discover that the release version of the film contained almost twice as many titles as the script. "This was done," grumbled Struss, "as a concession to the great public, which presumably cannot as yet take its entertainment by seeing and thinking for itself."

For instance, title #9, in which the vamp entices the young farmer to follow her to the city, was offered in multiple options:

"THE CITY! WAIT UNTIL YOU KNOW IT! LIGHTS AND MUSIC — EXCITE-MENT AND THRILLS — FREEDOM — LOVE — "

Or: "THE CITY! YOU DON'T KNOW IT! EXCITEMENT — THE JOY OF LIVING — LOVE — FREEDOM — "

Or: "THE CITY! WAIT UNTIL YOU KNOW IT! FREEDOM — LOVE — LIGHTS AND MUSIC — EXCITEMENT AND THRILLS — A MAD WHIRL — "

The adjustments went on until just two weeks before the film's premiere. After the film had already had its musical score recorded, the Caldwells revised the wording for title #2: "For wherever the sun rises and sets — in the city's turmoil or under the open sky on the farm — life is much the same; sometimes bitter, sometimes sweet — "

As they noted in a memo of September 12, "Title No. 2 is six words shorter than the one it replaces in the picture. As this picture has already been scored for MOVIETONE the new title should have the exact length in footage of the old."

Hilliker and Caldwell responded with such attentive detail because Murnau had created a masterpiece. It is ironic that one of the most pantheistically celebratory of all films is also one of the most synthetic. While the film mostly avoids stylistic expressionism, the tactics and impulses behind it are as overtly expressionistic as the twenty-pound weights Murnau forced George O'Brien to put in his shoes, so that his heavy, clomping tread physically expressed his emotional state.

(O'Brien's remarkable, daring performance during the film's first third, head down, shoulders thrown forward to ward off emotion and emphasize his hulking body, makes his metamorphosis from a brooding, would-be murderer to enraptured husband that much more exhilarating.)

Murnau's natural bent was toward the formal, the defined, the symmetrical, each shot perfectly composed and framed. Film is a two-dimensional medium, but Murnau creates a sense of three dimensions by using foreground objects — a lamp, a fountain — to give a sense of planes of action.

Murnau creates an entirely integrated work of art, not in spite of the lack of dialogue, but because of it. Silence gives the anecdotal story a timeless universality. In a scene near the end of the film, the wife sleeps peacefully in a boat as her husband battles a raging storm that has suddenly blown in. As William K. Everson pointed out, in a talking film, with realistic sound effects, it would be absurd for her to continue sleeping through a near-hurricane, but in a silent film, the moment works as a metaphor for her newly restored trust in her husband.

Dialogue is replaced by a subtle musical score by Hugo Riesenfeld, and some creative, symbolic sound effects — at climactic moments, church bells signal catharsis. Shot by shot, scene by scene, Murnau so unites material and technique that the audience must simply give itself over. Trick shots, tour-de-force photography, and, above all, the inexorable, fatalistic rhythm of Murnau's editing are in service of an emotional and aesthetic continuum.

What keeps an academic deadness from slowly obliterating emotion are the humane, impassioned performances Murnau draws from his actors, and his frequent use of what might be called a "bump," abruptly cutting to a shot where the emotion is already at a high point, as in the scene in the narthex of the church. For that matter, the entire film begins with a bump; a conventional director would begin with the woman from the city arriving in the country and seducing the man. But Murnau cuts to the chase, opening with the man already preoccupied by his affair, needing only a slight nudge to agree to murder.

Murnau is interested in texture, and the way it reflects emotional states; the rough wooden floor of the peasant houses, the slick, gliding glitter of the vast city. As the great cinematographer Nestor Almendros would note of *Sunrise*, "It was so atmospheric you could almost touch the air and smell it." And Murnau was after an emotional, not geographic, reality — in the famous tracking shot through the swamp, the audience gradually loses all orientation as the shot progresses, mostly because Murnau had two separate moons constructed for the shot. Our geographic disequilibrium equals the man's moral disequilibrium.

Murnau gives the dominant role to the woman — in the love scene in the swamp, the woman ends up on top of the man. Woman's wishes and needs dominate the passive man, which may or may not relate to Murnau's feelings about his own sexuality. What is certain is that in Murnau's films, whenever sensuality rears its smooth head, disaster is never far behind—witness *Sunrise, Tabu, Faust,* and so on.

The premise of *Sunrise* implies a simple city-country dichotomy, but Murnau is never that superficial. The vastness and diversions of the city, its innate impersonality, enable the couple to rediscover their love for each other. The city may be the origin of the bacillus, but it is also a healing medicine.

When the film opened in New York, on September 23, 1927 ("Destined to Amaze, Awe, and Thrill Millions in Search of Something New in Amusement," read the ads in hyperbole that was simultaneously vague and desperate), it was preceded by a fascinating match-up of Movietone shorts, one with Mussolini and the Fascist regiments, the other with the Vatican choir. *The Film Daily* noted that "the recording was splendid."

Sunrise bowled the critics over. Mordaunt Hall of *The New York Times* called *Sunrise* a "brilliant achievement," *The New York World*'s Quinn Martin said that it was "the best, most adult, and most satisfying screen play to come this way in a year," while Robert E. Sherwood in *Life* called it, "to my mind, the most important picture in the history of the movies."

Even the trade papers, normally the last bastion of a homespun preference for domestic "entertainment," thought it was wonderful, although they were hard-pressed to say why. The notably grumpy *Film Daily* called the film "amazing. It gets over to the audience an indefinite something; just what, it is difficult to describe."

There were only a few dissenters, most prominently *Photoplay* ("too arty") and John S. Cohen Jr. in the *New York Evening Sun,* who helpfully re-directed the film for Murnau when he wrote that the film was "lopsided . . . If *Sunrise* had been carried through in the proper manner, the wife should have drowned, the husband should have thrown the city gal out on her ear, and then, as the sun came over the hills, he should have been shown, his soul awakened, entering some tiny hillside church to pray, or else going to the top of a hill and stretching his arms towards the sun."

Sunrise would be hailed all over the world; in Berlin, the *Neue Berliner* would call it "the best, maturest and most artistic film of the world," while the *Reichsfilm Blatt* said that it was "not only a masterpiece [but] a great event."

William Fox had undertaken *Sunrise* on the assumption that it would be highly problematic commercially. In several cities, *Sunrise* was a road show: in New York it had the considerable run—for an art film—of twenty-eight weeks, in Los Angeles ten weeks, in Philadelphia eight weeks, in Detroit nine weeks. These were first-rate engagements, but outside the sophisticated markets, business fell off. In Pittsburgh, the film eked out one week, the same run as in Cleveland, where it had to compete with vaudeville acts on the same bill. The film played what the trade called a "grind" basis even in Boston, where it lasted only a week. Still, *Sunrise* did well enough in the large cities to justify itself financially. Certainly it did far better than previous Murnau films such as *The Last Laugh* and *Faust*—which barely struggled through a two-week run in New York.

Sunrise ended up amassing domestic rentals of $818,000. It was the third highest-grossing film Fox released that year, after Borzage's *Street Angel* and Ford's *Four Sons*. William Fox had earned at least as much prestige as he could have wished and, once foreign receipts were added, couldn't have lost much, if any, money. Still, he seemed dissatisfied about something; perhaps the idea of intentionally losing money was easier to countenance than actually doing it.

Murnau quickly began assembling the pieces of his next movie. Both men agreed on one thing: this one would have to be made for a lot less money and a bigger audience. Fox and Winfield Sheehan were pleased with the titling efforts of Katherine Hilliker and H. H. Caldwell. Their options were picked up, their salaries were raised to $1,000 weekly, and they were assigned to edit and title the most prestigious Fox films.

A December editorial in *Moving Picture World* commented that "from the Coast comes word that Fox is going right along turning out products like *What Price Glory* and *Seventh Heaven.*" No mention was made of *Sunrise*, which spoke volumes. In the meantime, Movietone was an even bigger hit than *Sunrise*. By November, Fox was running its Movietone newsreel all over New York, and it was doing well enough so that display ads included a list of the theaters in Manhattan and Brooklyn that were showing the newsreel, with no mention at all of the accompanying features. "Hear the news as well as see it!" proclaimed an ad in *The New York Times*.

❑ ❑ ❑

By now, many people in the business had seen at least some of the sound pictures that Warners was turning out. Their reaction was encapsulated by First National producer John McCormick, who said that talking and singing were good for short subjects, as a bonus for the patrons. But people, said McCormick, liked the dark quiet of the movie house, with the symphony orchestra underlining the emotions of the actors. Even comedy was better silent. Virtually everyone whose name wasn't Warner or Fox agreed with him.

Most filmmakers looked upon talkies with something between contempt and horror. "To compare *The Jazz Singer* with *Sunrise* ... was sheer blasphemy," wrote the actress and screenwriter Salka Viertel, the wife of writer-director Berthold Viertel. Even a lofty intellectual like H. G. Wells concurred. Talking to Terry Ramsaye of *Moving Picture World* (October 31, 1931), he said, "The talking picture—how often so absurd...They drag the infernal microphone around, and there is such an infinity of difficulty and labor that the entertainment is squeezed out."

Nevertheless, the evidence of the box office was clear. Sound was suddenly hot, and Al Jolson was now the biggest star in the world. Soon, he would sign a three-picture contract with Warner Bros. that paid him $225,000 per picture plus 10 percent of any film that grossed over $1 million. He was guaranteed top billing and the studio was forbidden to use any outtakes or scenes from the completed films in any compilations. It was the percentage agreement that made this such an astonishingly rich deal; it would help Jolson clear nearly a million dollars on *The Singing Fool*, the follow-up to *The Jazz Singer*.

❑ ❑ ❑

What exactly was the quality of the sound that audiences heard in 1927?

The Vitaphone discs had a frequency response that reached up to about 4,300 cycles per second (the range of human hearing extends to about 20,000 cycles per second); the rival optical-sound process bettered that, with a response that would eventually reach 8,000 cycles. Needles rode the record grooves with a thundering force of between three and six ounces. (Thus 78 rpm records of the same period are marginally superior to the 33⅓ rpm Vitaphone discs because their faster speed made it possible to record and reproduce higher frequencies.)

There were no bass or treble controls on the early Vitaphone control boards, nothing to guide the sound into some reliable middle range. Add to this the primitive tube amplifiers, the catch-as-catch-can quality of the speakers,* and the fact that most of the theaters in which Vitaphone was being shown had been built with acoustics designed for live, not recorded music, and the results must have been at least slightly problematic.

The microphones could also be troublesome; their active agent was carbon, which had a tendency to coagulate. Engineers learned to tap the mike to jar the carbon granules, but sometimes they forgot, or were using a bad mike. That said, Vitaphone sound could be remarkable; the early shorts and features in particular have excellent sound. Original Vitaphone discs of Jolson's *A Plantation Act* and *The Jazz Singer* offer remarkably clear sound. The disc for the initial sound sequence of *The Jazz Singer* records Jolson's finger-snaps with a clarity that makes it sound like he's in the room.

But, without very careful recording and playback, early sound

---

* The speakers marketed by Western Electric were of the horn type, which could be aimed toward the most absorptive areas of the theater, thus giving the best quality. But the RCA speakers were nondirectional, large cones mounted on both sides of the screen, and tended to spray the sound around. RCA was also working on devising their own sound system, a variation on sound on film. The system, called Photophone, was excellent. It was successfully previewed in February 1927 at the Rivoli Theater in New York, before an invited audience that was given strips of the film as a souvenir. The test films included a master of ceremonies talking, a film of a hotel orchestra from Schenectady playing several songs, and two reels of MGM's *Flesh and the Devil* as recorded by the orchestra at the Capitol Theater.

Unfortunately, the market had already been divided by Vitaphone and Movietone, and RCA couldn't find any buyers. David Sarnoff was forced to find a market for his system by creating one. In October 1928, he took over a small studio known as FBO and the considerably larger concern known as the Keith-Albee-Orpheum Theater Circuit and formed RKO Radio Pictures, setting up an interesting competition on Wall Street—RKO was largely financed by Rockefeller money, and Western Electric was largely financed by Morgan money.

could be on the thin, echoing side, with trebles emphasized. Seeing a movie on the third or fourth day of use of a set of discs was a guarantee of scratchy, sibilant sound. But none of this seemed to make any difference. So long as there was dialogue, and it was (more or less) in sync with the actors' mouths, the audience was not merely satisfied, but thrilled.

While audiences were lining up with the greatest enthusiasm, in the projection booths there was a constant state of low-level panic, caused by the incessant demands of the Vitaphone process, and by memos like this one from Warner Bros., containing the Thou Shalt Nots of Vitaphone:

> DON'T expect good reproduction if equipment is allowed to get out of order.
>
> DON'T allow discs to become warped. Keep in a cool place.
>
> DON'T use a disc that is dusty or dirty. Brush it off.
>
> DON'T use a needle more than once. Needles are cheaper than audience dissatisfaction.
>
> DON'T allow needles to become loose. Tight needles and tight electrical connections mean clear reproduction.
>
> DON'T fail to see that the needle tracks properly. If full-tone needle fails to track, use halftone needle.
>
> DON'T put the fader [volume control] on until the motor is at top speed.
>
> DON'T start the motor until the film is properly threaded and the record is properly set on the start mark.
>
> DON'T overlook the fact that good reels are necessary for take-up. Watch take-up reels to see that they are working properly . . .
>
> DON'T start a disc until the tone arm is properly in line.
>
> DON'T use a scratched disc. If any scratch shows, get a new disc.
>
> DON'T forget that the fader setting should be judged by the capacity of the theater and the number of persons in the audience.

Seeking to accentuate the positive, Warner Bros. didn't release any of these concerns for public consumption. Even within the trade, they sought to emphasize the positive benefits of Vitaphone, and they made it sound as though any idiot could run the system success-fully. As Porter Evans, a Warner Bros. engineer, said while delivering a paper to the Society of Motion Picture Engineers, "[Vitaphone] is simplicity itself. The only attention the reproducer requires in the projection booth is the insertion of a new needle with each disc. If anything goes wrong with the reproducer, a new one may be in-stalled quickly, easily and cheaply.

"The only skill required on the part of the projectionist is that required to select the correct record and place the needle on the start mark, and occasionally replace a section of damaged film by the same length of black leader. A little difficulty has been experienced in getting projectionists capable of doing this. It is much more diffi-cult to find men who can properly maintain the more complicated soundhead [with sound on film.]"

Evans went on to claim that when sound on disc was compared to sound on film in a blindfold test, participants invariably picked the discs because "it is firmer and clearer and contains more detail than the film." *

For their part, Fox claimed that the aural differences between the two systems were intentional. As Earl Sponable told the same group of engineers, "The Movietone has differed from the Vitaphone from the beginning. We ... do not want ... to simulate an orchestra but rather to serve as a frame for the picture ... We prefer to ... make the music part of the picture. We like to keep the volume low in order not to detract from the picture." Of course, this may have been an intellectual rationale for the ofttimes fuzzier quality of sound on film.

---

* This may in fact have been correct; James G. Stewart, the sound engineer who would record *Citizen Kane*, said that Vitaphone was superior to Movietone because of the absence of wow and flutter that plagued early sound on film, not to mention the back-ground noise caused by the light cell picking up the grain of the film emulsion. Robert Gitt at UCLA points out that the film stock of the period had a coarser grain than the modern variety.

Overleaf: Two examples of the duties expected of projectionists during the talkie revolution. "Fader" was an early term for volume control.

RULES FOR OPERATORS

1. Check film number with the record number to make sure they agree before threading the film or setting the needle.

2. Set the starting frame of the film in the aperture.

3. Make sure the needle (see paragraph 13 below) is firmly clamped in the reproducer and then set it within $1/4''$ of the start of groove.

4. Give flywheel several turns with left hand and watch needle at same time to make absolutely sure that it is "tracking" properly in the starting groove. This is very *important*.

5. Never remove or put the clamp on the record while the turntable is turning, since this may damage the springs which form the mechanical "shock absorber."

6. In making changeovers on orchestral accompaniment to feature pictures, *always* wait for last note of music from the old record before moving the fader over to pick up the music from the new one, regardless of which machine the picture is coming from. That is, there will usually be a short interval during which the music comes from one machine and the picture from the other.

7. When making changeovers, move fader as smoothly as possible. If you cannot make the complete changeover in one movement, *stop at zero* for a fresh grip. Be careful not to "overshoot" the setting and have to come back to it. *Never* have the fader on any point but zero unless the motor is up to speed, otherwise there will be a very unpleasant change of pitch in the sound coming from the horns in the auditorium. In case of a break, *always* bring fader to zero *before* stopping motor.

8. Keep volume of monitor horn down until it is just loud enough to follow the music after numbers have started, but turn it on sufficiently loud for cues (but not louder than necessary).

9. Mark each record *after* it has been played.

10. Always put records in envelopes with the playing side next to the felt and facing you. In using records during the show, place the empty envelopes in the back of the record cabinet; this always brings the next record to be played at the front of the cabinet.

11. Buzzer Signals — 1-Fader up one, 2-Fader down one, 3-Booth call.

12. In testing horns, try them one at a time, using for test purposes a record with which you are familiar.

13. Never use a Victor full-tone steel needle for more than one record. Where Tungsten needles are supplied they should be used in accordance with instructions left by engineer.

14. Every operator should know how to do the following: (a) Start the amplifier system, (b) Operate battery charging panel, (c) Test amplifier system on Monitor Horn, (d) Shut system down, (e) Test horns, (f) Run complete Vitaphone show, (g) Properly maintain Vitaphone equipment.

For D.C. Operation Only
CUE SHEET "BETTER 'OLE PROGRAM"

CODE SM Start Motor. CO Changeover. U-1 Fader up one.
                                       D-1 Fader down one.

HORN SETTINGS

Short Subjects 1—2—3— Feature 1—2—3— Overture 1—2—3—
               4—5—6—   4—5—6—   4—5—6—

RECORD	SUBJECT	FADER CUES FOR FADER CHANGES
263	Mignon	———
366	Aristocrats	——— U-1 for all close ups.
365	Warrenrath	———
355	Jessel	——— D-1 for song only.
339	Janis	——— U-2 when Elsie asks British soldier if he can sing D-2 immediately after answer.
349	Howard Bros.	——— U-1 on "I am shot." D-1 after pistol shots.

INTERMISSION

40-A-4 Bairnsfather———

BETTER 'OLE

369	Reel 1	CUE Explosion in Dugout.
	Fader———	SM Just after smoke clears away.
		CO On Fade out of Dugout.
370	Reel 2	CUE last Title "Major Russett" etc.
	Fader———	SM Next scene.
		CO As Major counts on fingers.
371	Reel 3	CUE last Title "That sure 'ad a kick."
	Fader———	SM As "Old Bill" goes toward two men
		CO As "Old Bill" exits thru door.
372	Reel 4	CUE last Title "I just captured a spy."
	Fader———	SM When "Ole Bill" pushes soldier in fountain.
		CO As "Old Bill" walks out of scene.
373	Reel 5	CUE Girl comes on stage.
	Fader———	SM On title "Daughter."
		CO As Father embraces girl and she looks up at him.
		NOTE U-1 for Tipperary song.
374	Reel 6	CUE As two soldiers shake hands.
	Fader———	SM As Two soldiers walk downstairs.
		CO Two soldiers in theatre.
		NOTE U-1 for cheers.
375	Reel 7	CUE Soldiers pull horse's head off.
	Fader———	SM As headless horse starts toward gate.
		CO As headless horse passes through gate.
376	Reel 8	CUE last Title "Du Verdammter Esel"
	Fader———	SM As "Old Bill" closes door.
		CO On close up of man behind prison bars.
377	Reel 9	CUE Soldier falls down ladder with "Old Bill."
	Fader———	SM as soldiers put "Old Bill" on table
		CO when "Old Bill" kicks man against wall.
378	Reel 10	Note: Two up on Orchestra.
	Fader———	END Title "The End."

❑ ❑ ❑

Cagey directors were beginning to give some thought to the proper use of sound. Josef von Sternberg instinctively understood that words could carry a plot and establish character, but were useless in providing atmosphere, the *ne plus ultra* of his art. "I want *immediate* sound," he proclaimed at a dinner table while planning his first all-talkie. "*Swamp* the audience immediately. *Envelop* them with raw sound...early morning sounds...hard heels on cobblestone streets, the slap of water thrown on a storefront from a metal bucket...dogs barking...rattle of thick breakfast dishes. A canary sings...From the first moment, the audience must be *deluged* with sound, conditioned instantly, it must learn to concentrate on hearing, to *listen* to dialogue *above* the *klang*."

Three days before Christmas, F. W. Murnau sat down and wrote a letter to his employer. "...The year 1927 is rapidly nearing its end [and] my not having communicated with you until now, weighs heavily on my mind...I intend to start on Tuesday, January 3, 1928, with my new production—*The Four Devils,* figuring a shooting schedule of about twelve weeks. I shall mail you a copy of my script and I certainly would like to hear from you and Mrs. Fox, as to your opinion about the story, and suggestions...

"I am greatly delighted with my story and with the forthcoming production, for the very reason that the characters have to be young, beautiful, wholesome people, which enables me to introduce and train a group of new and unspoiled talent...

"I am sure it will also be good news to you to hear that the estimated cost of the picture is reasonable, since exorbitant settings like in *Sunrise* are not required, and since I have also tried my utmost, in order not to be subjected to California weather-whims, to have all my settings on the Hollywood stages, with only a very, very few exterior shots."

He went on to say that the new John Ford film *Four Sons,* which he had seen in rough-cut form, would prove to be "one of

the greatest box office values that has ever been shown on the screen
... I certainly congratulate you on this picture." *

Murnau engaged in some further (mild) soft-soaping of the boss
by saying that Movietone was far superior to all the other talking
systems and "will very soon be hailed all over the world."

Murnau told Fox that he planned to use some Movietone sound
effects for "some of my circus scenes," and inquired about the possible use of the wide-screen 70mm process Fox was developing
for use in a picture he was already planning to make in the coming summer. The tentative title was *Our Daily Bread*: "A story that
will tell a tale about 'WHEAT' — about the 'sacredness of bread' —
about the estrangement of the modern metropolitans from —
and their ignorance about — Nature's sources of sustenance, the
story adhering to the stage play *The Mud Turtle*. I believe that
this theme would be a great starting vehicle for the Grandeur
Film."

After another inquiry about a new color process, Murnau closed
with "I am feeling fine. I like the lot and all my collaborators, the
spirit of co-operation. If I could move my beautiful Berlin home to
Hollywood, everything would be perfect."

Fox's reply, dated December 27, is similarly formal but friendly
and obviously concerned with limiting costs and steering Murnau's
choice of material into as commercial a path as possible. "After my
talk with you in New York I felt sure that you would make this
picture at a reasonable cost, as expressed by you at that time ... I
hope that when the scenario arrives it will contain not only the
screen drama which this story tells, but it will likewise contain pathos, thrills, well-timed and well-calculated comedy situations inter-
mingled with the other emotions which I am certain every large
picture requires ...

"I wish I could suggest how your beautiful Berlin home could be
transplanted to Hollywood. However, I am sure that ultimately you
will have a beautiful home in Hollywood and that it will have this

---

* Murnau's enthusiasm might have been stimulated by the considerable extent to
which Ford had been influenced by Murnau's style, up to and including shooting
some scenes from *Four Sons* on sets left over from *Sunrise*.

advantage: instead of it blooming only during the summer months as it does in Berlin, it will bloom all year."

□ □ □

The Jazz Singer opened at the Warner Theater on Hollywood Boulevard the last week of December 1927. The industry crowd was less demonstrative than the New York opening-night audience had been, but they were no less affected. As the film ended and applause grew with the houselights, Sam Goldwyn's wife, Frances, looked around at the celebrities in the crowd. She saw "terror in all their faces," she said, as if they knew that "the game they had been playing for years was finally over." In the lobby afterward, there was a buzz of excitement, but in the Goldwyn car on the way home there was dead silence. Also attending had been Irving Thalberg and Norma Shearer, and the mood in their car was far more soothing, as Thalberg told his wife that "sound is a passing fancy. It won't last."

For weeks afterward, remembered the journalist Cedric Belfrage, "If you had a press pass you could get in [to the Warner Theater], but otherwise you had to wait for hours. There was a line the whole way around the block, all day long. They started the show at about 9 A.M. and the lines were filling at dawn. It was the most incredible sight.

"You went in to see this thing, and it was the most appalling bit of shit, really, but here was Al Jolson, suddenly this voice coming out of the screen . . . and everybody was paralyzed with excitement. I made my contribution by predicting that the talkies wouldn't last very long."

When *The Jazz Singer* opened in Los Angeles, the screen competition included *Sunrise, The Gaucho, My Best Girl,* and, last as well as least, *Old Ironsides.* Lionel Barrymore was onstage in *Laugh, Clown, Laugh,* the Marx Brothers were onstage in *The Cocoanuts,* and Noël Coward's *The Vortex* was also playing. As in New York, Sam Warner's offspring instantly obliterated the competition and converted even hardened skeptics. Louella Parsons wrote that "*The Jazz Singer* and the Vitaphone are affinities that do not jangle out of tune . . . The combination exceeded this viewer's best expectations."

Nevertheless, Jack and Harry were not home free. By the end of 1927, ERPI had equipped only 157 theaters for sound, 55 of them with the new combination disc/film sound mechanism. Out in the field, exhibitors were expressing guarded optimism about the possibilities of talking pictures, especially in smaller towns where attendance needed all the goosing it could get. "The manager and operators," reported an ERPI service technician in Springfield, Massachusetts, "were quite anxious to know if I could tell them when the theater would reopen with Vitaphone. I was asking the same thing of them."

The royalty statement ERPI prepared for their parent company, Western Electric, showed that they had collected no royalties at all for talking pictures in 1926, but $187,000 for 1927, a good total for a mere handful of releases. (By comparison, phonograph royalties for 1927 amounted to just slightly over $1 million.)

Yet, back in Hollywood, far from the madding crowd, the industry remained unimpressed; they believed that sound films would, before too much longer, be firmly remanded to the category of fad. In their yearly editorial about the business, *The Film Daily* vented opinions about corporate mergers (good for the big, bad for the small), the orgy of stage presentations accompanying silent films (economically unsound), and various and sundry other ephemera. They said nothing whatever about Vitaphone, Movietone, or Al Jolson.

Likewise, in *The Film Daily*'s annual roundup of more than thirty industry heavyweights (Laemmle, Schenck, Zukor, Lasky, Mayer, DeMille, etc.) for the purpose of listing their predictions for the coming year, only William Fox, his employee Winfield Sheehan, and Harry Warner mentioned the coming deluge.

At the end of the year, the Motion Picture Producers and Distributors of America, headed by Will Hays, put out a promotional booklet citing the important events of 1927 in cinema. The MPPDA took careful stock and decided that financial consolidation and a willingness to experiment with style and technique were the hallmarks of the year. *The Jazz Singer* was relegated to the back of the book, behind DeMille's *The King of Kings,* and the movie industry's contributions to flood relief.

As far as the elite of the film industry was concerned, silent films had nothing to fear.

But Jack and Harry Warner and William Fox didn't care what Will

Hays and company thought. Sound was the future. They had bet their lives, their fortunes, and what they imagined to be their sacred honor on it, and they weren't about to back off now. Because of them, as 1927 became 1928, the limitless blue bowl of sky that habitually hovered over Los Angeles was about to start falling on explorer and homesteader alike.

PART THREE

1928

THE MOVING PICTURE SPEAKS,
AND HAVING SPOKEN,
THE SILENCE THAT ONE SEEKS
IN FILMS IS BROKEN.
ALAS FOR THOSE FAIR FACES
WHOSE BEGUILANCE
LAY IN THEIR THOUSAND GRACES—
AND THEIR SILENCE.

Welford Beaton
The Film Spectator,
January 5, 1929

Recording Leo the Lion's roar
for the MGM trademark in 1928.

CHAPTER 1

At the beginning of the crucial year of 1928, while Murnau was shooting *Four Devils*, while Vidor was tussling with his apparently intractable *The Crowd*, Harry and Jack announced that all Warner Bros. films would have, at the very least, Vitaphone sequences. Warners personnel rolled their eyes and set to work.

The Warners studio on Sunset Boulevard was, as cameraman Byron Haskin remembered, "a fairly decent studio . . . but it was all hit-and-miss. On the first Vitaphone shorts, we used automobile headlights [for lighting]." With Jack and Harry's decision, the studio was suddenly far too small for their plans.

Early in 1928, the studio was forced to sublease stages on another lot for a film called *The Lion and the Mouse*. Because the stage wasn't soundproofed, the film was being shot at night, when traffic noise was at a minimum. One night, Benjamin and Pearl Warner arrived to watch the sound film being shot.

"They gave Mrs. Warner a rocking chair," remembered May McAvoy, the picture's star, "and they made her very comfortable and she was enjoying it. Everything was fine and we got two or three takes . . . and we were just rolling . . . great in this one take and all of a sudden *squeak, squeak, squeak, squeak*. Mrs. Warner was so pleased and happy, she was rocking back and forth in her chair and it was making a large squeaking noise which ruined the film completely. So we had to do it all over again and put her in another chair so she wouldn't be inclined to rock."

McAvoy, a firm believer in the prevailing doctrine which held that sound would blow away in six months' time, found talkies more trouble than they were worth. "All the main characters would have one camera directed on him or her, for his close-up, then there would be another camera directed on two or three people who had some dialogue together, and then there would be one other camera, some way [back] so they could get the [master] shot.

"Hiding microphones was something else again. They could be under a pillow, hanging behind a chair, under a piece of paper, we never knew where they were. I mean, we did know where they were, and we had to remember where they were, so we could be heard, but also we had limits as to how far we could walk . . . and yet we'd have to be natural about talking to somebody who was sitting in another chair. It was a madhouse, just a madhouse, and the people were the guinea pigs and I was one of them."

Meanwhile, Roy Pomeroy, the technical adviser for the committee formed to study the new sound processes, weighed in with his decision. Faced with a choice between Western Electric's sound-on-film system, and RCA's sound-on-film system, the politic Pomeroy decreed that they were both perfectly satisfactory.

Despite the fervent wishes of the moguls, sound had not gone away; indeed, it had gained a perceptible momentum. Very well; they would stall some more. They began negotiating, playing off ERPI against RCA in order to gain the most favorable terms. That could take a few more months. Surely the public would grow bored with sound movies by then.

❏ ❏ ❏

The Hermann Bang novel called *Four Devils* captured the atmosphere of sawdust and tinsel, the excitement of bodies in motion. Four young people are adopted by an elderly circus clown and grow up together. All four become aerialists, and two of them fall in love. There is one sequence — a city coming alive as the main male character walks home at dawn — that directly prefigures the famous opening sequence of Rouben Mamoulian's stage production of *Porgy,* as well as his film *Love Me Tonight.*

As with *Sunrise,* the shooting script devised by Murnau and Berthold Viertel makes the magnetic pull of eroticism lethal. After an initial tryst with a beautiful woman who frequently attends the circus, the aerialist feels out of sync with his partner. During the performance, they are working well, but mechanically, without fire. The girl has a vision in which she sees the boy cold and still. Later, at a benefit performance, with his lover looking on from a box, the boy misses the bar and falls to his death; the girl sees him fall and intentionally lets go of the bar, also plunging to her death. In the box, the woman who has caused the tragedy goes into hysterics.

Murnau had actually begun the script of *Four Devils* only a few weeks after *Sunrise* had opened. Murnau's treatment is full of the evocative description that, alone among directors, he seemed able to transmute from the page to the screen: "As a contrast to these pictures from the lives of the artists, we see the lady from the box [the vamp who seduces the aerialist] who is still lying in bed and asleep in her darkened room. One sees vaguely shadowy, packed trunks standing about, articles thrown about, making the impression of a projected journey.

"The lady herself is asleep and sees once more in her dream the young athlete of yesterday, swinging gracefully, hovering above her, hanging from the trapeze by his knees. She is torn out of this enchanting dream by a knock, a maid is at the door, she calls to the gradually awakened lady. 'It is high time, the train leaves in an hour.' The lady answers 'I am not leaving!'

"She goes on sleeping and one sees in another room servants drawing covers over armchairs and opening heavy curtains, without once obtaining a more definitive impression of this house, which begins, as though from out of a darkness, to emerge into mysterious silhouettes."

Murnau was following Max Reinhardt—under whom he had studied as a young actor—in specifying an underlying emotional or psychological texture to accompany the narrative flow, which is all the stronger for never being overtly stated. For a scene in which the trapeze artist's girlfriend discovers that he is distracted, Murnau wrote a note to either himself or William Fox: "It must be commented here that there are numerous opportunities at hand for a number of details ... which will throw light upon the inward course of the drama of the soul which is spun between the four acrobats. It is just the vital execution of this line which is to form the fundamental character of the film, the convincing full-blooded daily round for which there is a plentiful supply of material at hand, to feed the dramatic tension even in the neutral episodes."

Murnau's script ends with a final page headlined THE SOLUTION OF THE DRAMA. Although the previous page ends with the unfaithful trapeze artist falling and hitting the ground, and the tone of the preceding pages implies a tragic ending consistent with the source material, Murnau has the boy survive. At least at this stage.

❏ ❏ ❏

King Vidor recalled that up to seven different endings were written for *The Crowd*, but it seems that only three were shot and only two were real possibilities: the right one, and a hilariously out of tone "happy" ending. It survives on paper in a studio cutting-continuity dated January 21, 1928.

The ending picks up at the scene in the last reel where Mary (Eleanor Boardman), urged on by her brothers, leaves her husband. The new footage begins as John (James Murray) gets into a fistfight with the brothers; then Mary walks out, but relents and rushes back to his arms.

"YEARS! FLEET YEARS!" announces a title. "THE CROWD THAT JEERS AT FAILURE IS THE SAME CROWD THAT CHEERS AT SUCCESS." It is Christmas, and the family, complete with now jovial in-laws and new baby, is gathered around the tree. "Here's to John and his latest advertising slogan," says a brother. *Baseball matches. They always strike!* John tells his wife, "You're the most wonderful girl in all the world." She responds, just before the fade-out clinch, with "Honest, Johnny . . . way down deep in my heart, I never lost faith in you for a minute." Fade out.

As a last-minute violation of the tone and spirit painstakingly established and maintained for the previous ninety-six minutes, one could hardly do better. Although Vidor would later claim that only one theater requested this absurd coda, he seems to have let wishful thinking color his memories. *Variety* reported that both endings were on view during the film's opening day at the Capitol Theater in New York, possibly so Vidor and the MGM brass could choose the one that seemed to play the best. Another trade paper said that the film was indeed released with the happy ending, but audience reaction was so bad MGM recalled those prints and sent the film out again with the original ending.

Some critics were, predictably, appalled. Where was the plot, the stars, the happy ending? "A drab, actionless story of ungodly length [ninety-eight minutes] and apparently telling nothing," snarled *Variety*. "As it is, 2,000 feet could come out of this picture, and the more the better." In regard to the ending, *Variety* suggested that "the one that will leave the film the shorter should be selected."

Other critics were only slightly more sanguine. In *The Film Spectator*, Welford Beaton said that "as art it is a success, but as [screen entertainment] it will be a failure." Despite the fears of the philistines, *The Crowd* did all right. MGM carried its negative cost at $551,380, with prints and advertising adding another $100,000 to that. The world gross was $988,169; subtracting studio overhead left MGM with a net profit of $7,526.57.

The Crowd received some Oscar nominations, but failed to win any. "Back then," Vidor recalled, "there were five people who would end any kind of a tie [in the Academy balloting]. They were Louis B. Mayer, Douglas Fairbanks, Joe Schenck, Mary Pickford, and Sid Grauman. They sat up all night and Sid Grauman called me up and said, 'I held out until five o'clock for *The Crowd*, but it didn't get it.' The reason was that Mayer did not want to vote for one of his own films."

Vidor was almost certainly being too kind; Mayer hadn't the least compunctions about voting for his own films. It's far more likely that he actively disliked a movie so dark in content and style. *The Crowd* was antithetical to the emerging MGM ethos, and Mayer didn't want it to have recognition as an MGM picture.

The film's events tend toward the mundane — a leaky toilet, marital spats — and the sudden, tragic death of a child, not as a forced climax, but in the middle of the picture, is the turning point that begins the deterioration of a marriage. Although the film is careful to concentrate on the ordinary occurrences of life, Vidor's film is never dreary reportage; he infuses each scene with his characteristic energy and vitality, and the location footage of 1927 Manhattan is carefully selected for its symbolic weight. Vidor had the eye, not merely of a poet, but of a great documentarian, for the New York scenes are perfectly chosen to symbolize the authoritarian nature of the modern city.

Under the influence of the German films that had struck Hollywood so forcibly in the previous few years, Vidor gave his film an expressionist tinge, utilizing forced perspective and stylization. Like *Sunrise, The Crowd* was a city film; the films share a common majesty, but Vidor's film is the more dissonant, for he consistently characterizes the urban landscape as monolithic and impersonal.

Vidor makes his main character a well-meaning but affectless, shallow man who feels entitled to success because of his supposed superiority to the masses. It's bred in the bone: "There's a little man the world is going to hear from all right, Doctor," says his father on the day he is born. A few years later, little John is telling his playmates, "My dad says I'm going to be someone big." In his spoiled fecklessness — amplified by the soft charm of actor James Murray — John is a middle-class version of Georgie Minafer in *The Magnificent Ambersons*. Only tragedy can make this big baby grow up, and maybe not even that.

Vidor's initial emphasis is on the rhythm of work, crowds being sucked into buildings every morning, being spewed out at night. Implicitly mocked is the myth of self-improvement. The city takes John and Mary's youth, their ideals, their optimism, and even one of their children. Man proposes, Vidor is saying — with the pragmatism of his Christian Science — but fate disposes. Later, as John falters, his optimistic belief in his own innate superiority beginning to fail, the film's rhythm slows, and the style subtly shifts to neorealism, charting a relentless, gimlet-eyed view of feckless human decline.

For a film made in burgeoning Hollywood during the sustained orgasm of the Roaring Twenties, *The Crowd* is audaciously downbeat in both style and substance. Vidor builds his characters and themes with brief scenes of telling detail, taking the marriage of John and Mary from rapture to boredom to hostility inside twenty minutes, bathing the film in the shabbiness of the lumpen proletariat, people living as best they can in a succession of seedy cold-water flats.

The Crowd's steely-eyed objectivity toward the cheerful mediocrity of an average American might have been inspired by the inquisitorial novels of Sinclair Lewis, but much of the tone derives from the fatalistic street films of postwar Germany. It also eerily anticipates the specter of the Depression that would strike in just a year. In addition, in mercilessly documenting the deterioration of John Sims and the steadfast strength and loyalty of his wife, Vidor is prefiguring the wisdom that would emerge later in the century: men break, women bend.

In the end, John and his wife tentatively reconcile. They sit in a theater laughing uproariously at a crude vaudeville act, heartened by seeing an ad in the program that uses a slogan Sims had devised. It's an equivocal happy ending, until Vidor suddenly pulls back for a chilling crane shot that goes back, back, back, until John and Mary are lost in the crowd of hundreds of people rocking back and forth in laughter, an abstract pattern of humanity that obliterates the individual.

The Crowd is not merely the best picture King Vidor ever made, it's among the best pictures anybody ever made. It had two great critics. The first was Ernst Lubitsch, who told a friend that "Americans will not understand this film. Europeans will not understand this film. Only Europeans who have lived in America will understand this film."

The second was Vittorio De Sica, who met King Vidor and threw his arms round him. "Oh, *The Crowd, The Crowd!*" he exclaimed. "That was what inspired me for *The Bicycle Thief.*"

❑ ❑ ❑

Since *Four Devils* took place in a circus, Murnau wanted a camera that could move easily and catch the excitement of the setting. "Naturally the camera must not stand stock still in one spot in such a gay place as a circus!" he wrote. "It must gallop after the equestrienne, it must pick out the painted tears of the clown and jump from him to a high box to show the face of the rich lady thinking about the clown."

The Fox technicians built what Murnau described as "sort of [a] traveling crane with a platform swung at one end for the camera" — in other words, a camera crane, a full year before Universal supposedly built the first one for *Broadway Melody.* Murnau's staff called the crane "the Go-Devil," and the director was enthralled with the crane's utility and grace. "The studios will all have Go-Devils, some day, to make the camera mobile," he commented.

Once again, Murnau chose Janet Gaynor. Once again, he gave her no quarter. For the climactic scene where Charles Morton had to hang from Gaynor while she hung from the trapeze, she was wired to the trapeze and rigged with a kind of saddle for Morton. With a heavy man hanging from her body, it felt to Gaynor as if "I was going to be cut in two. Murnau said let them go . . . and there I was, in such pain, and he hadn't told me one thing to do, what was going to happen or anything. I just hung there and I cried from pain and from anxiety. So finally they brought us down, and Murnau came over and patted me and said, 'Oh, Janet, just what I wanted.'

"So that was Mr. Murnau. But I have to tell you that after he put you through something like that, great American Beauty roses would be at the house, and the card would say, 'To Janet, the finest and fairest actress on the screen.' "

Murnau was no less ruthless and single-minded with extras. For a subjective shot from the point of view of a falling acrobat, Murnau rigged a camera to drop down from a great height toward the circus audience. He neglected to explain to the extras in the audience that the camera would not actually crash into them, so the shot contained a very authentic impression of panicked scrambling.

❑ ❑ ❑

By March, Publix Theaters sent out publicity manuals to their theaters concerning the right and wrong way to advertise Vitaphone. In essence, the right way was to banner the name Vitaphone over and above everything else. Hence, the shorts that accompanied the films were not just shorts, they were "Big Time Vitaphone vaudeville," and they were to be billed above the features. "Vitaphone ads, no matter how large or how small," the manual instructed, "must show at a glance the number of acts on the program. The word 'Vitaphone' should dominate everywhere in the ad."

The implications for the future were both ominous and obvious, for Publix Theaters was a subsidiary of Paramount Pictures, who were shortly to begin pedaling as furiously as possible in order to catch up to Warners and Fox. Yet, while the marketing department was gung ho for sound, the creative executives still couldn't bring themselves to realize what was happening. In early March, Jesse Lasky announced that "to make all pictures dialogue vehicles would be to turn the progress of the screen back at least ten years. The great power of the motion picture has been its power to touch swiftly upon action and then sweep away. This would be impossible were dialogue between the actors to be recorded . . ."

Lasky went on to say that the best use of sound was as in its present state, no more: "The use of sound will be dramatic, and will heighten intensely the effect of the picture. The hum of crowds, the roar of an angry mob, perhaps a shouted command, the shrill of a police whistle, the bark of a dog, a knock on a door when such a knock heightens the suspense . . ."

That March, Lasky stood steadfast. By August, he was just another tree in the Hollywood forest, toppling under hurricane winds.

❑ ❑ ❑

After much playing footsie and going back and forth, the producers' committee on sound elected to commit to the Western Electric sound system, partially because only ERPI would take the responsibility for the manufacturing and installation of the sound equipment in theaters, a job for which the studios were particularly ill-equipped. The contract with ERPI was signed on May 11.

John Otterson was a happy man, for he had gotten the best of both worlds. Manufacturing the equipment for the majority of the major studios that signed the agreement was good; having a monopoly on the lucrative business of wiring and servicing the nation's theaters for sound was much better, for it was a quick ticket to windfall profits. Not only that, but, in keeping with the phone company's tradition of leasing their products rather than selling them outright, ERPI would actually maintain ownership of the speakers and soundheads.

Still, ERPI had a problem in that it had to quickly find and train hundreds of technicians to install the new technology. Moreover, ERPI had to establish a network of engineers and supply warehouses in strategic spots around the country, for they intended to boast that no theater in the country was more than a half-day away from their service departments. Stanley Watkins, who had been loaned out to

Warner Bros., was called back to company headquarters to supervise training for the next year.

❑ ❑ ❑

While ominous industry rumblings were common in New York, they tended to dissipate before they could reach the sensitive antennae of the industry in Los Angeles. Unless someone wanted to spend $450 (in modern currency, several thousand dollars) to risk an airplane ride, it would take three days to cross the country by train. If the studio wasn't paying, most people were content to stay where they were. In 1927, sound had been a fad, and many people in the industry hadn't bothered to see *The Jazz Singer*. By the spring of 1928, the situation had changed, and movie people began lining up in front of the Los Angeles theater where Warners' *Glorious Betsy* opened on April 26, 1928.

"We had heard that there was some sort of newfangled sound effect connected with the production," remembered director/writer William deMille (elder brother of Cecil B. DeMille, he maintained the lowercase *d*). "We sat in the darkened theater and watched *Glorious Betsy* unwind herself. For several reels it was just a regular picture, the plot of which I have forgotten, but I shall never forget the moment when Andre de Segurola, playing the part of a military officer, stood in the middle of the picture to address the group around him.

" 'Ladies and gentlemen,' he said.

"*He said!*

"A thrill ran through the house... No one minded, at first, the gentle, crackling noise which pervaded the scene... [and] sounded like a grass fire. I glanced at Clara [Beranger, deMille's wife and a screenwriter]. She, too, was feeling the importance of the moment. I whispered to her: 'This is history, my dear; a new era,' and she nodded without taking her eyes off the screen."

❑ ❑ ❑

The film that truly began talkies was not *Don Juan*, not even *The Jazz Singer*, which was, after all, a silent movie with a few random songs. No, the film that sent the most flamboyant large industry in

America into convulsions was a dreadful little movie called *The Lights of New York*.

That February, Bryan Foy had convinced Jack Warner to let him make a dramatic two-reeler to add some variety to the profusion of musical one-reelers. Foy told him it wouldn't cost more than $20,000; Jack said, "Go ahead, but don't say anything about it," whereupon he left for Europe. Foy forged ahead and did what he had wanted to do for the last year and a half: make an all-talking feature. He reasoned that if he made it fast enough, it wouldn't actually cost any more than the agreed-upon $20,000.

Seven days and nights later, *The Lights of New York* was finished. Foy told his wife he was going to bed for twenty-four hours and not to bother him. Two hours later, he was awakened by the news that his father, the famed vaudevillian Eddie Foy, had died at the age of seventy-one. The Vitaphone short his son had planned for him was not to be.

After Foy got back from his father's funeral, and Jack Warner had returned from Europe, Foy told Jack that he had slightly over-shot the planned two reels by four additional reels. An exasperated Jack dragged Foy into Harry's office; Harry ordered Foy to cut it back to the planned two reels. Neither Jack nor Harry were interested in the picture, because, Foy believed, they had committed to Darryl Zanuck's plans to make their first all-talkie a prestige project.

A desperate Foy sneaked the picture to an exhibitor friend, who promptly offered to buy it outright for $25,000. That got Harry's attention, and he delegated his brother Albert to take a look at the movie. Albert Warner came back raving, and Jack and Harry decided that they might have been a little hasty. *The Lights of New York* was presented in New York at the Mark Strand Theater on July 6, 1928, as the first all-talking movie.

The Lights of New York ("... A STORY THAT MIGHT HAVE BEEN TORN OUT OF LAST NIGHT'S NEWSPAPER," proclaims an opening title) is a deeply unlikely tale about two innocent barbers gulled into fronting for gangsters. The film is schizoid. Half the scenes — those deriving from the two-reeler — are played fast, with zippy, almost hysterical exposition, and bouncy, vaudeville-style performances. But the added scenes are static filler, add-ons to fill out the running time, long single takes with actors conveniently positioned by microphones concealed in telephones. The only interesting things about the picture are the excellent quality of the sound and the nearly continuous musical underscoring behind the dialogue.* Warners figured that the final negative cost of the film was $23,000, surely a record for a studio picture of that era.

Everybody could tell that *The Lights of New York* was an appalling picture. Intellectuals in particular were unimpressed, and began to refer disparagingly to the "squawkies." Yet, there were lines of ungodly length at every box office where it played. It ended up grossing an amazing $1.2 million.

And now came the great panic. "*The Jazz Singer*," said Darryl Zanuck, "turned them to sound, *The Lights of New York* to talk. It turned the whole goddamn tide."

With that combination of bewildering illiteracy and folk wisdom that endeared him to an entire generation, Will Rogers reported in his column, "The whole business out here is scared cuckoo..." and not because "spring marrying is about over and summer divorces haven't quite got going good... In four or five years you will look back and laugh at yourself for ever having sit [sic] for hours and just looked at Pictures with no voice or no sound...

"I saw a picture the other night that used the talk. It's called *The Lion and the Mouse* and Oh! boy how the stage Actor does show up the Movie ones! Lionel Barrymore even as a Villian [sic], and Alec Francis, another splendid stage actor, just made you wish the others hadn't talked...

"The titles that the Actors speak have got to be something that the man would really say under those circumstances, and not something

---

* UCLA's Bob Gitt believes Warners might very well have recorded the music directly to their master discs and dubbed the dialogue over the music, rather than the other way around. At this stage, mixing fuzzed out music more than it did voices, and Warners was still under the impression that the music was more important than the dialogue.

that read good when the Title Writer 'Copped' it out of some book. It's going to make pictures about twice as Human." *

Whatever nervousness was being felt in the industry was only amplified by the comments of Roy Pomeroy, the special-effects technician who had been put in charge of Paramount's sound operation. "One year will be required to photograph a feature picture accompanied by a complete dialogue duly recorded by a sound track," he helpfully told *Variety*. "In the matter of speech between two persons in a 'two-shot' it is necessary to permit an appreciable lapse of time between the end of the remarks of one of them and the beginning of the other's, so that the audience may follow the change and have an opportunity to realize the shift of emphasis."

A contributor to *American Cinematographer* magazine nicely captured the panicked mood of Hollywood, a city under siege, in the summer of 1928: "One cannot pick up a daily paper, walk along Hollywood Boulevard, attend a meeting of any kind or even sit at a table at Henry's . . . One cannot do any of these things or follow the routine of his daily life, without reading, hearing a little matter of interest and a lot of nonsense on the 'talkies,' and without being questioned on their past, present and future . . ."

"The atmosphere was suddenly uncertainty and fear," recalled Joe Youngerman, a propman at Paramount at the time. "The soundman was up in the air, in a booth overlooking the stage, like God. Paramount started building soundstages, four of them, and before they were finished, they burned down, so they had to build them all over again. Those stages are now Stages 11, 12, 13, and 14 on the Paramount lot."

The tide had irrevocably turned. Warner Bros. and Fox, two second-string studios hungry to break into the big time, had done it via the back door; Vitaphone and Movietone were obliterating silent films with the same systems and the same kinds of films that the

---

* *The Lion and the Mouse* was a good example of the unhappy, herky-jerky compromises of the part-talkie. The first dialogue sequence came two minutes into the movie, as Lionel Barrymore planted the story. During the twelve or so silent sequences, the audience was in an odd state of unrest, wondering when the talking would start again. In all, there were about thirty-one minutes of dialogue in the sixty-five minutes of the picture.

public had freely yawned through or rejected outright as recently as five or six years earlier. What had changed?

Among other things, the audience. At the end of 1921, there were eight radio stations licensed for broadcast in America; a year later, there were 564. Radio exploded onto the American scene and whetted the audience's appetite for sound, any kind of sound. Radio also spawned a fascination with technology. By 1925, remembered actor Ben Lyon, "when radio became popular, attendance in the theaters dropped off to nothing." By October 1927, some fifty million people listened to Graham McNamee call the Dempsey-Firpo fight. For the first, but not the last time in their lives, Jack and Harry had the inestimable advantage of good timing.

Then there was the technology, which had improved since the last halfhearted attempt represented by Griffith's *Dream Street.* Finally, there was the nature of silent films. By 1927–28, with films such as *Sunrise* and *The Last Command,* they had reached a state of liquid perfection, a seamless, impeccable synthesis of style and storytelling. They had trouble indicating speech, but no trouble with anything else. To audiences used to constant, incremental improvements, perfection equaled stagnation. Sound represented what a later generation would call the Next Big Thing. It may have been an addition that was an artistic subtraction, a refinement that coarsened the storytelling, but it happened to be what the audience wanted.

The nature of the movie experience was about to be altered. A private, active experience, in which each viewer took a creative role in the structure and perception of the drama, was about to become collective and passive. The quiet communion between artist and audience, what writer Barry Paris called "the inviolable emotional trance," was about to be destroyed.

And that was just fine with critics like Robert Sherwood, by all odds the most amazingly prescient writer of the era. In June 1928, he wrote that "within the next year . . . we shall see some full-length talking pictures of more than passing merit—and from 1930 on, silent movies will be as obsolete as are cylindrical phonograph records or Model T Fords."

The audience responses were unpredictable and, to experienced filmmakers, deeply disconcerting. A Fox Movietone newsreel of an English soccer game showed a stadium full of spectators. In the foreground was a man unaware of the camera, who "begins to shout," reported Quinn Martin. "It seems his mouth will never stop opening . . . At each showing of the subject this scene attracts rounds of laughter." In other words, the audience was stimulated to laughter by a picture of a yelling sports fan. Critics were no less swayed than the public. "I have no backwardness in recording the fact that Movietone is to me one of the marvels of the age," concluded Martin. "In the final analysis it is nothing more nor less than the bringing of the whole wide world to your doorstep."

❑ ❑ ❑

In April 1928, before *The Lights of New York* was released, Adolph Zukor called a summit meeting of Paramount executives, berating them for their ignorance about sound. "Warners is making this picture," Walter Wanger recalled Zukor saying, "and what have we got? You don't know a goddamn thing about sound. A lot of dumbheads. We pay you all money . . ."

After listening to more in this vein, Wanger raised his hand and offered to spend the next six weeks adding sound to a Richard Dix baseball picture that had just arrived at the home office. In August, *Warming Up* premiered with music and sound effects. Working in the RCA plant in Trenton, New Jersey, Roy Pomeroy and Wanger had rigged up a Rube Goldberg device that involved two projectors running in sync — one for the picture, one for the sound — a stopwatch, and a metronome.

The results were predictably crude. "[It] appears to have been done in a little too much of a hurry," reported *The New York Times.* "The synchronization is . . . not well-timed in spots, the result being that the cheers for a good play can be heard some time before the play itself. And then there is a little too much noise in one or two scenes. Trying to watch the picture and at the same time hearing a terrific racket is a bit reminiscent of riding in the front seat of a roller coaster and listening to the frightened shrieks of the customers behind."

Zukor got more than he bargained for; before *Warming Up* opened, Paramount had been planning to use sound only for shorts and major road shows, such as *Wings*; the majority of the company's product would remain silent. But when *Warming Up* began showing in theaters, business was appreciably greater than for silent Richard Dix vehicles. It became clear that sound enhanced ordinary programs as well as reserved-seat "specials." Paramount promptly yanked *Abie's Irish Rose* out of release — it had been playing for eight weeks in New York, and had already grossed over $150,000 — called Jean Hersholt and Nancy Carroll back to the lot, and added a few dialogue sequences.

Although Paramount was leaning strongly toward sound on film, as of July 16, 1928, an internal memo stated, "For the [next] year Paramount will use the disc method exclusively for the recordings of sound or music." Because of the slightly different aspect ratio of a sound-on-film print, caused by the narrow section set aside for the sound track, the studio had to send out explanatory memos to theaters instructing them that if they were using discs with a print that also had a sound track, they had to "place a mask on the aperture plate of their machine. Unless this [is] done, the sound track would show on the screen. These masks, as advised, we will furnish free to our accounts . . . Once a print is converted for use with disc, it is to remain in use with disc only and is not, under any circumstances, to be sent out . . . as a sound-on-film print." While the studio was making up its mind, early all-talking Paramount pictures such as *The Letter* and *Gentlemen of the Press* were sent out as disc releases. It was estimated that it was costing the industry about $500,000 to operate the separate record system, not to mention a great deal of time-consuming paperwork.

The competition for wiring theaters began heating up as well. Western Electric, by virtue of its agreements with both Warners and Fox, had cornered the market, and were pricing the installation of their sound system at $19,800 for theaters with more than 1,750 seats, $15,300 for theaters seating between 1,000 and 1,750, and $11,300 for theaters of fewer than 1,000 seats. RCA was doing their best to undercut them; their top price was $17,000 for the largest installation, sliding down to $8,500 for the smallest.

Although Western Electric's installations far outnumbered RCA's, exhibitors noticed that the smaller company's sound process — a sound track that, to the naked eye, resembled the teeth of a saw, a kind of graph of the sound, rather than Fox's pattern of variable grays — yielded quieter sound tracks. "I have noticed [background noise] in almost every Fox film that I have so far reviewed," commented *Harrison's Reports*. "In *Win That Girl* it is very bad. In *Me, Gangster,* which is playing at the Roxy this week, it is 'terrible.' In fact, it is a great surprise to me that Mr. Rothafel, whose ears are so well tuned to music, could tolerate such noises."

□ □ □

The ever-present, self-appointed guardians of the industry wondered about a name for the new arrival. "Talkies" seemed uneuphonious, if not downright ugly, so the *Exhibitor's World Herald* suggested a contest to settle on an official, appropriately decorous name. Among the 250 suggestions that came in from both the public and the industry were things like "Actorphones," "Cinasound," "Dictodrama," "Dictocomedy," "Dramaphone," "Fonofilm," "Imagalive," "Kinephone," "Movietalk," "Oralfilms," "Phonoplay," "See and Hear," "Soundscenes," "Speakie," and the comparatively plainspoken "Talking Picture."

While pedants were quibbling over names, actors were being assigned voice tests. Mary Pickford, who had started on the stage when she was six and should have had little to worry about, trooped in to take her test and was horrified at the playback. "That's not me!" she protested. "That's a pipsqueak voice. It's impossible. I sound like I'm twelve or thirteen. Oh, it's horrible."

She was not the only one who was appalled. Jean Arthur listened to the playback of her voice and cried in dismay, "A foghorn!" At Fox, Victor McLaglen was extremely worried, fretting about his working-class English accent. "There were almost tears in his eyes," remembered soundman Bernard Freericks. "I kept saying to him, 'That's the one thing that's going to put you over, because you're not the run-of-the-mill actor." When William Powell, an experienced stage actor, listened to his voice for the first time, even he ran out the studio door, yelling over his shoulder that he was going into hiding.

Charles "Buddy" Rogers remembered that "over at Paramount, we'd been reading all about talkies and getting pretty nervous. Dick Arlen had been on the stage once, [Gary] Cooper never had, and I knew I had this corny Kansas accent. Dick and Coop and I made a pact to protect the one of us that we figured would turn out not to have a voice; the other two would give him a certain segment of our salaries until he could find something else to do.

"I'll never forget the time I was standing outside a stage, and the door burst open with some guy running out yelling, 'Wally Beery has a voice! Wally Beery has a voice!' It was a strange time in Hollywood."

It is not hard to imagine the stress felt by actors and actresses making between $2,500 and $10,000 a week who were forced to undergo intrinsically humiliating voice auditions. Understandably nervous, the vivacious Colleen Moore looked for some reassurance from her husband, production head John McCormick, or others at First National. They weren't even looking at her, but nervously staring at the sound engineer in the booth above the stage.

"He was about my age, twenty-five," remembered Moore. "He may have been twenty-eight, but no older. He wasn't a movie person. He wasn't connected with any of the arts. Nor did he know anything about acting . . . On this young man's judgment my whole career depended." Colleen Moore recited, "Little Bo Peep has lost her sheep . . ." The engineer leaned out of his window, smiled, and made a circle with his thumb and forefinger, appropriating the standard gesture used by cameramen to indicate a take that would be printed. One more career was temporarily safe; Moore's contract with First National was amended to pay her an extra $25,000 per picture for use of her vocal cords.

At Fox, Madge Bellamy recalled "panic, bedlam and enthusiasm." For their sound tests, Fox's actors weren't even given anything so formal as scenes to memorize, or suggestions about what not to do. Actors were told to say anything that came into their heads, which could include nursery rhymes or halting, awkward non sequitur phrases from people who hadn't had to speak to an audience in years.

Conversations among actors tended to center around two questions: Should I speak loud or soft? Will I make it or won't I? Louise Brooks and Clara Bow went in for their tests, and Brooks would later write Kevin Brownlow that she found Bow "stunned and helpless . . . She already knew she was finished." Bow played a scene from what was to be her first talkie, then had to engage in some impromptu chatter: "My name is Clara Bow," and so on. When Bow saw the test, she "screamed," said her friend Billy Kaplan. "How can I play . . . with a voice like that?" Late that summer, Bow gave an interview to *Motion Picture Classic* in which she blithely described the basic emotional state of everybody in Hollywood: "All of us in pictures are so frightened."

Some performers made only halfhearted attempts during their tests and their all-important first talkies. "I knew I was finished when sound came in," said Claire Windsor, a stunningly beautiful, second-string silent star. "I was never frightened of the motion picture camera, but the microphone scared me to death."

If the internal enemy wasn't bad enough, there were also external gauntlets to be run. Universal was the best friend of the small-town exhibitor, mass-producing a long list of routine programs, with just one or two prestige productions a year (*The Phantom of the Opera* for 1925, *The Man Who Laughs* for 1928, etc.) to break up the monotony. It was a production policy borne of necessity, for Universal had only one or two first-run theaters and had to cater to a less urban, less demanding market. The studio had its most profitable years from 1924 to 1926, and was thus even slower to adapt to sound than it would have ordinarily been.

Eventually, however, even Carl Laemmle tumbled to the new wave, and the studio's directors found themselves being interrogated by technicians who hadn't even been at the studio four months before. Director William Wyler was called into a conference with Roy Hunter, the new head of the new sound department. Hunter, as he did with every director on the lot, asked Wyler if he knew how to say "Good morning." Other directors had responded with a stunned stare, or admitted that, no, they weren't entirely certain about the best way to say it. Wyler stared at Hunter and said, "Sure, I know. I say it every morning." End of conference.

After every take, actors no longer looked at the director, but to the booth holding the soundman. It looked like the observation window of a dirigible nosing its way onto the stage, thirty-five feet above the floor. Against their instincts, against their will, directors — even producers — found themselves looking to the technicians for approval as well, for no one could offer a word of protest when the soundman leaned into his microphone and dispassionately barked the horrifying word "Cut."

"The soundman at that time was one of the biggest prima donnas you have ever seen," said Frank Capra. He remembered one technician who insisted on leaving the set every day at four to have his ears washed out. "He actually had us believing it! He'd leave the set and we would all wait while this man went to a doctor . . . Finally we said, 'We'll bring the doctor here.' He said, 'No, I've got to go to his office.' 'No, no,' we insisted, 'you bring the doctor here.' So the doctor came and did it in the dressing room. We saved a little time that way."

Another stalling exercise derived from listening to the playback. "We had a little playback room on each stage," remembered Hal Mohr, "and immediately following the conclusion of photographing a scene, everybody would rush back to the little room to play back the dialogue and see how the actors were doing . . . Half our time, instead of shooting film, was being spent listening to the mistakes that we had made so we could make them over again!"

The lack of direction during a sound scene was particularly noticeable. "There wasn't that help from the director," remembered Mary Astor. With silent film, "He'd say, 'You're doing fine, now you see him at the window, now run, now a little faster . . .' The verdict was that [my voice] was bottom of the barrel, absolutely too low, almost masculine." Which was not to say that there wasn't a place for Astor in sound pictures; Fox studio manager Sol Wurtzel said that if she'd be willing to cut her salary in half, the studio might stick with her. Astor refused and was out of work for ten months, until she did a play with Edward Everett Horton and proved her voice was perfect for sound.

Sam Jaffe, production manager at Paramount, would say that the studios made serious mistakes in this period by their own ill-considered lack of judgment in throwing their most valuable, if vocally inexperienced, stars into the breach. Speaking of Clara Bow, Paramount's most prominent imminent casualty, Jaffe said, "We didn't train her; we should've taken six months to send her to school, teach her how to speak. [But] we were bringing in all these Broadway actors and directors . . ."

Yet the studio wasn't so shortsighted with all their stars; Paramount hired a vocal coach for Esther Ralston to help her with the basics of pronunciation and enunciation, in case her nearly twenty years of stage work had been completely forgotten. The subliminal animosity the producers felt for the often willful, occasionally adolescent personalities to whom they had to pay thousands of dollars a week now began to emerge.

"It was a time when they [started] to favor . . . the stage people," remembered Budd Schulberg. "And the sound people had become a sort of god; all of a sudden the sound engineers were listened to a great deal . . . All the silent stars were being watched, I would say, somewhat suspiciously as to whether they could talk or not."

As always, it was easier to hire and fire than to manage and plan. The actors' problems were exacerbated by years of training, as well as their own inclinations. "When I arrived at Paramount," remembered Esther Ralston, who became one of Paramount's most reliable stars of the period, "I wished I could use my voice. But they taught you not to open your mouth, because they'd only cut to a subtitle. When you use your voice, you use your hands, and for silents they all but put my hands behind me. It was all in the face, the eyes."

Ralston had a year to go on her Paramount contract; since her deal didn't include a clause for sound pictures, her husband figured this was an opportunity to squeeze more money out of Adolph Zukor. (Up to this point, Zukor had taken a fatherly interest in his seraphically beautiful blond star. When she visited him at his estate in upstate New York, and wine was served at dinner, he would solicitously turn her glass over so she wouldn't drink alcohol.)

"My husband sent me in to ask for $100,000 to sign a talkie contract," remembered Ralston. "Mr. Zukor said, 'We'd love to keep you, but we don't know if they're going to accept your voice. I can't pay you that much money.' So, they canceled the contract that I wouldn't sign without a $100,000 bonus. At the time, I was making $3,500 a week. And then [a year later] the stock market crashed and my husband lost all my money."

❑ ❑ ❑

At the University of Southern California, a speech professor named William Ray MacDonald devised a six-page speech worksheet and a one-page speech diagnosis sheet, then began hiring himself out to the studios. The diagnosis sheet for MGM contractee Anita Page, done in three hours on July 7, 1928, assigned letter grades in a staggering seventy-one categories such as "Prosodic — Accent" (she got a C) and "Kinesophonic — Inflection" (she got a B). Overall comments were "Very good material, hard worker, intelligent-ambitious, learns quickly." For the nervous moguls, outside opinions were particularly valuable in the case of someone like Page, who had been with the studio for only six months and had no stage experience whatsoever. As it turned out, Page's lack of stage experience didn't prove a hindrance and she had a brief run of stardom in early talkies.

While the inhabitants of the Culver City lot struggled to control their panic, Douglas Shearer was in a New Jersey studio, adding sound to what would be MGM's first sound release. *White Shadows in the South Seas* began production in Tahiti, being codirected by Robert Flaherty and W. S. Van Dyke. But Flaherty was a brilliant amateur, not a professional filmmaker, and he quit. Van Dyke completed the film and returned to Hollywood in April, where the film was cut together and handed over to Shearer.

Shearer added a musical score compiled from standard program music, a new theme song by William Axt and David Mendoza, and some sound effects: a father moaning over the death of his son, pounding drums, clapping hands. *White Shadows in the South Seas* was and is a good film; it opened in New York on July 31, preceded by thirty-two minutes of Movietone shorts and newsreels, and was a large success, grossing nearly five times its cost. The final profits of $450,000 were ascribed to the novelty of sound rather than the film's serviceable story or its minor cast (Monte Blue, Raquel Torres). Two years after *Don Juan*, nearly a year after *The Jazz Singer*, Mayer and Thalberg finally girded their loins for an all-out assault on sound.

CHAPTER 2

Four Devils had two sneak previews in the first week of July, one in San Jose, and one in Fresno. At some point during the production, Murnau had decided to veer away from the happy ending that was so similar to the one in *Sunrise*. In the preview version, the two lovers died.

At any other time, the question of the ending would have been of major importance, but, in the summer of 1928, with talk all the rage, whether or not Janet Gaynor survived in a silent movie seemed slightly beside the point. Some additional silent material was shot in July and August, and, with what must have been considerable misgiving on the part of William Fox, *Four Devils* was prepared for release.

Four Devils did reasonably well, grossing over $100,000 in New York City alone, but the silent version was released in only a few markets. The film was then withdrawn while Fox tried to figure out what to do with it.

Thinking there was more money to be made with a sound picture than with a silent picture, William Fox ordered sound added to *Four Devils*. Since Murnau was already in the midst of the third picture on his Fox contract by that point, Fox delegated the job to Murnau's assistant director and one of the "dialogue directors" that were invading Hollywood by the dozens.

The resulting film, judged to contain about 25 percent talking scenes, ended up grossing a very modest $581,000. In either silent or sound form, it is no longer extant. The failure of *Four Devils* was an ominous portent, for the film Murnau was shooting in Oregon, far away from the studio, was yet another silent movie.

❑ ❑ ❑

In his 1928 memoir, *An American Comedy,* Harold Lloyd reported on the new sound phenomenon from the Hollywood front lines: "We are listening intently and moving cautiously. Our next picture will have a musical score and sound accompaniment; that we are agreed upon and we are more than half persuaded to try dialogue."

For comedians like Lloyd, sound posed particular problems; most silent dramas had complete shooting scripts, but Lloyd worked only from a detailed outline. "We had many notes," Lloyd said in a 1966 interview. "We had a pretty good outline of where we were going . . . but still when we started shooting the scene, sometimes even though we'd shoot the first scene maybe *exactly* as we wanted it, we would shoot it again, and maybe again and again, because we'd ad-lib and do something entirely different. And, maybe, by the time we'd shot the scene seven times, we had changed it around so much that you wouldn't hardly know it from the first scene."

Lloyd felt loyal to the traditions of his craft. In August of 1928, Lloyd began production on the film that was to become *Welcome Danger* as a silent picture. In this he was supported by Paramount, his distributor. Sidney Kent, Paramount's sales chief, wrote late that year that "personally, I believe the time will never come when the outstanding silent pictures will be out of the market. We are trying to work out the best possible combination of sound and silent."

❑ ❑ ❑

Sound was forcing cameramen to alter their carefully worked-out lighting methods. MGM had their staff cameramen attend classes taught by John Nickolaus, a Western Electric engineer. Only after they attended the classes would the cameramen be assigned to a sound film. It wasn't an easy transition; dollies and arc lights were gone. Cameramen now had to operate their cameras while sitting in insulated booths behind plate-glass windows, which had the general effect of turning superb lenses into mediocre ones. It also had the general effect of turning wide-awake cameramen into unconscious cameramen. "It was unbelievably hot and cramped," remembered the great Joe Walker, "with barely room for myself and a bulky camera." Ben Reynolds, a gifted but obese cameraman, quickly developed a reputation for dozing off inside the camera booth.

Joe Walker grew noticeably depressed and considered quitting the business, for the multiple cameras demanded a bright, uninteresting lighting scheme that Walker, and most other cameramen, loathed. The burnished, dimensional shadings of the late silent films were vanishing fast.

And, of course, there were the microphones themselves, dangling immobile about a foot over the actors' heads like the sword of Damocles. The microphones were heavy (over ten pounds), partially because of what one sound engineer would call "Western Electric's battleship mentality: there was an awful lot of bronze used." Actors who failed to remember they were no longer in silent movies could put themselves in peril; on a set at Columbia, Jack Holt stood up suddenly, slammed his head into the microphone he forgot was there, and was knocked out cold.

The reason for the mike's immobility was found not in the weight of the apparatus but in the early amplification process. The microphone, which had an effective radius of only five feet, had to be closely connected to the first amplifier. This amplifier was contained in a heavy wooden box that held a vacuum tube specifically developed not for sound recording but for telephone transmission. In other words, it was built to be immobile.

If the box was touched, or moved even slightly, there would be a large BONG resounding from the vacuum tube. "The tube itself was very microphonic," said sound engineer George Groves. "There was no way of moving the microphone and its associated microphone amplifier . . . [once] a microphone was located in a set, it could not be moved. . . . It had to be tied up with ropes, in a certain position, and anybody who talked or said or did anything had to go to the microphone. The actor went to the microphone, not the microphone to the actor."

Schemes for camouflaging microphones could range from the obvious — telephones, vases, lamps — to the creative. Some chunky actors had mikes strapped to their chests or backs and were given nonspeaking parts as immobile human mike-holders. Since every scene couldn't be structured with two actors standing by a conveniently located flowerpot, the Warner Bros. cameramen and engineers devised a method that utilized the two-dimensionality of the screen. In essence, it was a microphone matte; the microphone would actually be dangling down in full view of the camera, but the same wallpaper or covering that was in the background of the scene would be mounted in front of the mike and lit to blend in with the wall that was several feet behind. The result looked like an unbroken surface.

"Generally, you'd have five or six mikes in a shot," remembered the Warners cameraman Byron Haskin. "Behind them would be a medium-gray wall. The propman would . . . slip . . . a sheath . . . of a certain gray [onto the microphone], and if it matched the back wall, it was OK. I've lost as many as eleven mikes with these — blend them in with a little powder, and a little charcoal, and dust them into the wall, and you'd lose them. It was a matter of just shading them in the proper color."

In a rush to maximize profits before the sound fad burned itself out, the studios began working virtually around the clock. Warner Bros. often ordered their camera crews to shoot Vitaphone shorts on what were supposed to be their off-hours. "We'd be eighteen hours a day on the soundstage," remembered Byron Haskin. "There was no limit to the hours, no compensation such as time-and-a-half for overtime . . . To kill the pain of fatigue, many of us were half loaded most of the time. These excessive working hours brought the unions into the business to legislate tolerable conditions. So the abuse accompanying the coming of sound brought profound alteration of the whole movie business in every way."

❏ ❏ ❏

"We had an awful lot of people and a lot of equipment we'd never seen before," remembered Arthur Jacobson, who had worked his way up to assistant director during the transition period. "There was a man sitting at a little desk with things on his ears. We found out that was a mixing panel. They'd strung all these piano wires over the actors' heads . . . We didn't know what to expect . . . the mysterious soundmen were kings. We were being asked to do things we knew nothing about. Everybody was in the dark; it was a whole new world and nobody knew if it would exist next month."

Henry King, an experienced director of quality films (*Tol'able David* and the 1925 version of *Stella Dallas*), watched in amazement as the soundman hired by the studio walked through his location sets slapping his hands, saying that the sound wasn't usable: "He goes to the [other] set and [again] does the hand slapping and says the same thing. I got fed up and finally asked what the problem was. The soundman said that the sound would echo. I said that there was an echo in every room in real life . . ."

The soundmen were forcing so many arbitrary changes that a wag at MGM hired the famous prankster Vince Barnett to impersonate a sound expert. He walked around a half-constructed soundstage giving Louis B. Mayer doubletalk about the obvious errors in construction that made the acoustics impossible. Barnett finished by telling Mayer he would have to tear it all down and start over. Mayer was about to issue orders to do it when he was let in on the joke.

In defense of the soundmen, part of the problem was that their soundproof booths had been outfitted with theater speakers. In a small, enclosed room, the engineers heard noises that not only could not be heard on the set, but would never be heard in any theater with the slightest amount of reverberation or ambient noise.

"The soundmen had their troubles with the cameramen," recalled Joe Youngerman. "The soundman would want the mike *there* and the cameraman would say, 'It's in the picture.' They would get into squabbles." According to the regnant new ideology of sound, if movies were to be heard, they could not move.

Then Paramount's B. P. Schulberg came up with what must have seemed a declaration of war. He began importing theater directors from New York to work side-by-side with experienced filmmakers. The idea was that the veteran moviemakers would direct the camera, and the *arrivistes* from New York would handle the actors and the dialogue. It seemed a fortuitous idea; the movie director knew what to do with a camera, the dialogue director knew what to do with talk. As far as the pecking order on the set, "the movie director had the power," said Arthur Jacobson. "The other guy was a specialist, and there were a lot of things to do with making a movie besides dialogue." Some of the dialogue specialists that Schulberg hired

(George Cukor, John Cromwell) would go on to considerable careers of their own, although none would ever be noted as a visual stylist.

"It was in a sense good luck for me because it was the opening of the Red Sea, and so we could all come in," George Cukor told Kevin Brownlow. "People who had not had any stage direction, stage experience, they were baffled. They'd say, 'Now he speaks his title here' and 'he speaks his title there.' I was supposed to do a picture with [Adolphe] Menjou. He said, 'But my reactions, my reactions . . .' He'd planned to do very suave things between each line, and he had to get over that."

The response of the entrenched Hollywood veterans to the implicit message being sent was predictable. "They saw an opportunity to put all us arrogant, overpaid sons of bitches out of their way," snorted Clarence Brown, the best director on the MGM lot next to King Vidor. "There must have been a hundred of them [theater directors]."

Howard Hawks, in the middle of shooting an aerial picture called *The Air Circus,* was rudely asked by Fox executives, "What do you know about sound?" All Hawks could say was, "I just know how people speak." That didn't seem good enough, so Hawks was assigned a dialogue director named Lew Seiler, characterized by the angry Hawks as "a burlesque comic for Minsky's." It was Seiler who shot the sound scenes of Hawks's picture. "You have never *known* such bad dialogue," groused Hawks. "We all had a hell of a time."

But Brown, Hawks et al. had an edge. Theater directors knew how to stage a dialogue scene, but that was all. As Clarence Brown put it, "We learned their business in three weeks, but they couldn't pick up ours."

Most directors made the transition; others weren't so lucky or skilled. Major commercial directors like Fred Niblo *(Ben-Hur, The Mark of Zorro),* Clarence Badger *(It),* Marshall Neilan *(Stella Maris, Tess of the D'Urbervilles),* Rex Ingram *(The Four Horseman of the Apocalypse, Scaramouche),* and Herbert Brenon *(Peter Pan, Beau Geste)* would see their careers plummet, and for good reason; even by the severely limited standards of early talkies, their efforts are particularly awful.

Neilan's *The Vagabond Lover* features the adenoidal singing and ungodly dance-band music of Rudy Vallee, who displays the preoccupied concern of a man trying to pass a kidney stone; his acting ability was of the sort usually found only in sixth-grade plays. Vallee makes Crosby look like Cagney and plays the kind of music that Spike Jones mercilessly parodied. It's the film of a director at a total loss; actors stumble over their lines but plow gamely ahead, and Neilan keeps the footage in the film.

It might not all be Neilan's fault; the original negative of the film was burned in a studio fire, and the film survives today as reconstructed with outtakes. But Neilan's *Tanned Legs,* of that same year, is nothing more or less than *The Cocoanuts* without the Marx Brothers, and includes a nondescript score by Oscar Levant and only trace elements of Neilan's once-vaunted airy charm. Neilan directed only a few more pictures for major studios before being relegated to Poverty Row, then permanent unemployment.

Most of the men who failed to navigate the shoals of sound were older, more set in their ways, and probably couldn't have directed a screen test in three weeks, let alone an entire film. Neilan was an alcoholic and may have been too far gone to make the adjustment. "Rex Ingram, pageant-master," as James Joyce referred to him in *Finnegans Wake,* made only one talkie, an independently produced Foreign Legion romance called *Baroud.* Beautifully photographed in North African locations, and surprisingly nimble in terms of sound, Ingram himself played the lead to save money. Had *Baroud* been made as a silent, Ingram's black-Irish good looks would probably have made the picture a success; in sound, his flat, awkward phrasing and the film's theme and setting — clear throwbacks to the silent days — made *Baroud* a humiliating financial failure.

But even a director like James Cruze *(The Covered Wagon, Old Ironsides),* talented, fast, facile, eager to work — and also an alcoholic — had major career troubles after sound. He tried independent production and failed, went back to the studios, and, with the exception of his work on Universal's lavish disaster *Sutter's Gold,* bounced around on projects of declining prestige. He finished his career grinding out B movies at Republic. After four years of unemployment, he committed suicide.

Some idea of the difficulties that filmmakers faced can be gauged by looking at comparable films from a rising young director. Tay Garnett's 1928 circus picture, *The Spieler,* although a B movie, is energetic, with a vigorous narrative and elaborate camerawork (and it was made for the extremely modest cost of $95,597). *The Flying Fool,* his first talkie, released only six months later, is a dire aviation picture with William Boyd and an overweight Marie Prevost mouthing the words while someone else sings a song. Pathé was falling apart at the time through lack of capital—there are no extras in street scenes, for example—which probably didn't help Garnett any. Still, sound threw most directors—good, bad, or indifferent—off their rhythm.

Some of the more intelligent members of the Hollywood community could see what was about to happen, but were powerless to prevent it. In the *American Cinematographer* of August 1928, a pseudonymous column writer predicted with remarkable accuracy that "the panicky rush into talkies is just going to set our dear little picture business back about two years...In the second place, the helluva rush to beat the other fellow in getting talking pictures out is going to mean lousy pictures—no two ways about that...

"Go to any talking picture, shut your eyes, and if you don't get exactly the same effects as in a theater, there's something wrong that somebody's gonna get heck for. For the ideal they're working for in speech from the screen is to duplicate as far as possible the stage voice quality, the stage spacing of words, the stage delivery of speech, and the stage construction of sentences. All of which is the rankest kind of hooey—for pictures. Now reverse yourself and stop your ears, and see if you don't see the punkest kind of movie action you've seen in all this world.

"The poor, helpless movie industry is in for two years of tooth-cutting, measles, housemaid's knee, whooping cough and all sorts of childish woe. For they won't be sensible. They've got talkies and they're going to make 'em talk or die...In short, we're in for a new deal, and the game is dated right back to the rules of 1915..."

Some members of the industry correctly apprehended the essential nature of the alteration, but misunderstood its transcendental import. Conrad Nagel, who had been in silent films since the teens to no particular notice, had a resonant baritone that was perfect for the early sound equipment. In July 1928, he wrote an article for *The Film Spectator* in which he theorized that Hollywood had grown flabby with success, that "stories have become such familiar formulas and casts so stereotyped, that a picture-wise audience can tell just what will happen after seeing the first reel of an average production ... The industry has allowed itself to slip into a rut so deep that a cataclysm is needed to jar it free ...

"The talking picture [will] slowly make a place for itself without disrupting the motion picture industry. The silent picture will always be made — at least for many years — to supply the great foreign market and the thousands of small theaters that cannot afford talking equipment as it is now installed ...

"Let those who doubt that the talkie is here to stay, go into any theater that is running one of the latest talking pictures. Watch the audience lean forward and listen with rapt attention while the players are speaking. Watch the audience relax — sit back and whisper comments when the talking ceases and the old familiar printed title is flashed. The picture is once more a dead thing — without life, until another talking sequence occurs."

For all of his smugness, Nagel was on to something; silent films *were* inherently artificial and talkies *were* inherently realistic. Silence abstracted stars and stories, and had a way of making actors seem younger than they were. Sound reversed this, and demanded an entirely different manner: sass from people who had seen and done it all and were eager to talk about it. Sound was the first wave in an onslaught of surface reality that would eventually disfigure film almost beyond recognition, make it a slave to the most prosaic elements of objective reality.

Since Nagel had the good fortune to appear in some of the earliest Warners Vitaphone features and his voice was obviously OK, he worked furiously, appearing in around thirty pictures in two years.

"To us, [the early days of sound were] a great adventure," remembered Nagel years later. "It's like crossing the ocean on a big liner. It's so easy and comfortable, but the first person who tried it had only a little ship called the *Santa Maria* ... We were just a bunch of

Columbuses — we had no rules to go by and no technical advantages to help us.

"I remember doing a picture with William deMille and another one at the same time with Cecil DeMille. I'd work with William in the morning and Cecil in the afternoon. I'd have to ask myself, 'Gee, what part am I playing now?' Then I would work with Fred Niblo in the evening. And the next morning I would go out with Harry Rapf . . . When I got to where I was only working on two pictures at once, it was practically a vacation."

On those rare evenings when Nagel wasn't working, he and his wife would want to go to a movie, only to discover that he was in the picture at Grauman's, Loew's, and the Paramount as well. "We couldn't find a theater where I wasn't playing. So we'd go back home. I was an epidemic."

□ □ □

The die-hard adherents of silence grew fewer in number, although they popped up in the oddest places. In June, dear old Carl Laemmle ran an open letter in the trade papers proclaiming that "I will not be stampeded [by talkies] into forgetting the needs of the small exhibitors." Fox's Winfield Sheehan, undoubtedly talking out of both sides of his mouth, proclaimed in August that there was room enough for both forms, that there would be just as many silent pictures as there would be talkies.

In the fall of 1928, Joe Walker was photographing *Submarine* for Frank Capra at Columbia, and idly mentioned that a scene wherein a submarine crew was rescued by tapping on the side of a submarine with a wrench was a great opportunity for sound. Producer Sam Bischoff glared at him. "Columbia will *never* make a sound picture," he snarled. By the time *Submarine* was released late in the year, with Capra directing with all the roughhouse vitality of Raoul Walsh, the director had amplified the rescue sequence into an impressive *tour de force* that was accompanied by a sound track. The effect of the wrench tapping on the hull was a crude but eerie approximation of the sound (more like metal on wood, not metal on metal), but nobody seemed to mind.

The audience's preferences were further amplified when Warners' follow-up to *The Jazz Singer* was released in September. Oddly, Jack and Harry made *The Singing Fool* as another part-talkie, albeit one that's a good 70 percent sound as opposed to *The Jazz Singer*'s 15 percent. The entire first two reels are silent, and feature some stunning, elaborate tracking shots by Byron Haskin.

The story is a fervently lachrymose concoction about a pop Pagliacci, a singing waiter who rises to fame and fortune but whose son dies after his wife leaves him. Al Jolson gives not one but two encores of "Sonny Boy." The score is a virtual compendium of Jolson standards ("It All Depends on You," "I'm Sitting on Top of the World," "There's a Rainbow Round My Shoulder"), but the film's most notable feature is Jolson's alarmingly overwrought performance. Sound, which made Jolson one of the primary movie stars of the entire world, also ensured that his reign would be brief, for he was a maniacally overbearing actor.

The Singing Fool is cunningly constructed to give the effect of offering more synchronized sound than it really has; large-scale long shots and crowd scenes are mostly shot silent, but Warners had become sufficiently adept with music and sound effects to have over-dubbing give the effect of synchronized sound. *The Singing Fool* also features one of the first times the bulky camera booth was moved during a scene. It clearly shows why it was so seldom done, for the image — a medium shot of Jolson singing that moves into a close-up — goes noticeably, if temporarily, out of focus.

"After seeing and hearing *The Singing Fool*," wrote the critic for *Harrison's Reports,* an exhibitors' trade paper, "I could not help becoming convinced that talking pictures are here to stay . . . *The Singing Fool* . . . will be to talking pictures what *The Birth of a Nation* has been to silent pictures . . ."

From a strictly commercial standpoint, *Harrison's* was right. First-night tickets at the Winter Garden, the theater where Jolson had had his greatest theatrical successes, cost an enormous $11 top. Despite the film's manifold drawbacks, the audience reaction was thunderous. SINGING FOOL A WOW, screamed the banner headline in *Variety* ("Jolson [is] the tragedian as well as the comedian . . . Jolson showed them that he was the greatest entertainer in the world . . ."). With Jolson's relentless plugging of "Sonny Boy," *The Singing Fool* amassed a staggering worldwide gross of $5.8 million against a cost of $388,000.*

The pattern of mediocre sound films outgrossing good or great silent films was being repeated everywhere. "[Sound] was a great hypo [to business]," said Eugene Zukor, the son of Paramount's Adolph Zukor. "Attendance just picked up tremendously," commented William Mitchell, the president of Interstate Theaters in Dallas. *Variety* estimated that sound had increased business in some cities by as much as 15 to 20 percent, all at the expense of the theaters that could only play silent pictures.

A William Haines vehicle for MGM called *Excess Baggage* was released with music and sound effects, but exhibitors found that wasn't good enough. "Played to the poorest Sunday crowd we have had for months and months," reported one small-town Illinois exhibitor in *Motion Picture Almanac.* "The Madison Theater in Peoria ... opened with ... *The Singing Fool* the same day and turned hundreds away and that is what became of the biggest share of our crowd ... Let us hope that the rest of the Vitaphone pictures will not have the drawing power that *The Singing Fool* has, or we will never survive until the sound pictures are available for us."

As that letter suggested, small-town exhibitors were in especially difficult circumstances. The agreement that the major studios had signed with Western Electric ensured that their chain theaters would be wired first; the massive cost was at least partially balanced by jettisoning live acts and musicians. Daily operating costs, without the stage shows, actually went down. But fringe or independent theaters, which had to struggle to get a bank loan, were imperiled. In Paris, Texas, the locals were driving to Dallas to see movies, which hurt the local economy; the Chamber of Commerce loaned money to the owner of the local theater so he could install a Movietone system.

---

* Behind the scenes, the relationship between Jack Warner and Al Jolson was beginning to fray, for they were two competing egotists who habitually sucked up all the air in whatever room either of them happened to be in. One day Jack noticed an exceptionally red Cadillac limousine parked on the street outside his office window. Informed that it was Jolson's new car, Warner immediately phoned the Cadillac sales department and ordered the same car, "only redder."

Every week, the trade papers' tallies of grosses from around the country delivered devastating news to silent-film partisans. For the week of September 19, *Variety*'s report from San Francisco was "Straight talkers here and records go by boards"; in Kansas City it was "Loew's Midland had its first 100 percent talker, *The Terror.* The lines were long and frequent. Saturday and Sunday openings were turnaways and the balance of the week good. Funny thing, that while practically all the fans continue to razz the talkers and kick about the noise and gratings of the machines, they stick for the complete show." Meanwhile, Lubitsch's *The Patriot,* universally applauded by critics but carrying only music and sound effects, was termed a "disappointment all around."

For Jack Warner this was not just validation, it was a millennial triumph, and he reacted accordingly. "It is not the novelty of the talking picture that will pass," he crowed to the Los Angeles *Times's* Edwin Schallert, "it is the novelty of the silent film that *has* passed."

CHAPTER 3

In the fall of 1928, MGM, along with the other studios, began to get in line with the prevailing winds. They announced that, of the next season's program, forty pictures would have sound, and nineteen of those would have dialogue. Nick Schenck, the head of Loew's, Inc., was a believer. But over at United Artists, his brother Joe Schenck was still holding out for silence, a disagreement that was mirrored in the two men's politics — Nick had contributed $25,000 to Al Smith's presidential campaign, while Joe was an ardent Hoover man.

Paramount was shooting *Interference,* its first talkie, and was building four new soundstages as quickly as possible. Warners had three stages running full-time, with a fourth about to be opened, while laggards like U.A. and Universal were contenting themselves with two.

As for Fox, production of the Movietone newsreel was being stepped up to twice a week, and William Fox had financed its expansion to the tune of thirty mobile units scattered throughout the world. On the home lot in Hollywood, with just two exceptions, every director was making a talkie, and production supervisor Winfield Sheehan expected to release five talkies before year's end. Those two exceptions were Frank Borzage, who was wrapping up work on *The River,* and F. W. Murnau, on location in Oregon with a film he was calling *Our Daily Bread.*

The latter property was to undergo a series of adaptive agonies unusual even by Hollywood standards, and it involved a subject much on the minds of Hollywood in the late 1920s: the dangers of the city, and the homicidal small-mindedness of the country. Whether it was Fox's *Sunrise*, MGM's *The Wind*, the DeMille Corporation's *White Gold*, or *Our Daily Bread*, the studios were awash in stories about a woman from the city who comes to a rural environment where her innate erotic charge disrupts the social and familial order, usually with disastrous results.

These films depict a society at odds, not merely with sex, but with both halves of its population. *Our Daily Bread* concerns Lem, a young farmer who travels to the city to sell his father's wheat crop. While there, he meets Kate, a waitress, falls in love, and gets married. They return to the family wheat farm, where his father, an authoritarian patriarch, begins a relentless campaign to destroy Kate, thereby reasserting his control over his son. After Lem has a fistfight with a hired hand who has taken a yen to his wife, the couple reconcile and prepare to stay on the farm with the now-chastened father.

Willis Goldbeck had completed a scenario for *Our Daily Bread* by August 1926, but by the time *Sunrise* had been completed Murnau was already interested in the property, which required jettisoning Goldbeck's script. On came Berthold Viertel, working with Murnau. Viertel did two drafts, the second of which ends with a particularly luminous scene: the couple, now reconciled, are in the barn. Outside, it's raining. They embrace and she takes his hand to lead him back to the house, but he pulls away and gets a pitchfork. He begins working the hay into a pile. His wife looks on, her expression moving from puzzlement to acceptance to joy. He finishes arranging the hay and they embrace, as the camera retreats into the rain outside the barn. In June, another screenwriter, named Marion Orth, came on for a final polish, and, in the latter part of August Murnau took his cast and crew to Pendleton, Oregon, for the location photography.

Murnau was perched on the edge of the volcano, for *Our Daily Bread* was a silent picture just entering production at a time when the grosses of silent pictures were plummeting, a time when all anybody wanted to talk about was sound.

□ □ □

Although Joe and Nick Schenck were brothers, they were not above poaching on each other's territory. One of MGM's most valuable assets was John Gilbert, whose contract was expiring in March of 1929. In the late summer of 1928, Joe Schenck moved in and offered Gilbert a berth at United Artists.

A draft contract outlined a six-year deal under which Gilbert was to deliver twelve pictures at his own expense, an arrangement similar to that of the other partner-producers in U.A. such as Chaplin, Fairbanks, and Pickford. In return, Gilbert would receive a sliding scale of the gross, topping out at 70 percent in America and England, 50 percent in the rest of Europe. Douglas Fairbanks assumed a primary role in the negotiations and helped negotiate the rights to the first two prospective Gilbert/U.A. productions: *The Virginian* and *Cyrano de Bergerac,* both of which were to be talkies.

Given the rising tide of sound, it was a complicated proposal; Arthur Kelly, Chaplin's man at U.A., pointed out that Gilbert should be obliged to furnish three different negatives per picture — a sound print, a silent print, and another negative for foreign use, conformation to be determined.

"We don't believe [Gilbert] has any idea of [financing the pictures] personally," wrote Clarence Erickson, Fairbanks's man at U.A., "but [would] make arrangements through [Joe Schenck's] Art Cinema." Fairbanks was obviously in danger of letting his enthusiasm run away with him: "Gilbert would undoubtedly be great asset to United," continued Erickson, "but we will advise Douglas against assuming personally any financial responsibility in connection with same."

As the deal evolved, Joe Schenck's Art Cinema Corporation agreed to assume the financing of Gilbert's pictures, up to a cost of $750,000 apiece, with Gilbert having director and cast approval, or even the option of directing himself. Although Gilbert had often played around with writing and direction — and had actually directed at least one film, before his acting career took off — as negotiations stretched on into the winter of 1928–29, it must have seemed like an intimidating responsibility for the mercurial actor, whom nobody had ever considered likely producer material.

Gilbert finally opted for the devil he knew, re-signing with MGM for a staggering $250,000 a picture. He had no discretion as to story or director, but MGM capitulated to the extent of agreeing that the contract was essentially unbreakable on their part; so long as Gilbert made his two pictures a year and didn't violate the standard morals clause, MGM was obligated to pay him $500,000 a year for the next three years.

Gilbert was ecstatic — it was more money than any actor had ever been paid by anybody. Nick Schenck was also delighted — one of his primary corporate assets had been protected and bound to the company for the foreseeable future. Gilbert was golden at the box office, and all that money was going to keep coming in. What could possibly go wrong?

□ □ □

By mid- to late 1928, Warner Bros. had worked out a brutally complicated method of editing sound on disc. Actually, they had done it as early as mid-1927, in *Old San Francisco,* when sound effects for the earthquake sequence were dubbed over the original orchestra recording. In essence, it involved multiple turntables. One turntable held a counting record, which counted every revolution for ten minutes. This was the timing matrix that determined the precise moment when the other records were to be started and stopped to dub down the required sound to the picture sequence, which had already been edited. Each record was started and stopped by hand.

Even with all the precautions, exact synchronization was impossible to maintain, and the film reel would often have to be slightly recut to synchronize with the sound disc. Something more exact was required.

Warners came up with a system of automatic machinery that would start and stop as many as eighteen turntables on preset cues, sending each cue to the master disc. "It was like a telephone dialing system," said George Groves. "A system of relays and selector switches was used that would release the turntables, and they would start to spin on preset cues. If there were more records to be dubbed than available turntables [Groves recalled that as many as one hundred discs could be used to compile the final master record for one ten-minute reel], a crew of men would stand there with the next records in a rack, select the next record in sequence, take the old one off, and reset the footage counter so that each turntable operated at the right time."

For example, if the engineers determined that turntable #9 had to deliver its cue at 64 revolutions plus 4 frames, a special platen would be placed over that disc that showed the start point of 60 revolutions plus 35 frames. The needle would go down at 60 plus 35, the turntable would get up to speed and deliver the cue at 64 plus 4, which might take, say, 12 revolutions plus 34 frames, until the out point of 72 plus 34.

Of course, once the train of dubbing turntables was started, it had to go through all the way to the end; should a mistake be made — synchronization be off, the wrong disc be put on the right turntable, whatever — they had to go back to the beginning of the reel and start over. "If they'd had computers," mused sound engineer (and later director) Edward Bernds, "they might have been able to do it, but [that system] was hopeless." The ironic end-result of all this killingly arduous labor to create a rerecording and dubbing system was that each generation of dubbing made the sound seem more remote, made the overall quality appreciably worse.

"By using that kind of equipment," says Robert Gitt of UCLA, "it sounded like it was coming through cardboard. A Vitaphone film from 1929 has a more primitive sound than one from 1927."

On the exhibition end, discs also complicated the process. While Warners, out of proprietary pride in Vitaphone, released their films with sound recorded on just one side, United Artists and Paramount sent out discs recorded on both sides, probably to save money. Side A would have the sound for reel one, side B would have the sound for reel three, and so on.

The discs came packed in very heavy flat, wooden cases, with corrugated paper between each disc. Breakage wasn't the problem — the boxes were solid and absorbed most shocks, and the discs weren't as fragile as most people thought. The real problem was mix-ups: the wrong discs, or even one wrong disc, with the right film. To minimize these mistakes, the release number of the film, prominently emblazoned on the leader and trailer of every reel, was likewise rubber-stamped onto the label of every disc. Because the discs wore out so quickly, distributors had to have multiple copies of each set of discs on hand.

"It was doing a job the hard way," admitted George Groves. Even die-hard Warners loyalists were forced to look longingly at the competing Fox sound-on-film system, where all you needed to edit sound was a pair of scissors, and all you needed to ship it was a few metal cans.

□ □ □

"The biggest change I noticed with sound was the absence of mood music," remembered Frank "Junior" Coghlan, a child star of the late silent era. "The music was such a big aid." On the first audition Coghlan went on after the arrival of sound, he was handed a script and told to give a reading, that is, scan it and give a rough performance. Coghlan, without stage experience, just read it aloud as if it was a newspaper story. He didn't get the job.

"It made me realize that this was a whole new ball game. You had to think about what you were doing. The director couldn't talk you through a scene. If you missed a word, it meant another take; in silents, who knew? In silent pictures, I don't think we ever did more than six takes; you didn't have to worry about perfect diction and the director could talk to you, so his ego was assuaged."

Coghlan was thirteen years old when he made his first talkie, and, he remembered, "If I'd been a married man with kids, I'd have been terrified." As it happened, children's light voices were difficult for early sound equipment to record; whenever possible, child actors were avoided, so Coghlan's employment opportunities began falling off.

□ □ □

As Paramount prepared *Interference,* its first all-talking picture, it was determined that it would be codirected by none other than Roy Pomeroy. (Lothar Mendes had completed *Interference* as a silent, and Pomeroy reshot the picture, re-creating Mendes's original with dialogue.) Although Pomeroy was regarded as "brilliant," he was not without his eccentricities. An Englishman, Pomeroy's subsidiary passion was archery — he kept a large collection of bows in his studio office. Also, Henry Hathaway remembered that Pomeroy "spit—he'd talk to you, you'd get wet."

A trade paper enthusiastically, if somewhat incoherently, proclaimed "the . . . sound chief of Paramount to be a dual human center of double abilities . . . 1. He is a picture technical expert; 2. a camera expert; 2. [sic] a sound engineer; 4. a director; 5. an oil painter; 6. an electrical engineer; 7. a mechanical expert; 8. a mathematician. He is also widely read on history, literature, drama, music and kindred arts."

The notice, the deference, went to Pomeroy's head. He proclaimed himself the wellspring of all knowledge about sound. "He threw his weight around," remembered propman Joe Youngerman. "He claimed he knew all about it." Because hardly anyone knew more than Pomeroy, and most knew much less, Paramount gave him whatever he wanted, including a mammoth raise that took his salary from $250 to $2,500 a week. "We couldn't have treated him with more awe and homage if he had been Edison himself," Jesse Lasky remembered.

Along with the native caution of the engineer, Pomeroy now began displaying the haughty insolence of the neophyte expert. Pomeroy began directing *Interference* in early September 1928. His first decree was that no outsiders were to be allowed on his set. The sole exception was William deMille, who had volunteered his services as Pomeroy's assistant. "Within [the set's] enclosure Roy was king," wrote deMille in *Hollywood Saga*, his superb volume of memoirs. "Even the heads of the Company had to ask permission to enter this sacred and mysterious domain, where strange and exciting miracles were being wrought. When the four-toned automobile horn had signaled for silence and the massive doors were closed, everyone in the building froze into immobility, hardly daring to breathe. A cough or a sneeze might cost several hundred dollars. There was no ventilation, and powerful lights soon made a turkish bath of the place; the whole atmosphere was that of medieval necromancy."

When *Interference* arrived in theaters, one of the more prescient reviews came from the New York University *Daily News*, wherein one Henry Levy wrote, "We should say that it is more nearly a play than a cinema. If you take the dialogue from the finished product and show only the silent film you have nothing; if you remove the cinematic element and leave only the dialogue you have the equivalent of the reading of a play."

The trade paper *Billboard* reported that "Before [Jesse] Lasky saw *Interference,* his opinion was that the average star's voice would record satisfactorily and that the difference between the voice of an untrained film star and that of an artiste who has had stage experience or is not particularly adapted to histrionics, was not so great.

"He has now changed his mind . . . *Interference* proved to Lasky that only the best trained voices are of any use." Lasky decreed that the slogan for all Paramount talkies was to be the oxymoronic phrase "With Casts That Can Talk." As *Billboard* noted, the clear implication was that "Paramount stars, no matter how big they are, will not have a ghost's chance in talking roles if their voices are not sufficiently trained for proper reproduction." *

William deMille's younger brother Cecil was a loyal silent-movie man. Cecil looked on glumly as he was forced to add a talkie sequence to his production of *The Godless Girl,* a richly absurd ragout about wayward youth — fundamentalists versus atheists in high school — that encompasses morality, melodrama, sadism, and muscular narrative dynamics. The opening title reads: "IT IS NOT GENERALLY KNOWN THAT THERE ARE ATHEIST SOCIETIES THROUGHOUT THIS COUNTRY ATTACKING THROUGH THE YOUTH OF THE NATION THE BELIEFS THAT ARE SACRED TO MOST OF THE PEOPLE."

Shot in early 1928, *The Godless Girl* premiered in August at the Biltmore Theater in Los Angeles. Reviews and business were substandard; the picture had cost a weighty $722,315, and DeMille's own company was financing, with Pathé releasing. But Pathé was faltering (they would soon be absorbed into RKO). DeMille bailed out, selling a batch of stock and signing a three-picture deal with

---

* *Interference* was a film of no particular importance, but its premiere in London provided audiences with much hilarity. Clive Brook's mother went to see her son's first talkie and reported back to him of the ensuing disaster. There was an episode in the film in which an anonymously written postcard arrived, which Brook tore up with the words "Another one of those damn postcards." At that point, the needle got stuck, endlessly repeating "Another one of those damn postcards . . . Another one of those damn postcards . . ." as the scene continued into a murmuring love scene of Brook kissing his wife.

MGM. Correctly realizing that silent pictures had a limited audience in the early winter of 1928, Pathé panicked, pulled the silent version, and hired Paul Bern, Barney Glazer, and Jack Jevne to cobble together a couple of talking sequences.

Although DeMille was already on the MGM lot, his secretary sent him a note accompanying some script pages in late November: "Please make a point of okaying [by] tomorrow, Saturday, so they can shoot it Sunday, which is the only day they can get people and equipment together." The talking scenes were shot — without DeMille, under the supervision of character actor Fritz Feld — on November 25.

For most of its running time, *The Godless Girl* is a silent film with a synchronized score and sound effects: sirens, marching feet, and so on. After the climax, a brilliantly staged fire sequence that's among the most dynamically shot and edited action sequences in cinema, the film concludes with two tacked-on dialogue scenes. The first is an add-on to the silent footage, as the characters debate whether or not to kill the evil Noah Beery character. Most of the sound is dubbed over silent footage.

There follows a tag scene wherein there is much debate about how to spend the rest of their lives.

"What are we gonna do and where are we gonna go?" says one.

"I know what I'm gonna do," announces another triumphantly. "Sell hot dogs!"

The hopeless, anticlimactic triviality of the dialogue — the scene has nothing to do with the plot, the characters, or the admittedly giddy mood DeMille has spent two hours establishing — would be replicated dozens of times in so-called "goat-gland" * movies, silent movies that filmmakers attempted to rejuvenate by surgically grafting a dialogue scene onto them.

DeMille must have been maddened by the entire experience; earlier in the picture, during a scene when the two main characters

---

* "Goat-gland" referred to a surgical procedure developed around 1920 by one Dr. J. R. Brinkley of Milford, Kansas, in which Brinkley surgically implanted goat testes into humans. It was thought to be a cure for impotence, with possibly beneficial effects on insanity and influenza. The procedure sparked intense coverage and debate in the Sunday supplements.

escape and are pursued by the police, he double-exposed a shot of alarm bells into the upper corner of the screen while Lina Basquette reacted to the sound in the lower half of the shot, an effective way of visually suggesting the panic caused by the teenagers' escape. But the sound track redundantly accompanies the image with the sound of bells, banishing suggestion, literalizing the moment.

When it finally limped into release, the sound version of *The Godless Girl* was a commercial and critical failure, grossing less than $500,000. *The New York Times* said that "the story, which stretches from unexpected ludicrous slapstick through scenes in a burning reformatory, the intensity of feeling of which equals motion picture depictions of the French revolution, is punctured with vapid, religious admonitions and strange, heavenly warnings in the form of crosses burnt into the palms of the heroine . . ."

In later years, DeMille would grouse about the demands of early talkies: "To leaf through my shooting script of *Dynamite* [his first all-talkie] is to see at a glance what sound had done to films. The dialogue, typed in red, is the outstanding feature of each page; and some of the dialogue in the first reels seems . . . painfully bright and brittle, as if we were dinning into the audience what good playwrights we were, now that they could hear as well as see."

That was DeMille speaking some thirty years after the event. At the time, his reaction was encapsulated in a glum remark to his brother: "It looks to me, Bill, very much as if we [are] all going to work for the electric companies."

❏ ❏ ❏

The most unfortunate example of a goat-gland movie is Paul Fejos's *Lonesome*. Essentially, *Lonesome* is *The Crowd* without expressionism. In telling the story of a machinist and a telephone operator who meet on a bus to Coney Island, fall in love during the long day, and are accidentally separated to the requisite emotional devastation only to find they are next-door neighbors, Fejos anticipates rigorous neorealism twenty years before De Sica. Other than some flashy montages and the sophisticated camera work — Fejos was clearly in awe of the possibilities of the camera, and moves it in every scene — the film is relentlessly deglamorized.

Much of the film was shot among large crowds, which presented cameraman Gilbert Warrenton with a problem: "The requirement is to identify them immediately in every scene and without conscious effort. Otherwise . . . the feeling of reality is lost." Warrenton imperceptibly focused a key light on the two principals at all times in the crowd scenes, brightening them, forcing them into the visual foreground even if they weren't in the compositional foreground.

But Fejos's entirely fluent, effortless film is interrupted three times for a total of about six minutes of banal chitchat:

"Nice day, isn't it?"

"It's sweet."

"Just like you."

"Shut up."

Or:

"Gee, we're alone . . . Gee, it's funny how lonesome a fella can be, especially with a million people around him . . . All my life I've wanted a little white house out in the country with blue shingles."

"I hate blue shingles."

And so forth.

All the dialogue scenes are shot in single-camera setups that could have been photographed in one day and probably were. The dialogue relentlessly reiterates what Fejos and his actors have already communicated perfectly well without words. The talking scenes don't destroy the film, but they do mar it.* *Lonesome* isn't as good as *The Crowd*—it lack Vidor's conceptual and stylistic grandeur, and it steals several tropes from *Sunrise;* Fejos used studio artifice realistically as opposed to impressionistically. Nevertheless, it is a small classic that suffered from the random defacement of irrelevant sound. It deserves a wider audience today.

For that matter, *Lonesome* deserved a wider audience in 1928;

---

* Tay Garnett was put through the same penance as Fejos.

"Congratulations, it just arrived," the Pathé production manager told Garnett.

"What has just arrived?"

"Our sound equipment . . . You start shooting sound tomorrow morning."

In October, a full month after he had completed the silent version of *The Spieler,* Garnett shot two days' worth of talking sequences, spending an additional $13,663. While Pathé's recording facilities had arrived, they still had no music or sound effects departments, so the musical score was recorded back in New York.

despite raves from people like René Clair ("originality, freshness and enterprise ... [showing] that intelligence and daring are not as rare [among American producers] as many of us have been inclined to believe"), *Lonesome* grossed only $227,318 — a fourth of what *The Crowd* made — a disparity pointing up the differences between releasing companies. MGM could release a defiantly uncommercial art movie and, with its powerful chain of theaters, snare a decent gross; Universal could release an art movie, and the film could disappear without a trace.

❏ ❏ ❏

From being a fairly low man on the studio totem pole, Roy Pomeroy was now the single most important man on the Paramount lot, and he meant to keep it that way. When Victor Fleming and his assistant Henry Hathaway went to check out the production of *Interference,* they were stopped by a policeman at the stage door. "[The] test stage was guarded like the Bank of England," recalled Hathaway.

An outraged Fleming went to production head B. P. Schulberg: "Look, this guy's got locks on his doors! Jesus Christ, are you only going to have one director for sound? What the hell is this, Ben? We're all going to have to know about it. This son of a bitch, he can't direct all the pictures."

Fleming had a point, and Schulberg knew it. The *Interference* set was opened up. "From then on," said Hathaway, "Vic and I spent most of our time on that one ... stage, learning the equipment." *

Even other studios had to cope with Pomeroy's grab for power; MGM borrowed Paramount's single soundstage to shoot a reel of

---

* Since Fleming had been an expert auto mechanic and had a technical bent, he picked up the essentials of sound quickly; the perennially underrated director's first all-talkie, *The Virginian,* makes extensive use of locations and ambient sound. The dramaturgy is a trifle stiff — villain Walter Huston wears a flamboyant black mustache, and barely manages to restrain himself from twirling the tips — but the film's lack of music in conjunction with the thunk of boots on wooden sidewalks, the persistent bellowing of cows, the off-screen sobs of a man about to be hanged, give *The Virginian* a documentary authenticity that transcends the stock story and bad dialogue ("You gol-darned, mangy, soup-fed buzzard").

Alias Jimmy Valentine in sound, and, true to form, Pomeroy refused to permit people on the stage.

In preparation for *Alias Jimmy Valentine*, Louis B. Mayer insisted that star William Haines take elocution lessons from an elderly teacher who forced him to utter lines from classical drama in the requisite pear-shaped tones. (Haines would later compare the arrival of sound at MGM to "the discovery of clap in a nunnery.")

Because Paramount was making its own films during the day, the sound scenes for *Valentine* were shot in the middle of the night. "You are confined to working quarters . . . that are almost airtight," Haines reported. "You can hardly breathe, and in the hot weather it's like working in a boiler room . . . The sweat rolled off me until I could hardly stand it, and once I nearly felt like fainting."

Pomeroy finally overstepped himself when a young executive named David Selznick told him about a casting decision. Pomeroy curtly told Selznick that the sooner the executives realized that there could be no talkie casting conducted without his prior approval, the better off everybody would be.

Lasky, Zukor, and Schulberg looked around and saw that, as other studios were somehow managing to make talkies without Roy Pomeroy, there was a good chance they could too. The last straw was Pomeroy asking for yet another raise, this time to $3,500 a week. Pomeroy's next film was promptly assigned to William deMille; Schulberg contacted Western Electric, who sent out a couple of technicians with no ambitions to run the motion picture business. Roy Pomeroy disappeared from the Paramount lot; after directing one more film at RKO in 1931, he disappeared from filmmaking altogether.

The Pomeroy pattern was repeated all over Hollywood. At the Hal Roach studio, the head of the new nine-person sound department was a man named Elmer Raguse. As the editor Richard Currier recalled, "In pictures, if you can't get an effect one way, you figure out another way of getting it. But with Raguse, there was only one line you could follow, and that was that."

One day Currier wanted to record a gunshot, but Raguse wouldn't let him shoot a gun near the microphone on the grounds that the loud noise would break the light valve. Currier asked Raguse how much the valve cost. $150? $200?

"Oh, no," replied Raguse. "It probably only costs twenty cents."

Currier promptly fired the gun, and got his recording of the shot.

Around the Roach lot, a low-key, mom-and-pop operation, Raguse was distinguished by being antisocial. "He was totally technical," said one Roach staffer. "In his own little world." Until the shakeout between the two competing sound systems, Roach was distinguished by recording both ways, sound on film *and* sound on disc. The latter came in handy, as Stan Laurel had disliked his voice since he was a teenager and was extremely nervous about sound. "I had quite a lisp [as a teenager]," he remembered in 1957. "My voice was kind of broken." "Every take we'd make, [Laurel] wanted to hear a playback on it," said Roach technician Thomas Benton Roberts.

Hal Roach remembered that his studio had sound equipment a good six months before MGM (in fact, a slight exaggeration): "For two-reel comedies in sound, they were paying us more than they were paying for features ... The theaters were paying enormous amounts of money for our comedies. That was the first time we changed from our original idea of selling the whole year's package at one time [i.e., block booking]; we started selling these sound comedies by themselves."

The figures bear out Roach's claim; Laurel and Hardy made eleven silent shorts during the 1928–29 season; the collective profit was a mere $35,000. Their first five sound shorts alone made a profit of $43,000.

❏ ❏ ❏

Vaudeville grew out of early variety shows, which tended to be performed in waterfront dives and frontier honky-tonks. In 1883, Benjamin F. Keith, a former circus performer, combined variety shows with some of the traditions of the English music hall and came up with vaudeville, carefully pruning away anything that might offend a family audience. Keith, in partnership with Edward F. Albee, eventually presided over a chain of a thousand theaters, with one located in every city with a population of at least one hundred thousand.

A vaudeville program was constructed in modular form, six to ten acts of no more than twenty minutes apiece. The acts were combined to create an overall effect of novelty and variety. "In the end," wrote historian Henry Jenkins, "what vaudeville communicated was the pleasure of infinite diversity in infinite combinations." Because Keith-Albee entertained two million people daily in the United States and Canada, there was a consistent market for talented specialty acts who could work "clean": jugglers, acrobats, singers, magicians, comedians, monologuists, and so on. By 1928, the National Vaudeville Artists Association Inc. had about fifteen thousand members.

One of the major joys of the vaudeville proving ground was the multiplicity of skills that it taught. Comedians could, of course, learn jokes and, more important, timing, but they could also pick up dancing or, if they were interested, juggling, singing, whatever. Although George Burns and Gracie Allen became famous for ritualistically detailed two-handers between a calm, bemused husband and his deeply confused wife, they were actually all-around performers —in the 1937 *Damsel in Distress* they do a spectacular production number with Fred Astaire. "When I met Gracie," remembered the ninety-seven-year-old George Burns, "she was a dramatic Irish actress. [Vaudeville taught her how to] *play* the part of a comedienne."

Even the people who worked within vaudeville were conscious of its slightly surreal nature. It was more than acrobats and magicians. Jugglers followed animal acts who followed monologuists who followed singers who followed comics who followed acts that didn't really fall into any known category. No matter what form the act took, time was of the essence; as Eddie Cantor told an interviewer, "A [perfomer] in vaudeville . . . is like a salesman who has only fifteen minutes in which to make a sale. You go on the stage knowing that every minute counts. You've got to get your audience the instant you appear."

Among the legendary oddball acts was Swayne's Rats and Cats, the favorite act of both Groucho Marx and George Burns, in which Swayne trained rats to chase cats around a circular enclosure. There were the Siamese Twins, a pair of circus freaks who played saxophone-and-clarinet duets, impersonated other sister acts, sang songs, cracked jokes, and tap-danced. (*Variety* noted that they were "not bad for an act of this type.")

There was Think-A-Drink Hoffman, who would come out with a

portable bar and one single cocktail shaker. Without ever being seen to add any ingredients, he would make up any drink anybody in the audience desired. "The audience loved it," remembered Donald O'Connor, who began his performing career as a child in vaudeville. "They were getting smashed, but they loved it. Or maybe they loved it *because* they were getting smashed."

Or there was the great Hadji Ali, Judy Garland's favorite vaudevillian. The Egyptian had a unique regurgitation act in which he would consume large amounts of water or walnuts, then bring it all up in a different order than he had swallowed it. The topper to Hadji Ali's act involved his drinking water followed by a smaller amount of gasoline. His assistant would set fire to a model house, after which Hadji Ali would bring up the gasoline, spitting it over the model until it threatened to turn into an inferno likely to consume the theater. Hadji Ali would then bring the water up to quench the blaze. Pandemonium, followed by wild applause.*

"A great act in vaudeville was made up over the years," remembered Donald O'Connor. "It was never written down. So, when vaudeville died, there was nothing to preserve." It is for this reason that the Vitaphone and Metrotone shorts provide a truly invaluable documentation of the performance styles and manners of show business in the first quarter of the twentieth century.

MGM's Metrotone shorts feature acts like the Ponce Sisters (two singers with good harmonies), the Reynolds Sisters (dancers), Joseph Regan (an Irish tenor who was all throat), innumerable sopranos that are all trills, the Five Locust Sisters (singers singularly unblessed by nature in every possible way), a profusion of dialect patter songs, a performer named Johnny Marvin who switches from a ukulele to the musical saw, Leo Beers ("World-Renowned Whistling Songster"), and, in a "Gus Edwards Kiddie Revue," a girl who tap-dances while bending over backward until her palms are flat on the floor.

Then there are the MCs, vending venerable wheezes from *Joe Miller's Joke Book*. Sample patter from MC Jack Pepper, a nervous, would-be charmer who served a brief tour of duty as Ginger Rog-

---

* Fortunately, Hadji Ali's act was filmed and preserved in a Spanish-language Laurel and Hardy movie entitled *Politiquerias*. No verbal description can quite encompass the act's rich absurdity, not to mention Hadji Ali's virtuosic esophageal control.

ers's first husband and who seems to have been a road company Cliff "Ukulele Ike" Edwards: "Why, she's so dumb that she worked in a five-and-ten-cent store, the Woolworth's, and was fired because she couldn't remember the prices ... I will now play the Scottish national anthem: 'I Can't Give You Anything But Love.' "

Every once in a while, something interesting or startlingly awful happens. The Metrotone shorts feature several appearances by a middle-aged black man billed as "George Dewey Washington, the Voice of the South." Washington's persona is that of a tramp in ragged clothes, and he sings the requisite songs of melodramatic passion, such as "The Road to Mandalay," in a trained, neo-operatic baritone. At one point, he goes down on one knee à la Jolson, and for just a second the surrounding tackiness of the born second-raters is dispelled by a performer of compelling passion and charisma.

On the other hand, there is an MC named Harry Rose, a mincing, smarmy horror who might have served as the inspiration for Joel Grey's capering grotesque in *Cabaret*. (Sample lyric: "Even on Yom Kippur / I would have to slip her / Frankfurter sandwiches, frankfurter sandwiches / All night long.")

The music in most of these acts is trite and hackneyed, and in theme and manner goes back to Stephen Foster. How revolutionary the Gershwins and Cole Porter must have seemed once radio and the talkies began penetrating the hinterland!

The Warners Vitaphone shorts offered more variety and a higher class of performer, from Willie and Eugene Howard to Ernestine Schumann-Heink (singing "Danny Boy" and "By the Waters of Minnetonka," among others). Warners didn't know what would work, so they tried everything. The music ran the gamut from Tin Pan Alley to folk songs, spirituals, and jazz; there were monologuists and sketches, impersonations and recitations.

The legendary World War I entertainer Elsie Janis, featured in a 1926 short entitled *Behind the Lines*, had personality, brio, a relaxed, one-of-the-boys manner that must have delighted soldiers, and a high kick the equal of Charlotte Greenwood's. A short entitled *The Office Scandal* stars a young Edgar Bergen, complete with Charlie McCarthy minus monocle or formal wear, dressed instead like a ragged member of Our Gang. Otherwise, the McCarthy character is already fully formed: naughty and smart-mouthed, with lots of rapid cross-talk with Bergen.

Among the most interesting of the hundreds of novelty acts Warners featured was the cartoonist Bruce Bairnsfather drawing his character "Ol' Bill," an actor impersonating Lincoln doing the Gettysburg Address, and comic and dramatic playlets with new-to-Hollywood actors such as Pat O'Brien and Spencer Tracy. Because of the necessity of cramming a great deal of narrative into ten minutes or less, these dramatic shorts tend to resemble tabloid versions of O. Henry or, at their best, Griffith's Biographs.

There are great musicians such as Noble Sissle and Eubie Blake, not to mention Eddie Peabody and his banjo, and legendary performers such as Weber and Fields. Warners even tried Cantor Josef Rosenblatt ("BOOKED ON REQUEST ONLY" the catalogue warns) singing "Omas Rabbi Elosor." One of the most popular Vitaphone attractions was the Metropolitan Opera's Giovanni Martinelli, who made over a dozen shorts for the company.* The key, then, was variety for its own sake. Past the initial rush of Jolson, Martinelli, et al., Warner Bros. didn't treat the Vitaphone shorts as motion picture events so much as a circulating library of recorded performances—phonograph records that happened to have a visual component.

The performance styles in the MGM and Vitaphone shorts understandably tended toward the theatrical proscenium, which occasionally resulted in dueling conventions of the stage and screen. Many of the 1926 and 1927 shorts end with the performer taking bows, sometimes two or three. The trade papers commented that the performer milking the house aroused titters in the audience. One commentator noted that shorts "should be cut off [early] to make a proper closing." By the end of 1928, bows in short subjects were mostly a thing of the past.

* Warners' allegiance to classical music wavered only during the summer of 1927, when they transferred the production of shorts from the Manhattan Opera House to their new Sunset Boulevard soundstages. Since most of the opera stars refused to travel west to record, in the winter of 1928–29 the studio resumed East Coast production at the refurbished Vitagraph studio in Brooklyn, and classical music was once again a regular attraction of the Vitaphone program.

One popular vaudevillian, the impressionist and singing comedienne Irene Franklin, left an invaluable record of the tense, uncertain process of making a Vitaphone short. The most important thing, she wrote, was to develop a sense of being "mike-wise. [Mike-wise] is the knowledge of how much lung-power *not* to put into the microphone, how long to pause and time a supposed joke for the laughter of the invisible audience . . . Mike-wise means to just about whisper your own songs, but not to take on the depressing drone so natural in dropping the voice, to keep the voice natural, expressive, vivid, to keep the letter *S* clear, the *R* from hardening, and the pitch slightly nasal for distance. And, at the same time, keep the over-taxed mind off the deadly mike-fright."

Franklin found the actual production arduous. The offstage orchestra was hedged in by scenery that also served as a sound baffle. First, Franklin ran through her routine for purposes of timing, because the director told her she could not run over eight minutes.

The rehearsal was recorded and Franklin went into another room to listen to the playback. "Gosh, what a funny voice! Did I really sound like that? Ah! There was that darned letter *S* — I was a little too fast on that line — that's better — that's clearer — oh, how I blurred that word — and it would be the one that made the joke — must remember — must remember — must remember — what a spiral you made of that *S*, old girl, and oh, God, how unfunny you sound to yourself."

It was time for a take. "The quiet hurt my ears, the heat was frightful. I swallowed. Heavens, I had an Easter egg in my throat . . . then a tiny sound, the husky little grind of the recording machine . . . good Lord, my throat began to tickle. I must clear it or I would cough. It was getting worse. At the end of the chorus there was a second's pause. I managed to clear my throat. I could hear the faintly smothered cough. Had anyone else noticed it?

"Our little army marched back to the room to hear the playback. It was a bit clearer, the muddled words were a bit overstressed, the boys were laughing; I could feel my head swelling. Suddenly a bloodhound barked from the machine. The crowd roared. I turned to [director] Roth, bewildered.

" 'That was your little smothered cough,' he said. 'Without it this would have been a perfect record. We'll do it again, and try not to cough . . .' "

Vitaphone and Metrotone shorts soon began to supplant live variety acts. Throughout 1928, the pages of *Variety* were full of reports of exhibitors abandoning vaudeville or "prologues" that accompanied the features, in favor of the less expensive shorts. At the same time, fringe vaudeville houses and "vaudfilm" houses began switching over to the canned entertainment.

Watching hours of surviving shorts from MGM and Warners gives one the uncomfortable feeling that what killed vaudeville was vaudeville; when medium-sized cities and small towns saw what constituted the authentic Big Time, the Harry Roses and Jack Peppers were doomed. Where did they go? How many dancing schools could they open? These shorts make it clear that people like Jack Benny, Bob Hope, and Burns and Allen were not typical of their peers, but, rather, the very best of the breed. (Poor Irene Franklin was typical of many; born in 1876, she died in poverty at the Actors' Fund Home in 1941.)

The 1929 stock-market crash and the ensuing Depression made the economics of vaudeville increasingly untenable, and the business began narrowing; each time a performer made a short, it reduced the audience for a live performance of the same material. The conundrum was not lost on the vaudeville community, and they reacted with appropriate hostility. Technicians engaged in wiring theaters for Vitaphone often needed bodyguards to protect them from threatening performers, stagehands, and musicians.

To modern eyes, the most interesting acts tend to be the most contained, the ones with the quiet self-confidence to let the audience come to them, precursors of what a later generation would call the "cool fire" of the good television performer: Cliff "Ukulele Ike" Edwards, Van and Schenck, Jack Benny. Benny's appearances in MGM films reveal that most of the essentials of his character were already in place by the time he graduated from vaudeville: aggrieved, saturnine, disgusted, used to being ignored. The refinements — his vanity and overwhelming cheapness — would come later.

CHAPTER 4

Ifter *The Crowd,* King Vidor quickly shot two Marion Davies films, *The Patsy* and *Show People,* a delightful satire on moviemaking. Davies was always a problem for MGM because, while her connection to William Randolph Hearst was impeccable, her grosses seldom were. Her previous two films had lost a total of nearly $250,000, but the two snappy comedies she made with Vidor earned a cumulative profit of over $320,000.*

* *Show People* and many other MGM silents were issued with a good music-and-effects track, an effective halfway measure that at least preserved the visual aesthetics of silent film. Unfortunately, sound's impact quite obliterated the audience's interest in visuals. Ironically, a mass-market silent spectacular like William Wellman's *Wings* effortlessly showcases far more visual variety than mainstream American films have offered since: it displays shifts from brutal realism to nonrealistic techniques associated with Soviet avant-garde or impressionistic French cinema — double exposures, subjective point-of-view shots, trick effects, symbolic illustrations on the titles, and so on. Sound made American films far more stylistically rigid, while at the same time enlarging the money stream, but in only one direction. Between 1927 and 1929, net profits for exhibitors went up 25 percent; for producers, they rose nearly 400 percent.

Not all synchronized music-and-effects tracks were as effective as those for *Sunrise* and *Show People.* Tod Browning's *West of Zanzibar* features a lugubriously heavy track of jungle drums that weighs down the film. Yet, Browning's gleeful Grand Guignol seldom dawdles, and *West of Zanzibar,* while not as memorably

While Vidor's stock with his employers was very high, his roving eye was already weakening his private life. His marriage to Eleanor Boardman was already a formality — Wanda Tuchock, who worked with him on the script for *Show People,* was his new companion. Already comfortable with the ratio of two films for MGM, one for him, Vidor embarked on a European vacation ready to begin another personal production upon his return.

When he left in the spring, the matter of sound versus silents had been up for grabs; when he returned in midsummer, he found that the matter had been decided. His new film, he realized, would have to be a talkie.

A Texan, Vidor had long been interested in black culture. He argued with Thalberg that if novels, and plays like *Porgy,* and, on an entirely lower level of accomplishment, short stories by Octavus Roy Cohen, could be successful with white audiences, why couldn't a movie? Despite his dislike of sound, the Gospel-based musicality of rural black life seemed to Vidor to constitute a viable reason for the use of sound in a movie.

The film that would become *Hallelujah* began life in September 1928 as an outline entitled *The Negro Story* that closely follows the finished film. Despite Vidor's enthusiasm, there was no way that Mayer and Thalberg would approve such a story, if for no other reason than it would be impossible to get bookings south of the Mason-Dixon line. So Vidor went over their heads and proposed his all-black film directly to Nicholas Schenck, pledging to defer his salary of $100,000 against any profits. Vidor had some evidence on his side; Fox was embarking on a similar project entitled *Hearts in Dixie.*

Schenck knew a committed employee when he saw one, and reasoned that the popularity of jazz and spirituals combined with the

---

demented as *The Unknown,* is a better film than its cheap score indicates. Early scoring ensembles were fairly standardized, as this memo sent to First National's Leo Forbstein indicates: "Let it be understood for the silent pictures, the following instrumentation will be used until further notice: 3 violins, 1 violin (second), 1 viola, 1 cello, 1 tuba and string bass, 2 trumpets, 1 trombone, 1 flute, 2 clarinets, 1 piano, 1 drum."

novelty of an all-black talkie might carry the picture over the top. He took Vidor up on his offer. *Variety* announced the project with a nervous qualification: "It will have an all-Negro cast, but is not going to be a propaganda film."

Once again, Vidor insisted that location work was necessary. On September 18, he began a location search in Beaumont, Texas, then proceeded on to Natchez, Mississippi, three days later. For once, MGM was probably glad to see him go; although *Hallelujah* was to be a talkie, MGM still didn't have a soundstage of their own. While Vidor was shooting his location footage silent in October and November, MGM was rushing to complete their first soundstage.

The male lead, Daniel Haynes, was an understudy in the Broadway production of *Show Boat*. Other actors had no theatrical experience at all; Harry Gray, who played the patriarchal Parson, was a porter at the *Amsterdam News*. Since the cast was all black, Vidor also attempted to integrate the crew, appointing Harold Garrison, a black employee of MGM, as his assistant director. Although Garrison's hiring was reported in the black press, he didn't receive any screen credit.

While Vidor was away filming, back at MGM production manager J. J. (Joe) Cohn was wrestling with problems of the sort that didn't happen in Culver City. Because of the prevalent Jim Crow laws, the black actors had to be content with traveling in chair cars, not sleepers, all the way east of El Paso. If they traveled via Kansas City, the actors could have sleeper cars, but, as Cohn wired the *Hallelujah* unit production manager, "troupe would arrive 935 PM instead of 640 AM." Ever the efficient manager, Cohn made his own preferences clear: "Am certain colored actors would not object to riding chair cars."

Hallelujah was given an overly optimistic forty-day schedule. Vidor began shooting October 23 in Memphis and by November 2 was two days behind schedule. Some sense of the confusion of the industry at this pivotal time can be gauged by a plaintive wire Vidor sent to Joe Cohn: "Please let me know if you anticipate changing method of [synchronizing] releases from records to Movietone so I can allow space outside of frame [for the soundtrack]." MGM still hadn't committed to one system or the other, but Cohn wired Vidor

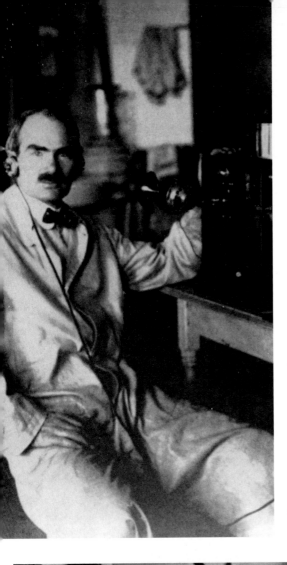

Left. Lee De Forest.

Above. Frames from a De Forest
Phonofilm of Elihu Root; the
sound track is the wavy area
between the sprocket holes
and the image on the left.

Below. Shooting a De Forest
Phonofilm in 1925.

Top. An early example of what would later be termed Vitaphone, with the record running, it was hoped, in tight coordination with the projected film.

Middle left. The brothers Warner. From left: Harry, Jack, Sam, Albert.
Middle right. William Fox (left) and secretary.

Below. Mary Astor and John Barrymore in 1926's *Don Juan,* the first Vitaphone feature.

The front page of the special section *Variety* issued to celebrate the debut of Vitaphone in Los Angeles.

A production still for one of the early Vitaphone shorts with Anna Case. The location is the Manhattan Opera House. Sam Warner is the man with his coat on in front of the camera booth.

AT&T ARCHIVES

Making *Sunrise*. Cameramen Charles Rosher (hand on camera, other hand obscuring face), Karl Struss (in long coat, looking at notebook) and director F. W. Murnau (behind Struss, face partly obscured by extra's hat brim) rehearse what looks, on screen, to be a simple shot.

KEVIN BROWNLOW
COLLECTION

Two shots of the vast city set for *Sunrise* designed by Rochus Gliese, lit by Charles Rosher and Karl Struss.

The night of October 6, 1927.
Sam Warner has just died.
Talkies have just been born.
SCOTT MACQUEEN
COLLECTION

Jolson sings for the first time
in *The Jazz Singer*. The
songs are "Dirty Hands,
Dirty Face," and the
considerably more
memorable "Toot,
Toot, Tootsie."
SCOTT MACQUEEN
COLLECTION

May McAvoy comforts Al
Jolson just before he goes
onstage as *The Jazz Singer*.

The stylized art direction of the city that dwarfs the characters melds beautifully with the seamlessly realistic portrayals that King Vidor extracted from James Murray and Eleanor Boardman in *The Crowd.*

Shooting sound on location in February 1928 for *The Lights of New York.* The booths, called "iceboxes," each hold one camera and one cameraman. KEVIN BROWNLOW COLLECTION

King Vidor's 1928 film *Show People* (with Marion Davies on left) is an extremely accurate portrayal of the verities of silent film production—interior sets were built adjacent to each other. Musicians were used for the dual purposes of drowning out the competing din of carpenters and directors from other movies, and to provide a semblance of emotional underpinning for the actors.

March 1929—actor Lane Chandler shows off a new housing that stifled enough
of the camera noise so that the cameras could emerge from the stultifying
iceboxes. Movies slowly began to move again.

King Vidor (glasses, under the microphone) talking to Daniel Haynes during production of
Hallelujah on the MGM backlot. MUSEUM OF MODERN ART STILLS ARCHIVE

Lionel Barrymore (beneath camera)
directing *His Glorious Night,* the
film that helped destroy the
career of John Gilbert,
and a scene from the film.
MUSEUM OF MODERN ART
STILLS ARCHIVE

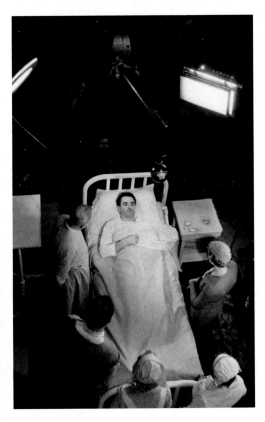

Poor, doomed John Gilbert, with the
paraphernalia that destroyed his
career, and his life.

Apparently helpless Ronald Colman and Joan Bennett in a still that nicely captures the light, quizzical, James Bond-ish charms of 1929's *Bulldog Drummond.*

Charles Farrell and Mary Duncan on location in Oregon for Murnau's doomed *City Girl.*

Among the dozens of vaudevillians who rushed to the movies after sound were George Burns and Gracie Allen, here in a scene from a short entitled *Lamb Chops*. SCOTT MACQUEEN COLLECTION

The production of Ernst Lubitsch's *The Love Parade* was typical for 1929. The orchestra at left is playing a live accompaniment for a musical number being performed by Lupino Lane and Lillian Roth, while the ubiquitous pair of booths holds the cameras and the sweating cameramen. ROBERT S. BIRCHARD COLLECTION

Other early talkies didn't have to worry about recording every little sound. The glorious tracking shots showing off the splendid art direction of the Douglas Fairbanks (bottom center) and Mary Pickford version of *The Taming of the Shrew* were shot silent, with the sound dubbed in later.

The first talkies of great silent stars were a sometime thing, but few of them are as catastrophically dull to modern eyes as Mary Pickford's *Coquette,* which even reproduced some of the stage lighting of the George Abbott stage success.

Contrary to popular legend, many of the early sound efforts of the silent idols were financial—and critical—successes, if for no other reason than the audience's curiosity about how their favorite stars sounded. The crowds in front of the United Artists theater in Los Angeles and the Loew's Stillman in Cleveland attest to Pickford's and Lloyd's commercial power in 1929. The rapid audience erosion for both stars only set in with their second talkies, after the audience's curiosity was satisfied.

Chorus girls in Universal's *The King of Jazz,* a fairly typical musical monstrosity.

Bessie Love and Anita Page in MGM's *The Broadway Melody,* among the more charming of the early musicals, and the Best Picture of 1929.

The Metropolitan
Opera's Lawrence
Tibbett, who had
everything necessary
for screen stardom
except a chin, shoots
a scene for MGM's
The Rogue Song.
ROBERT S. BIRCHARD
COLLECTION

Helen Morgan
(above right) in
Rouben Mamoulian's
1929 film *Applause*, one
of the first truly
good talkies.

The startling, original
Jeanne Eagels killing
the man she loves
in *The Letter.*
MUSEUM OF MODERN
ART STILLS ARCHIVE

Making William Wyler's *Hell's Heroes* in 1930 on the edge of Death Valley.
Pity the poor cameraman in the box. MUSEUM OF MODERN ART STILLS ARCHIVE

Talkies seemed to mandate the production of multiple-language versions of
prestige films, so as to equal the revenue that had accrued to silents by merely translating the
titles. On the left, a scene from the American version of Garbo's *Anna Christie,* directed
by Clarence Brown; on the right, the same scene in the German version, directed by
Jacques Feyder, with a more garish wardrobe and expressionist makeup.

the next day, "Will not do picture with Movietone. Recording on wax."

A far more vexing problem was the casting of the pivotal part of the temptress, Chick. The actress Vidor wanted was not the actress Thalberg wanted. Vidor originally cast a woman named Honey Brown, but, as Thalberg wired Vidor after looking at the rushes, "Terribly disappointed in Honey Brown. She has lots of pep but very little if any sex. Great for first part with comedy scenes but afraid audiences would laugh at the sex scenes and question whether they would believe sincerity of story which is strong sex attraction between the two." *

Thalberg preferred Nina Mae McKinney, but Vidor felt that "she didn't compare to Honey Brown." He prepared another test of Brown while continuing production of the picture in an attempt to convince Thalberg. "I will personally guarantee we will never have any lack from her on this score," Vidor wrote. "Now and then I have been right and I believe this is one of the times."

Thalberg was prepared to be convinced ["Sincerely hope this can be one of the very few times in which you are right . . ."], but, on November 1, when he compared the tests, Thalberg still favored Nina Mae McKinney. Stubbornly, for the next three weeks of location work, Vidor made all the location scenes twice, once with Honey Brown, once with Nina Mae McKinney.

Vidor and company finally arrived back in Culver City and began work on the sound sequences on November 23. It was at this point that Vidor acquiesced in Thalberg's decision and fired Honey Brown. There were some problems with the new sound system, but there were even more problems with leading man Daniel Haynes. By December 12, Haynes still hadn't memorized his dialogue, and a week after that he missed at least three days of shooting due to illness. On January 3, he was late to the set because some of his wardrobe had been misplaced. Vidor finally wrapped production on

* In a later letter, Thalberg made explicit his objections to Honey Brown with the cold-blooded objectivity for which he was famous: ". . . a certain ugliness particularly around her mouth, her flat-chestedness, and her upper lip has very outstanding hairline." Other than that, he thought she was swell.

January 14, fourteen days over schedule. *Hallelujah* amassed a negative cost of $320,150, not counting Vidor's deferred $100,000 or the
$4,500 license that MGM paid to Western Electric for every talkie
they made.

As Vidor began editing his film, he told Thalberg that he wanted
to dedicate *Hallelujah* to a black woman he had adored in his child-
hood. Thalberg absolutely vetoed the idea, and Vidor had to content
himself with planting a tree in her honor. "I don't know what will
happen to [the film] of course," Vidor told *The New York Times*,
"but I think it either will be one of the greatest hits of the year or
one of the greatest flops. I'd certainly hate to have it turn out to be
just one of those pictures."

❏ ❏ ❏

Of all the directors brought to movies by sound, none demonstrated
more fearlessness than Rouben Mamoulian. "You couldn't scare me
with dialogue," recalled Mamoulian. "What fascinated me in the
movies was obviously the camera. That's the magic of the movies . . .
I thought the fascinating part was to use sound imaginatively. I
don't believe in naturalism on the screen or the stage. I believe in
stylization, which if properly done comes over as greater truth than
reality. It's really [the] inner reality of things."

The son of a bank president, Mamoulian was educated at the
Moscow Art Theater. Coming to America in 1923, he spent three
years in Rochester directing operettas and musicals at the George
Eastman Theater. In 1926, he went to work for the Theater Guild,
directing their triumphant 1927 production of *Porgy*, which began
with a spectacular scene in which syncopated naturalistic sounds
moved from $\frac{4}{4}$ time to $\frac{2}{4}$ to $\frac{6}{8}$. (Mamoulian would reproduce the effect
in the remarkable opening of 1932's *Love Me Tonight*.)

Mamoulian had always been interested in using sound for dramatic effect. During a quiet, dramatic scene in a stage production
called *Wings Over Europe*, he had the stage manager carry a loud
metronome from way backstage down to the back wall of the set;
the ticking seemed to emanate from a clock on a mantel and slowly
enveloped the audience.

Signed up as one of the Astoria studio's experiments in cross-
pollination, Mamoulian wandered around the Astoria studio for five

weeks watching how other people made movies. Jean de Limur was directing one picture, and Herbert Brenon was struggling with another. Mamoulian didn't like what he saw. "I learned *ad adversus*, as the Latin puts it — by the contrary. Whatever they did, I did the reverse; what was black to them was white to me, and vice versa."

Mamoulian peppered cameramen with questions about lenses. He went into cutting rooms, story meetings. What he saw were crews making plays into movies by photographing each scene with three cameras: two close-ups and a medium shot. "They could shoot the whole scene and cut that in the cutting room, and the result was what people in their wisdom called 'talkies.' I resented that very much. I thought that was so unnatural; it was like having a racehorse push a baby carriage in a park."

After five weeks, Mamoulian walked into Adolph Zukor's office and told him he was ready. "For what, lunch?" asked Zukor.

Mamoulian worked with Garret Fort for five weeks on the script for his first film, a seedy slice of life about an aging burlesque queen, her sheltered daughter, and the backstage milieu. As production of the film that would be known as *Applause* got under way, Mamoulian encountered the usual incessant demurrals from the soundman. "The soundman . . . was a dictator. They had one microphone hanging, and if you rehearsed a scene he would say, no, he has to come closer, and he can't sit down, he has to stand . . . Whatever I asked for, they said 'That's impossible.' "

Mamoulian suggested that the camera booth be mounted on rollers so six men could push it where he wanted it to go. Everything was a struggle, and this temperamental, egocentric man used to getting his way was getting nowhere; as the third day of production dawned, Mamoulian decided he had to work his way or not at all.

The scene involved the burlesque queen (Helen Morgan) and her daughter (Joan Peers); Mamoulian wanted the camera to start on a long shot, come in to a medium shot, come in further to a close-up, then go back to the original position. He further suggested that, because Morgan was to sing a lullaby and the young girl was to say her rosary, the sound be recorded on two different microphones, relayed to two different strips of film (or records), and put together in the laboratory.

The technicians laughed. Mamoulian threw a tantrum and ran

upstairs to the front office. A meeting was called with Zukor, producer Walter Wanger, cameraman George Folsey, and the soundman. The technicians all said that what Mamoulian was asking for was impossible. Mamoulian played his last card and offered to take full responsibility, which, in a bureaucracy, meant he was willing to be fired. It was a gamble, but not a suicidal one, for he could always go back to his thriving theatrical career.

"It was a hunch," Mamoulian would confess in his old age. "I wasn't quite sure if you could put two celluloid sound-tracks together . . . I wasn't 100 percent sure." Mamoulian shot the scene his way, and went home thinking "this is probably my last day in movies."

The next day, when Mamoulian's taxi let him off at the studio's front door, the usually surly security guard took his cap off and ushered him in with a bountiful good morning. Mamoulian was met by his assistant, who told him that Wanger had given the lab a rush order for the scene in question and the brass had previewed it at eight that morning. The camera had moved, and the two-track sound had worked as well; the word going through the studio was that what Mamoulian wanted, Mamoulian would get.

He nodded, walked onto the set, and promptly ordered four cameras for the day's work, one of which he wanted placed six feet below the floor. When he was told that the concrete slab the studio rested on was two feet thick, Mamoulian persisted. A little later, large, burly men lugging pneumatic jackhammers arrived on the set, whereupon Mamoulian held up his hands and explained that he had only been joking.

The same battle for artistic innovation was being fought everywhere, at all the studios, but not with equivalent results. The fact that it was being fought in the midst of oppressive silence only made it worse. Actors who had no stage experience found the basic technique of talkies difficult. There was no more comforting low murmur of voices on the set, no more director to say, "Fine, now you hear the footsteps — and *freeze!* Over to the window, lift it up, run. Fine." The deathly silence was a hollow void. A silent set was a study in controlled bustle, but with sound, when the red light went on, everybody froze in position. "It was like a quick switch from a bleacher seat at Ebbets Field to a box seat at a Wimbledon tennis match," wrote Frank Capra.

❑ ❑ ❑

At Paramount's West Coast studio, 3,000 miles away, William "Wild Bill" Wellman, the underrated director of the silent classic *Wings*, was trying to make his first talkie.

They didn't call him "Wild Bill" for nothing. Wellman was a rough-and-ready character whose idea of humor was goosing stuntmen with a bamboo stick as they climbed a wall, causing them to lose their balance and fall. As Wellman's assistant Arthur Jacobson remembered, "Wellman was really crazy around this time. He'd made Paramount's biggest hit, *Wings,* and . . . could do whatever he damn well pleased. He used to stand outside the front office and yell obscenities up at the executives."

The combination of a volatile temperament like Wellman's, a primitive technology, and rigid technicians was sure to bring about an explosion. Wellman's *Beggars of Life* had been shot as a silent picture; just before it was released in September, in the wake of the hysteria created by *The Lights of New York,* B. P. Schulberg got the idea of adding at least one talking sequence to the hobo drama. The dreaded Roy Pomeroy wanted Wallace Beery to enter the scene and stand in the midst of a group of hobos while singing "Hark the Bells." Pomeroy insisted that the microphone had to remain static. "That burned me up," remembered Wellman. "You can't make a picture that way. You've got to have some flow. So I came in and said, 'I've got some news for you soundmen this morning. I'm moving that goddamned mike.' "

As David Selznick, the picture's associate producer, recalled it, "Wellman . . . took the microphone himself, hung it on a broom, gave orders to record — and moved it." *

As *Beggars of Life* hit the theaters, the order came down to halt

---

* The invention seems to have been simultaneously and independently devised at a number of studios; at MGM, Douglas Shearer gave credit for the idea of the mike boom to studio general manager Eddie Mannix; other candidates for the invention include Dorothy Arzner and Lionel Barrymore.

production on a silent picture Wellman was making called *Chinatown Nights.*

"We were a third of the way through the picture as a silent when they called it off," recalled Jacobson. "It was a Saturday. In four days, they wrote out a dialogue script and we went back to work on a Wednesday to make it as a talkie.

"Wellman adjusted very simply. The first night we went back to work, we were shooting a Chinese wedding. The scene called for Wallace Beery and Florence Vidor to walk the length of a street while talking. We suddenly had all these people we knew nothing about—soundmen, mixers—and they knew as little about our business as we knew about theirs.

"Well, the microphone, which was on an overhead pulley, squeaked. They tried Vaseline, grease, everything, and the piano wire still squeaked. So they set up a series of overhead mikes and the actors could only talk while directly underneath [each microphone].

"The soundman came up to Wellman and told him he had to have the actors walk, then stop and talk, walk some more, then stop and talk. They couldn't talk and walk at the same time. 'Why does the microphone have to be overhead?' Wellman wanted to know. 'Why can't it be underneath?' He was getting very angry.

"Wellman demanded that they take a microphone off the wire and hand it to him. He sat down underneath the camera, Indian fashion, and stuck the mike between his legs, and said, 'Get me a pillow, for Chrissakes, this hurts.' And he aimed the mike at the actors as the camera dolly tracked with the actors. He was inventing the shotgun mike!

"The next day we go in to see the rushes and the soundman's there. The scene comes up and Wellman turns to the soundman and says, 'Did you understand them?'

" 'Yes, but the decibels . . .'

" 'I don't care about the decibels, did you understand what they said?'

" 'Yes, but the quality . . .'

"And Wellman said, 'Bull,' and that's how we converted to sound."

Wellman received no credit for the innovation; rather, he received credit for making the picture. His impatience was born as much from ego as artistry. A man who ran roughshod over actors and producers was not about to let a little microphone dictate his method of working.

Despite directors like Wellman and his vaulting impatience, making *Chinatown Nights* didn't get any easier. "It was still a hard show," Jacobson told John Gallagher. "Beery and Vidor were not used to learning lines. We'd do a take and they'd have their lines, but it would be no good for sound and we wouldn't know it until the dailies next day. It turned out the traffic noise out on Melrose Avenue was screwing us up, since they didn't have soundproof stages yet. So we had to shoot the picture at night."

Florence Vidor was so appalled by the process of making talkies that she promptly retired and married Jascha Heifetz, doing it so abruptly that Wellman was forced to use a voice double for some of her scenes.

With his next talkie, a boxing drama called *The Man I Love*, Wellman kept expanding the possibilities of sound, pulling off a couple of tracking shots of extraordinary virtuosity; one shot moved through three rooms, down an arena aisle, then tracked along the front row to the other side of a boxing ring. As Frank Thompson has observed, it's a shot that would have been formidable in silent films; doing it with synchronized-sound equipment was miraculous.

❑ ❑ ❑

In the latter half of 1928, Hollywood was a town besieged from within and without. As Leonard Sillman wrote, "One half [of Hollywood's] occupants were contemplating vistas of a brave new world, the other half — suicide." With little warning, the larynx was deemed to be the most important part of the human body, and suddenly the town was crawling with pedagogues. As one observer noted, "A broken-down British beldame I knew who had been cackling on the lecture circuits for years was now a teacher of articulation and elocution. A carnival hustler who could do a slow soft-shoe was one of the town's leading teachers of the dance."

For anyone who had ever been on the stage, Hollywood was the new Klondike. Stage actors began flooding in. Some were good, some were bad, and most of them gave carefully studied stage performances. "I never paid any attention to [the camera]," said Pat

O'Brien in 1975. "I just played it like I was onstage . . . It never bothered me at all. I never bothered on which side you'd find a light or anything else. I said that's the cameraman's job."

Felix Hughes Jr., an uncle of Howard Hughes and, until the advent of his nephew, the family playboy, became one of the more successful vocal coaches in town. Felix was not a fraud; Mary Garden told Felix's brother Rupert that she considered him the best singing teacher in the world. Before long, his elocution pupils included Anita Page, Hoot Gibson, Jean Harlow, and Alice White.

MGM was rumored to be preparing an all-star musical revue, as were a number of the other studios. Leonard Sillman, a vaudevillian himself, opened a dance studio. His first client was Carmel Myers, a second-string leading lady of enormous personal charm and kindness. Sillman bartered instruction for Myers's voice test in exchange for introductions to nervous stars who might need a crash course in singing and dancing. Soon, he had Patsy Ruth Miller, Laura La Plante, Bessie Love, and ZaSu Pitts under contract for voice lessons. The fee was $125, and he taught them a song-and-dance routine. Each pupil got exactly the same routine: "Ten Cents a Dance."

Not all the studio heads thought elocution lessons were a good idea. Charles Farrell was from Cape Cod, so he took some lessons to get rid of his accent, which had made "park my car" come out as "pahk my cah." At his suggestion, Janet Gaynor also enrolled, but Winfield Sheehan at Fox called her into his office and told her, "We don't want you to. We want you to be just [what] you are."

The massive influx of talents both dubious and authentic demanded a support system. *Sound Waves*, a specialized trade publication, began publishing in August 1928. The twice-a-month paper, full of hortatory enthusiasm for the new medium and its practitioners, was soon full of classified ads for voice coaches ("Louis Aschenfelder, Eminent Vocal and Musical Comedy Coach") and supposedly renowned singers ("Ludovico Tomarchio, formerly leading dramatic tenor of principal opera houses of Europe, will be available for sound motion pictures until April 15"). Equipment was also advertised, from microphones ("from $25 to $250") to complete sound outfits that could be rented by the day by low-budget independent producers.

Sound Waves had a slight but prematurely sophisticated political bent. In one issue, in a column otherwise devoted to sound reproduction in the town of Azusa, editor Cedric Hart mentioned that a color line was enforced for Mexican patrons. "[That] they are forced to sit in one side of the house is something our 'free and equal sense' rebels against.

"This is a subject too lengthy for us to go into, being also out of our domain. But we do want to go on record as saying that this attitude is as much a blot on the sun-kissed township of Azusa as is the eternal glory of their progress in beautiful homes and farms a credit in the other way."

Technicians also began pouring into Hollywood; most of the nascent sound technicians derived either from the telephone company or radio. Taking as many people as the studios actually needed would have denuded Bell, Western Electric, and General Electric of most of their staffs, so the studios quickly established informal apprenticeship programs that could be taught by the few key men that came to California.

The studios needed warm bodies; their background was irrelevant. For example, Ralph Butler, a common laborer around the studios, got a lead to talk to a man who had just arrived in Hollywood from the Victor Talking Machine Company's headquarters in Camden, New Jersey. Butler was asked a few questions about basic electricity —he had played around with crystal and single-tube radios—and was hired for $25 a week and assigned to the Hal Roach studio.

If a laborer could become a successful sound technician at $25 a week, a trained radio man could do much better. Edward Bernds was born in 1905, and was part of the first wave of movie soundmen. "I was working as a radio engineer at WLS in Chicago, where I met the chief engineer, an arrogant, cocky little man named Howard Campbell," recalled Bernds in 1994. "He was paying me $65 a week, then I went to WCFL for $75 a week.

"Campbell had been in the Signal Corps during World War I, and had gotten tight with guys in Western Electric. In 1928, Campbell was offered the job of head soundman at United Artists through those people at Western Electric. He needed a staff of thirty technicians. Where to get them? Campbell offered jobs to everybody at WLS. And he called me; I'd only been at WCFL for three and a half months, and I grabbed the job. He offered me $65 a week, but I was already getting $75. He matched it, so I came out to California for $75 a week."

Bernds and his wife drove out from Chicago in an Essex 4, still venerated as the ugliest car ever made. The Essex broke down in Benton, Arkansas, so Bernds and his wife doubled up with their traveling companion, another engineer hired by Campbell, who was driving a 1928 Nash. Leaving behind most of their clothes, and all of their household goods, Bernds and his wife arrived in Hollywood in October of 1928.

While the preferred lodgings for new arrivals was the Roosevelt Hotel on Hollywood Boulevard, other, slightly more downscale establishments put in their bids as well. The Gardiner Hotel Apartments, 5165 Fountain Avenue, advertised that they were "a five minute walk to Fox Studio" and offered "Frigidaire . . . Maid Service . . . and 24 hour telephone service," not to mention reasonable rates.

Bernds and his wife rented an unfurnished house at 1305 North Sycamore Avenue, within walking distance of the Pickford/Fairbanks/United Artists studio. The house rented for $35 a month, and they furnished it with orange crates. Bernds reported for work . . . or tried to:

"My first task was to roam around watching them shoot silent films. The sound equipment hadn't been installed yet. The early sound recording machines were on cement pedestals — it was ridiculously cumbersome, unnecessarily so — and the cement bases were still in their forms, poured and drying.

"Ernst Lubitsch was shooting a silent called *Eternal Love*, with John Barrymore, when an assistant director incorrectly cued an avalanche and dropped all this fake snow on Barrymore. First, Barrymore dropped Camilla Horn — BOOM! Then he lit into the assistant. 'I'll take that goddamn gun from you and shove it up your ass!' and so forth. U.A. catered to visitors and we had a bunch of middle-aged ladies who heard his whole tirade. He went on for a couple of minutes, a very long time to sustain a tirade with any originality."

Once the cement pedestals finally dried — U.A.'s sound installation would cost $250,000 — Bernds found that U.A., unlike the far more industrial-minded Paramount or Warners, was all dressed up with no place to go. U.A. had hedged their bets and installed both disc and sound equipment, although, as it worked out, almost all

U.A. talkies were released as sound on film — discs were only used for playback on the set to check a take.

"They had three or four times as many people as they needed; they couldn't make more than one sound picture at a time because they had only one soundstage," Bernds recalled. "Pickford, Fairbanks, and Goldwyn weren't competing for that stage, they were trying to avoid getting onto it. Aside from that one stage, there was practically no back lot; to build the mountain set for the Lubitsch picture, they had to use the parking lot."

Because there wasn't really a lot of work to do, the U.A. lot was a rat's nest of backbiting and factionalism. After a while, soundmen were given alternate days off, then alternate weeks off, all on full salary. No one was let go, because the executives didn't have the vaguest idea what might happen next week or next month. The rumor around town was that RKO was offering soundmen $250 a week, and the rumors might have been true.*

Although Ed Bernds was young, he had grown up idolizing silent stars like Douglas Fairbanks and was uncomfortable about some of the compromises his own job was forcing on tried-and-true production methods. "I could understand why the old-line . . . directors hated us, with our obnoxious microphones and two-ton camera booths and camera motors that ran backward. We were interlopers, a bunch of young upstarts who were destroying the beautiful art form they had spent years perfecting."

As it happened, Bernds did not lack for powerful allies. One day during the production of *Bulldog Drummond*, Bernds was working in the sound booth when Sam Goldwyn got into a violent argument with his assistant, Mike Levee, about sound. Goldwyn didn't like the way *Bulldog Drummond* was going and felt that sound was ruining Ronald Colman's acting (!). As for Joan Bennett, "such a

---

* The average pay for a salaried job such as assistant director at the beginning of the sound era was $60 to $65 a week; as Arthur Jacobson would recall, "There was no overtime, no vacations, no pension, no nothing. You worked twenty-eight hours a day, nine days a week, thirty-four weeks a month. You went home, ate, went to the bathroom, and went back to the studio." When the studios were unionized in the 1930s, the pay for an assistant director immediately went up to $137.50 a week, with benefits.

beautiful girl, she don't look so good when they have to photograph her out of those goddamn doghouses." Levee insisted that sound was here to stay, that the quality of the sound and photography would improve, and that they could never go back to making silent pictures.

Indeed, Goldwyn, along with Joe Schenck and directors Fred Niblo and Herbert Brenon, were continuing to tell anyone who would listen that the rush to sound was a hysteria that could endanger the movie industry. One director told Mordaunt Hall of *The New York Times* that talkies were a million-dollar idea that the industry must be careful not to make worth twenty cents.

The stolid but prestigious Niblo wrote an article for *The Film Daily* and desperately cast about for reasons to ignore the obvious. "Frankly, I am afraid . . . I do not believe that the public interest in the silent film is flagging to the point where innovations are demanded. The trouble lies in theater overdevelopment, more seats than can possibly be filled. Turn half our theaters into garages and there will be no more complaint on the score of patronage.

"The silent drama has a great clientele. Shall we jeopardize this by tinkering with the type of picture that has built up this following? Shall we drive film patrons from theaters by presenting them with mediocre talking pictures? . . ."

The fear and frustration was understandable; the industry had millions of dollars' worth of product on the shelf and the customers were suddenly asking for something else. As William A. Johnston, editor of the trade paper *Motion Picture News,* pointed out late in the fall, "Just the other day, I spoke to a worried-looking executive of one of the big companies. 'You're terribly busy,' I said. 'Busy!' said he. 'We're crazy.' "

The cameraman George Folsey enjoyed telling a story about Jean de Limur, a fairly gifted director who had apprenticed under Chaplin on *A Woman of Paris.* "He knew that certain things [in sound] were very difficult, and he was most reluctant to give anybody any trouble," remembered Folsey. "It was very important for me to find out if the scene we were about to do was a sound shot or, in some cases, a silent shot. So I would try to get Jean to tell me and he knew it was a great deal of trouble and he would say, 'Well, just a little bit of sound . . .' "

"So many silent-film directors were phonies," said Ed Bernds. "I didn't think highly of Herbert Brenon, for instance. He was the old, imperious type of director. Lordly, demanding. There was a scene in *Lummox*, where Winifred Westover was supposed to be betrayed by Ben Lyon, who has gotten her pregnant. He throws some money down and she takes the money and tears it up with her teeth.

"Well, Brenon demanded real money! And several takes. The poor propman was going around borrowing money from the crew. It was the Imperial syndrome of silent-film directors."

Sound demanded a more fluid grasp of drama, if not of camera effects, and the ideal studio director for talkies would prove to be the equivalent of a solid repertory company director, someone who could get a script up and running on time and with a minimum of introspection. The dramatic affectations encouraged by the essentially plastic nature of silent filmmaking now seemed ill-judged, if not grotesquely absurd.

The quintessential director of talking pictures turned out to be a phlegmatic personality like Raoul Walsh, who didn't know much about the stage but knew how people talked. Rarely artistic, a resolutely competent, unpretentious man making top pictures since 1915, Walsh's first talkie showed the way. His preferred recollection was that *In Old Arizona*, in which he was starring as well as directing, began as a two-reel short that expanded during production. Walsh took one of Movietone's newsreel sound trucks on location, and, as he remembered it, "After they had seen the first rushes, the studio bosses called me and said, 'Fantastic. Keep it up and make us a feature.' I thought I was going to faint."

Unfortunately, Walsh was a flamboyant fabricator. The script for *In Old Arizona* prepared in September 1928 (now preserved at the University of Southern California) is a full sixty-eight pages long and follows the film more or less as it was released. To help the director keep this newfangled sound business straight, the script offered the helpful heading "List of Characters," then, below that, "List of Characters Who Talk."

After the sound equipment broke down near the end of location work, Walsh and company were headed back to Hollywood when a jackrabbit leapt through Walsh's windshield, driving glass into the director's right eye. The eye had to be removed. Fox recast the part with Warner Baxter and had Irving Cummings complete the direction.

❑ ❑ ❑

As the tumultuous year of 1928 moved to a close, MGM's Irving Thalberg decided that it was time for Norma Shearer, his wife and supreme object of contemplation, to take the talkie plunge.

The Trial of Mary Dugan was approached exactly like a play; rehearsals were scheduled for twenty-one days, actual shooting for only twelve, although some of those days seem to have been double shifts, with 10 A.M. calls on one stage, and 7 P.M. calls on another. On December 17, after three days of rehearsal, what MGM production records referred to as "the first act" was recorded for sound (as if it was a radio show), so Thalberg could approve the voices and overall dramatic approach before photography. Three days later, production began. Sound equipment was still at a painful premium; on December 29, the *Mary Dugan* company sat around until 9:45 in the morning because the sound system was in use by the trailer department.

By the end of the year, even part-talkies were becoming less frequent. Many of the industry leaders couldn't bring themselves to believe that their industry was truly involved in such a precipitous sea-change, even as it was happening all around them. Every year, the *Film Year Book,* published by *The Film Daily,* asked industry leaders their predictions for the coming year. Adolph Zukor prophesied that "by no means is the silent picture gone or even diminished in interest or importance." He believed the industry could exist quite comfortably as half-talking and half-silent. Jesse Lasky agreed, and Carl Laemmle went even further: "The silent picture technique is too well established and its popularity too widespread to permit a variation of its form, no matter how interesting it is to the public, to dominate the thing itself."

Hindsight is 20/20, so these comments sound ostrich-stupid. But Lasky, Zukor, and Laemmle believed sound to be a prestige technology, not a fundamental part of mainstream filmmaking. They could easily have been right, for movie history is replete with prestige technologies (various and sundry wide-screen processes) that have been used or ignored as the occasion warrants. As for an outright gimmick technology, there is the perennial example of 3-D.

In any case, more than forty other industry luminaries disagreed with the three loyalists and believed that that particular train had long since left the station.

□ □ □

During the calendar year 1928, ERPI wired 879 theaters for sound, for a total of 1,046. During that same year, as the Fox empire increased exponentially, William Fox raised the amount of life insurance he was carrying to a total of $6.4 million. He sardonically told one trusted employee that "if nobody else grieves my passing I can at least depend upon the president of every large insurance company in the world."

That December, Winfield Sheehan (on the West Coast) placed a phone call to William Fox (on the East Coast). Sheehan was overflowing in his enthusiasm for the recently completed *In Old Arizona*. Sheehan claimed that there had been *The Birth of a Nation*, and now there was this, something just as startling "in an audible form for the present day." Fox, smiling, nodding, affirmed that, yes, "things move fast in this business."

How fast, even William Fox had no idea.

PART FOUR

1929

Twinkle, twinkle, movie star,
In your fancy motor car:
When the talkies make the grade
You will be a chambermaid.

"A.S.C."
Life magazine
January 11, 1929

Of course, not everybody thought talkies
were a good idea . . .

By the beginning of 1929, Harry and Jack Warner had Vitaphone, First National, a burgeoning chain of theaters, and the considerable satisfaction of forcing the industry that had patronized them to play 52 pickup.

They wanted more.

In January, they began discussions with Joseph Schenck, the universally loved and respected godfather of the film industry, for the purpose of merging with United Artists. The initial proposal seems to have come from Schenck, and it was carefully couched so as to appear nonthreatening to the eminent group that had founded U.A. ten years before: Charlie Chaplin, Douglas Fairbanks, and Mary Pickford — Griffith having flown the coop some years earlier. Under the proposed merger, Warners and U.A. Consolidated (the proposed new name) would retain their separate corporate and production identities. However, to save on distribution costs, the sales forces would work together. The U.A. partners would sign contracts obligating them to deliver two pictures a year apiece for five years, a greatly increased rate of production that, in addition to the lowered overhead, would make them millions.

It was, more or less, a decent deal for all concerned; Warner Bros. stood to gain incalculable prestige, while U.A. would get access to Warners' three hundred theaters. But it was submarined by the maddeningly solitary Chaplin, who told Schenck in April that if the deal went through, he would withdraw from U.A. and distribute his pictures on his own.* Pickford and Fairbanks were both furious with Chaplin, but then realized that the loans that would be necessary to finance U.A.'s end of the deal would inevitably water down their ownership percentages in the company they had created, leaving *de facto* control in the hands of bankers. A disappointed Joe Schenck grudgingly called off negotiations.

According to *Variety*, between June 1928 and February 1929, $24 million was spent to install recording equipment in movie studios. That was more than a third of the $65 million that had been estimated as the entire investment in the structure of the movie business at the end of 1927. As for the theaters, about $300 million would be spent to wire them for sound. All that money came from banks, and to protect their investments, bankers started appearing on studio directorates; by the start of 1929, more than forty banking and electrical company presidents were on the boards of the ten largest film companies. Paramount had eight bankers on their board, and RKO, a child of several allied business interests, had nineteen. The people who actually made films began to feel far more hot, supervisory breath on the back's of their necks than they ever had before; the bankers' interest in seeing their investments pay off meant that production philosophies began veering away from anything that smelled too strongly of taking chances, or of art.

By late February 1929, sound equipment was being installed in 250 theaters a month. Western Electric reported that they had 1,082 back orders in the United States, 37 in Canada, and 125 in other countries. The company figured that if they could ratchet supply up to the level of demand they would gross about $40 million in 1929. Likewise, an L.A. city survey showed that 48 separate stages or producing units had been built in the city the year before, nearly 50 percent more than the previous year, an increase totally attributable to the need for new soundstages. The pages of *The Film Daily* featured entire columns of theaters both urban and rural that were wiring for sound.

---

* A contributing factor in Chaplin's obstinacy might have been his realization that producing two features a year was impossible; Chaplin invariably took three and four years to make a single movie.

Despite all this, Warners made placating, blatantly disingenuous moves toward industry Luddites. Albert Warner wrote a piece for *The New York Times* that February in which he said "the silent film is too firm of foundation, too stanchly [*sic*] embedded in the esteem of patrons, to be even remotely disturbed by the first tremors and upheaval ... of the new medium ... It is preposterous to suppose that the time will ever come when all the houses, the length and breadth of the United States, will be [equipped for sound]."

In Culver City, MGM undoubtedly hoped that Albert Warner was right. They were still making only slightly more than half their pictures with sound; the emotionally — and politically — conservative Mayer and Thalberg couldn't bring themselves to make the necessary leap. A story made its way around MGM asserting that the deciding factor was a Vitaphone short featuring Giovanni Martinelli. It had taken days of persuasion to get Mayer to see a talking program, and he finally went under protest. Like almost everyone else, he came away babbling enthusiastically.

Mayer asked to meet with sound engineer Stanley Watkins. MGM general manager Eddie Mannix escorted Watkins into Mayer's office and said, by way of introduction, "Louis, I want you to meet the Pope." What Mayer et al. didn't know — and what Watkins was careful not to tell them — was, as he would recall, "how little we still knew, and how much we had to find out as we went along. I had to make decisions based upon some pretty unsupported guesses ..."

Part of MGM's slow response was due to their corporate culture, and part was class-based; as far as Mayer and Thalberg were concerned, Warner Bros. were beneath notice, just low-rent upstarts. "Warners paid as much attention as they could [to technical details]," said MGM production manager J. J. Cohn, "but they didn't care about external noises or anything else, so long as they could [record] it and shove it in the theaters that were overflowing."

Nevertheless, this sound thing seemed to be doing lots of business, so even the most innately conservative of the major studios edged toward the precipice. As Cohn sagely observed in his ninety-sixth year, "Money has a peculiar way of talking ... We resorted to all sorts of things, including putting padding on the settings, so you wouldn't have resounding external noises. And then we built probably the best soundstage in California. We went down something like sixteen feet to lay the concrete foundation, to eliminate the vibrations from Washington Boulevard."

In January, MGM released *Alias Jimmy Valentine,* an adaptation of the stage melodrama that had been previously filmed — and rather well — by Maurice Tourneur in 1915. For their first film with dialogue, MGM devised a *coup de théâtre;* although mostly a silent picture, *Alias Jimmy Valentine* uses sound for its climax, when Jimmy, a reformed safecracker, relents and opens a safe in which a small child is trapped. While Jimmy frantically works to open the safe, the only sound to be heard is the child crying to be let out, followed by a short dialogue scene between Lionel Barrymore, as the detective, and William Haines, as Valentine. The film, shot for the modest cost of $208,000, grossed $1.1 million worldwide, a very rich return for Haines, a second-echelon star usually paired with a more widely known costar (such as Lon Chaney or Marion Davies).

Dialogue obviously held few terrors for Lionel Barrymore, and he helpfully explained the new world the unwary Columbuses had discovered: "As an old and experienced hand to whom nobody has paid any attention these many years, let me explain. Sound won't make quite as much difference as you fearfully expect. Action will remain the chief ingredient of these cultural dramas of ours. The main difference will be that the titles will from now on be uttered — hopefully in something approximating English — rather than printed."

This sounded good to Louis B. Mayer, so he promptly made Barrymore a director; he quickly proved himself one of the worst in the business. After directing six pictures, the best of which was mediocre, and two of which helped torpedo the career of John Gilbert, Barrymore wisely gave up the director's chair to concentrate on acting.

MGM was a studio of fiercely guarded fiefdoms, separate and theoretically equal craft guilds, each of them run by a man with a good deal of power within the studio, all existing in an uneasy feudal court ruled by Mayer and Thalberg.

"We were very particular in our studio," said J. J. Cohn. "Mayer believed completely in building, not buying. He'd rather develop people. It was a comparatively loosely run studio, with certain strictures. Mayer had a very strong feeling about never denigrating a mother. But [neither] Mr. Mayer [n]or anyone else told me what I could or could not do." Cohn learned to be careful about the sensibilities of prestige MGM directors such as King Vidor. "You had to be sure that when you said no to people like that that you had a good reason. [Vidor] had a better reason for doing it than you had for not doing it. I was never in a discussion with Irving Thalberg over whether or not to do something. We had Cedric Gibbons and his marvelous crew. You had to be careful because a lot of people knew more than you did."

To head up the sound department, Mayer and Thalberg tapped Douglas Shearer, brother of Norma, and a longtime employee of the studio. "He was a very ingenious fellow, and kind of fell into it," said Cohn. "*Everybody* fell into it. I could spell s-o-u-n-d, but that's all." Originally coming to Hollywood to visit his sister, Shearer soon had landed a job at Warners, where, he would later remember, his primary chore was cleaning up after the livestock used in Rin Tin Tin pictures.

Moving to MGM, Shearer was working in the special effects department, where he showed an aptitude for trick photography and engineering. "What I knew about sound you could have put in a nutshell," he later said. "Overnight I became the one-man sound department. They ordered me to do the job, they didn't just give it to me. And probably they wouldn't have given it to me except that they were desperate."

Shearer headed by train for New York, to the Bell Labs, for a crash course in Sound 101 from Stanley Watkins. ERPI headquarters was close to Central Park, and Watkins and Shearer would frequently walk over, lie on the grass, and discuss sound technique. By the time Shearer arrived back at the studio he had picked up a skeleton sound crew, stealing men from Bell, from other studios, even from colleges.

While construction of the soundstages was under way, MGM was beginning to add music and sound effects to most of their movies. A February release, Sidney Franklin's *Wild Orchids*, with Greta Garbo, was a riot of sound effects, from crowd noises to doors slamming to hands clapping to a theme song crooned during a love scene in the manner of Borzage's *Seventh Heaven*. The noise is so profuse that it becomes intrusive, for the essence of silent films was an impressionism that met the audience halfway, made them a cocreator of the film's emotional effect. One Javanese dance number has such realistic voices and sound effects — it may even have been recorded live, while the scene was being shot — that the transition back to the surrounding silent film is uncomfortably stark.

All this raises the question of why Thalberg and Mayer didn't go all the way and make the movie as a talkie. Franklin moves the camera much more than was normal for MGM, and he softens, eroticizes, the usual staccato dreariness of MGM editing, taking his rhythm from Garbo's languidly erotic performance.

If MGM was embracing everything but the actual voices, Paramount was still warily circling. Their production of *Four Feathers* had a score that underlined the emotions and action more heavily than background scores would just a few years later. But the directors — Lothar Mendes (the drab interiors) and Merian C. Cooper and Ernest Schoedsack (the insanely risky and destructive location footage shot in the Sudan) — missed some opportunities for the creative use of sound.

There are gunshots, drums, and the roar of hippos. But there is also a sequence where the hero — Richard Arlen, that profile on legs — is trying to sneak through an enemy encampment and dislodges a rock. The sound of the rock dropping in the midst of dead silence could have — would have — created an effective dramatic moment. But Paramount stuck with what they knew: silence.*

Paramount's schizophrenic indecision is puzzling; that spring they were releasing full talkies both competent *(The Dummy)* and almost distinguished *(Gentlemen of the Press)*. Although *The Dummy* offers little in the way of a believable story, and complicates things further by casting Jack Oakie and ZaSu Pitts as gangsters, the direction breaks up its essentially theatrical scenes by effective cutting between the various camera booths.

The picture, a three-hander between the cops (John Cromwell, who would begin directing later in the year), the distressed parents (Fredric March and Ruth Chatterton), and the kidnappers, offers some random pleasures — Cromwell gives a lean, incisive perfor-

---

* According to Keven Brownlow, who knew Merian Cooper well, he and Schoedsack had no idea they were working on a sound film; they were glorified second-unit directors on what they imagined to be a silent adventure spectacular.

mance, and there is an effective musical score — but there are inevitable drawbacks as well. As always, Chatterton is hopelessly mannered, trilling her *R*s in the worst barnstorming way, and the violence is a clumsy and unconvincing blur, as it often is on the stage.

In May, Paramount released the startling good, cynical all-talkie *Gentlemen of the Press,* a relentlessly downbeat look at the grubby underside of journalism and a direct precursor of Billy Wilder's *Ace in the Hole.* Wick Snell (Walter Huston) is a workaholic reporter; when his baby daughter is born, he's covering a fight. She grows up and he's still working — he only finds out she's married by reading about the ceremony in a wedding announcement in his own paper.

To help out his struggling daughter, Snell quits journalism and takes a cushy PR job for the National Mausoleum Association, only to find that he can't countenance working for a corrupt man. He quits and goes back to being a night city editor. Wick is working late putting out an extra about a sinking ship when his daughter dies in childbirth. (As she expires, cameraman George Folsey throws the image out of focus.)

Finally awakening to his failure, Snell cries out to a young reporter who asks for professional advice, "Get out of it. Get a gun. Rob, steal, but get out of it!"

Gentlemen of the Press has some of the airless stiffness of the early talkie — an absence of music, no exteriors — but director Millard Webb gets maximum variety out of his three-camera setups, and the maturity of its theme, the resolute underplaying of the great Walter Huston, and the unflinching execution make it a very impressive picture, the kind of movie that wouldn't have been half as effective as a silent. It was urban, sardonic, and *real.*

Cynicism and urban harshness would prove particularly well-suited to sound. Von Stroheim's work excepted, silents didn't offer anything as scabrous as a wisecrack in the middle of a movie called *Pointed Heels,* a backstage romance written by Charles Brackett. As a group of chorus girls clomps to the beat, a cigar-chomping Eugene Pallette snarls, "You can't tell me that infantile paralysis is not on the increase in America."

Released six months after *Gentlemen of the Press, Pointed Heels* shows how quickly the studios were forcing technical advancements. Director Eddie Sutherland, an amiable hand who had matriculated as an assistant to Chaplin, pulls off a genuinely impressive crane/ tracking shot that moves over the heads of dancers and circles around a table during a conversation, as well as a nicely impressionistic montage, all whip pans, fancy angles, quick cuts, and rapid tracking shots.

Some scenes are clearly shot with a blimped single camera, while others are done with the conservative three-camera technique. The hesitant but perceptible leading edge of style helps take the mind off an otherwise flat narrative that not even William Powell, as a Ziegfeldian producer, can save, what with the resistible, one-note brass of Helen Kane and Richard "Skeets" Gallagher, and the moist Phillips Holmes, who plays a society wimp struggling to be a composer. "Something of the quality of Stravinsky," murmurs Powell upon hearing a sample of his *echt*-Gershwin.

Good or bad, these are all astringent city movies, full of a cheap street slang that would date them in just a few years, but which thrilled audiences of 1929, made them feel like they were in on something racy and dangerous. Words like "doublecross," "yegg," and "beezer" had a vibrant immediacy that made the ardent romance of silents seem Victorian.

□ □ □

It was William Fox, as always lunging to the point while others were still idly contemplating their options, who dropped the other shoe. On March 25, Fox announced that he was discontinuing the production of silent pictures. Playing catch-up, Harry Cohn said that Columbia was also going into the talkie business full-time. Fox was verbalizing what was already *de facto* industry policy; all the companies, with the exception of two or three films they were wrapping, were making only sound movies, but almost all of them were also producing silent versions of those talkies for foreign markets and smaller domestic theaters that weren't as yet wired for sound. Of the thirty-one films Paramount had on their schedule at that point, seventeen were scheduled to be released as both sound and silent.

While others pondered, William Fox *moved*. "The change in Fox policy," reported *The New York Times* with chilly precision, "will affect thousands of actors, title writers, directors and supervisors. Screen favorites unable to measure up to the new vocal requirements will probably lose out as a result of the altered production policies . . ."

Winfield Sheehan, Fox's production chief, predicted that by January 1, 1931, there would be as many as three thousand theaters wired for sound. (As it happened, by the end of 1930, the number of theaters equipped to show talkies would grow to ten thousand.) As *Fortune* magazine wittily described the situation, "The producers were in the condition of learning on Tuesday that what they thought might occur a year from Tuesday had actually happened a week ago Monday."

At the time Fox announced he was abandoning silents, the studio was signing Will Rogers, Willie Collier, George Jessel, Pulitzer Prize–winning playwright Owen Davis, the songwriting team of DeSylva, Brown, and Henderson, and about ninety others.* Although Will Rogers had had an indifferent silent screen career, his years onstage for Ziegfeld and other producers made him an obvious hot ticket. Rogers's contract, outlined in March 1929, proved that timing is indeed everything. Beginning June 1 and continuing for sixteen months, Rogers was to act in and assist with the construction and writing of four talking pictures. He was to be paid a staggering $150,000 for each of the movies.

In 1928, Fox had released fifty-five features and had stepped up production of Movietone News to two reels a week, distributing to theaters in more than thirty countries. He had studios in New York, Hollywood, and Europe and owned over three thousand theaters in America alone.

None of it was enough. It was at this point that William Fox irrevocably defined himself as the single most acquisitive man in the history of the motion picture industry: he decided that if he couldn't beat them, he would buy them.

Marcus Loew had died in 1927, and, as the estate wended through probate, his widow decided to sell the shares of stock that gave her

---

* One estimate had it that more than a thousand screen tests were made in New York in 1929, a figure that sounds low. "The moment you made a hit in a play, everybody was after you," said Lloyd Nolan of this period; Stuart Erwin remembered that when he left New York to go to Hollywood, most of the passengers on the train were actors.

control of Loew's, Inc., which included Metro-Goldwyn-Mayer. Her asking price was $50 million. Both Adolph Zukor and Harry Warner went after the deal, but they didn't move as fast nor spend as much as William Fox. On March 3, Fox bought 443,000 shares, a one-third interest, in Loew's. The purchase price was $125 a share, about 50 percent over the market price of $84.

Nicholas Schenck, knowing a good thing when he saw it, sold out his private shares in Loew's as well, accepting cash and Fox stock in exchange. Schenck's personal profit was in the vicinity of $10 million. In return for Schenck being so agreeable, it was decided that he would stay on as president of the new company. Louis B. Mayer, outraged at being kept outside the loop, regarded Schenck's behavior as a personal betrayal.*

Including Schenck's shares, Fox bought another 227,000 shares for an additional $20 million. In one afternoon, William Fox had spent more than $50 million for slightly more than 50 percent of Loew's, Inc., making it, in effect, a subsidiary of Fox and doubling the size of Fox's film business. But he wasn't through yet. Fox then purchased British Gaumont for yet another $20 million. It was all an astonishing role of the dice, for Fox had a limited time in which to start spinning money; he had a $15 million AT&T note due in only a year, in March 1930.

Mayer was not without solid ground from which to wage a retaliatory campaign. Among other things, there was his friend Herbert Hoover, who had bestowed on him the status of honored guest at his inauguration in January 1928. The White House guest book shows that Mayer was there twice within a ten-day period in July 1929. With good reason, Fox began to believe the Justice Department had him in their sights for potential antitrust action. He offered Mayer a $2-million payment to ease his anger and, hopefully, convince Hoover that the merger was a fine idea for American business.

---

* The Fox-Loew's deal instigated a minor passion for mergers. On September 1, Paramount and Warners announced a new consortium called "Paramount-Vitaphone," which would exceed the asset base of either Fox-Loew's or RCA-RKO. The company would own 1,400 theaters, six movie studios, CBS radio, and Columbia Records. A month later, Herbert Hoover's Justice Department threatened an antitrust suit, and the merger was unceremoniously canceled.

According to the account Fox gave his biographer Upton Sinclair in a very curious 1933 book entitled *Upton Sinclair Presents William Fox*, Mayer agreed to take the money. Bosley Crowther, Mayer's biographer, talked to a Justice Department official who remembered being astonished when Mayer's opposition to the merger magically melted away. For his part, Mayer always denied that he did anything but fight William Fox. The two accounts are not, of course, mutually exclusive; Mayer could have agreed to take the money, then continued working to submarine the merger. What is certain is that, money aside, Mayer had nothing to gain by becoming Fox's employee. He was, moreover, psychologically incapable of ceding any of his power or authority, which were far more important to him than wealth.

Fox's plan for his new conglomerate was to close two hundred duplicate distribution offices, which would bring an annual savings of about $17 million, and to use his three movie studios to control the product distributed to the Loew's and Fox theaters. With one hawklike swoop, William Fox had become the most powerful movie magnate in the world, then or now. Yet, as *Fortune* magazine wryly observed, "Comparing him (probably not to his displeasure) with Napoleon, 1929 might be termed his Moscow year . . ."

Up until his purchase of Loew's and Gaumont, Fox had financed his acquisitions via mortgage bonds, but the new purchases demanded more capital. At first he resorted to short-term notes; since his credit was excellent, the primary lending banks of London and New York were soon awash in Fox paper.

But even bank loans weren't enough to cover $90 million of purchases. That spring, Fox borrowed $10 million from Harry Stuart, of Halsey, Stuart & Co., and another $15 million from ERPI's John Otterson. No collateral was offered or requested and, even more strangely, no permanent financing plan, in the form of a stock option, was offered.

Besides the outlay for Loew's and Gaumont, Fox was finishing construction of his new 180-acre Movietone city on Pico Boulevard, complete with twenty-five recording units. In contrast to the large, open expanses of silent studios, where sets were built side by side, the new sound studios were constructed of a double wall of cement block more than a foot thick, with six inches of air between the blocks. On the inside of the studio walls, sound-deadening drapes were hung. Fox even soundproofed his old Western Avenue studios; nearly forty years later, they still had the original soundproofing on the walls: mattresses, strapped to the concrete walls with wire.

In that deep, hazy summer of 1929, the shrewd, suspicious William Fox controlled thousands of movie theaters, two of the primary movie production companies in the world, and access to exhibition in England. He bestrode the world of American movies like the proverbial Colossus. But none of it would make any difference — for, in the entire history of industry and finance, no one would ever have worse luck than William Fox.

❏ ❏ ❏

In October 1927, Howard Hughes had begun production on a film intended to obliterate the triumph of Paramount's aerial spectacular *Wings*. With the monomaniacal attention to irrelevant detail that would mark his entire life, Hughes spent $2 million of the fortune that derived from the Hughes Tool Company to employ thirty-seven pilots, seventeen hundred extras, thirty-five cameramen, twelve editors, and several directors (Marshall Neilan, Luther Reed) to make the film he called *Hell's Angels*. After some fifteen months of production, resulting in miles of footage and three deaths, Hughes looked up and noticed that talking pictures were all the rage. Since his picture was silent, Hughes realized, some six months late, that he had an unreleasable movie on his hands.

Hughes decided to keep the excellent aerial sequences — which had no dialogue anyway — and reshoot all of the surrounding story footage, which had been the responsibility of Luther Reed, a journeyman director who had been the aviation reporter for the *New York Herald-Tribune*. To write the new material, Hughes hired Joseph Moncure March; to direct, James Whale. March screened the silent version and, as he remembered, "with the exception of the air sequences and the final dramatic scene in which Jimmy Hall shoots his brother Ben Lyon, to keep him from telling all to the Hun, I thought the film depressingly bad. I had to contrive a story better than the one Hughes had, but still manage to have it logically embrace the sequences that were good enough to keep."

While March rewrote through the summer, Whale and Hughes worked on recasting the female lead; Greta Nissen, the woman in

the silent version, had a heavy Norwegian accent that rather miti-
gated against her playing a British tart.

Ann Harding and Carole Lombard (Carol Peters at the time) were
tested and rejected, as was June Collyer. Arthur Landau, the agent
who represented Ben Lyon, the picture's star, then offered up another client, a young actress named Jean Harlow. Hughes liked what
he saw and hired her. She had white-blond hair, a pouty little Peking-
ese face, and a luscious body. Unfortunately, she couldn't act at
all, as James Whale discovered when he began shooting the talking
sequences in early September.

Two months later, Hughes finally ended production and began the
arduous process of editing the talking footage and dubbing the silent
footage. Joseph Moncure March discovered that the actors playing
the German officers in the silent version had ad-libbed their lines,
and nobody was able to remember just what they had said.

"Undaunted by this complex problem," remembered March, "we
brought in a German by the name of Julius Schroeder. He and I sat
down at a Moviola and ran the zeppelin sequences till our eyes
dropped out . . . Schroeder tried to determine from the lip movement
just what each man had said. I would then decide what he ought to
be saying to make sense, and Schroeder would try to find a way of
saying it in German that would fit the lip movement of the actors."

While all this was going on, Hughes's accountants realized with
mounting horror that their exceedingly odd employer had spent $2.8
million on *Hell's Angels.* Hughes promptly announced that the cost
of the film was $4 million, about the same amount that MGM had
spent on *Ben-Hur.* Hughes wisely realized that nobody would be
interested in the second-most expensive movie ever made; for publicity purposes, *Hell's Angels* was to be the most expensive movie of all
time.

❑ ❑ ❑

Of the forty-two actors on Paramount's contract list, thirty-nine had
stage experience. Yet, the studio was engaging in strategic press leaks
to put perceived marginal talents on notice that their days were
numbered. MENJOU AND OTHERS IN DOUBT WITH PARAMOUNT, read
a headline in the March 30 issue of *Billboard.* The "others" included
Florence Vidor, Fay Wray, John Loder, Jack Holt, and Emil Jannings.

It was clearly understood that most, if not all of these people, would soon be following closely behind the departing Bebe Daniels and Louise Brooks. Actors whose low vocal undertones were regarded as perfect for sound included George Bancroft, William Powell, and Clive Brook. Most of the people on the endangered list would in fact go on to long and successful talkie careers; clearly, the problem was not so much the voices of Menjou, Holt, Wray et al. as it was their hefty salaries — Menjou, for one, got $5,500 a week.

Because of the increased emphasis on stage writers and actors, Paramount's Astoria studio found itself a hotbed of activity. Paramount had opened the studio in 1920, in order to take advantage of the fact that it was just a short ride over the Queensboro Bridge from Manhattan. Broadway talent could shoot a movie during the day and still make their evening performance, a luxury Hollywood couldn't offer. Astoria quickly became the favored production center for Gloria Swanson and W. C. Fields, among others. Paramount made more than a hundred features there in seven years, but had abandoned the studio in April 1927, in order to centralize all production on the West Coast. Little more than a year later, sound forced Paramount to reverse itself.

Paramount put Monta Bell in charge of the newly revitalized studio. Bell was a former reporter for *The Washington Post* who had ghosted Chaplin's 1922 book *My Trip Abroad,* before going on to serve as "literary editor" on *A Woman of Paris.* A charming, likable, sophisticated man, Bell was fond of telling stories about the days before he met Chaplin, when he was so broke his wife would send him sandwiches through the mail.

After his time with Chaplin, Bell had gone on to direct a series of very good pictures, including *A King on Main Street* and *Man, Woman and Sin.* With his appointment as executive producer at Astoria, Bell took a beautiful apartment on Fifty-seventh Street, on the East Side of Manhattan, and moved in with his beloved pet schipperke, whose party piece was a trick Bell called "Hollywood." "He would say, 'Come on, do Hollywood,' " remembered Helen Laidlaw, whose husband was one of Bell's writers. "And the dog would lie down on its back and spread its legs."

Bell moved quickly in spite of the fact that he had seen only about six talkies, signing up directors like Robert Florey because the novel technique he had displayed in his avant-garde shorts made him seem a promising talent.

Initially, Astoria had only one soundproofed stage, a small space in the basement that was hot in the summer and freezing in the winter. Florey frantically set to work making tests, dozens of them, from eight in the morning till midnight. All sorts of people trooped before Florey's camera, from Ethel Barrymore to Edward G. Robinson. For those who seemed to have some possibilities — such as Eddie Cantor, Borah Minevitch, and Lillian Roth — Florey would film one- and two-reel shorts, usually making them on Sunday, as many as three a day.

Florey tried to convince Bell to make "drama, action, or mystery pictures, with a minimum of dialogue simply replacing the subtitles of the silent films . . ." But, with Zukor and Lasky breathing down his neck, Bell felt a residual caution. He would prefer, he told Florey, emphasis on "talk" only. Bell eventually assigned Florey to top-of-the-line productions like *The Cocoanuts,* the movie debut of the Marx Brothers, who were paid $100,000 en masse. When Florey wanted to go on location to Florida for greater realism, Bell inquired as to why Florey felt authenticity was an issue, when one of his stars was wearing a greasepaint mustache.

Although Groucho and Morrie Ryskind would later claim that Florey's obliviousness to the humor of the Marx Brothers was nearly equal to Margaret Dumont's, Harpo remembered Florey flying into hysterics at their routines, ruining take after take. In order to get the film made, Florey had to move into the tiny little camera booth. "We still played to Florey," remembered Harpo Marx. "When he flew into a fit of silent convulsions we knew we had done something good. It was the weirdest audience we ever played to."

The Cocoanuts was nothing more than a photographed version of the play, and wasn't even slickly done; props drop out of the frame, actors disappear, lines are blown. But audiences had never seen anything like the Marx Brothers. *The Cocoanuts* opened on May 3, 1929, to enthusiastic responses from audiences and critics ("It sets out to achieve one purpose, that of making the audience laugh, and as I laughed during almost its entire showing I must credit it with having scored a success," wrote Welford Beaton in *The Film Spectator*).

"I feel like an amateur in my own business," groused Bell, who was nothing if not honest. "At the time I came east [to take over Astoria] I did not like talking pictures. I do not like them today." For the next few years, until financial difficulties again forced Paramount to abandon the operation, Bell and Walter Wanger set a distinctly literary tone that rarely became dry or stultified. Bell believed that "we were still making motion pictures; that if we continued to keep that fact in our minds and use sound and spoken dialogue where the effectiveness of motion pictures would be enhanced, we were on the right track." Bell never forgot the Astoria studio's reason for existence — its proximity to Broadway. Nearly every Astoria picture would be either a direct adaptation of a Broadway play, or a testing ground for newly acquired New York talent.

For new blood, Paramount eagerly signed up the tempestuous stage star Jeanne Eagels to star in an adaptation of Somerset Maugham's *The Letter*. To direct, Bell hired Jean de Limur. Although she looked like a fragile blond flower, Eagels could curse like a longshoreman and had a steely sense of her own worth. When Florenz Ziegfeld offered her $1,500 a week to help him glorify the American girl, she curtly refused, saying that she was a dramatic actress and not a chorus girl.

Although she had made several films before and during World War I, Eagels had not really been counted a success until she made 1927's *Man, Woman and Sin,* in spite of the fact that her part was secondary to a brilliant performance by John Gilbert. After that, she went back to her first love, the stage, but, in April 1928, the increasingly erratic star was suspended by Actor's Equity for her unprofessional behavior — once, she lowered the curtain during a performance of *Rain* until a door backstage was shut; on another occasion, she halted a performance of *Her Cardboard Lover* by demanding that costar Leslie Howard get her a glass of water.

At the very least, Eagels was a raging alcoholic; at the most, a drug addict. Her widely reported nickname of "Gin" Eagels referred to her habit of drinking hot gin, supposedly because it helped kill the pain of persistent neuralgia. Because at that point she couldn't work on the stage, Paramount's offer of a three-picture deal was heaven-sent.

Compared to the later William Wyler version, Jean de Limur's film of *The Letter* is a tab version of the Maugham story, albeit without the ridiculous censorship that mandated the death of the adulterous Leslie Crosbie. As a film it's of minor interest; as a record of Jeanne Eagels, it's invaluable.

Looking like a youthful Gladys Cooper, with a smoky voice that simultaneously suggests sachets and wild nights, Eagels flaunts a faultless English accent — rare among women born in Kansas City. Unlike the drearily statuesque ladies who commonly infested the movies in the days of early sound (Diana Wynyard, Ann Harding), she has a jittery, vibrating, febrile quality that could be either a function of her acting persona or a reflection of a woman in dire need of a drink. She listens to the other actors with intense concentration, and carries off the great curtain line ("With all my heart, I still love the man I killed") with a bloodcurdling flourish.

Eagels's already perilous physical and emotional states could not have been improved by the ardors of a talkie production; microphones were still being hidden in flower arrangements, and numerous takes were usually required. Also causing difficulty was the fact that Astoria was using a variation on the Movietone system, in which the sound was recorded on the same piece of film as the picture, a different method than used by Paramount's Hollywood studio, where the sound was recorded on an entirely different strip of film, to facilitate cutting and mixing.*

On October 3, 1929, a few months after finishing *Jealousy,* her second Paramount feature, Jeanne Eagels died at the age of thirty-five from what was initially reported to be "death by alcoholic psychosis." Upon hasty reexamination of the evidence, undoubtedly spurred by threats from Eagels's lawyer, her death was officially attributed to an overdose of sleeping medicine, specifically chloral hydrate, a popular sedative with unfortunate delirium-inducing capabilities. Unofficially, her death was assumed by those in the business to be the result of a heroin overdose.

❑ ❑ ❑

---

* Astoria maintained this arduous process until Ernst Lubitsch arrived in early 1931 to make *The Smiling Lieutenant* and demanded the double film system. He got it.

By the early part of 1929, sound engineers were successfully dubbing sound. For *Innocents of Paris,* the initial starring vehicle of Maurice Chevalier, Paramount utilized an old stock shot of a Paris street. On a darkened, draped stage, an orchestra huddled under one microphone, a group of voice extras gathered underneath a second, while three men with bird whistles stood below a third. The orchestra played "Louise" as musical background, while the voice extras interpolated random sentences such as "What pretty flowers! How much are they, please?" and the men playing bird whistles burst into twitterings.

Because all this had to be recorded simultaneously, on a single track, balances were difficult to get right; several rehearsals and several takes were necessary, but eventually the grainy silent footage sprang to life. From there, it was a short, obvious step to dubbing sound over new footage.

Another new wrinkle, but with greater creative impact, was the movement of journalists and playwrights to the West Coast. "With sound came the Jew," was the pithy summation of Joseph L. Mankiewicz. The migration was inevitable, but the pace was increased by the efforts of Herman Mankiewicz, who was put in charge of writer recruitment by Paramount. A hard-drinking gambler, a dedicated, self-destructive underachiever, Mankiewicz hired men in his own image: Ben Hecht, Bartlett Cormack, Edwin Justus Mayer, writers comfortable with the iconoclasm of big-city newsrooms who would introduce their sardonic worldliness to movie audiences.

Writers with a different persona could have a difficult time fitting in. Among the early imports was Zoë Akins, who wrote what Joesph Mankiewicz categorized as "terribly elegant imitation Maugham plays." Although born in Kansas City, Akins affected a phony British accent that other writers found maddening. One day she poked her head in Mankiewicz's office and asked about the "shedule" on a picture that was about to start production.

Mankiewicz, Grover Jones, and William McNutt glanced at each other. Grover Jones did the answering for all of them when he sighed, "Oh, skit!"

❏ ❏ ❏

It was all changing so fast. In 1928, Paramount had released seventy-eight movies, all silent. In 1929, it would release sixty-seven, only twenty of them silent. The studio would probably have released an all-talkie program but for a catastrophic fire on January 16 that destroyed their new talkie soundstages. A distraught Adolph Zukor asked studio manager Sam Jaffe how long it would take to rebuild them. "Mr. Zukor, these are cement buildings, it isn't like putting up a set. It's going to take six months if we work day and night to put up these stages," Jaffe told him.

"If we can't make sound pictures," retorted Zukor, "we're out of business. In six months all the companies will have finished their stages and they will be making hundred-percent talking pictures, and we will be making only pictures with sound effects."

A few days later, Jaffe was working late at night when it hit him. "I thought, 'Why do we need soundstages if we turn *day into night?*' We could have actors come and start at night, at nine o'clock. Break for lunch at one or two, and work until six in the morning when there's no noise, no trucks or lorries. If you go out to the desert where there's no noise, you could make interiors without a sound-stage."

Jaffe consulted with the sound department, which told him to buy up all the blankets in Los Angeles for use as sound baffles. The four remaining silent stages were quickly converted into makeshift talkie stages, and, for the next several months, Paramount nervously tap-danced through dusk-to-dawn production schedules and hoped audiences wouldn't notice.

"The sound wasn't as good, from a technical point of view as, say, Metro sound," remembered Jaffe, "but we had more pictures being made, and the public didn't know any different because as long as the voice came out and it synchronized, it was perfectly OK. Instead of being out of business, we were making more sound pictures than the other companies."

A year after devising the scheme to shoot at night, Sam Jaffe's contract came up for renewal; Zukor offered him $1,250 a week, up from $1,000. Jaffe countered by saying that wasn't much of a raise for the man who had saved Paramount. Zukor swallowed and gave him $1,500.

The remaining inventory of silent pictures would be released grudgingly, with a minimum of promotional effort. The studios began cleaning out actors who couldn't talk well or who had the misfortune of undesirable accents. Paramount let go of Emil Jannings, Goldwyn abandoned Vilma Banky, and Universal said farewell to Conrad Veidt. "Indirectly," said one trade paper, "he is a victim of the talkers."

Some of the actors went quietly, others with a show of defiance. Lya De Putti, the Hungarian star of E. A. Dupont's *Variety* for Germany's UFA studio, had come to Hollywood to work for Griffith in *The Sorrows of Satan* and had been mildly successful, until her accent rendered her *hors de combat*. "Talkies are the bunk," she snarled to the press on her way to England in February 1929. "They will pass and there will be much disappointment over them. I am not alone in my opinion ... America will realize its folly and the producers will be clamoring for us to come back." De Putti's Norma Desmond–like disaffection would be permanent. For her only part-talkie, the 1929 adaptation of *The Informer*, she had to use a voice double; she died of pneumonia in 1931 without ever attempting another sound film.

Actors who still had jobs knew what was going on and reacted with appropriate displays of deference, which seemed insufficient to counter the prevailing paranoia. Even at lowly Columbia, "The soundman was the president of the United States he was so important," said actress Dorothy Revier, one of Harry Cohn's mistresses. "I was doing *The Donovan Affair* ... with Frank Capra. Agnes Ayres, who was playing my stepmother, was very mean to me because I was a newcomer. I was nothing. I saw her lunching with the soundman and then we did our voice tests.

"Agnes sounded fine but I sounded insane, like this [a chipmunk squeak]. My enunciation was gone and my voice was shattered ... I always thought Agnes Ayres had something to do with this. Later on she and I became good friends because I learned how to handle her. I flattered her by saying, 'You were so wonderful in ... *The Sheik*.' But she never admitted if she sabotaged my test."

Early in 1929, as Richard Dix and Esther Ralston were making their first talkie, *The Wheel of Life,* Dix paused during a love scene and said, "Esther, see that man up there in the booth?"

"You mean the soundman?"

"Yes, and you'd better be nice to him."

"Oh. Why?"

"Because he can make a baritone out of you and a soprano out of me."

Not all actors were nervous. During production of *Betrayal,* a part-talkie directed by Lewis Milestone, a scene called for Esther Ralston to emote over an unconscious Gary Cooper. "Wait, don't shoot yet," the soundman ordered. "I keep hearing this strange noise." After much delay, it was finally discovered that the rattling buzz the microphone was picking up was Cooper snoring.

As it happened, the man in the glass booth didn't stay there for long. As director Allan Dwan described it, "These idiotic rooms away at the top of the building were supposed to look down on the stages so the sound mixer could see what was going on. But they forgot that the sets were high and that the windows he looked through would be blocked, so he couldn't see the stages at all. There he was, sitting alone, and he didn't know what they were doing below. Things ran down to a halt. We had to dispense with the big expensive rooms upstairs and put the man down at a table [near the set], very much as he is at the present moment."

As Cecil B. DeMille arrived at MGM to begin production on *Dynamite,* his first talkie, he found "everybody was sort of in a crouched position ready to spring." Because of the location of the camera, in the dreaded icebox, "you could not pan the camera. You could not move the camera. You rehearsed the first act of a play because everybody rushed to New York and bought plays . . . and then you turned the camera all the way through the first act. Everything that the silent screen had done to bring the entertainment and the beauty . . . of action, was gone."

DeMille described the tormented first week of production on *Dynamite* to George Pratt: "I said, 'No. Take the camera out [of the booth] and put it on the stairs.' And they said, 'Well, you can't take the camera out of this room because it makes so much noise you can't shoot.' I said, 'Take it out and put it on the stairs, or *I* will take it out and put it on the stairs.' "

The sound engineer promptly walked off the set. Unfazed, De-Mille sent the propman for a couple of blankets to wrap around the camera. DeMille asked the soundman to come back and listen.* The soundman said he could still hear the camera. DeMille sent the propman back for two more blankets. The soundman said he could still hear the camera, but not as loudly. Once again the propman returned, this time with two bed quilts. "We turned it with difficulty and the [soundman] said, 'I don't hear it. It's all right.' Well, everything was fine, except that you couldn't get at the camera to turn it or focus it or lower it or anything else. But you couldn't hear it."

Douglas Shearer stopped by the set to see what the imperious DeMille had wrought. Shearer immediately grasped the idea, and asked DeMille to wait a week while he built MGM's first camera blimp, in essence nothing more than a box large enough to envelop the camera magazine. A hinged door allowed access, and the interior was lined with blankets to absorb the sound of grinding gears. The camera was freed from bondage.

❑ ❑ ❑

As Will Rogers arrived that summer to begin his Fox contract, he found that "the whole business out here is just scared cuckoo. You meet an actor or girl and in the old days where they would have just nodded and passed by, now they stop and start chattering like a parrot. Weather, politics, Babe Ruth, anything just to practice talking, and they are so busy enunciating that they pay no attention to what they are saying. Everything is 'Annunciation.' I was on the stage twenty-three years and never heard the word or knew what it was."

Even technicians were finding it difficult. The young cameraman James Wong Howe had amassed major credits in silent films and spent the summer of 1928 in China, shooting background footage

---

* That a mere technician walked off a set commanded by the lordly Cecil B. DeMille and, rather than being summarily dismissed, actually returned to his job, gives some idea of how the balance of power had shifted.

for a film he wanted to direct. "When I came back, I couldn't get a job," he remembered. "They'd say, 'Have you photographed a sound picture?' I'd say, 'No.' They'd say, 'Well, it's all different.' "

After what he remembered as a year out of work (it was actually closer to six months), Howe finally got lucky, although he had to swallow his pride and take a major pay cut. " 'Pop' Sherman [producer Harry Sherman] was going to make a picture with Conrad Nagel and Catherine Dale Owen. It was called *Today* and William Nigh was directing. He said, 'We're going to have to make it in seven days, Jimmy.' I said, 'I don't care; we'll work day and night on it.' So finally, when we finished it [on schedule] 'Pop' Sherman took me aside and said, 'I can't pay you until I get the picture released.' I said, 'OK' but I still got the credit, which was the most important thing."

"There was such a feeling of apprehension on the part of producers," said the actor William Bakewell. "They felt that anybody in silent pictures couldn't talk, which was ridiculous, although some successful actors, like Gary Cooper and Loretta Young, had never been in the theater at all."

But there were also other actors who had never been in the theater, and it showed. Stars making at least $5,000 a week, such as Norma Talmadge, Corinne Griffith, Tom Mix, and, to a lesser extent, Colleen Moore, would find that sound revealed, if not outright vocal inadequacy, plebian voices that detracted from their allure.

A far odder failure was that of Lillian Gish, whose first starring talkie, *One Romantic Night*, an adaptation of Molnar's *The Swan*, was a complete financial — and, according to Gish, creative — disaster. "I'd seen *The Swan* in the theater with Eva Le Gallienne," Gish remembered in 1979. "I liked the Molnar play. I was seeing a great deal of George Jean Nathan in those days and he thought it would make a good talking picture."

But Gish didn't like the director — an obscurity named Paul Stein — and didn't particularly like talkies. "I thought talking pictures would shrink our audiences," she said. Gish was an experienced stage actress — she would go on to play Ophelia opposite John Gielgud's Hamlet, in addition to enacting a long series of distinguished supporting film performances — so her voice was not the problem. It's more likely that audiences had grown tired of an actress they had been watching since 1912, and used the pretext of sound as an opportunity to seek out new faces.

Gish had a contract with United Artists for three pictures at $50,000 per picture and half the profits. Since there were no profits to be had from *One Romantic Night* — it grossed only $400,000 — Gish elected to cancel the remainder of her contract and to work on the stage.

Studios were only too glad to get out of munificent contracts and replace old stars with new ones that could be had for much less. (John Gilbert was making $250,000 a picture in 1929, with two pictures a year; Clark Gable, his eventual replacement as primary leading man at MGM, never made that much when he was under contract, topping out at $7,500 a week.)

Eleanor Boardman, who gave such an indelible performance in *The Crowd*, saw her first part-talkie — *She Goes to War* — gross an anemic $485,000 domestically; a popular leading man like Rod La Rocque saw talkies like *The Locked Door* ($470,000 gross) lead him into supporting parts. Norma Talmadge, one of the primary commercial icons of the silent era, made two sound flops in a row, one of which, *Du Barry*, barely grossed $400,000.

Of all the idols of silence, none would be so positively transformed by sound as Ronald Colman. In silent pictures, the actor had been successful enough, his gentle, beautiful eyes and handsome features obscuring the fact that he was as facially inexpressive as Clive Brook. Yet, the reticent, deeply shy Colman was unsure of his own perfect voice.

When Sam Goldwyn sent him a standard rider to his contract to cover talking pictures, a panicked Colman replied to his employer: "I would rather not sign this. Except as a scientific achievement, I am not sympathetic to this 'sound business.' I feel, as many do, that this is a mechanical resource, that it is a retrogressive and temporary digression insofar as it affects the art of motion picture acting — in short, that it does not properly belong to my particular work (of which naturally I must be the best judge)."

Despite his reservations, Colman signed, but continued to worry. Although Colman had been appearing in a series of exotic romances opposite Vilma Banky, by heritage and inclination he was a reserved

Englishman. Goldwyn first tried to buy *Arms and the Man* for Colman's talkie debut, but Bernard Shaw quickly quashed that idea. Goldwyn then hired Sidney Howard, who had already won a Pulitzer Prize in 1925 for *They Knew What They Wanted,* to adapt the invariably successful Bulldog Drummond stories, which Goldwyn already owned. The H. M. "Sapper" McNeile stories were a good combination of urbanity, wit, and adventure, and they didn't need any of the love scenes that seemed to be causing audience laughter.*

Director F. Richard Jones, a former supervisor at the Hal Roach studio who had directed *The Gaucho,* a very stylish Douglas Fairbanks film, rehearsed Sidney Howard's script for two full weeks. Cameras finally rolled on January 28, 1929, and production of the talkie version was completed in four and a half weeks; another two weeks was spent shooting a silent version nearly a half-hour shorter than the ninety-three-minute talking version. *Bulldog Drummond* wrapped on March 18.

The rehearsal period proved invaluable in speeding up actual production, as did the bulky sound equipment, which virtually mandated longer takes, hence fewer total shots. To a great extent, art director William Cameron Menzies preplanned the picture — most of the interior sets were partials, designed to be seen from a specific camera angle. A visiting architect found that the sets resembled "the inside of a Coney Island crazy house. Vanishing points are all wrong; windows slant unaccountably . . ." Because of the careful preparation, production costs for *Bulldog Drummond* were a very modest $550,000, at least $150,000 less than Goldwyn had been spending on the Colman/Banky silent pictures.

Bulldog Drummond emerged as a commercial matrix for the shotgun marriage of image and sound. Its stylish, well-spoken dialogue and Menzies' eye-popping sets made *Drummond* far more polished than the average film of the transition period. The *dégagé* elegance of Sidney Howard's dialogue is summed up in one line of Colman's,

---

* KIDDING KISSERS IN TALKERS BURNS UP FANS OF SCREEN'S BEST LOVERS, read a page-one headline in *Variety* that year. "In the silents," the article explained, "when a lover would whisper like a ventriloquist, lips apart and unmoved, and roll his eyes passionately, preparatory to the clinch and then kiss, it looked pretty natural and was believable. [But now] the build-up to the kiss . . . makes a gag of the kiss."

when he idly mutters at a bar that he's "too rich to work and too intelligent to play." Howard's scenes tend to be shorter and punchier than the usual film scene of 1929; the rhythm is not that of the theater, but of the movies. When the scenes are lengthy, they're saved from ponderousness by sharp cutting or humor. Goldwyn, Jones, and company only tip their hat to the novelty of sound by inserting close-ups of such innocuous — to later generations — actions as pouring a drink into a glass.*

Bulldog Drummond matches a polished, sophisticated hero against polished, sophisticated villainy, something Hitchcock was to do for the next half-century, and whenever the tone threatens to get too trivial, Menzies' ominous, expressionist sets serve to ground the proceedings and keep the film from floating away on arch clouds of stiff-upper-lip Englishness.

Most important, *Bulldog Drummond* offered the audience the crushed-velvet voice of Ronald Colman, a voice that matched his already established urbane screen personality. This would prove to be the key to survival for silent stars attempting to make the transition. If their voices fit their personalities — Laurel and Hardy, Colman, Victor McLaglen — then they would triumph. But if there was a misalliance between image and voice . . . disaster.

Bulldog Drummond opened in New York in May, the same month as Vilma Banky's part-talkie *This Is Heaven*. Banky's heavy Hungarian accent was the focus of every review; likewise Colman's mellifluous British intonations.

"He has a cultivated and resonant voice," said the *Los Angeles Times*. "He loses nothing by the transition but rather gains a great deal . . ." *Photoplay* proclaimed that "he's suave and easy before the terrorizing mikes. Voice gives him a new charm . . ." *The New York Times* said that "Mr. Colman is as ingratiating when he talks as when he was silent." As for Banky, "[she] is heard to talk in several places,"

---

* This sort of thing reached its loony height in a Paramount picture called *The Mysterious Dr. Fu Manchu,* in which a marching band that has, oddly enough, accompanied troops freeing the British legation during the Boxer Rebellion continues marching and playing for minutes, stopping the narrative dead, for no other reason than to give the audience the unfamiliar thrill of hearing a marching band on the screen.

wrote the trade paper *Harrison's Reports*. "She has a decided accent and her punctuation is not very good. It might have been better to have left the talk out entirely."

The Banky picture lost $200,000; the Colman film made $750,000 profit. "What Chaplin is to the silent film," exulted Goldwyn, "Colman will be to sound." Banky made one more Hollywood picture, on loan-out to MGM. Her costar, Edward G. Robinson, would remember that "it did not take long to realize that Miss Banky was seriously out of her depth. The glorious creature . . . was seized with stage fright and inability."

That picture, *Lady to Love*, is a hapless, interminable adaptation of Sidney Howard's *They Knew What They Wanted*, with Robinson doing some frenzied overacting. (The living-room set for Robinson's character ominously displays pictures of both Herbert Hoover and Mussolini.)

MGM knew they had a problem; Banky's first three scenes give the placid blond beauty no dialogue. When she finally begins talking, her Hungarian accent proves heavy but perfectly intelligible. Perhaps because she had to concentrate so hard on the words, Banky's performance is actually superior — quieter, far less bombastic — than her costar's, but it didn't help. The audience would accept an accent from a star, but it had to accompany a smoldering, mysterious sensuality — Garbo, Dietrich, Boyer — and all Banky radiated was a maternal *gemütlichkeit*.

Even though she had two years remaining on her Goldwyn contract, at $5,000 a week, Banky never made another movie. Goldwyn paid her off and Banky retired, comfortably well off, with her husband Rod La Rocque.

❏ ❏ ❏

Exhibitors were struggling to catch up with the new sound phenomenon, just as were the studios, actors, and directors, and often they got very little help. "In the beginning," remembered Alvin Sloan, a projectionist who became a theater owner, "if a picture talked, that alone would make it do business." Different terminologies arose to help the audience make their moviegoing decisions. "The marquees in those days were limited; you wouldn't have room for more than the star, the name of the picture, and maybe one other word. So we would put up SOUND if the picture had no talk, just music. Otherwise, it was TALK on the marquee."

The public quickly grew adept at tripping up those theaters that tried to fudge the issue. "[People] would call up and want to know, 'Is this a talking movie?'" remembered Dallas exhibitor James Cherry. "And you'd say, 'No, it's with music.' Well, they wouldn't come, because [they'd] already heard [talkies] and [that's what] they wanted." The critics carped, but the audience didn't care. "Criticisms terrible," read one telegram to a producer, "business tremendous."

Although the Vitaphone discs were made of shellac, they were of a softer mix than conventional 78 rpm records, and, because of the heavy wooden crates they were packed in, Sloan recalled never having a broken record. He did, however, remember other disasters that came with the territory.

"One day I was working in Caldwell, New Jersey, running a Buck Jones western. We were supposed to start at 2 P.M. and the film and discs were delivered about noon, with no time to test everything out. Comes two o'clock, I cue up the film and disc. Everything was fine, except that they'd sent me discs in Spanish for the film! Since it was a double feature, I put the other picture on, jumped in the car, and got into New York, got the right discs, and got back in time to run the Buck Jones picture on schedule."

Exhibitors found that there were two inherent problems with the Vitaphone system: splices and skips in the records. Splices meant that the film could only be kept in sync by inserting a length of black film that was precisely the same length as the section that had been damaged and removed. For first-run theaters, this wasn't much of a problem, but second- and third-run houses often got rough, choppy prints that had a plethora of places where the picture went blank and the dialogue imperviously ground on.

As for record skips, a problem most common when discs had been well-used, projectionists grew fairly adept at coping with the situation. "We would hear a repeat," remembered Alvin Sloan, "and count how many times it repeated until we could get to the machine and pick up the needle. Then we'd put it down that many grooves ahead. Then we'd look at the screen to see if the sound was late or early; it was usually close, but not quite on. Then we'd move the needle one more time and that would generally do it; we grew quite proficient at it.

"What else could we do? You're halfway through a reel; if you stopped the show to rewind the reel and start all over again, it wouldn't solve anything, because when the record got to that same point, it would stick again. Of course, every time this happened, all sorts of things were going on downstairs with the audience . . ."

❏ ❏ ❏

Some directors coped with using sound by doing their level best, others flailed hopelessly, and still others displayed an attitude that, at least in retrospect, managed to lighten the static visuals and fuzzy recording. Josef von Sternberg's *Thunderbolt,* released in June 1929, displayed only shards of that gifted director's unparalleled visual instinct, and all of his perversity. A light rewrite of his silent film *Underworld*—with the booming George Bancroft as a good/bad gangster who proves himself a decent guy just as he's bundled off to the electric chair—the sound version lacks von Sternberg's customarily rich chiaroscuro, flattened by the necessity of shooting through plate glass.

Although variety of setting was stifled by the immobility of the microphone—the filmmakers coped by setting half the film in a prison cell—von Sternberg immediately seized on the contrapuntal possibilities of sound and image; when Bancroft runs from a police raid on a Harlem bar, guns fire offscreen, but von Sternberg keeps his camera focused on Fay Wray clutching her furs. (Even in his first talkie, von Sternberg had no interest in the wave of literal naturalism that sound was bringing to the movies.)

Like many of the films he would make with Marlene Dietrich, the script for *Thunderbolt* grafts conventional morality ("I wanna be decent again," moans Fay Wray) onto multiple opportunities for flamboyantly baroque, decadent images. But, with those images limited by circumstances beyond his control, von Sternberg's dramaturgy proves insufficient. He fills in the creative gaps and keeps himself amused by indulging his taste for straight-faced absurdity. Richard Arlen and his mother have a grab-ass romp on the bathroom floor; Bancroft demonstrates his essential good nature by adopting a bedraggled stray dog, which he keeps in his cell (nothing if not egalitarian, von Sternberg also gives Bancroft a cat squeeze toy); and, supremely, when Bancroft enters death row, we hear a barbershop quartet singing "Sweet Adeline."

Von Sternberg's haughty disdain could hardly be more obvious, but just in case anybody didn't notice, he made his sympathies plain in an article he wrote for *Esquire* in which he defined talkies as "a visual skeleton clattering with voices." Later, in his autobiography, he would speak icily of the "redundance" of sound, of the way "the camera had been able to impose a viewpoint on the image by a control of scope, angle, lens and light, but the . . . microphone . . . had no viewpoint . . . To be correctly and effectively used, sound had to bring to the image a quality other than what the lens included, a quality out of the range of the image . . . [but] sound became a blatant addition, a saccharine, charmless frosting . . ."

❑ ❑ ❑

A shapeless but bizarrely entertaining series of one-reel shorts called *The Voice of Hollywood* began production on Poverty Row at this time, featuring a conglomeration of second- and third-tier silent stars doing what amounted to voice tests, cheek by jowl with radio personalities doing what amounted to screen tests. *The Voice of Hollywood #9* featured Dorothy Jordan, the cowboy star Ken Maynard and his horse Tarzan, Marceline Day, Wesley Barry, and the evangelist Aimee Semple MacPherson, who ardently tells the audience that she is "hoping that talking moving pictures shall not only bear entertainment, but shall bring education to many, many thousands of people heretofore unreached."

The Voice of Hollywood #13 offered as hostess the serial star Ruth Roland, who does a tap dance; Charles King, who recites a poem; and (thank God!) Jack Benny, who dissuades Estelle Taylor from singing or dancing. The essential novelty of sound was rarely made more explicit than in these cheaply made, ramshackle shorts.

❑ ❑ ❑

Meanwhile, in July, shortly after completing his acquisitions of Loew's and Gaumont, William Fox was being driven to a Long Island golf date with Adolph Zukor, when he was broadsided by an inexperienced driver. The crash killed his chauffeur and put Fox in the hospital with multiple injuries. As far as Fox was concerned, it was deeply unfortunate, but not tragic. The doctors expected him to be on his feet around the first week of October 1929. Everything, he was assured, would be fine then.

CHAPTER 2

In terms of career and social politics, the closest thing Hollywood had to royalty were Douglas Fairbanks and Mary Pickford. They both confronted sound at the end of 1928 — Fairbanks gingerly, Pickford wholeheartedly.

Fairbanks had essentially completed production on *The Iron Mask,* a sequel to *The Three Musketeers,* by the beginning of 1929. But by that time, as William Bakewell, who was costarring with Fairbanks, recalled, "every silent in production had to have a sequence in sound. Fairbanks decided they ought to have a prologue, with a tapestry featuring D'Artagnan and the musketeers. There was a fanfare, Doug leans down, whips his sword around, and begins to speak.

"Well, everyone was nervous about it. [On the day it was shot] people were coming in from all over the lot but they wouldn't let them in. Doug was a professional man of the theater, and [even] he was uptight about it."

With good reason. A ten-foot-high blowup of a page of the Dumas novel simulating old parchment was mounted in a frame; Fairbanks was to slash through the page with his sword, leap through, and deliver his prologue speech.

"We did the scene over and over," recalled soundman Edward Bernds. "Even after all these years, I can remember Doug's lines: 'Out of these shadows of the past, as from a faded tapestry dim and vast, I bring you a tale of long ago.' Finally, we got a complete take, and, as was the barbaric custom in those days, we played it back. Sound equipment was touchy and inefficient then. Sometimes speed would go out of control. When we made that playback for Doug, we had a 'runaway' on the wax playback machine, just fast enough to give Doug a girlish falsetto. I was standing near him when that mincing gibberish came from the loudspeaker. He turned, not pale, but green. Mercifully, somebody pulled the loudspeaker plug, but I think Doug never really recovered from the shock of hearing that gibbering runaway version."

Fairbanks's voice turned out to be a serviceable, barking light baritone, slightly out of key with his glorious physicality. As an experienced stage actor, he could easily have modulated it, or projected less, but he didn't seem to care. It wasn't that Fairbanks was scared of technology; he had used the expensive, difficult, two-color Technicolor process to stunning effect in his 1926 film *The Black Pirate,* and he was a producer of integrity who firmly believed that innovation was a primary component of superior filmmaking. No, it was *this* technology he found lacking.

"He didn't like sound pictures," remembered his son, Douglas Fairbanks Jr. "He had a sense that his time of mime and ballet — and I use the phrase deliberately because he thought of silent films that way — were over. He liked telling a story visually, on the quite correct theory that the impact on the eye is greater than the impact on the ear."

Fairbanks had given sound a good deal of thought and instinctively understood that something different was going to be required. He told one critic that he had been "looking for a new formula. The old patterns will not fit . . . Just as Griffith showed us the essence of the silent picture technique in *The Birth of the Nation,* someone is going to create a standard of talking picture method. It has not come yet, and when it does arrive, it will be shaped either consciously or unconsciously by rhythm."

He pointed to the sprightly cadences of Walt Disney's experiments in character animation as the best example of what he thought talkies required. "These cartoons get their tremendous appeal from the perfect rhythm, in comedy tempo . . . It is not mere synchronization; it is more than that; it is a rhythmic, swinging, lilting thing, with what musicians call the proper accent-structure."

On some instinctive level, Fairbanks must have known that the needed innovation would have to come from someone besides him. At the age of forty-six, he had already given the best that was in him. *The Iron Mask* was one of the last silent — or, technically, part-talking — pictures that could be termed a financial success. Although Douglas Fairbanks would go on to make almost a half-dozen talkies, it was the last picture he would make that could be considered up to his standards.

Although more emotionally conservative than her husband, Mary Pickford elected to plunge into sound, not with anything as paltry as a single sequence, but with an entire movie, and one based on a successful Broadway show at that. George Abbott's production of *Coquette* had made a star of Helen Hayes, and this story of a head-strong young southern girl who is matured by tragedy was Pickford's choice for her talking debut.

Pickford's first sound-test was horrible, especially visually — at the age of thirty-seven, she was attempting to play a girl/woman of eighteen or twenty. Although it had been shot by her personal cameraman, Charles Rosher, the new lighting threw Rosher off his game. Rosher made a second test, this time without the diffusion filters on the lens, and it still looked bad. A desperate Pickford realized she couldn't afford an indifferently photographed debut in talkies and fired Rosher, who had been with her since 1917.

Pickford tried to hire George Barnes, but he was unavailable. The equally expert Karl Struss, who had collaborated with Rosher on *Sunrise,* and on Pickford's *Sparrows,* was brought in. Pickford retreated to her stage training and had the cast and crew in for two weeks of rehearsals. On the last several days, positions for four cameras were pegged for each scene. Most of the scenes ran for between three hundred and four hundred feet of film (three and a half to four and a half minutes), and sometimes the cameramen had to change their lenses in the middle of a scene in order to accommodate director Sam Taylor's unimaginative, stage-oriented blocking.

The picture climaxed with a ten-minute trial scene, which Struss and Taylor sought to shoot "in one," that is, playing it straight through, much as it would be done on a stage, but with six cameras to capture all the angles and shots that would be needed in the cutting room. The main fear was a power outage, as the lights for the six cameras were drawing 2,500 amps, and the feed-cables of the time were not equipped to handle such an influx of electricity. "However, the lights burned fifteen minutes," Struss would say, "and it took ten to get the scene from all angles. Everything went great and timed to perfection." The scene had been scheduled to be shot with conventional methods in five days, but Struss and Taylor managed to complete it in two.

Coquette was shot sound on film, with discs used only for playbacks on the set. As the film was being edited, Pickford realized she had a serious problem with one scene. "I just adore red roses" was her line, but with the panchromatic film, the roses, which were indeed red on the set, looked a pale cream on the screen. Pickford gave orders to rebuild the set and reshoot the scene, but soundman David Forrest saved his boss both time and money by taking the film back to the cutting room and managing to cut out the single word "red." Forrest's standing on the U.A. lot took a sudden upward swing.

When *Coquette* was released in March of 1929, it was an enormous hit. "Mary Pickford has made the transition to the new medium with flying colors," enthused Edwin Schallert of the *Los Angeles Times*, who called it "a great picture . . . *Coquette* [is] the first real star picture, outside of the two Al Jolsons, to appear in the new spoken word form. It is the first big film produced by a big old-line picture star and favorite."

In fact, *Coquette* was and is witheringly bad, with performances that derive from the Belasco era of American theater. Even the great William Cameron Menzies is reduced to replicating stage sets. Director Sam Taylor resorts to stage techniques, such as gradually darkening the set — to indicate sunset — until the actors are in silhouette, and not cutting until an actor completely exits the frame, instead of cutting on the initial forward movement, as was common in silents.

Nevertheless, the public, curious about the voice of an old favorite, attended in sufficient numbers for the film to gross $1.4 million domestically (it cost a nominal $489,000), providing Pickford with her biggest hit ever — and the illusion that sound might lengthen her career rather than brutally shorten it.

But her next production, *The Taming of the Shrew*, costarring

Fairbanks, had only a minor success, despite the fact that it was quite an entertaining, if slight, abridgment of the Shakespeare play. "We didn't use booms on *Taming*," remembered Ed Bernds. "We hung multiple mikes." Douglas Fairbanks quickly gave Bernds the nickname of "ERPI," and demonstrated for the delighted young soundman his dexterity in goosing unsuspecting people with the scabbard of his sword.

Despite its breezy charm, *The Taming of the Shrew* was the beginning of a downward spiral for both stars that would never be reversed. Each of Pickford's four talkies grossed less than the one before it. She made her last, *Secrets,* in 1933; Douglas Fairbanks's final film, *The Private Life of Don Juan,* was released a year later.

❑ ❑ ❑

The new technology quickly spawned new slang terms. "Spot the mike" meant to place the microphones; if an actor was booming his lines, he was "over-shooting"; if he wasn't projecting enough, he was "under-shooting." "Lock 'em up" was the command to close the doors of the airless camera booths, entombing the cameramen like unfortunates in a story by Poe. "Marked up" meant that the cameras and recording machines were ready for electric current; "turn 'em over" was directed to the recorder to complete the synchronization of camera and recorders.

The studios were now required to hire all sorts of people who had never been necessary during the days of silent pictures. MGM hired a piano tuner to tend its thirty-seven pianos, from grands to uprights. Paramount found itself with nineteen projectionists and fifty sound engineers. Each studio hired a full assemblage of sound effects technicians, but their jobs were hampered by the primitive quality of the microphones. Someone quietly shelling peanuts next to an open mike contributed a sound that resembled sharp crashes of thunder and lightning. A woman wearing silk stockings and crossing her legs produced something akin to the noise of a Kansas cyclone.

Often, the technicians had to devise synthetic noises to replicate real ones that were either too explosive or somehow sounded false when recorded. Rifle fire was faked by breaking kitchen matches; wind through the trees was produced by the old stage technique of revolving a canvas strip over a cylinder of wooden slats; a falling body was simulated by dropping a ripe pumpkin; collapsing buildings were replicated by tearing heavy paper very near the microphone. As for cyclones, well, the technicians took advantage of serendipity and rubbed silk stockings together.

While new departments were springing up in every studio, old departments were changing both practically and metaphorically. Scripts changed, became far more specific, far less impressionistic. Here, for instance, is page 5 of the shooting script written by Carl Mayer for Murnau's *Sunrise* of 1927:

> Fading in from lit candlestick
> Simple rustic room
> Wardrobe open.
> Dresses hanging inside.
> Valises and trunk in b.g.
> Now:
> The vamp walks into the picture.
> In very short negligee, with limbs exposed.
> A typical creature from a big city.
> Beautiful.
> Racy.
> Coquettish?
> Just lighting a cigarette at the burning
> candle.
> Now smiling and looking around.
> What should she wear?
> So — scrutinizing her dresses.
> Very self-centered and coquettish . . .

Later in the film, after the wife realizes the husband has meant to kill her, they scramble onto the shore and she flees.

> Continually after her!
> With hands stretched out toward her.
> Yelling after her from the
> depth of his soul.
> And then:

Awful!
Did she fall?
Entangled in the reeds?
He falls down before her.
Terrified — trying to calm
her.
But quickly she gets to her
feet, away from him.
Awe-struck — slightly
trembling.
Like an animal about to be
slaughtered.
Terrified — benumbed — escaping
him.
He, who has no more strength
left.
Now shocked — cowering in the
reeds.
His hands empty.
From which she escaped.
Quick cut again.

The Mayer script is impressionistic blank verse, concentrating more on emotional tone than on specific visuals or acting gestures. Give it to five different directors and you'd get five radically different films. And there are no words. "For silent pictures," explained writer-director Frank Tuttle, "writers made their characters speak by their actions."

But talkies demanded a far more specific foundation; give the script for an early talkie, even a good one, to five different directors and the differences would be far less severe. Compare Mayer's poem to this excerpt from the script of Paramount's 1929 *The Studio Movie Mystery:*

OUTSIDE BORKA SET — close shot
Helen, staring through the aperture into the set, covers her face with her hands, and starts to sink slowly to the floor, her body shaken by great sobs.

> Tony rushes out from the set to her, and
> catches her in his arms.
> TONY: (Whispering) Helen! You knew all about this—
> Helen, baby—tell me!
> HELEN: (Moaning) No—no—I didn't know anything—
> what is it?

Beyond the banality of the dialogue and the strong stage directions, the nature of the dialogue in a given scene implicitly demanded
a certain style of presentation. Add to that the producers' demands
in shooting style—to give them choices in the editing room—and
the result was that movies became more heavily indicative, less atmospheric . . . and far more under the sway of producers.

"You could change the entire meaning of a scene [in a silent screen-
play] with a subtitle," remembered producer David Lewis. "Frances
Marion once told me how many silent pictures she had twisted and
turned with subtitles." Lenore Coffee was famous for being able to
completely reverse the meaning of a silent film with a title or two,
and she remarked that "a silent film was like writing a novel, and a
script [for a talking picture] was like writing a play. That's why
women dropped out. Women had been good novelists, but in talking
pictures women were not predominant."

But where silent screenplays could be likened to a skeletal map,
pointing the direction without specifying the route, sound screenplays
became exhaustively complete road maps, providing all sorts of sug-
gestive routes and signs by which the dramatic trip could be made,
often reducing the director to the status of glorified traffic cop.

"In silent films, meaning was more abstract," remembered King
Vidor. "Take a [scene with a] crap game. In silent pictures, it could
be taken that they were betting five or ten dollars, or even five or
ten cents. It was wide open, but with sound, I realized that I suddenly had to pin the exact figure down . . . We were going from an
abstract, impressionistic mood, to saying things in exact terms.

"It took years to get back to having pictures that left some things
unsaid. In a silent film you couldn't leave to get popcorn because
you might miss something. The minute sound came in, you could
get up, walk around, maybe go out and buy some ice cream, and you
could still hear the sound track and you wouldn't miss anything."

Because words were more important now, a script that might have made do with one or two writers now took four or five, all of them working to the specifications of the producer. MGM assigned eleven writers to a musical called *It's a Great Life*. Some worked for as many as twenty-six days, some for as few as three. Associate producer Lawrence Weingarten complained to Thalberg that "[Al Boasberg, Ransom Rideout, Frances Marion, and Lew Lipton] have not worked on story since I've been here. I note that they have charged both Lipton and Marion to the story but I think this must be an error." Assuming Weingarten was right, that still leaves seven writers hashing over a backstage musical.

Subtly but irrevocably, sound shifted film production from the personal to the industrial, moved the balance of power from director to producer. Great directors like Ford, Capra, and Wyler would still maintain control in the sound era, but to cut through the accreting layers of management and supervisory personnel a director increasingly had to rely on his intimidating personality or the success of his films, rather than the divine right of his job title.

As for audiences, they no longer had to concentrate actively on the movie before them; watching silent movies was and is a far more tiring experience than watching talkies. Now, the convenient expedient of words could do all the work for both technicians and audiences.

But there was a way out: not the conventions of silence, certainly not stage technique, but, rather, a hybrid. *Bulldog Drummond* and Fox's 1929 release of *In Old Arizona* seemed to point the way, for the latter picture startled critics and audiences by its use of outdoor sound.*

"I was prepared to hear people speak," recalled one amazed audience member, "but the other sounds surprised me — a train whistle,

---

* The extensive, natural location sound was also made possible by Arthur Edeson, a great, if largely unheralded, cameraman who had personally reengineered his camera till it was about 50 percent quieter than the conventional Mitchell camera. With the addition of a single heavy blanket, Edeson was able to leave behind the camera booths, which he called "sound houses." Edeson imperiously claimed never to have used one, because "you couldn't get good photography." He would utilize the same camera for *All Quiet on the Western Front*, which would have been impossible to photograph otherwise.

the bark of a dog, the hoofbeats of horses we could see." What proved especially amazing was off-screen sound: the audience heard the footsteps of a man before they saw him.

What with the sudden immobility of the camera and the preponderance of dialogue, movies were becoming an adjunct of radio. A reporter from *Sound Waves* (February 15, 1929) visited Universal's new talkie stages, and, in a remarkably detailed I-am-a-camera article, observed "cameras . . . in sound-proof cages, five feet square and seven feet high. These are padded cells set on rollers with two plate glass windows in the front, one for the camera to shoot through and the other for the director to observe the action. The door is of the refrigerator lock type and makes the cell air tight . . .

"A series of a half dozen microphones are held out over the set by long counter-balanced arms. They are just above the camera range . . . Other microphones are set off-stage near various sound devices. In this scene there is a storm outside. There must be lightning, the roar of thunder, the patter of raindrops on the windows and room, and the whine of wind. One microphone is set near a suspended sheet of tin, which gives the thunder; another near a sprinkler [that] gives the patter of rain, and a third near a canvas roller wind-effect machine . . .

"On the balcony on one side of the stage is a glass-enclosed monitor room where the sounds from the various microphones are properly mixed. Each microphone is connected with a rheostat by which the volume of sound from that particular microphone can be regulated . . .

"In another recording room, at the same time the sound is being recorded on the film, it is being recorded on a wax record. Immediately after the scene is completed this record, which is a test record, is played back to the director and if it is satisfactory and contains no flaws in speech, lost syllables, mispronounced words, poor pausing between words or hesitation on an actor's part in recalling his lines, the scene is approved and production progresses to the next scene."

Actors with stage experience could adjust to the lack of spoken direction during a scene, but those who were too young to have spent much time onstage could be unstrung. Alice White, a jazz-baby actress at First National, was particularly stunned. At the best of times, White wasn't much of an actress — she had been a script girl for Charlie Chaplin only a few years before—and director Mervyn LeRoy remembered that "you had to tell her everything you wanted her to do, and then go out and practically do it for her." For a dance scene in an early talkie called *Naughty Baby,* a desperate LeRoy resorted to waving a handkerchief at her when he wanted her to move her arms. If semaphores worked for the Navy, they could work at First National.

Over at Paramount, the predominant cause of worry seems to have been not sound effects, but laughs, that is to say, the timing of pauses so that audience laughter wouldn't drown out the next line of the comedy called *The Dummy.* Director Robert Milton devised a special loudspeaker that fed out of the mixer's booth. When the actor delivered his line, the laughter from the technicians in the booth feeding onto the stage helped set the actor's timing. But before he began laughing, the mixer had to hit a circuit breaker so that the microphones on the stage cut off and wouldn't pick up laughter from the loudspeaker.

Of course, this wouldn't work on the second or third takes, after the joke had ceased to be funny; nor would it work if the technicians had a defective sense of humor, or were too late to cut off the actor's mike, or too quick to turn it back on, while the mixer's laughter was still being absorbed by the mattresses that lined the soundstages.

Where directors had been able to talk actors through their scenes, gently guiding them via the verbal pulling of strings, now they had to remain quiet during the take. Even Lionel Barrymore, who had never directed theater or silent films, found it difficult. Pondering the question of communicating with his actors, the apparently inarticulate Barrymore came up with the worst possible solution, deriving from an old scam used by stage mind-readers, in which answers were sent to fake psychics through small electrical shocks in telegraphic code. He installed a small medical battery that would send out just enough voltage to give the actors mild jolts in prearranged signals.

This was madness, life in moviemaking hell. That any good movies were made at all amid such conditions of physical claustrophobia, narrative obfuscation, and an unimaginably confusing technical nightmare of crossed cables and purposes, was a heroic feat. And sometimes even a bad movie was so interesting that quality was irrelevant.

The future screenwriter Sidney Gilliat *(The Lady Vanishes)* adored silent films and hated the first few talkies he saw. Then he saw a Ruth Chatterton film taken from James M. Barrie and felt the future wash over him.

"It was a complete thing on its own," says Gilliat. "The lighting was different from what you got on silent films because of the incandescent lamps, which they used because of the sound track, and that gave it a different look. I still felt that talkies had nothing to do with art, but did have something very immediate. The audience felt a part of a whole new medium. Looking back, it was probably like a photographed stage play, but when I came out of the cinema, I said, 'Talkies are here and they're here to stay!' That totally forgotten film was the one that convinced me."

❏ ❏ ❏

On May 19, 1929, on the occasion of the very first Academy Awards ceremony, Warner Bros. was given a special Oscar for their trumping of the industry. Jack was out of town — the ceremony, held at the Hollywood Roosevelt Hotel, was no big deal, not at first — so Darryl Zanuck accepted the award for him. "This award," said Zanuck in acceptance, "is dedicated to the late Sam Warner, the man responsible for the successful usage of the medium."

After all the speeches had been made, Al Jolson got up to entertain. "I notice they gave *The Jazz Singer* a statuette, but they didn't give me one," he said. "I could use one; they look heavy, and I could use another paperweight." And then Jolson lunged: "For the life of me, I can't see what Jack Warner would do with one of them. It can't say yes."

Although never regarded as a particularly penetrating intellect, Jolson had a gift for prophecy. His line about Jack Warner would prove as prophetic as "You ain't heard nothin' yet."

CHAPTER 3

It was not enough merely to fine-tune the lists of desirable actors and directors; the specific kinds of movies that were made began to change. First National had long had a mildly profitable sideline in series westerns starring Ken Maynard, a gifted trick rider with a serious drinking problem. (Sober, Maynard was a nice guy; drunk, he was a truculent wild man, given to shooting at coworkers with live ammunition.)

Upon taking possession of First National, Jack Warner ordered the Maynard company back to Burbank from location in Ogden, Utah. At first they tried shooting around planes coming and going from Burbank Airport, but the Maynard company was soon forced to work nights, outside, while construction began on First National's soundstages.

After Maynard finished his contract, Jack let him and the rest of the western unit go. The Vitaphone engineers had informed him that, because of the mainly outdoor production requirements, talking westerns could be an expensive proposition. Actually, Jack had little interest in westerns and used sound problems as a good excuse to cut them out.

MGM did the same thing with Tim McCoy, the studio's only western star, despite the fact that his pictures, made for the rock-bottom price of less than $50,000 apiece, were consistently profitable. McCoy spent six months out of work ("Nobody had ever

heard of me," McCoy remembered. "I was out of the business . . . "),
but he finally caught a break and went over to Universal and made
The Indians Are Coming, the first sound serial and a highly profitable one. With the majors deciding B westerns were too much
trouble to bother with, and with big-budget westerns being commercially iffy, production of westerns shifted to the low-budget studios
on Hollywood's "Poverty Row." Westerns were still made, but the
genre entered a period of decline that wouldn't be arrested until
1939, with Ford's *Stagecoach.*

Nothing was safe—not genres, not directors, not dogs. Warner
Bros. decided to release Rin Tin Tin because, as one company lawyer
wrote in a memo, "The making of any animal pictures . . . is not in
keeping with the policy that has been adopted by us for talking
pictures, very obviously, of course, because dogs don't talk . . ."

In the late summer of the year, the young Universal contract
director William Wyler made his first all-talkie, an adaptation of
Peter B. Kyne's venerable drama *Three Godfathers.* The title was
Hell's Heroes; the locations were the Mojave Desert and the Pana-
mint Valley, on the edge of Death Valley. Although the camera was
still in a big box, Wyler refused the easy alternative of immobility.

"The camera had to keep moving," explained Wyler, "because the
nature of this story was such that the men who were being pursued
had to keep moving. When they stopped and talked, we had to bury
a microphone in a cactus. And we had to push that [camera] box
without making any noise. It was tough, with a guy on top of the
box and a microphone hanging over and guys pushing the box in the
sand in 110- or 120-degree heat. One time we opened the box and
the cameraman had passed out, because inside it was 150 degrees."

Sound altered cinematography for the worse, but it hadn't done
film editors any favors either. Formerly working strictly for pace,
rhythm, and storytelling, editors working with the Movietone system now had to learn to handle precisely twice the amount of film
they had before, as well as how to match up sound with image.

Sound Moviolas hadn't been devised yet, so editors were forced
to become reasonably proficient lip-readers and, to a lesser extent,
to be able to read the sound track by the look of the modulations.
"Most of us learned to distinguish the different categories of sound,"
remembered Edward Dmytryk, "such as dialogue, music, or crowd

noise (called 'walla-walla' in the cutting rooms) and to pick out certain spoken consonants, of which . . . S was the easiest to identify."

Hardly anybody seems to have been happy at this stage. Like Wyler's unfortunate cameraman, like harried editors, exhibitors were squeezed and producers were scared. Costs had risen 15 percent since 1927, an increase attributable to the price of sound equipment and the skyrocketing demand for film stock needed for multiple cameras. Economy became a watchword. Paramount issued an edict limiting the number of takes a director could print to two.

Business had never been better for projectionists, however; they had the strongest labor union in motion pictures, a branch of IATSE (International Alliance of Theatrical Stage Employees). By 1929, the number of projectionists had doubled, courtesy of the labor-intensive nature of Vitaphone, and projectionists' earnings rose nearly 15 percent.

But musicians, both inside Hollywood and out, took a terrible hit. One of the selling points Western Electric would use in pitching sound to theaters was that the cost of wiring a theater for sound could be almost instantly covered by the elimination of house orchestras. Midway through the year, the American Federation of Musicians held its annual convention, and the primary topic of discussion was the loss of jobs due to the talkies. A position paper decreed that the nation's culture was in jeopardy from the "mechanization" of recorded music, which was replacing live performances.

"As soon as sound was definitely in, all the theater orchestras were let go immediately," remembered Gaylord Carter, who was the organist at the Paramount Theater in Los Angeles. "I recall a headline in the *Los Angeles Times:* SOUND DRIVES ORGANISTS FROM THEATERS, MANAGERS REJOICE. They hated to pay us, you see; I was making $100 a week. Even so, a few of the name organists, Jesse Crawford, me, were kept on.

"The whole thing collapsed. The Los Angeles Theater Organist Club had about forty members, and I don't know where most of them went. Some went into teaching piano; one guy went into insurance and became a millionaire. I ended up going into radio, on *The Amos and Andy Show,* for twice as much money."

Jack Caldwell, an organist at the Palace Theater in Dallas, remembered that "we had forty men, good musicians. And they said, 'Aw, it won't ever happen.' Well, it did happen . . . 'That's just a fad,' [they said.] 'It'll be good to be off two weeks, then we'll be right back in the pit.' Well, they haven't been back there since!"

Loew's New York theaters eliminated all orchestras and organists as early as November 1928; other cities quickly followed suit. Musicians hired to keep actors in the proper mood on the set also disappeared; MGM estimated that set musicians, making about $90 a week apiece, had cost them $52,000 in 1927. By 1929, that expense was down to zero. In the country at large, during the 1928–29 season, more than 2,600 musicians lost their jobs as theaters were wired for sound. One conductor, whose theater had just done away with an orchestra that cost $2,850 a week, went to the president of the distribution company and, in a burst of desperation, threatened to put sound pictures out of business via strikes.

"Good," was the answer. "If you can do that, I'll give you a million dollars."

Some musicians relocated to Hollywood to work in studio orchestras. Broadway composer/arranger/conductors such as Max Steiner and Herbert Stothart, journeymen professionals experienced in all areas of musical theater, came west to adapt the music that was familiar to them, and many stayed to become composers of film music.

Some musicians weren't that lucky; the unemployment rate at many local unions went up to 50 percent. "I played the violin in a theater in Camden, New Jersey, for $125 a week," recalled a musician named Albert Green. "It dropped to $30 a month playing for the WPA in a government-provided orchestra. This was a wound to my self-esteem that tormented me for the rest of my life. Musicians who had only one skill to contribute to the labor market . . . were shoved out of the way [and could no longer] make a living."

The musicians blamed the exhibitors, but the exhibitors had problems of their own. Almost all of them had outfitted themselves with Vitaphone turntables, and now rumors were beginning to spread that Vitaphone was doomed, and that Movietone, or some variation thereof, was the system of the future. Trade papers began to fill up with ads offering small-town exhibitors the best — and in some cases, the worst — of both worlds. A sound-on-film projector and amplifier could cost as little as $1,995 ("For as little as 50 cents a day . . ."), while a projector with attachments for both systems could run as high as $6,500.

Off-brand turntables could be had for as little as $500 a pair, while off-brand equipment that could completely equip a small-town theater could be had for as little as $775 ("Includes two Mellaphone turntables, two dynamic cone speakers, Sampson six-tube amplifier, tubes complete, pick-up and fader"). For a small-town theater, buying two of any of these units was a serious investment; the money was about the same as buying a house, but with less possibility of appreciation. Still, it was either invest or get out of the business. According to historian Douglas Gomery, about five thousand of the twenty-five thousand total theaters (a figure that includes open-air and traveling exhibitors) did pull out, leaving the twenty thousand best-financed exhibitors still standing.

❑ ❑ ❑

The production of sound shorts proceeded at a nominal pace. While the shorts weren't as important as had been thought in 1926–27, the studios believed that audiences had been conditioned to expect them as part of the cinematic experience, and responded accordingly. Yet, the shorts were treated with an increasing casualness.

"I was having dinner with Jack Benny at Arthur Lyons's, Jack's agent's, house," remembered George Burns. "At that time, Jack was getting about $500 to 700 a week in vaudeville, and Gracie and I were getting $350.

"Arthur came over to Jack and said, 'How would you like to make $1,800 tomorrow?'

" 'How?'

" 'Fred Allen was supposed to do a short for Paramount and he fell out.'

"Well, Jack couldn't do it, but I said I could. We were set to do our street-corner act, but when we arrived at the studio, they had set up a living-room set for Fred Allen. We had to ad-lib.

" 'Gracie, if we can talk for five minutes, we can make $1,800.'

" 'Where's the audience?'

" 'See the camera? The audience is there. Do you think you can talk for five minutes?'

" 'Ask me how my brother is.'

"After that we signed for four shorts at $3,500 a short."

And what did the practiced vaudevillian think of himself when he first saw Burns and Allen on the screen?

"I thought I was great. I asked me for my autograph."

❏ ❏ ❏

King Vidor had returned from location work for *Hallelujah* to find MGM spreading and darkening in all directions. Twenty-two sound-stages were hurriedly being constructed; cement-block hangars were replacing the six glass-fronted stages that Mayer and Thalberg had taken over five years earlier. New buildings for sound and music were going up, and existing departments for wardrobe, props, research, and so on were being enlarged. The space for all this came at the expense of acres of landscaped gardens that had given the Culver City studio a relaxed, sylvan atmosphere. A factory that looked and often felt like a country club now looked like . . . a factory.

Vidor attempted to synchronize the silent footage he had shot in Tennessee and Arkansas with dialogue tracks and quickly ran up against nearly insurmountable obstacles. In long shots, it was impossible to read an actor's lips to determine just what line they had been speaking, and, in any case, much of the on-location dialogue had been improvised. Vidor tried rigging a push button from the projection room to the booth. When an actor in the silent footage began speaking, Vidor would push the button and the projectionist would make a grease-pencil line on the film that could be a starting point for the dialogue.

When they checked the synchronization, they found that they were anywhere from two to six feet off — the lag time between Vidor pressing the button and the operator reaching into the projector mechanism with his grease pencil. After much improvisational effort in the primitive art of dubbing, the film was finally finished.

Hallelujah was released in August 1929. Paul Robeson loathed the picture; W. E. B. Du Bois endorsed it. *Variety* smacked its lips over

Nina Mae McKinney, saying that "she comes closest to being the Clara Bow of her race," and thought that the picture would "to the whites [be] a big, entertaining picture. To the negroes it will either be a gigantic sensation . . . or looked upon as holding up some of the ancient sacred rites of the race to ridicule. Most likely the former." *The Film Daily* liked it ("Notable and, in the main, impressive . . .") but thought it had dubious potential at the box office.

Because exhibitors anticipated a large black turnout, they were terrified that white patrons would stay away. This dilemma was resolved in New York by holding the premiere at two theaters: one in midtown Manhattan, the other in Harlem. Blacks who came to the Manhattan theater had to sit in the balcony.

While *Hallelujah* usually played good theaters in the north — the Capitol in New York, the Stillman in Cleveland, the Fox Palace and Criterion in Los Angeles — in Boston both the Loew's and the RKO circuits refused to play it. As a result, the film ended up playing in Symphony Hall, the home of the Boston Symphony, in April 1930, almost a year after it was first released. *Billboard* reported the box-office results as "good." As Mayer and Thalberg had feared, *Hallelujah* appears to have received no bookings at all in the South, outside of a date in Dallas. It ended up with a world gross of $725,049 — not a great hit, not a great flop, just "one of those pictures."

Vidor's film examines the connection between the dual ecstasies of religion and sex with considerable cunning. The basic tale — a good, hardworking man is brought low by a Bad Girl, but he recovers and struggles his way toward respectability — aims for and attains the quality of archetypal folk-fable, and it's no accident that the film captures much of the operatic quality of *Porgy* while retaining a documentary directness. With the exception of Nina Mae McKinney and the dignified Daniel Haynes, the acting tends toward the apostrophic, but Vidor's sense of landscape is worthy of Corot, and sound enabled him to give a voice to the devil he always saw in nature, and in the primary temptation of sex.

The first half of the film is a quasi-musical, with four song numbers, including two contributed by Irving Berlin at Thalberg's request. As it happens, the songs are good; "Swanee Shuffle" in particular has the authentically sleazy feel of a juke joint at 3 A.M.

Later in the film Vidor does what Rouben Mamoulian would be overpraised for: he uses a song as a transitional device, and carries its performance through different locations (Daniel Haynes begins a number on a levee, continues it riding on a train, and completes it on a country road).

Because so much of the film was shot silent, Vidor takes his rhythm from the cutting of the silent footage, and the sound editing is far in advance of the time. One scene, a tracking shot of a wagon moving down the street, with the music changing from barrelhouse to blues depending on what bar the wagon is passing, must have been maddeningly difficult for the sound editors; the orgasmic revival sequence, shot at the studio, is a high-water mark of early sound montage.

With these scenes, and with the chase through the swamps at the end, Vidor doesn't attempt exact synchronization, but rather an impressionistic effect of appropriate sounds: slurping mud, slapping water, panting, bird cries.

Vidor's vision of the black man as a primitive hedonist who finds salvation in singing locks the film in its time, but Vidor was always drawn to pagans, and the way in which the characters' sexuality is subsumed by the ardor of their revivalist religion seems remarkably prescient. The director's attitude is attentive, affectionate, and never patronizing. The film's sense of texture, of dusty roads, rough-hewn log buildings, shacks, and grief, is remarkable.

The wonder is that, having seen *Hallelujah,* so many filmmakers continued the stylistic pedantry that was increasingly unnecessary. By any standards, *Hallelujah* is a fine film, but it is inestimably superior to the other all-black film, Fox's *Hearts in Dixie,* which beat *Hallelujah* to the marketplace in March. Preceded by a prologue in which it is helpfully explained that all people feel the same emotions, *Hearts in Dixie* is a story of singin' songs, pickin' cotton, and eatin' chicken on de ol' plantation. Blacks are portrayed as illiterate primitives ("De doctor ain't no good 'cept for white folks" is a sample of the folk wisdom imparted), and the proceedings are only partially redeemed by a musical number in which Stepin Fetchit sings, "I'm sick, I'm weak, I'm feeble." At the end, Clarence Muse, playing the main character, sells his mule in order to send his son to college. Throughout *Hearts in Dixie,* minstrel-show condescension drips from the screen.

Beyond the Reconstruction-era racial politics, *Hearts in Dixie* is technically quite good; Fox's location sound is superior to MGM's or Paramount's. Moreover, *Hearts in Dixie* utilizes overdubbing, and there's a long tracking shot with synchronized sound that was surely one of the first uses of the boom mike. Interestingly, this movie, which combined the innocuous and the awful, struck a particularly deep chord with William Fox, who ran it over and over again at the projection room of his mansion, Fox Hall.

❏ ❏ ❏

Of all the MGM stars, the most profitable, in terms of cost-to-gross, was not John Gilbert, not Norma Shearer, Joan Crawford, or Greta Garbo, but Lon Chaney. Chaney's MGM films were invariably B movies whose sole distinctions were their under- (and sometimes over-) tones of the grotesque and the arabesque, and the charisma of their star. Costing between $200,000 and $300,000 apiece, the films each reliably netted about that much. Since Chaney made four pictures a year, MGM was making a minimum of a million dollars a year on him, a very satisfying return on Chaney's salary of $3,750 a week as of March 1929.

Despite his salary, Chaney was far from being a company man; indeed his manner and value system were rigorously and proudly working-class. While he never complained overmuch about scripts, basically taking what he was given, he refused to give the company anything beyond what he was contractually obligated to, and he had the workingman's instinctive distrust of his bosses.

In April, MGM studio manager M. E. Greenwood shot off a memo to L. B. Mayer about a proposed Chaney talkie, saying that "one of the things Lon Chaney was extremely concerned about yesterday was why [Laurence] Stallings should be writing dialogue on the Foreign Legion [picture] when nothing has been said to Lon as to whether he would consent to talk. His contract does not provide for his talking . . ."

Before he would make a talkie, Chaney wanted to renegotiate his contract. He didn't want a spectacular jump in salary; he did want a

$150,000 cash bonus. Clearly, Chaney had either managed to sneak a look at the company books or had very good instincts for his worth. But the actor's negotiating position was complicated by his failing health; cancer had been discovered in his bronchial area, and, during the latter part of 1929, MGM took him off payroll for several months because he was unable to work.

MGM refused to pay a bonus, any bonus, until Chaney took a voice test they could classify as successful—a transparently phony negotiating ploy, as Chaney's voice, a deep baritone with a slight rasp from his years of heavy smoking, was precisely the kind of voice they already knew recorded well.

MGM counteroffered a bonus of $25,000 for a five-year deal that would ultimately bring his salary to $11,250 a week, but they still insisted on a voice test. Chaney agreed to all the provisions but the bonus, which he insisted must be no less than $50,000. Louis B. Mayer then countered with an offer of $75,000, of which $25,000 would be a bonus and $50,000 would be paid back to MGM over two years. That is to say, the same offer they had made originally, together with a no-interest loan that Chaney didn't need and hadn't asked for.

Chaney was adamant; no bonus, no deal. Thalberg and Mayer's petty avarice was—and is—bewildering. MGM was haggling over $25,000—$500 a week—for a star who was bringing them a clear profit of a million dollars a year, and was likely to bring them even more. Was their obstinacy psychological, or were they afraid of setting a dangerous precedent that other stars would seek to replicate?

MGM was also engaged in similar tussling with a star who carried more prestige than Chaney's bread-and-butter appeal: reigning diva Greta Garbo. MGM wanted to get Garbo into a talkie as quickly as possible. They had tentatively planned on using her in their all-star *Hollywood Revue*, but were stymied by her contract, which provided that "she shall be starred or costarred, but if costarred, with a male star only." Half the actors in *Hollywood Revue* were female, thus costars. In addition, Garbo obstinately refused to sign a rider to her contract covering dialogue. "In this respect," said an internal MGM memo, "she is the one exception in our stock company. The question of her signing was discussed ... but she declined to sign, giving as her reason, as I recall it, lack of confidence in the English tongue."*

Garbo procrastinated endlessly; *The Kiss,* her last silent film, wasn't released until November 1929. Eventually, even Garbo realized that she could not be the only star in pictures — always excepting Chaplin — to continue basking in silence. Chaplin worked for himself and could do what he liked; Garbo worked for MGM and, ultimately, did what they liked. Louis B. Mayer got her to agree to make *Anna Christie* by allowing Jacques Feyder, a favorite of hers, to direct an export version in German, a language with which she was comfortable, costarring her friend Salka Viertel in the Marie Dressler part. First, however, she had to make the film in English, to be directed by Clarence Brown.

Anna Christie went into production on October 7, with Thalberg allotting eleven days for rehearsal and nineteen for production. Shooting was uneventful, even though the picture shot some exteriors in Venice, California; the production wrapped on November 18, only one day behind schedule. The German version was shot as a separate film in December and January, with supervision by Paul Bern, and the O'Neill translation in the hands of Frank Reicher (who would later play the ship's captain in *King Kong*).

Feyder's version is superior to Clarence Brown's, in spite of the fact that Salka Viertel's Marthy lacks Marie Dressler's ravaged humanity. The German adaptation is less stagy, more cinematic — Feyder tosses off a few innovative deep-focus shots worthy of William Wyler and Gregg Toland — and Garbo gives a performance that is simultaneously freer and more focused than in the first, English version. This could be because the first version in effect served as a lengthy rehearsal, but Feyder also costumes her to look more like an authentic prostitute than was thought acceptable for American consumption. Feyder's version is eight minutes longer but seems ten

---

* In fact, Garbo never did sign the rider; MGM decided not to press the matter, for, as a legal memo stated, "by her talking in *Anna Christie* ... she has construed talking as part of her contract. [MGM's lawyers] feel that if she refused to talk now, we would have the same rights as though the talking provision was in her contract. Furthermore, it is to her interest to talk."

minutes—at least—shorter. None of these differences really mattered, of course. The only question anyone wanted answered was, Can Garbo talk? In any language, Garbo's deep, throaty contralto added a grave, musical inevitability to the fateful quality already embodied in her silent performances.

Other MGM stars sailed into sound with no apparent cares. Joan Crawford's all-talkie debut, *Untamed,* begins as a drama with music set in South America, then makes a choppy transition to a society romance in which the lovers are reconciled only after she attempts to murder him. The film's tone shifts with every new scene. At no time does any character in *Untamed* resemble any human being who ever lived, but its flamboyant unreality gives the film a vaguely comic, unintentional charm.

Crawford's costar, a polished new contract player named Robert Montgomery, on his way to a respectable career and an off-screen reputation as one of the chilliest, most pompous actors ever to find his way to Hollywood, slid effortlessly into the brash-but-decent slot that had heretofore been relegated to William Haines. As for MGM's leading ingenue, Crawford proved only that, while her acting was shaky, it was better than her singing and dancing.

Clearly, Thalberg and company wanted to try Crawford out in a variety of material and didn't feel they could afford to take a few years to do it. Were it not for Crawford's boundless energy, flashing sensuality, and popularity with the shopgirl audience, Thalberg might have given her up as a bad job.

❑ ❑ ❑

It was always easy for actors, writers, and directors to mistake Irving Thalberg for the good cop, if only because he was the alternative to Louis B. Mayer's blatantly manipulative, Darwinian bad cop. Simply because Thalberg had read some books made him seem like a brother-in-arms to the waves of writers that were being signed to contracts. As Jim Tully, who knew and liked Thalberg, wrote in a *Vanity Fair* profile, "Thalberg . . . has a quick mentality that runs in narrow grooves. If it were deeper and vaster and more profound, he would be a financial failure in the business of films."

True, Thalberg did have a boyish charm he could turn on when it suited him. On one occasion at Universal, before he went over to

MGM, Thalberg was casting a William Desmond picture, and was attempting to calm a director worried because Esther Ralston was taller than Desmond. "Come here, Esther," said Thalberg, standing up behind his desk. Ralston walked over to him and for the first time noticed that she and the small Thalberg were the same height.

"You see? You know that Bill Desmond towers over me," Thalberg assured the director. Looking down, Ralston saw that Thalberg was standing on his tiptoes. Ralston got the part.

"Unlike Selznick, he was not a memo writer," remembered David Lewis, an associate of Thalberg's. "Things were discussed face to face . . . Occasionally, he would write a memo, but he was not at his best with the written word. Sometimes, he would even try to write a scene. But while the idea was generally excellent, the delivery was invariably disastrous. He wanted to be a writer more than anything in the world, but he just didn't have the flair for writing, and he was too stubborn to admit it. But the way his mind moved and the depth of his character understanding [were] magnificent."

In regard to Thalberg, the experiences of J. C. Nugent, an old vaudeville and theatrical hand of no particular distinction, were indicative. While Nugent had no interest in movies and couldn't tell John Gilbert from Adolphe Menjou, he had a modest, demonstrable gift for dialogue and had been recommended by Robert Benchley. MGM signed him for $1,500 a week. Arriving in Hollywood, he was driven to MGM and, after the usual wait, was told that "Mr. Thalberg will see you now."

"And who is Mr. Thalberg?" inquired the terminally ignorant Nugent. Nonchalantly barreling past the ensuing deadly silence, Nugent was shown to Thalberg's office and saw only a slender, boyish figure shuffling through some papers while seated at one corner of a large desk. "I came to see Mr. Thalberg," said Nugent.

The man rose, walked behind the desk, sat in the chair, and looked at his visitor. Nugent realized with a sinking heart that "the glance in his eyes seemed to come from away back somewhere in the centuries and to look clear through me."

"Sit down," the small man said. "I am Mr. Thalberg." For about a full minute, the two men enacted the ritual of the rabbit and the snake, neither one saying a word. Finally, Thalberg said, "Well, I don't know that I have anything to say to you, Mr. Nugent." More of the cold stare, more silence. "I think you will like California after you have been here a while. Very few people like it at first."

Nugent was struck by Thalberg's impersonal tone. The by-now desperate Nugent attempted to recoup his losses. "I thought that you were a much older man," he said by way of apology. "I can't help that," replied Thalberg. Nugent gave up and waved his white flag. "Well, have you got any work for me to do?" he asked weakly.

Work. Something Thalberg understood. He suddenly lit up. "Oh yes, we have work for you at once. I will take you over to [producer Bernie] Hyman. He will explain everything to you." Then, and only then, did Thalberg smile. "And I think, after a while," he said by way of dismissal, "Mr. Nugent, you will like us."

So long as an employee was obedient, Thalberg and Mayer were supportive and even avuncular. It was only when individuality or self-interest were asserted that all smiles stopped. When MGM offered Edward G. Robinson a contract, the actor wanted time off every year to do a play. Thalberg curtly informed Robinson that the theater was about to be replaced by talking pictures and that MGM had no intention of signing a nonexclusive contract with anybody. Plays fail; failure might endanger MGM's carefully orchestrated buildup of a potential star.

"The temperature in the office was below zero," remembered Robinson. "I compromised on some minor points, certainly demonstrating some goodwill. Thalberg compromised on nothing; he sat there, stern and immovable . . . I disliked him thoroughly. His eyes showed me that an actor was beneath contempt." Robinson refused the contract, left Thalberg's office, and managed to get out of the building before he vomited.

CHAPTER 4

Of the dozens of people who knew John Gilbert socially, of the hundreds who worked with him professionally, not one thought he had a high-pitched voice. MGM production manager Joe Cohn used to spend a lot of weekends playing tennis at Gilbert's house on Tower Road in Beverly Hills, and remembered nothing out of the ordinary about his voice. Anita Page said that Gilbert's voice "sounded all right to me. He was a fine gentleman; he'd invite me to his bungalow and never make a pass at me. I admired him; once I asked him, 'John, how is it that you can lie down and weep on cue?'

" 'If the scene plays true, I can do it every time,' he told me. 'If it doesn't, I can't.' If a scene had anything false about it, he couldn't do it."

"Gilbert was a very impetuous, actorish man, very immature," asserted director Clarence Brown, who was helming *Flesh and the Devil* when Gilbert and Garbo fell in love. "She had him under her thumb. They were in love, although he was more in love with her than she was with him. He was always proposing in front of people, trying to coerce her into accepting, but she always kept him at arm's length."

In addition, Gilbert was a heavy drinker and self-destructive to a degree rarely encountered even among actors. "I remember him as a hysterical person," said Eleanor Boardman, his costar in *Bardelys the Magnificent*. "If he had good reviews, he hit the ceiling, and he was the happiest man in the world. But if he had a bad review, he got in the dumps and you couldn't get him out of it. A strange fellow."

Given Gilbert's personality, and Mayer's long-standing dislike of the man — they had at least two physical altercations — only Gilbert's apparently unassailable commercial appeal indemnified him against disaster. *Redemption,* Gilbert's first talkie, was shot in the early spring of 1929 by Fred Niblo and Lionel Barrymore. Scheduling a morose drama about a dashing wastrel for Gilbert's first talkie was not as illogical as it sounds; as the reader's report of August 8, 1928, said, "Tolstoy has already given Gilbert two successes [which] makes this powerful and rather heavy story worth consideration."

Redemption isn't terrible, but it lacks dramatic tension. Gilbert was once again playing one of the losers he was drawn to — the performance gets better as the character goes downhill into degradation and squalor, but it's a nonstop slide from gambler and rake to wastrel, compulsive gambler, and eventually derelict suicide. The presence of Renée Adorée in the cast provokes inappropriate memories of their work in *The Big Parade* and other, better days. Moreover, the film's ragged production (Barrymore took over for retakes) is glaringly obvious; scenes change from daylight to darkness midway. Kevin Brownlow places the blame firmly on Barrymore; in the Niblo footage, "Gilbert is relaxed, his voice is strong . . . Then the lighting changes, and Barrymore's stuff takes over. Gilbert's elocution was a little too pear-shaped in Niblo's scenes, but in Barrymore's he is acutely embarrassing — like a parody of himself."

Once they saw a rough cut of the lugubrious drama, MGM had second thoughts. They decided to rush a lighter, more romantic picture through as Gilbert's first talkie and release *Redemption* later. They quickly settled on a 1928 Molnar play entitled *Olympia* that was characterized by a studio reader as "the least interesting of Molnar's books . . . [although] Sidney Howard has done a fine translation . . ." Unfortunately, the studio didn't use Howard's version, but a script devised by Willard Mack.

Lionel Barrymore began directing the Gilbert film, initially under the original title, which was later changed to the quaintly antiquated *His Glorious Night,* in mid-June. Although it is invariably reported that the picture was rushed through in thirteen days, MGM production records show that rehearsals began on June 11, and production wrapped precisely a month later, three days over schedule. It was a schedule commensurate with those for Norma Shearer's early talkies, and a reasonable one for a drawing-room romance that presented no particular production difficulties.

The response when *His Glorious Night* was released in September was immediate and unmistakable: "A few more talker productions like this and John Gilbert will be able to change places with Harry Langdon," wrote *Variety*. "His prowess at love-making which has held the stones breathless takes on a comedy aspect . . . that gets [them] tittering at first and then laughing outright . . ." The film was profitable, but trouble was clearly afoot.

Various conspiracy theories have been floated through the years, mostly centering on a vendetta on the part of Mayer. Hedda Hopper, who played Gilbert's mother in *His Glorious Night*, blamed the film's failures on the inexperienced Lionel Barrymore. Certainly, Barrymore was no asset to the production; between his directorial awkwardness and a reported drug dependency, he presented considerable problems. (Production records for *His Glorious Night* show that Barrymore was constantly late in the mornings, while Gilbert was late only once.)

But this theory presumes that Mayer would have decimated one of his studio's most valuable commercial assets out of personal pique, and that Nicholas Schenck and Irving Thalberg would have let him.*

Yet, beyond the unfortunate choice of director and the absurd title of Gilbert's first released talkie, the truth of the matter is that Gilbert's breathy, slightly nasal voice didn't have a "bottom" and lacked chest tones, and it was very difficult to modify voices with the primitive control boards of 1929.

Gilbert was destroyed by a pair of subtle, but nonetheless fatal, misalliances: the gulf between what his audience imagined he sounded like and what he actually did sound like, and the gap between the kind of movies that were particularly well-suited to silence and the kind that were well-suited to sound. The dialogue in *His*

---

* For the record, soundmen who were familiar with the situation at MGM resolutely deny that Gilbert was intentionally sabotaged by MGM's mixers. "He just had a bad voice for that period [of sound]," said Irving "Buster" Libott, an expert soundman at Columbia who knew and worked with Gilbert.

Glorious Night is as richly florid as the titles in *Love*, the silent Gilbert/Garbo adaptation of *Anna Karenina*. It is rife with stylized dialogue that can be read (barely) but spoken only at considerable peril: "Oh darling! Oh darling, dearest one, what have I done but wait, wait, wait ever since I've known you" is a regrettably typical sample.

To add insult to injury, *Redemption*, released after *His Glorious Night* had aroused titters, offered Gilbert in yet another passionately purple love scene: "Even while my mind tells me I'm doing wrong, my heart tells me I'm doing right" is one representative line, while the scene's end is punctuated by Gilbert ardently murmuring "Tomorrow . . . tomorrow . . . tomorrow." Gilbert was the only swashbuckling lover MGM had on their roster, and nobody had thought to modulate his style of presentation.

In truth, Gilbert's voice was a perfectly good light baritone — "He had as normal a voice as Gary Cooper," said William Bakewell — and it would have been a good fit for an actor with the wry, ironic screen personality of Robert Montgomery or David Niven. But for a hypermasculine, passionate lover? No.

Actors in silent movies had no specific identity; they lived the emotional lives that audiences chose to project onto them. In contrast, sound forced actors to declare themselves, define their personalities, their relationships to each other and to the audience, and a perfectly pleasant light baritone was not what John Gilbert's fans had fantasized about.

Harold Lloyd had intuited the tenuous hold that silent stars had on the capricious imaginations of their fans as early as 1924, when he told *Photoplay* editor James Quirk, "The fans don't like us at all. They like the idea they invent around us. They doll us all up with black eyes, golden hair, six feet of brawn, and a voice like Caruso's. Then we come out with red hair, green eyes, freckles, and a squeak in the upper register. But if we turned out to be Apollo someone would be disappointed; someone would have expected Adonis or Hercules."

"It was very unfair," said MGM production manager Joe Cohn of the Gilbert situation. "It was a miscarriage. Today, his voice problem would have been rectified in five minutes."

Beyond the question of the specific timbre of Gilbert's voice, there was also the question of Gilbert's acting style, which tended toward the emphatic. Left to his own devices, he delivered a passionate style that verged on barnstorming. When working with a top director — King Vidor or Clarence Brown, for instance — or in a film he was emotionally involved with — such as *Man, Woman and Sin* — Gilbert could deliver a performance of amazing subtlety and depth. Absent one or both of those factors, Gilbert would resort to stock displays of his star persona: flashing eyes, gleaming teeth, slight tosses of his head, radiating a shallow charisma that even his friend Vidor found irresistible material for parody, as in his delightful film *Show People*.

"[Gilbert's career ended] because he didn't know how to adapt his aggressive lover to sound," insisted Vidor. "It would have happened to Valentino had he lived. They were both intense lovers. In silent pictures audiences would wonder what they were saying and would fit their own words to the action. But suddenly they had to speak and say things like 'I adore you, I worship you, wait till I get you in bed tonight.' And it became laughable."

In truth, Gilbert's acting style had occasioned some disparaging remarks even at the height of his career. John S. Cohen in the *New York Sun* of January 15, 1927, wrote of Gilbert's performance in *Flesh and the Devil*: "Thereupon he gives her a look of utter contempt, mingled with pain and disgust — in other words, a dirty look — and at that tense moment the audience . . . fairly howled with laughter . . . The audience laughed openly at what was supposed to be its heaviest, most dramatic scene . . . Healthy American lads like Mr. Gilbert can't get away with such tactics . . . [like] German actors [who] are marvelous at this sort of thing."

The financial returns tell the grim story. *His Glorious Night* cost $210,000, and grossed $726,000 [about $100,000 less than Gilbert's silent vehicles were grossing], for a tidy profit — once distribution costs were deducted — of $202,000. But the audience hadn't liked the picture, and, more important, they hadn't liked Gilbert. His next release, the heavily reshot *Redemption*, cost $561,000 and grossed $652,000, losing $215,000. After that, no starring Gilbert vehicle grossed more than $654,000, and most did about half that. Given Gilbert's salary of $250,000 per picture that kicked in with *Redemption*, MGM couldn't make one of his pictures for much less than $500,000. This meant, in round numbers, that every time they made a Gilbert picture they had to be prepared for a loss of between $250,000 and $500,000.

A panicked MGM tried to get Gilbert to terminate his contract, but he flatly refused. "I'll work out the contract cleaning spittoons, if they make me, for that kind of money," he told Ralph Bellamy. Without any possibility of profit to motivate the star's vehicles, MGM didn't exactly throw in the towel — they gave Gilbert solid directors like Mervyn LeRoy and Tod Browning — but they didn't go out of their way to give him much-needed prestige properties either. In any case, in a year or two Gilbert's confidence was irrevocably shattered, and the actor was the most obvious burned-out case on the Metro lot.

MGM obviously had internal debates on how much good money to throw after bad. At one point, they announced that Gilbert would star in an adaptation of *A Farewell to Arms,* to be written by Laurence Stallings, Maxwell Anderson, and Dale Van Every. That was followed by an announcement that he would star in an expensive film about the 1849 Gold Rush. But it wasn't long before MGM got conspicuously cold feet. Only a month after the announcement about the Hemingway adaptation, MGM shelved it (the property was later sold to Paramount); a week after that, they shelved the Gold Rush story. Clearly, prestige properties were not to be wasted on John Gilbert.

It was at this time that Howard Hawks wanted to star Gilbert in his production of *The Dawn Patrol* at Warner Bros. Hawks, with Gilbert in tow, went to see Mayer about a loan-out. Mayer turned to the actor and said, "I understand you'd like to do this picture?"

"I'd do it even if I didn't get paid for it," said Gilbert.

"I don't care a bit whether you get paid for it or not," retorted Mayer. "I wouldn't give you a nickel to make a picture." Hawks realized that Mayer had only agreed to see him in order to insult and humiliate Gilbert. "They wouldn't let [him] work," said the director.

Actually, under his contract, MGM had to let Gilbert work, but they didn't have to let him work in anything anybody would want to see. *Red Dust* was dangled in front of him, only to be snatched away and given to Clark Gable, the young bull of the lot.

Saddled with second-string scripts for movies that audiences consistently stayed away from, the actor grew desperate and wrote a story of his own. *Downstairs* was a fascinating, resolutely downbeat film about a rapacious chauffeur in *mittel*-Europa, but the actor's incipient self-loathing led him to cast himself as one of the screen's most scabrous characters. That one Mayer let him make. No actor in whom MGM had a long-term interest would have been cast in that picture. Failed marriages (with Ina Claire, Virginia Bruce) followed Gilbert's failed films. A costarring part opposite Garbo in 1933's *Queen Christina* failed to stem the indifference with which Gilbert was regarded by audiences.

"You couldn't talk to him too much about [his vocal troubles]," remembered Mervyn LeRoy, "because he was very self-conscious about it." By the time Gilbert's contract expired, for all the self-respect and professional standing he had left, he might as well have been cleaning out spittoons.

Gilbert proceeded to amplify his own tragic circumstances by drinking himself to death. By the time he came to make his last film, 1934's *The Captain Hates the Sea*, alcohol and bitterness had reduced a gregarious *bon vivant* to a dark, brooding shell. "He was a quiet, strange man," recalled Irving "Buster" Libott, one of the soundmen on the film. "And he drank *all* the time." In 1936, just before he was to embark on a comeback in Ernst Lubitsch's production of *Desire*, John Gilbert died of a heart attack. He was forty-one years old.

While Gilbert was embarking on the gaudiest and most precipitous decline of his era, other actors were also struggling. Charles Farrell, a gorgeous, gentle actor who had starred in a series of exquisite romances for Frank Borzage, such as *Seventh Heaven* and *Lucky Star*, had the build of a linebacker but a truly odd, inappropriate voice, with the quality of a street sharper, a Lee Tracy-ish hustler. He could just about get by in quiet, *sotto voce* scenes, but in a noisy scene, where he had to raise his voice, he sounded as if he'd been inhaling helium. Farrell worked out his Fox contract, but to steadily diminishing returns.

Richard Barthelmess — an actor of attractive sensitivity, a producer of integrity — had been among the most reliable of all silent leading men since his beautiful performance in Griffith's *Broken Blossoms* in 1919. One of his biggest hits, 1927's *The Patent Leather Kid*, had grossed the very considerable amount of $1.6 million. But sound meant that Barthelmess's career would begin a slow, steady decline, with the actor reduced to supporting parts.

Barthelmess's talking career got off to a rocky creative start with a film about a convict who becomes a radio star called *Weary River.* The press unhelpfully leaked word that Barthelmess couldn't really play the piano and someone else had dubbed his singing voice. The public, curious about the voice of a longtime star, came out in droves, giving *Weary River* a world gross of $1.7 million on a cost of $333,000. The follow-up, inauspiciously titled *Drag* (think of the marquee . . .), grossed less than half that, and his next picture, *Young Nowheres,* grossed a quarter million dollars less than *Drag.* With the exception of the Howard Hawks aviation spectacle *Dawn Patrol,* which again grossed $1.6 million, Barthelmess was marginalized by sound.

The demands of a declining career—and an affair with journalist Adela Rogers St. Johns—led Barthelmess to develop a greater affection for brandy than was entirely healthy, and the alcohol began to etch its effects onto his face. He decided that a facelift was the answer.

"He went to Budapest to a plastic surgeon," remembered his publicity man Joseph Steele. "It didn't work. He went to one in Paris, he went to one in Berlin, by the time he got back he had no expression. Ronald Colman and he were great friends, and it used to upset him that Colman took care of himself and had that beautiful voice. Dick couldn't stand it. He said to me, 'I can't live here, I've got to go away,' and he picked up and went to Long Island and lived there."

There was nothing wrong with Barthelmess's voice, but there was nothing right about it either. It was inexpressive, ordinary, and Barthelmess didn't know how to use it. Sound revealed that his actor's gift resided in his face and eyes, which had been frozen by the facelifts. Even if Barthelmess's face had remained pristine, however, dialogue had taken the place of action, and the facial intensity of the silents had been immediately jettisoned; actors like Barthelmess were robbed of their primary tools and asked to replace them with implements with which they were not expert.

If sound could disrupt the technique and dislodge the career of a good actor like Barthelmess, less talented people were in dire danger. Rod La Rocque had been a successful leading man since World War I, but early talkies like *The Delightful Rogue* stimulated him to some outrageously bad acting, with sideburns shaved to a Valentino-ish point and the Spanish accent of a rank amateur.

The film itself — Zorro in the South Seas, directed by Leslie Pearce, with "Pictorial Director" Lynn Shores — has flamboyant flourishes, such as a few elaborate tracking shots and quite good exterior sound. It's the sort of lighthearted exotic romance ground out by the yard in the silent days, suddenly rendered absurd by the humorless heaviness of actors who persisted in giving a silent-film performance in a talking picture.

"Some actors might have been afraid of using their voice, and it showed," recalled Esther Ralston. "Sound changed acting techniques. You gave a different performance in a talkie. Your facial expression wasn't as important as the fact that you were using your voice. Your voice was more important than your expression, and the reverse was true in silent movies."

Another career that was suddenly endangered was that of Clara Bow. With the exception of *Wings,* Paramount had milked her stardom by casting her in relentlessly ordinary B movies, movies brought to life only by her personality. Although Bow was from Brooklyn, and had only a minimal education, *The Saturday Night Kid,* her third talkie — a remake of the Louise Brooks silent *Love 'Em and Leave 'Em* — reveals that there was nothing wrong with her voice. There was, however, a great deal wrong with the picture, as, once again, Bow plays a poor but honest girl working in a department store — a plot identical to that of *It,* Bow's biggest hit.

Most of Bow's silents had taken their rhythm from the star's effervescent performances, but the strictures of early sound made that impossible. The editing rhythm of *The Saturday Night Kid* is painfully attenuated, and, as a result, Bow's performance seems pitched too high. Moreover, her emotional problems show up in her pudgy figure. Movies like *The Saturday Night Kid* couldn't be saved by the glistening, empathetic star quality of Bow, or anybody else. To survive sound, Bow — or John Gilbert — would have needed good pictures; neither got them, and emotional instability finished the job studio incompetence started. Clara Bow became yet another creature of silence whose magic dissipated beneath the microphone.*

The law of compensation being what it is, for every Richard Barthelmess or Rod La Rocque there was a William Powell or George Arliss. In silent pictures, Powell usually played skulking heavies, but sound revealed his resonant baritone, and it also seems to have freed him as an actor. Watching Powell in silent pictures, one searches in vain for the blithe irony that was a resolute characteristic of his sound performances. He seems a journeyman actor, nothing more. Yet, in early talkies like *The Canary Murder Case* and *Street of Chance* Powell is reborn: deft, incisive, suavely sardonic, quietly memorable.

Another, far more unlikely star created by talkies was George Arliss, who was born in London in 1868 and made his stage debut at eighteen. He first came to America in 1902 and then stayed for twenty years, carving out a niche playing famous historical figures: Voltaire, Richelieu, and, supremely, Disraeli. Arliss had made a few silent films to no particular response, but, like many others adept with dialogue, he was hired by Warners in early 1929 to do talkie versions of a couple of his stage hits. He quickly shot adaptations of two of his theatrical perennials, *The Green Goddess* and *Disraeli,* the former a remake of a silent film he had made some years before, the latter a part he had been playing since 1911. Although *The Green Goddess* was made first, Arliss thought *Disraeli* was the better film, and pressured Warners to release it first.

For Warners, signing Arliss had been a low-risk act of hubris, for the actor conferred a certain prestige, and his pictures could be made relatively inexpensively. Jack and Harry were probably hoping for little more than a break-even proposition, but they quickly found themselves with another star on their hands. *Disraeli* cost little more

---

* One actress whose career should have been destroyed by sound was Marion Davies, whose difficulty was revealed in an offhand remark to a studio publicity man at a screening of *The Jazz Singer:* "M-m-m-m-m-Mister Voigt, I-I-I-I have a p-p-problem." Luckily, Davies' stutter vanished when she spoke memorized dialogue, so her career was able to continue, although only by grace of her alliance with William Randolph Hearst. (Of Davies' eleven MGM talkies, precisely three made money, and piddling amounts like $18,000 and $20,000 at that.)

than $300,000, grossed nearly $1.5 million, and won Arliss the 1929
Academy Award for Best Actor in the bargain. None of Arliss's
succeeding films had anything approaching that kind of success, but
they did well enough to keep him at Warners through 1933 and in
America through 1935.

"I played the part [of Disraeli] exactly as I had acted it in the
theatre," Arliss wrote with some satisfaction, and he wasn't kidding.
Disraeli — Arliss is billed as "Mr. George Arliss" — is a film of stage
groupings, stage exposition, and stage acting, but, in Arliss's case
at least, rather attractively old-fashioned stage acting. Arliss was
endearingly homely — he looked like one of the higher amphibians
— but he was an engaging old ham, with a good line in foxy grandpas
who could preserve empires while bringing young lovers together.

Moreover, he leavened his characters with brisk, self-deprecatory
humor. The drama in *Disraeli* consists almost entirely of hoary conventions — lurking spies and overheard conversations, with Big Moments emphasized by raised fists — and Arliss's twinkle occasionally
grows rather too studied, but he is a fascinating relic of the vanished
tradition of Henry Irving and Beerbohm Tree.

❑ ❑ ❑

MGM had been preparing *The Broadway Melody* since August 1928,
with Thalberg sitting in on story conferences with writers Edmund
Goulding and Sarah Mason and director Harry Beaumont. By September, they had an outline for a backstage musical about vaudevillian sisters whose act is broken up by the attentions of a genial
songwriter. Thalberg thought it would be an ideal subject for a half-
talkie, but when he read James Gleason's dialogue for the film, all
slang and up-to-the-minute Broadway jargon, Thalberg revised his
plans and decided to make it an all-talkie.

The finished film followed the outline quite closely. Although
Rosetta Duncan would later claim that the film had been designed as
a vehicle for her and her sister, by November 1928, Anita Page and
Bessie Love had been chosen to star in the film (Love was the current
girlfriend of songwriter Arthur Freed, while Page would become
Mrs. Nacio Herb Brown). That month, Page was given the tryout
scene to rehearse, with a note from Jack Cummings: "Anita baby —
read these and don't worry — "

Despite Thalberg's clearly stated preference for Page, director Harry Beaumont was displeased. "[Harry] Beaumont didn't want me," said Anita Page. "He went in to see L.B. [Mayer] and said, 'I need a consummate actress.' And L.B. said, 'Take her, she's a Bernhardt.' "

Thalberg clearly saw *The Broadway Melody* as a test case. "Thalberg was a darling, a love, so very clever," remembered Anita Page. "We were doing the film, and he began coming onto the set, which he rarely did. Pretty soon he began to see that it had great possibilities, and we began to get more and more [production] time. It was difficult, because at that time, MGM only had one soundstage; Norma [Shearer] got it in the morning and we had it at night."

The Broadway Melody took three months to make, three months of what Anita Page remembered as "just plodding along," especially when compared to the brisk four- and five-week schedules of the silent films she had been making a few months before. Charles King caused some problems because of his inability to remember dialogue (the studio resorted to cue cards), but mostly the difficulties arose because of the new technology.

"We would do a scene," remembered Bessie Love, "and then they'd listen to it, and it would sound horrible. Then we'd all go off the set, and they'd take up everything, take up the carpets, the furniture, everything. And they'd get rows of carpenters to hammer, hammer, hammer, to get the floor down. Then they'd put everything back again and we'd do it again and then they'd listen, and they'd say, 'Oh no, there's something wrong.' So they'd hang drapes around the place, maybe behind or above, they'd try anything to get the sound a little better. And at the end of the film, they had got it better than it was in the beginning, so that it really didn't match, but by then, of course, it didn't matter."

Since the studio had no music department, an orchestra was recruited from the pool of musicians in the area. After one of the first recording sessions, Thalberg asked Douglas Shearer how it had gone.

"We had a lot of problems," replied Shearer.

"Why?"

"Because there's no system here!" exploded Shearer. "Every time we need some music we have to go out and hire musicians."

"You're talking to me like I was an office boy," said an irritated Thalberg.

"You're talking to *me* like *I* was an office boy!" Shearer retorted.

There was a steely pause, finally broken by an admission from Thalberg that Shearer was right. "What do you suggest?" he asked.

Shearer proposed telephoning the Loew's-owned Capitol Theater in New York and having them ship out their music library, arranger, music librarian, and conductor. It was the beginning of the MGM Music Department.

According to Bessie Love, *The Broadway Melody* began production using the Vitaphone system, but ended using sound on film. Because prerecording had not yet been devised, an offstage orchestra was in place for each musical number, which only complicated the recording process further. The responsibility of recording the orchestra, the singer, and the dancers in a decent balance was brutal. It couldn't be fixed in the mix, because the initial recording *was* the mix.

"All this made for a long day," remembered Bessie Love, "ten, twelve or more hours at a stretch, all without overtime payment." The actors were troupers; as soon as dinner was over, Anita Page would produce a script and begin running her lines for the next day's work.

Despite this eagerness, some of the dialogue bothered her. "I hated to say, 'Gee, ain't it elegant!' remembered Page. "I'd been brought up to speak proper English, and I had to say that sentence four times. Of course, when the picture won the Oscar, I began to like the sentence."

When Thalberg saw the completed picture, he approved everything except the finale, the lavish "Wedding of the Painted Doll" number. He ordered it reshot, whereupon the innovative Douglas Shearer suggested that it didn't need to be rerecorded. "We've got a perfectly good recording of the music. Why not just play the record and have the dancers go through the number? Then we can combine the film and the sound track in the lab." *

* Across town at Universal, bandleader Paul Whiteman was making the same suggestion to Carl Laemmle. Whiteman was relying on the technology familiar to him through making records, while Shearer's bright mind was intuitively leaping to the next level.

The Broadway Melody opened at Grauman's Chinese Theater on February 1, 1929, and proved a sensation. There were fourteen live stage acts preceding the movie, from George Gershwin playing *Rhapsody in Blue* to Edith Murray and her Torrid Ensemble performing a number called "Hot (Positively!)." Dimitri Tiomkin conducted and directed the finale, as the movie's stars descended a staircase designed by Cedric Gibbons. Afterward, there was a lavish party hosted by Mayer and Thalberg across the street at the Blossom Room of the Roosevelt Hotel.

Bessie Love's memories of the opening night were of a gorgeous apotheosis of glamorous show business. "When the picture turns out to be good — just right — the way you meant it to be — and this elephantine cinema in 'the town where they made 'em' comes to life from cellar to rafters, with everyone applauding and shouting their appreciation . . . in the middle of the film, it is something. I tell you, it really is."

The Broadway Melody grossed over $4.3 million worldwide, and showed a net profit of $1.6 million. It remains entertaining in spite of the fact that the technology isn't appreciably better than that of other films of the period. There are superfluous scene-setting titles left over from silent storytelling ("A theatrical hotel on 46th St. . . ." "The girls' apartment"). The mike boom hadn't yet hit MGM, for when the actors move off their spots, their voices fade appreciably. But the storytelling is brisk and professional. There are no dawdling gaps between lines and scenes, each sequence advances the story, and the actors pick up their cues with snap. The performances, especially the adorable Bessie Love, are scaled for the camera, not the stage. Also, the score by Nacio Herb Brown and Arthur Freed (with the title song, "You Were Meant for Me," and "Wedding of the Painted Doll") is excellent.

As was typical at the time, a silent version was also prepared, by the old Paramount director George Melford. Obviously, all the songs were cut, but the rest of the film was also quickened; the silent version was three and a half reels shorter than the talkie.

It was not long after *The Broadway Melody* that Anita Page ran headlong into a stony casting couch, when Louis B. Mayer asked her for "special favors." Page refused. "I could break Garbo in three pictures and I can make you in three pictures," he snarled. Her refusal, coming on top of a request for a raise, was undoubtedly interpreted by Mayer as disloyalty, and Page's career went into a steep decline. Mayer slotted her into indifferent vehicles, and even began loaning her out, something MGM almost never did except as a punishment to a recalcitrant star. "They weren't going to do me any favors anymore," Page sadly reflected, more than sixty-five years later.

Although Mayer clearly frightened her, she tried to be fair to him. "If he hadn't forced [director Harry] Beaumont to take me, I wouldn't have had the career I had." She believed that it was not refusing Mayer's pass that blunted her career so much as it was asking for more money. Given Mayer's personality, she may have been right. "If we hadn't [asked for more money] they would have taken care of me and built me up. I might have been one of their top stars."

CHAPTER 5

The success of *The Broadway Melody* clearly indicated that if audiences were happy to hear people talk, they were ecstatic to hear them sing. All the studios quickly geared up for all-star musicals. Even actors who had no demonstrated affinity with musicals were pressed into the effort. The casts of these films fell, roughly, into three categories: Broadway stars who knew what they were doing (Jolson, Cantor et al.), silent stars who sort of, kind of, knew what they were doing (Gloria Swanson, Bebe Daniels), and silent stars who were dubbed.

MGM decided to produce the equivalent of a Broadway revue without even attempting any connective tissue beyond that of a master of ceremonies. *The Hollywood Revue of 1929* began rehearsals on February 4, 1929. When production began a month later, Christy Cabanne was the director. By March 27, producer Harry Rapf had taken over directorial duties, possibly because after only two weeks of production a rough cut totaling 9,172 feet had been assembled, and major numbers from Norma Shearer, John Gilbert, Marion Davies, and Laurel and Hardy hadn't even been shot yet.

Other numbers took several days to rehearse and shoot, but Laurel and Hardy's contribution was completed in six hours on May 27. Two days later, John Gilbert and Norma Shearer were scheduled to shoot their takeoff on *Romeo and Juliet*. The original call was for 10:30 A.M., but Shearer, by this time Mrs. Irving Thalberg, called and asked that it be postponed for an hour; Gilbert didn't show up until 11:45. The scene would be rehearsed, re-rehearsed, and tested for sound for another week until it was finally completed to Harry Rapf's satisfaction on June 7. The unusually ragged production finally wrapped on June 11.

When the film opened only three weeks later, *Variety* correctly opined that the film would be a smash hit if only because "it's going to play for 50 to 75 cents in spots where they've never seen those ballets which open the second half of any Shubert extravaganza." The film's opening number, a tap routine that switches from the conventional positive image to a negative one, "froze the easterners in their seats because of the immediate thought on how is the stage going to compete with such effects, and if this were merely a sample of what was coming during the evening the ship has sailed."

As it happened, the ship was still in port; the negative image was as creative as *The Hollywood Revue* ever got. Although *Variety* thought that "Miss [Marion] Davies doesn't appear at ease" and "[John] Gilbert appeared a bit nervous," the film's novelty value overwhelmed the fact that nobody was doing anything particularly interesting in and of itself. The fact that it was John Gilbert or Joan Crawford or Marie Dressler doing it was sufficient, as MGM would prove over and over in the next few years.

If the lead-footed dancing of Joan Crawford—introduced as "the personification of youth and beauty and joy and happiness"—wasn't enough, the apache dancers and acrobats, along with the elemental time-steps and syncopated arm-wavings that passed for choreography in the pre-Astaire era, would sink any picture, as was Charles King singing a paean to mother love—undoubtedly inserted as a sop to Louis B. Mayer.

The film is not entirely without interest. Bessie Love is brisk, charming, and virtually the only cast member to avoid coyness. The comedian Karl Dane appears but says not a word; MGM was obviously terrified of his heavy Danish accent. The studio dropped him in 1930; by 1934, shortly before Dane committed suicide, he was working at a hot dog stand.

There is a briefly interesting scene where Charles King dubs Conrad Nagel during a love scene; across town, Richard Barthelmess was mouthing the words to somebody else's song in *Weary River*. He was presumably unamused by the *Revue*'s revelation of how easily such trickery could be accomplished.

The Gilbert-Shearer version of *Romeo and Juliet,* done in vintage 1929 slang ("Julie baby, I'm ga-ga about you . . . you're the cream in my mocha and java . . . "), ends with poor Gilbert declaiming in pig latin. It is shriveling in its failure. To modern eyes, *Hollywood Revue of 1929* is a (mild) curiosity crossed with a (complete) fiasco, but to audiences in 1929 a curiosity was what they wanted. *The Hollywood Revue of 1929* grossed $2.4 million worldwide, earning a clear profit of more than $1.1 million.

Other studios decided to get into the act, and, throughout 1929, each studio presented an all-star musical revue. The best of them was probably *Paramount on Parade,* if only for a couple of amusing scenes with Maurice Chevalier. The worst of them . . . well, take your pick among all the others.

Warners' *The Show of Shows* has a particularly bizarre opening non sequitur, a French Revolution scene in which H. B. Warner, playing an aristocrat, has his head cut off, whereupon Hobart Bosworth, as the headsman, turns to the screaming crowd and yells, "Prologue is dead; on with *The Show of Shows.*"

The MC is the charmless Frank Fay, overflowing with dismal self-satisfaction. Most of the overlong (two hours plus) production has the vaguely charming, underrehearsed air of ramshackle vaudeville, which occasionally kicks into authentic surrealism, as in a sketch wherein Ted "Is Everybody Happy" Lewis shows up on a pirate ship commanded by Noah Beery and Tully Marshall.

Fay's mustache comes and goes without explanation, and the primary interest in this succession of pasted-together shorts is the opportunity to see what screen dancing was like before it was invented by Busby Berkeley and Fred Astaire: dumpy chorus girls in syncopated, rhythmic numbers. The idea of geometric patterns à la Berkeley is occasionally suggested in the choreography, but the immobile camera can't accommodate it, let alone amplify it.

The film appears to have undergone a shuffling that would become *de rigueur* for these all-star efforts; George Arliss was supposed to appear, as were Al Jolson, Marilyn Miller, and the great English song-and-dance man Jack Buchanan. In addition, John Barrymore's presence was to be far more pervasive than it is in the finished film. Whether or not Arliss and Barrymore vetoed material deemed undignified is unclear. Premiering in November, *Show of Shows* continued the Warner winning streak, grossing slightly over $1.5 million on a cost of $795,000.

Over at Universal, Carl Laemmle agreed to pay Paul Whiteman, the leading bandleader of the day, a whopping $440,000 — $200 a week for each musician, plus $200,000 for Whiteman in addition to a percentage — for a movie to be entitled *The King of Jazz,* the name inappropriately bestowed on the bandleader because of his commissioning and premiering Gershwin's *Rhapsody in Blue.* Although Carl Laemmle had originally scheduled production for the summer of 1929, the assigned writers didn't quite know what to do with Whiteman. He couldn't act, and, at over three hundred pounds, he could barely move.

Production snafus of this nature were common at Universal, for Laemmle Senior was one of the more sweetly idiosyncratic of the moguls. Universal was well-designed to make cheap program pictures, but their yearly "event" movies always consumed too much money and threatened to paralyze the badly managed studio. Laemmle had bought the rights to Edna Ferber's novel *Show Boat* as early as 1926, and spent two years developing upward of ten scripts before production finally began in July of 1928. In the meantime, the Jerome Kern/Oscar Hammerstein II musical adaptation had made theatrical history. By the time Universal had completed their silent version of the Ferber novel in November, they realized they had to do something about a sound track.

It was not until January 1929 that Laemmle paid $100,000 for the musical score, and he quickly premiered the film in March at the Paramount Theater in Palm Beach, probably because it was Florenz Ziegfeld's favorite winter haunt. Despite their access to the immortal Kern melodies, Laemmle was maladroit enough to interpolate nondescript, non-Kern music (such as "The Lonesome Road," "Love Sings a Song in My Heart") into the background score.

The same pattern of initial indecision followed by bad decisions would be repeated with *The King of Jazz*. After much expensive delay, it was decided to turn the film into a revue. Laemmle tried to get Ziegfeld to stage the film, but settled for John Murray Anderson as a second choice, paying him $50,000. Anderson had never made a movie, but he had produced and directed dozens of theatrical productions. Universal then paid George Gershwin $30,000 for the rights to *Rhapsody in Blue;* when Anderson asked the composer if he had any ideas about the staging of the number, Gershwin responded with the verbal equivalent of a shrug, leaving Anderson even more at sea.

Upon arriving in Hollywood, Anderson made it a point to consult with the most highly regarded people on the Universal lot, asking cinematographer Hal Mohr and trick cameraman Jerry Ash if they had any pet ideas they had thought of but had never been able to use. Ash suggested that the opening of the picture could be Whiteman carrying a small suitcase, out of which would emerge, one by one, the members of the orchestra.

Production finally got under way in the fall, with the entire film to be made in Technicolor. Since the process at that time was limited to red and green, shooting *Rhapsody in Blue* presented an insurmountable challenge to the nonplussed Anderson, who ended up attempting to achieve the illusion of blue by utilizing a silver-and-gray background with a touch of green shading. It wasn't blue, but it wasn't bad.

As an experienced recording artist, Whiteman was aghast at the network of hanging microphones by which the sound engineers proposed to get a balanced recording of his orchestra. He instead proposed building a recording studio on the soundstage, prerecording the musical numbers and playing them back as the scene was photographed and the band faked it. "Let's do their ears a favor," he said. "It's bound to be an improvement." Whiteman had been successfully making records for ten years; as musical authority Miles Krueger points out, he was probably far more interested in making his recordings perfect than he was in making his movie perfect.*

Whiteman's plan was adopted for all the musical numbers in the film. Laura La Plante, one of Universal's few female stars, made a guest appearance in the film. She later recalled that while performers were miming to the musical playbacks, carpenters were noisily hammering on sets barely out of camera range, just as in the silent days. Only the comedy sketches and dialogue scenes were shot live.

Production on *The King of Jazz* was further complicated when the heavy-drinking Bing Crosby, one of Whiteman's vocalists, was arrested for reckless driving. Crosby drew a sixty-day jail sentence, but Whiteman managed to get him released during the day to work on the film. At the end of each day's shooting, he would return to jail. After forty days, his sentence was commuted. But the production wasn't without its recompenses. At Christmas, Whiteman gave each of his musicians a Ford automobile and Anderson a gold cigarette case worth $3,000, complete with a caricature of Whiteman made out of diamonds.

What with the rigors of its apparently endless production, *The King of Jazz* ended up costing $1.65 million, most of it invisible on the screen. Yet, Whiteman's stay in Hollywood wasn't a total loss. He spent most of his off-screen time in ardent pursuit of Margaret Livingston, the actress who had played the vamp in Murnau's *Sunrise.* They eventually married.

❑ ❑ ❑

Toward the end of 1929, movies finally began to move again, however tentatively. A Fox musical called *Sunny Side Up,* released in October, opens with a *tour de force* crane shot that examines a tenement block, roaming up the street, rising to peer into windows,

---

* *Viennese Nights,* which engineer George Groves remembered as being the first Warner Bros. picture to involve prerecording, was made a few months after *King of Jazz.* Paramount continued recording musicals live at least through 1932's *Love Me Tonight,* complicating the performer's job considerably, for people like Maurice Chevalier had to give what amounted to a precisely timed live performance without an audience as a gauge. A year later, Warners prerecorded all the numbers in *42nd Street,* and that led the way for the rest of the industry.

falling to examine the passersby on the sidewalk. The film is otherwise interminable and quickly declines into stylistic orthodoxy, but
changes were clearly coming, and not a moment too soon.

As for *The King of Jazz,* which came out too late in the cycle of
musical revues to make much of an impact, it was loosely organized
as "Paul Whiteman's scrapbook . . . full of melodies and anecdotes."
It has animation courtesy of Walter Lantz, loony specialty numbers
— a violinist who also plays the bicycle pump — and a mind-boggling
finale: a tribute to the American musical melting pot, literally portrayed as being about thirty feet tall, into which Whiteman stirs the
various ethnic melodies, out of which comes what Whiteman insisted
on calling "jazz," although it sounds mostly like big-band dance
music.

Despite the agonies of the production, Whiteman seems to be
enjoying himself; he looks a great deal like Oliver Hardy and proves
a genial *compère.* The film itself is more slickly produced than the
other revues, and is somewhat akin to MGM's *Ziegfeld Follies* of
sixteen years later.

The problem with revues like *The Show of Shows* and, to a lesser
extent, *The King of Jazz,* is their wild variation in tone; low-rent
vaudeville cheek-by-jowl with attempts at sophisticated drawing-
room skits, and musical numbers that quickly degenerate into exhibition marches. As Ethan Mordden notes, these films are not only
messes, they "lack character . . . [borrowing] Broadway's output but
[marketing] it for a public not entirely used to Broadway ware."

The proliferation of musicals should have been a windfall for Flo
Ziegfeld, but his habitual financial crises forced him to sell his finest
properties at fire-sale prices. Ziegfeld's money from *Show Boat* had
to be divided among Jerome Kern, Edna Ferber, Oscar Hammerstein
II, and the music publisher T. B. Harms, as well as Ziegfeld—so he
couldn't afford to sit tight and count his spoils.

He sold *Sally* to Warner Bros., announced plans to create a *Follies*
film, and, on June 13, signed a deal with Sam Goldwyn to be equal
partners in the production of musicals. It would never happen, of
course; Goldwyn couldn't work on an equal footing with anybody.
Nonetheless Goldwyn now had the rights to *Whoopee!* and its star
Eddie Cantor, making his talkie debut in return for $100,000 and a
10-percent cut. In return Goldwyn helped out the overburdened

producer by assuming the salaries of a number of Ziegfeld's employees, paying him for the property, and promising him 20 percent of
the profits . . . after Cantor's 10 percent was deducted.

Since Goldwyn had carefully reserved creative control for himself,
Ziegfeld could do little but fret while Goldwyn cut most of the
show's sixteen original songs, retaining the show-stopping title song
and the wonderful "My Baby Just Cares for Me." On the other
hand, Goldwyn did agree to at least one of Ziegfeld's ideas, that
of using a slightly improved two-color Technicolor for the entire
picture.

Whoopee! confirmed Goldwyn's instincts. It introduced Busby
Berkeley's goofily intoxicating erotic geometry. Equally as important, it offered Eddie Cantor. The diminutive actor had made a
few silent films, but in silence he had to play his comedy straight. In
sound, his essential playfulness came out; Cantor indulged in blackface, in-jokes, and topical humor, and even broke into Yiddish.

Cantor hasn't worn particularly well — he exhibits nearly as much
self-approbation as Jolson — but his role-playing and roaring appreciation of his own performance were nominal parts of Broadway
musicals of the period, providing oases of relief from the tiresome
plots. This genial undercutting of one's own vehicle, an attitude also
prominently displayed by the Marx Brothers, was a revelation for
the movies, and Cantor embarked on a successful film career.

Whoopee! was Ziegfeld's last hurrah. Although he sent a series of
telegrams to Goldwyn, the subtext of which was a pathetic begging
for continued partnerships, and he even tried (unsuccessfully) to con
a 20-percent piece of future Goldwyn/Cantor pictures, Goldwyn
wanted nothing more to do with a producer who was every bit as
single-minded and intransigent as he was.

❑ ❑ ❑

During the production of *Coquette,* Howard Campbell had been
dissatisfied with the sound quality of some test footage and had
ordered the tests embargoed. When Mary Pickford wanted to see
the footage, she was told that Campbell had forbidden it. It was
an arrogance typical of the soundmen, but it was a fatal mistake.
"Campbell," remembered Ed Bernds, "was as dead as a man who has

just been stabbed through the heart; he just hadn't fallen down yet." Pickford did not scold, threaten, or explode; a security man from the studio drove a car around to a fire exit on Santa Monica Boulevard and helped Campbell move his personal belongings out of the studio. Nobody in the U.A. sound department ever saw him again.

A man who disliked Bernds was put in charge, and both Bernds and his friend Dave Forrest were marked for slaughter. Forrest applied for jobs at Warners and Columbia, and was hired by Warners, which left the Columbia job for Bernds. "Dave had been in publicity and knew his way around. He told me that I should ask Columbia for a raise, otherwise they'd want to know why someone would leave U.A. for Poverty Row. I asked for $85, which they said they'd give me if my first picture was OK. So that's what happened. I went over to Columbia in August 1929."

At Columbia, Bernds found that the atmosphere was markedly different than at U.A. Practicality and efficiency reigned, because people were allowed to work out their own problems. Columbia's ace cameraman Joe Walker was, said Bernds, "one of the greatest men and greatest cameramen that ever lived. Joe would be willing to rearrange his lighting so we could get that clumsy old microphone closer to the actors. They wouldn't do that at U.A.; the cameramen were used to a high-key light, and they didn't want to change that to allow for the placement of the mike. Joe would use multiple key-lights if necessary, even though it took more pains to do it and we were making quickies."

On Stage 5 on the Columbia lot, a young director named Frank Capra was shooting process shots for a picture called *Flight*. Bernds quickly realized that the decisive Capra possessed the elusive quality of leadership. This was no passive Dwan, no absurdly peremptory Brenon, but a whirling dervish who handled his actors and crew with dispatch and camaraderie. "Capra was in charge of *everything*," recalled Bernds, who became a trusted member of Capra's crew until the director left Columbia.

Flight was shot in the late summer of 1929, and the ponderous equipment was still imposing a congealed production pace. On location at the San Diego Air Station, Joe Walker noticed a gorgeous composition of a row of parked airplanes against a setting sun. Capra wanted the shot, but thought the image was too strong to waste on a throwaway. He quickly gave the actors some lines and told the sound crew to set up their recording equipment.

"They . . . got to work laying cables, putting sound motors on the camera, placing the mike, warming up amplifiers, checking the sync of the motors," remembered Joe Walker. "By the time they were ready, the attendants had rolled the planes off the line and back into hangars, the sun had set, the blaze of clouds had grayed, and it was getting dark. Instead of our pictorial shot, we ended up with nothing."

Flight, essentially an uncredited remake of the Lon Chaney vehicle *Tell It to the Marines,* which was itself a variation on *What Price Glory,* ended up as a mildly diverting reprise of overly familiar themes. Capra shot most of the picture on location (once in a while crowd noise drowns out dialogue), and if the script and characters are strictly stock, the surroundings are authentic, and Capra's typically imaginative use of his camera and actors make it easy to overlook the cheerfully xenophobic script.

❑ ❑ ❑

By mid-1929, F. W. Murnau and his screenwriter Berthold Viertel were no longer connected with *Our Daily Bread* (which would have its title changed to *City Girl*). Sheehan and Fox were still trying to do the right thing, for among the first writers to work on the planned reshoots were Katherine Hilliker and H. H. Caldwell, who had titled *Sunrise.*

Hilliker and Caldwell's plans are outlined in a seven-page memo dated August 2, and involve shooting some new footage, to be sandwiched between existing Murnau material, which ended with the fierce old patriarch firing his gun and shattering a lantern. The suggested new material — which never mentions Murnau or any other director — ends with a quick scene of reconciliation that could have been shot in one day.

"Son, you know I . . . I wasn't meaning to shoot *you,*" says old man Tustine. The son refuses to accept the father's apology, and demands the Iago-like farmhand Mac admit his guilt in front of his farmhands. With Lem acting the self-sufficient man for the first time, the other men go back to the harvesting of the wheat. Lem says he's going back to the city with his wife, only to have her tell him his place is on the land. "You have Lem and so do I," she tells the old man. "Can't we make a go of it . . . for his sake?" Fade out on the now-happy group.

Sheehan must have thought there was a better solution, for he continued beating the bushes. By the latter part of 1929, *City Girl* was an orphan being passed from hand to hand. Junior writers at Fox were enlisted to try to come up with a way to cobble the footage together in a way that would please talk-crazed audiences while retaining as much Murnau footage as was dramatically and finan-cially practicable. Sheehan even assigned several writers to the film at the same time, hoping one of them would hit on something.

One approach, labeled "Final revised" and dated November 1, is by Elliot Lester, the author of the original source play. It includes a final dialogue scene that reconciles Kate and Lem's father:

"KATE: You know — this world's like a big restaurant. You come into it — you order — and what you get depends on how you ask for it. Old man, you've always been the grouchy customer — the kind that gets the burnt toast and the stale eggs . . . But we ought to help set things back. The wheat's got to make our daily bread, hasn't it? But not as it was, old man — to grow between those who love each other. If we stay, that's understood, ain't it?"

All of the dialogue scripts include much Murnau footage, but they also add comic relief and numerous suggestions that would water down Murnau's original conception and make the film less severe, less rigorous.

By this time, Sheehan and Fox undoubtedly both wished they had never heard of Murnau or *Our Daily Bread;* in November, sound material was shot quickly and cheaply by A. H. Van Buren and A. F. "Buddy" Erickson, an assistant director on the Fox lot. With what must have been a good deal of fatalism, the film was cut to-gether for its premiere in the new year.

Meanwhile, critic Robert Sherwood had turned his powers of prophecy to the problems of renowned silent-film writers like Hil-liker and Caldwell. He didn't like what he saw in his crystal ball. "Consider . . . the continuity writer who has been in the business since the old Biograph days and has worked his way upward to a $1,500-a-week job and attendant luxuries . . . He now finds that because he doesn't know how to write dialogue he must yield his salary, his office and his comely stenographer to an obscure playwright from New York.

"The continuity writer has been identified with some of the most tremendous box office successes that the movies have known. His successor . . . has written two plays, one of which ran for eleven performances on Forty-sixth Street, and the other of which perished miserably in Providence, R.I., before it had even been permitted to see the light of Broadway."

Sherwood was disgusted, Hollywood was trembling, and who could blame them? Even in that summer of 1929, there were those who were confidently sitting back and waiting for the novelty to wear off, for the audience to demand the return of silence to the screen. Royalists under Cromwell could not have waited any more impatiently for the return of Bonnie Prince Charlie.

❏ ❏ ❏

Harold Lloyd had been calling his new silent film *The Butterfly Collector,* then *T.N.T.* A talented ex-gagman named Ted Wilde directed for the first month, then was replaced by Mal St. Clair. When production ended in February 1929, Lloyd had a rough cut of two hours and forty-five minutes. Previews helped Lloyd get the length down to about a hundred minutes, but, by April of 1929, Lloyd and his crew had bigger problems than the picture's length. That month, noted Lloyd's office in a cautionary memo, 89 percent of pictures in release had dialogue and/or sound effects; outright silents accounted for a mere 4 percent of pictures in release.

During one of the previews of his new picture, Lloyd saw a two-reel sound comedy. "They howled at this," he glumly remembered. "They had the punkest gags in it, but they were laughing at the pouring of water, the frying of eggs—it didn't matter—the clinking of ice in a glass. We said, 'My God, we worked our hearts out to get laughs with thought-out gags, and look here: just because they've got some sound in it, they're roaring at these things.' "

Lloyd gathered his crew around him. One way or another, he announced, the film that was finally titled *Welcome Danger* would be released as a talkie. Mal St. Clair was let go, and Clyde Bruckman was brought on. For the next five months, Lloyd and company diddled with their picture, dubbing half of it and reshooting the other half as an outright talkie.

The dubbing experience was appalling; "it was like an insane asylum," said Lloyd. "We had seven or eight different people that were all making different effects. One man was walking upstairs and back down, another one was rattling, another one was hammering... another one was coughing... They [once] wanted to get some ice in a glass to sound natural. And after going through one effect after another, someone came out with a glass of ice water and clinked the ice in the glass. Someone said, 'My God, that's it!' "

The picture that emerged in October was a spectacularly charmless construct, overlong and full of wisecracking dialogue antithetical to the decent, rather sweet charm of Lloyd's long-established character. Paramount didn't like what they saw, and one executive even suggested that "we screen it before an audience both in the dialogue version and in the silent version. If the silent version is up to the standard of previous Lloyd pictures, I feel certain that it will please the public much better than the dialogue version."

Lloyd's instincts were superior to Paramount's; the sound version of *Welcome Danger* was the one released, and it grossed nearly $3 million worldwide, against a very high negative cost — because of the reshooting — of $979,828. Lloyd's profit was over a million dollars. Ironically, although Lloyd would make far superior films in the future, *Welcome Danger* would be his last great success; he had a slightly thin voice, and the audience preferred the fresh face of Eddie Cantor and his ilk.

"Sound," Lloyd would decide in retrospect, "didn't actually kill our kind of comedy; sound divorced it ... Stage techniques were used because performers had to remain close to the microphone. Sound tended to freeze actors and actresses in place ... Sound became a verbal medium, depending on jokes instead of pantomime ... Producers found it cheaper for comedians just to tell jokes, rather than to go out with sound equipment and try for action.

"Our silent comedies had, of course, been basically *motion* pictures. Action was everything! They couldn't have been done on the stage or in any other medium. But the new comedies ... could usually have been done in stage productions."

The end of silent film meant the end of comedians like Harold

Lloyd, simply because the new medium had little use for their skills. Silent film demanded a virtuosic level of physical comedy, because its primary tools were movement and rhythm. Silent clowns like Chaplin and Keaton created their own reality, which was rendered impossible by the objective reality brought by sound. Sound comedy would not be physical, but structural, situational; the writer became as important as the director, whereas, in silent films, the comedian and the director were the most important creative components.

□ □ □

When Rouben Mamoulian's *Applause* was released in October 1929, the general reaction was that it was too good to have been made by a first-time director. "No doubt," carped Sime Silverman of *Variety*, "Mr. Mamoulian did direct the stage work of the burlesque show and the attendant scenes back-stage, but to ask one to believe that a stage director on his first picture try could turn out this film as it has been turned out is asking one to believe as big a lot as a studio occupies." Silverman then went on to give credit where he believed it was due: "Monta Bell is the picture's producer." Silverman's churlishness was entirely misplaced; Bell had only a nominal, supervisory role in the production.

Even the initial sequence of *Applause* throws down the gauntlet — movement, not just sound; cinema, not theater. A desolate city street. A dog scrounging, papers blowing. Among them is a poster advertising "Kitty Darling, Queen of Hearts." A dog tears at the poster; a little girl stops the animal. We hear a brass band. People begin running to see the source of the music, which grows louder. We cut to Kitty Darling leading a parade to the burlesque theater. Inside, the camera moves past the pit musicians and tracks along the cinema's oldest, fattest, least appetizing chorus girls.

Aside from its innate stylishness, the rhythm of the cutting harks back to the silent films, with sound added for atmospheric details. Mamoulian sets the mood masterfully, creating the air of dingy hopelessness that will move the material beyond melodrama into near-tragedy.

Kitty gives birth to a baby. Realizing that the burlesque atmosphere is no place for a child, she sends the child to a convent. Fade out. Fade in, years later. Kitty brings the teenager out of the convent. The daughter has idealized her mother and is shocked to find a blowzy, over-the-hill embarrassment shacked up with a cheap ham who promptly sets his sights on the daughter.

Applause has been thought out in terms of cinema. The child playing with a necklace dissolves to the child playing with a rosary in the convent; the *Ave Maria* is interrupted by the crash of an arriving subway. The city is revealed largely through noise unaccompanied by images—the off-screen sound Josef von Sternberg regarded as the ideal. Mamoulian uses sound to anticipate a scene change (sound from the upcoming shot beginning during the final frames of the previous shot). To this day, however, Mamoulian has been credited with other innovations for which he wasn't really responsible; recording sound on location, for instance, had been done as early as *The Lights of New York.*

Applause is not without its faults—Helen Morgan is clearly not pregnant in the opening scene, just fat, and the radical contrast between the convent and the burlesque theater feels forced. Moreover, some of the film's virtuosity is extraneous, movement for movement's sake, the first appearance of the Look-Ma-I'm-Directing attitude that would trivialize many of Mamoulian's films—the director's innovations were rarely expended on good scripts. But Mamoulian's flourishes in *Applause* are understandable when understood as acts of defiant liberation—from camera iceboxes, from sound engineers, from the stultifying conventions of the previous two years.

Time's passing has only intensified the pungent atmosphere of the picture, the stark contrast between the roaring vitality of the big city, and the aura of peanut shells, stale beer, and grifters that make up cheap burlesque.

If nothing else, Mamoulian helped reestablish the primacy of the visual over the verbal. In later years, as Mamoulian's career stalled, then stopped entirely, the director's claims for his innovations grew ever more insistent and slightly frantic, as if he was claiming to be the Zeus from whose brow all talkie innovation sprung. His claims of being the first to use multiple microphones are, for instance, demonstrably false; Warners had been using them for two years.

But it should be remembered that Mamoulian didn't know what was being done on the West Coast; he had been given his indoctrination and was making his directorial debut at the Astoria studios, 3,000 miles away from Hollywood. The desperate ego needs of an old man should not obscure the very real style and audacity with which he adapted to a new technology while in his creative prime.

That said, an unfortunately little-known Paramount film released in August called *The Dance of Life*, codirected by John Cromwell and Eddie Sutherland, takes at least some of the shine off *Applause*. It's a character study of the people inhabiting tank-town burlesque, and the atmosphere—dingy railroad stations; venal managers; slothful chorus girls—is observed with gimlet-eyed objectivity. There's a wedding-party scene in which boorish, drunken performers compete with each other that's quietly hair-raising, eerily reminiscent of the corresponding scene in Tod Browning's *Freaks*.

The tone is very similar to *Applause*, but without Mamoulian's relentless flamboyance. Cromwell and Sutherland mesh well, the performances of Hal Skelly and Nancy Carroll are resolutely authentic—there are zooms, tracking shots, even some snappy montages in the manner of Slavko Vorkapich, and the twenty-three-year-old Oscar Levant pops up briefly. Unfortunately, *The Dance of Life* ultimately falls short of Mamoulian's accomplishment—it drags on too long, offers too many musical numbers, and gets grotesquely maudlin.

A more mid-range musical achievement was Warners' adaptation of the Jerome Kern–P. G. Wodehouse musical *Sally*, starring Marilyn Miller. Florenz Ziegfeld premiered the play—about a hash-house waitress who becomes a famous dancer—in 1920; it ran for three years and became a cornerstone of his theatrical empire, as did its star, the hard-drinking, temperamental Marilyn Miller, who also served as Ziegfeld's mistress for a time.

When she arrived in California to make movies, Miller refused to get off the train in Pasadena until there was a Rolls-Royce to meet her; she insisted on a new wardrobe and a remodeled dressing room, complete with paneled walls, French antiques, and a sunken tub. She loudly complained about having to work nights (the studio was working double shifts), because it put a crimp in her social life.

Miller was a prima donna, a drama queen, and spoiled rotten. She was Jack Warner's kind of woman, and they quickly began an affair. As directed by the journeyman John Francis Dillon, Miller and the rest of the cast of *Sally* essentially give theatrical performances, but the staging is fairly limber. Joe E. Brown plays a goofy playboy as a dry run for his inspired turn years later in *Some Like It Hot,* and Ford Sterling gives the same broad performance he was giving in 1910, comedy's Bronze Age. As for Miller, she's not much of a singer, but she's a piquant, effervescent dancer, with remarkable charm. *Sally* was an enormous hit, grossing nearly $2.2 million on a cost of $647,000.

The achievement of *Applause* and the more modest accomplishments of *The Dance of Life* and *Sally* are all the more startling when one looks at a comparable film released only a few months earlier. MGM's *Madame X* is a landlocked, paralytic antique whose grotesque style only emphasizes source material that was passé even then. Production, which began January 15, was difficult. The very first day, actor/playwright Willard Mack replaced Brandon Hurst in the role of the doctor and was simultaneously given the task of rewriting the script, which kept him up till three the next morning.

The theatrical nature of early talkie production is made clear by the fact that MGM allotted fifteen days for rehearsal, and only eleven for shooting. Since MGM had only one soundstage at this point, the *Madame X* company was sharing the facilities with other movies, and was forced to work different shifts. The regimen was brutal. Sometimes they would start their day at 8 P.M., finishing up at 11:45 the next morning; other days would start a little after two in the afternoon and wrap at almost three in the morning. Eventually, this began to take its toll on the actors; Ruth Chatterton called in sick; Raymond Hackett called in exhausted.

As with *The Broadway Melody,* Thalberg kept a very close watch on the production, coming on the set to observe final rehearsals rather than gauging the film in the rushes, as was his usual habit. The picture finally wrapped on February 16, a full eight days behind schedule.* Willard Mack took a credit for the screenplay but he used the pseudonym of John P. Edington for his performance.

Madame X represents a silent-film partisan's worst nightmare about sound. Ruth Chatterton pronounces every syllable ("Cru-ell") in a prime example of the insufferably mannered diction William Wellman called "Kansas City British." The hapless Lionel Barrymore, directing yet again despite his lack of vocational ability, gives the actors only nominal blocking and no business whatever.

There is no music, not even over the opening titles, and no thought given to devising action that might obviate the need for so many words. Between scenes, the sound disappears, as if the needle has been lifted from the groove. As with other movies of the period based on plays *(The Locked Door, Coquette),* no attempt is made to disguise the material's theatrical origins, for those origins were thought to be the major selling point. Slow fade-outs substitute for curtain falls between acts, and even entrances and exits are essentially theatrical.

The production problems encountered on *Madame X* were not at all unusual. MGM's *The Last of Mrs. Cheyney,* shot a few months after *Madame X,* also came in a full nine days behind schedule, partially because star Norma Shearer was a half-hour late every morning, reflecting either her star's prerogative or her difficulty in learning lines.

Interestingly, however, Thalberg was hedging his bets with his wife, and ordered production of a silent version of *Mrs. Cheyney.* This was not, as with *The Broadway Melody,* merely the talkie with titles in place of the dialogue, but a separate film shot in eighteen days until 11:45 every night. The day after the silent version was

---

* Although most of the time lost was because of script problems and exhausted actors, problems with sound levels were also giving MGM technicians terrible headaches; the only scene involving exterior sound is barely audible because of background noise from children that overwhelms the foreground dialogue. (Initially, the problem of recording location sound hadn't been that of balancing competing sound levels, but airplanes flying over the Culver City lot. MGM finally began hoisting a "silence" balloon warning aircraft to stay at least 2,500 feet away.)

completed, the company spent six days rehearsing the talkie version, then began production.

The talking version of *The Last of Mrs. Cheyney* offers some of Frederick Lonsdale's studied, deeply irritating sub-Wildean *bon mots* ("To accuse a beautiful woman of being likable is to suggest her underclothes are made of linoleum") and provides the unusual and not altogether satisfactory sight of Basil Rathbone playing a romantic lead. Shearer is less mannered and more likable than anybody else in the cast; her lack of stage training means she doesn't try to affect the brittle *hauteur* cultivated by the other actors. Director Sidney Franklin offers his customary understated elegance and tries to break up the lengthy drawing-room conversations with some camera movement.

For all the filmmakers' best intentions, movies like *Madame X* and *The Last of Mrs. Cheyney* proved that sound had altered the essential composition of film. Since Griffith's incremental innovations at Biograph, the primary building block of a movie had been the individual shot. *Sunrise* and *The Crowd,* not to mention hundreds of lesser films, were full of compact, radiant, emblematic shots. A conjoining of these shots — the montage — suggested, evoked, pushed open all the right doors for the audience while simultaneously omitting ordinary reality.

But, for several horrible years, the component part became not the shot but the scene, the *theatrical* scene, endless conversations with actors in dressing gowns sipping morning tea, or, if the scene was to take place at night, in evening dress sipping wine. Words introduced a less incisive quality into the art of film, if only because it was now possible to tell instead of show. The movies returned to the grim days of Adolph Zukor's Famous Players in Famous Plays, turning away from imagination, away from the development of their own intrinsic resources.

Gilbert Seldes pointed out the stultifying lack of structural motion in movies like Universal's *Broadway,* in which an attempted gangland hit is shown, after which the survivor troops into a nightclub and redundantly describes exactly what the audience has just seen. Whereas on stage the action had never been seen, the dialogue scene itself was from the play, and was therefore sacrosanct.

The success of movies like *Madame X* meant that the studios began the assembly-line conversion of theatrical antiques that had long been the province of provincial stock companies: *The Home Towners, The Green Goddess, The Last Warning, The Bat, Lightnin', Rain, Smiling Through, Liliom,* and so on. These were perfect properties in that they had modest production requirements and could be produced quickly, if only because there were very few actors over the age of thirty who hadn't played in them at one time or another.

If all this had been pointed out to Thalberg or Mayer, they would undoubtedly have responded by saying that what the people wanted was photographed melodramatic conversation, however cozy or familiar, and they believed in giving the people what they wanted. Case in point: *Madame X,* which cost a nominal $183,000 and amassed a worldwide gross of $1.2 million; MGM's net profit was $586,000.

"MGM is still behind the other studios in sound production," Mayer wrote Thalberg in October, "but quantity is not important ... What matters is that MGM becomes identified with the quality talking picture!"

For both Mayer and Thalberg, quality meant not the movies, but the theater. And so the movies died a little.

❏ ❏ ❏

The studios now had to cope with the dilemma of foreign markets. Silent films had been easy: ship the foreign negative to Europe, where the titles would be translated. Sound presented serious problems. An internal memo from Paramount's foreign-sales department stated, "One or two producers have tried [dubbing] on their pictures with a slight degree of success. We too have tried it with several reels of our pictures and found the result a very amateurish one and hardly worthy of further experimentation. Unless this method reaches better perfection [*sic*] it is unlikely that we shall ever use it."

It was because of sound that the long-lasting halfway house of subtitling was invented. Paramount split their efforts in two: some countries would see complete English-language films with subtitles; for the newly popular musicals, foreign markets would see weird hybrids in which, as a memo stated, "we take out the dialogue, retain the dance numbers, and then synchronize the entire picture to a musical score."

The results must have been interesting to behold. For the Marx Brothers film *The Cocoanuts,* Paramount told foreign exhibitors that "if we had this picture to do over again we would have eliminated the dialogue entirely, taken out some of the purely American comedy scenes, and would have synchronized the entire picture, retaining the musical numbers. It is too late for us to attempt this work now." Harold Lloyd's *Welcome Danger* was shipped out in three versions —Lloyd's original silent version ("not a re-edited version of the talkie"), the all-talking version ("suitable only for English-speaking countries"), and, for foreign markets, the silent version fitted with a music-and-effects track that Paramount trusted "should be a sensation."

Foreign-language films provided a fortuitous lifeline for a few lucky actors like the multilingual Adolphe Menjou. He went to France and made a film shot in both English and French for director Jean de Limur, who had quickly returned home after directing *The Letter.*

Upon Menjou's return to Hollywood, he made the French and Spanish versions of a Paramount B movie called *Slightly Scarlet.* Clearly, there was nothing wrong with his voice, and his acting was as polished and restrained as it had always been, so MGM signed him up . . . at half his previous salary. Paramount then borrowed him for von Sternberg's *Morocco,* and Menjou was off on the second half of a career that would flourish into the 1960s.

The studios then embarked on a wildly expensive program of remaking each picture in three or four different languages. In November 1929, MGM announced a $2-million program to replicate features in three languages: French, Spanish, and German. Paramount followed suit in the winter of 1929, when it assigned producer Robert Kane a Paris studio and gave him $10 million to produce films in five languages. By March 1930, Kane would have sixty shorts already made and ten features in production.

At Warner Bros., William Dieterle was imported from Berlin to make German-language versions of films deemed ripe for export. Long shots and action scenes from the English version were maintained, while the foreign-language dialogue scenes were shot on a rapid ten-day schedule; a big picture like *Moby Dick* might be allotted as much as fourteen days for translation into another language.

Comedy producer Hal Roach went along for the foreign-language ride, and enlisted his biggest meal tickets, Laurel and Hardy, in the battle. "We'd make the picture first entirely in English, naturally," remembered Stan Laurel. "Then we'd preview it. Then we'd get it cut and all ready for shipping. That way, we knew exactly what we were going to use of the film. If we hadn't previewed it, we may have reshot a lot of stuff that we weren't going to keep . . .

"So, then we brought in French, German, Italian, and Spanish interpreters. And they translated our dialogue into each language. Each interpreter brought his own company. . . . Then we'd set up a camera for the first scene. He'd tell us what our dialogue meant in English, then he'd tell us in French, for instance, and we'd write it phonetically as it sounded to us. And knowing the meaning of it, we got the correct intonation, which was helpful.

"We'd set up the camera, and we'd do the French version of the first scene. After the first scene, we'd hold the camera, and we'd do the German scene. And each scene we did four times, before we moved the camera . . . "

All of this was extremely time-consuming, which is to say expensive, but worth it. An executive at Paramount's Mexico office forwarded to New York a newspaper cartoon that featured two peasants. "I don't think you love me anymore," the woman says. "How can that be, sweetheart?" asks the man. "I have already told you that for your love I am capable of sitting through five English dialogue pictures." "The prices we got in South American countries and Spain were fantastic," said Hal Roach. "A Laurel and Hardy short in the Argentine would be like a feature picture."

A few of the films have survived, and movies seldom offer a richer experience than Stan Laurel attempting to wrap his Lancashire accent around sensuous Spanish vowels. (Oliver Hardy, on the other hand, launches himself into it with a flourish, complete with rolling *R*s.) The response was appropriately appreciative; one trade paper noted that "our correspondent in Barcelona informs us . . . that, after the first words, the audience howled so long and loud they never got the rest."

❑ ❑ ❑

With the exceptions of Sam Warner and William Fox, the producers had fatally underestimated the viability of sound, and they knew it, which only increased their ever-present paranoia. They had no intention of being caught so flat-footed ever again, so they began casting anxious glances at experiments in wide-screen photography.

Film that was 35mm wide had been arbitrarily established as the norm for theatrical photography ever since W. K. L. Dickson, working for Edison in 1891, had decided on the gauge after a long series of experiments with various widths and permutations of film. In 1907, an international agreement was drafted making 35mm the standard commercial film gauge, and experiments in wide-screen photography were largely the province of fringe inventors for the next fifteen years.

By 1923, George Spoor, late of the Essanay Company, and John P. Berggren were working on a 63mm film they dubbed Natural Vision. To attract interest, they rather desperately claimed that it produced a stereoscopic effect, when it did no such thing. A year later, Paramount began playing with something they called Magnascope, using it for the battle scenes in *Old Ironsides,* the elephant stampede in *Chang,* and William Wellman's magnificent *Wings,* which actually had more than half its footage projected in the process.

In essence, Magnascope was a zoom lens; at a prearranged signal, the operator would switch over to a projector equipped with the Magnascope lens, while the black masking of the square silent movie screen would pull back to a ratio remarkably similar to the modern, rectangular screen area of 1.85:1. The operator turned the lens and the picture grew gradually larger. The total enlargement was about four times the size of a normal picture.

Turning up the fire was Abel Gance, whose *Napoléon* opened in Paris in April 1927, with several sequences in what Gance dubbed Polyvision, a precursor of Cinerama that was marred only by Gance's placement of the three cameras above, rather than next to, each other. Because the three cameras didn't have the same horizon line, there was a perceptible misalignment problem in the triple-screened panoramic shots.

Nudged by these experiments, and by their stark fear of once again being caught unprepared, the moguls made a virtually unanimous decision to make a preemptive strike on the wide screen. The problem with Magnascope was, obviously, the increased grain of the projected image as the 35mm frame was enlarged; the only way around that was to increase the size of the film itself. Paramount began working on Magnifilm, which was 56mm wide.

With the help of the Mitchell Camera Corporation, which had devised 70mm cameras, William Fox began experimenting with what he called Grandeur, 70mm film with sufficient space on the side for an enlarged Movietone sound track that increased the aural fidelity just as the larger frame increased image definition. Grandeur gave a picture that projected at twenty feet high and forty-two feet wide, an unprecedented size for motion picture exhibition of the day. In April, Fox released Fox Grandeur News, which was nothing more or less than a Movietone newsreel shot in 70mm. Fox followed that with the May release of *Movietone Follies of 1929*.

Mayer and Thalberg moved quickly, an unaccustomed mode for them. Purchasing some of the Mitchell cameras, they dubbed their process Realife, while Warner Bros., latecomers for once, called their 65mm process Vitascope. The newly founded RKO contracted with Spoor and Berggren for Natural Vision. Wisely hedging their bets, the studio had most of the films that were put into production shot in a simultaneous 35mm version as well, with the normal cameras alongside the new Mitchells. All these varying processes required new projectors, new screens, new cameras, new printing machines, larger sets, and increased lighting. In mid-1929, Mayer, Warner, Zukor et al. had even more to worry about.

The onslaught of musicals meant that the time was right for Technicolor to come to the foreground, making use of a new and improved process. Instead of release prints consisting of a red strip and a green strip cemented together—the process in which *The Black Pirate* had been released—the Technicolor technicians had devised the imbibition process, a system much like lithography in which the individual strips of film representing the process's primary colors were brought into contact with a blank gelatin-coated filmstrip to which the dyes adhered.

Because the release prints were on a single strip of film, the focus problems that had plagued *The Black Pirate* were vanquished. The new Technicolor process was used for sequences in *The Broadway Melody* and Warners' *The Desert Song*, but the first major production was Warners' 1929 *On with the Show*, the first all-Technicolor, all-talking musical. A follow-up, *Gold Diggers of Broadway*, was shot that same year and grossed $3.5 million.

The color was still delicate, closer to a watercolor wash than to primary hues of vibrant intensity. Although the primary colors — red/orange and blue/green — were ersatz primaries, with a spectrum unknown to nature, the delicate unreality seemed to add to the musicals the process was used for. There may not have been blues, yellows, purples, primary reds, or primary greens, but it was yet another new wrinkle, a novelty to draw the public to the theaters.

The studios tumbled over themselves like circus clowns to ingratiate themselves with Technicolor founder Herbert Kalmus, even though using Technicolor meant spending about 20 percent more per film; Technicolor cost eight cents a foot for prints, as opposed to two cents a foot for black-and-white.

Demand was so great that Technicolor began requiring nonrefundable advances of $25,000 per picture as earnest money, amassing a total of $1.6 million. Jack Warner contracted for twenty pictures all by himself. By March 1929, Technicolor had commitments for the next ten months that entailed delivering the footage equivalent of seventeen feature movies. (A year after that, the footage equivalent was for thirty features — 12 million feet of negative, 60 million feet of prints.) Almost all of these pictures were musicals, and many of them were successes. Kalmus himself thought that the high-water marks of the process were *Whoopee!* and Warners' *The Mystery of the Wax Museum*.

Lighting style was complicated by the limitations of the process. Besides carefully painting all the sets — brighter, more vivid colors in the foreground, more neutral shades in the background — Warners took to spraying a light coat of silver paint on all trees, shrubbery, and plants so that the Technicolor cameras would pick up a surface sparkle. Factory lots of rouge were applied to the cheeks of actresses and the knees, elbows, and ankles of chorus girls.

As always, however, there was a worm in the apple. The amount of light needed to get a successful exposure was staggering; on *The*

King of Jazz, the lights were so hot that the varnish on the musicians' violins would bubble and peel. During production of Technicolor musicals at Warner Bros., George Groves saw smoke rising from men's pomaded hair. "You could light cigars in the beam of those things at a hundred yards," recalled cameraman Byron Haskin. "Hottest things you ever saw in your life." At Warners, a thermometer was placed on an unventilated stage lit for Technicolor, and the temperature rose, it was reported, to 140 degrees.

Technicolor's Hollywood lab was so overwhelmed by the rush that workers had to struggle to turn out acceptable prints while the rooms they were working in were being torn apart for expansion. Cameras were operating day and night, lab crews were working around the clock in eight-hour shifts.

But after little more than a year of boom came the bust. The deposit money dried up, and Kalmus and company began hearing demurrals such as "the public doesn't want color," "it detracts from the story," "it's too expensive," and, horrifyingly, "it hurts the eyes."

Kalmus correctly believed that most of the problems derived from the inherent limitations of the two-color system; three-color Technicolor would become the company's — and, eventually, the industry's — Holy Grail.

❑ ❑ ❑

The troubles with the Vitaphone disc system were systemic; refinements couldn't do much good. *Broadway Melody* had encountered the usual rash of trouble. A reporter from Chicago noted that "the reproduction was fairly passable until the final reel began, when the synchronization suddenly went bad, the spoken words being several seconds behind the lip movement on the screen." The audience began clapping, and the projectionist stopped the show, rewinding the reel and starting over, "repeating action we had seen before. A girl behind me giggled and said — referring to the entry of Charles King into a room, 'I guess he went out and came back in.' After fifteen seconds, it was obvious that synchronization was again off, the picture was stopped, and, shortly thereafter, begun for the third time."

By the end of 1929, all the studios but Warners had begun to make the transition to sound on film, and even Warners was dabbling in recording on film, although they continued to release strictly on disc.* It was largely because of that very quiet capitulation that the company could crow that "there are no longer any mechanical limitations to Vitaphone's scope," as a company ad proclaimed in October 1929. "Whether it is an outdoor picture, a color picture, a musical picture, a straight drama, Vitaphone retains all the flexibility of the silent film and adds to it all the realism that is possible only through the perfect reproduction of the human voice."

But the engineers and craftsmen were at work. The multiple microphones that had been hung over sets on ropes had necessitated the use of long poles to move them between scenes. This procedure was promptly dubbed "fishing," but, toward the end of 1929, the conjunction of pole and microphone gave someone at MGM the idea of constructing a long pole with a floor support in the middle, a counterweight at one end, and a microphone at the other.

Angled correctly, this mike could hover over the actors and even follow them, for the length of the boom's extension could be controlled by a crank, which gave actors and directors more freedom. Not only that, but the mike could swivel from actor to actor, thus negating the strict directional characteristics of the microphones — turning the mike back and forth to follow a conversation produced better sound than just hanging the mike in a strategic spot midway between two speakers.

Tracking shots, however, could still be dreadfully difficult. During the production of a film called *Mamba*, director Al Rogell got a brainstorm. For a walking scene with Jean Hersholt and Eleanor Boardman, Rogell had a hunchback walking in front of them. Actually, the "hump" was a microphone; when Hersholt talked, the man

---

* Dubbing sheets survive for both obscure movies, such as *Under a Texas Moon*, and famous movies, such as *Little Caesar*. For *Under a Texas Moon*, an unknown sound editor snarls, "Noah Beery's voice must carry over dialog and music which, unfortunately, were recorded on same record . . . not that anybody gives a #%&! . . ." In the case of *Little Caesar*, all sound effects — street noises, wind, and machine-gun fire — were still being recorded directly onto discs. The dubbing sheet for reel 8 of *Little Caesar* specifies, among other things, that wind begins on revolution 217 and ends on revolution 287, that machine-gun fire goes in at revolution 255 and out at 258, and so on.

was supposed to swing his hump in the actor's direction, then swivel over to point it at Boardman when it was her turn to speak.

In Hollywood, then, slowly, incrementally, things were changing. On Wall Street, the rate of change was slightly faster. On October 29, the great bull market exploded in a series of cataclysmic reverberations. The companies controlled by William Fox were among the first victims. The Loew's shares he had bought slumped in value from 64¼ to 49⅝ and kept dropping. (Within a year, Loew's stock would be down to 16.) Fox's immediate loss was in the vicinity of $50 million, and short-term notes began to come due in droves.

Fox was forced by his brokers to either cover the margins or sell and forfeit his dream of hegemony. He covered, spending $4 million of his personal funds in a single day. Fox's brokers demanded millions more. Fox, desperate for cash, was about $65 million short of his obligations. He utilized all of his personal fortune to try to avoid selling his hard-won holdings.

Fox's planned takeover of Loew's/MGM was canceled, as the debtors began gathering on the horizon. (Cash-rich studios like Warners and MGM would not feel the effects of the crash for a few years, when the ripple effect would decimate theater attendance by a full one-third.) All his efforts were in vain; Fox signed over voting control in his business to a board composed of himself, Harry Stuart, and ERPI's John Otterson. Stuart and Otterson soon composed a majority of two, and proceeded to take control of Fox's companies in what Fox believed to be an anti-Semitic putsch. (Fox, like Harry Warner, came to regard Otterson as the Wall Street equivalent of a Russian Cossack.) Even Winfield Sheehan, Fox's trusted lieutenant in production matters, went over to the enemy, taking much of the production personnel of the studio with him.

But Fox did not go without a fight, one that would consume years, dozens of lawyers, and millions of dollars. At one board meeting, things got so heated that one of the lawyers, a man named Berenson, became ill. Berenson said that Fox had better not try to put him in an ambulance, whereupon Fox snarled that that would be pointless, for the trustee would instinctively chase any ambulance as soon as he heard the siren. Fox ended up taking $18 million for his holdings, then launched a fruitless attempt to regain control of his empire.

❏ ❏ ❏

As 1929 drew to a close, producers, exhibitors, and stars were compelled to look about them at both rubble and shining new edifices. "A trying time for hundreds of exhibitors was 1929," wrote Ben Shylen in *The Exhibitor's Forum* of December 28. "Sound was a devastating scourge to many heretofore profitable theaters . . . Those exhibitors who have fought a game battle for survival until the fog cleared and the barometer pointed clearly to them which way they should go; who are now ready to go after their full share of prosperity they deserve, they too are to be congratulated. The year just closing is also an important one because it created a new type of showman—a picture merchandiser—who sold his wares like they were never before sold. Welcome 1930."

The novelty value of talkies meant not only that virtually everything the studios released made money, but that attendance increased substantially. Average weekly attendance increased from 50 million in 1926 to 65 million in 1928 (and would skyrocket to 90 million in 1930). Compare the net profits for the four major companies for 1929 with those from 1928, the last year of across-the-board silent production:

	1928	1929
Warner Bros.	$2,044,842	$17,271,805
Fox	5,957,217	9,469,050
Paramount	8,713,063	15,544,544
Loew's/MGM	8,568,162	11,756,956

As far as the moguls and their stockholders were concerned, sound was worth whatever its aesthetic cost.* Even in Europe, which was making the transition to sound very slowly, mostly because of inde-

---

* Once the novelty wore off, the situation proved eminently temporary, as *Variety* noted in a story from June 21, 1932. The headline was SOUND FILMS SHY BIG SILENT SUMS: "Silence in pictures, after all, was golden. It represented in money from some individual pictures much more for their makers than any talker to date . . . "

The article compared the grosses of *City Lights* ($4.2 million) and a host of silent pictures—*Seventh Heaven* at $2.5 million, *The Four Horsemen of the Apocalypse*

cision and lack of capital, business was good. And this in spite of the fact that few of the twenty-seven thousand European theaters were wired for sound. England had only about four hundred sound theaters by the end of 1929, compared to America's six thousand, and France had only about ten theaters capable of showing sound films.*

MGM released their last silent film, the Garbo vehicle *The Kiss,* in November of 1929. In this variation on *The Paradine Case* (a woman on trial for murdering her older husband), Jacques Feyder's camera swoops and glides through Cedric Gibbons's stunning deco sets in what is, for the stylistically austere MGM, an unprecedented display of camera style. Although the film is brief — sixty-four minutes — it's as long as it needs to be and is shot in a way that clearly indicates it was planned to use synchronized sound effects†: as two men struggle, Garbo rushes into the room and the door swings shut, blocking

---

with $4 million, *What Price Glory* with $2.4 million — with financial results for talkies in the midst of the Depression, where million-dollar grosses were few and far between, and $2-million grosses were as frequent as solar eclipses. Only *Whoopee!*, *Palmy Days* and *Trader Horn* came close to the halcyon days of *The Singing Fool.*

The trade paper ascribed the difference to "the gigantic possibilities of silents, with the world market to pick from, as against talkers with outlet narrowed . . . Figures on [*City Lights*] show that Chaplin was right about silence on the screen, at least in his case."

* England was so technologically backward that when British director Victor Saville's *Kitty,* produced as a silent, needed sound added for its June 1929 release, the film had to be shipped to New York, where the music and effects were added, as well as a new ending shot with sound. Nevertheless, Alfred Hitchcock managed to make *Blackmail,* begun as a silent, and reshot with dialogue. *Blackmail* also opened in June of 1929 and was, with only slight exaggeration, called "The First Full-Length All-Talkie film made in Great Britain." In spite of the fact that Hitchcock was, along with Vidor, among the first to make sound impressionistic — playing with it, distorting it, using it to create the effect of a greater silence — the London *Times* preferred the silent version; Kevin Brownlow considers that version the finest surviving English silent.

† MGM was clearly doing specific sound cues as a matter of company policy. *Our Modern Maidens,* a drama of the young and the restless with Joan Crawford and Douglas Fairbanks Jr. that was released in August, is a silent film with a synchronized

our view. The camera slowly pulls back until we hear a gunshot, whereupon the camera suddenly stops — the sound of the gun placing an emphatic period on the gliding sentence of camera movement. All in all, *The Kiss* is a fitting farewell to the silent film from the studio that made the most glamorous use of it; Garbo's commercial allure helped the film make a $448,000 profit.

In 1927 and 1928, Hollywood camera crews had always made it clear that the soundmen were unwanted interlopers. But, by the end of 1929, the balance of power had shifted. "We'd say, 'Well, you wanna go back to making silent pictures?' " remembered soundman Buster Libott. The answer would be an abashed headshake or a stony silence.

The audience had spoken: silent films now belonged to the permanent, irremediable past. All that was left was to see what kind of permanent shape talkies would take.

---

score and effects. One of the latter is a radio broadcast giving the time, after which the characters, who have stayed out too late, react with alarm.

Yet, such was the inconsistent state of MGM's commitment to sound that *Mysterious Island,* a part-talkie released in October, is a particularly chaotic example of the changeover. Lionel Barrymore is obviously using cue cards, unlike the actor that shares his scenes, the deliciously named Montagu Love. Their eyes meet only accidentally. Sometimes Lloyd Hughes talks into a microphone on board a submarine and we hear him; sometimes we don't. It's a deeply incoherent, shoddy — but not cheap — film, with roughly six directors manhandling an otherwise promising subject during a chaotic period.

PART FIVE

1930

and After

Silent films were like a beautiful
child playing in the sun, but . . .
when today's youth discovers the
cinema from back then . . . they
will be surprised at the melancholy
of their ancestors.

René Barjavel

Location work at MGM circa 1930. The camera
is out of the icebox, but the aerial balloon is still present,
warning airplanes to stay away.

ROBERT S. BIRCHARD COLLECTION

CHAPTER ONE

Sound was still something that had to be carefully handled, like nitroglycerin. For its January release of *The Rogue Song*, MGM sent out the requisite cue sheet specifying the amplifier setting for virtually every moment of the film. The projectionist constantly had to ride herd on the volume control, raising it for the sound effects that punctuated the gags of Laurel and Hardy and the singing of Lawrence Tibbett, lowering it for dialogue scenes.

"The desired volume during certain parts of *The Rogue Song*," instructed the cue sheet, "is considerably louder than has ever been considered conventional or necessary in the running of any sound picture, with the exception of gun shots or explosions. Do not be alarmed ... you will find that the audience will be thrilled by the effect, and you will also notice that the loud sections are short and are purposely followed in every case by low-volume scenes which afford a relief and contrast to the picture ...

"High volume is not in the least disturbing or objectionable when there is no distortion present in the sound. This is shown by the fact that an audience can listen [to] and enjoy a hundred-piece orchestra playing as loudly as possible."

Laurel and Hardy had been added to an operetta at least partially because audiences had quickly grown bored with the sameness of the musicals that flooded the market in 1929. *The King of Jazz* was finally released in May of 1930 to an unfavorable critical response, with *Variety* summing it up: "What this picture muffed is a pity." The film ended up earning less than $900,000 domestically, although the considerable loss was covered by the success of *All Quiet on the Western Front.* A disgruntled Universal nevertheless threatened to sue Whiteman for the twenty-two blue tuxedoes he had charged to the studio, along with numerous telegrams and food bills.*

As indifferent as *King of Jazz* was, it seemed a masterpiece alongside something like Warners' stupefying *Golden Dawn,* the only extant musical about the slave trade in German East Africa. The music—by Emmerich Kalman and Herbert Stothart—is not bad, but the libretto—by Otto Harbach and Oscar Hammerstein—sinks the enterprise. *Golden Dawn* offers such treats as a rare film appearance by Vivienne Segal, lines like "woman gives and remembers; man takes and forgets," and Noah Beery in blackface singing to his whip ("Listen little whip / while you're in my grip . . ."). Lupino Lane, who had made a hit in Ernst Lubitsch's *The Love Parade* the previous year, does one of his amazing acrobatic specialty numbers, which turns into a tribute to the benefits of going native ("Don't propose a limousine / To your dusky jungle queen . . .").

MGM's *Good News* likewise came too late to make an impression, despite the presence of Ukulele Ike and a classic DeSylva, Brown, and Henderson score. MGM was still using live recording for their musical numbers, and made effective use of the new mike boom to follow the singers. But the style remains presentational, the choreography designed for the proscenium rather than the screen. It doesn't come across and the filmmakers knew it; director Nick Grinde tries vainly to make the "Varsity Drag" number come alive by inserting shots of dancers' feet beginning to smoke, as well as superimposing

---

* The English revue film *Elstree Calling* is considerably more interesting than its American counterparts, if only because it lifts a good many of its performers and material from contemporary stage shows and music halls, while the Hollywood films basically made do with movie stars singing and dancing. Since most of them had limited talents in those areas, films such as *The Hollywood Revue* and *The Show of Shows* seem to last roughly as long as the Wars of the Roses.

a thermometer with the temperature rising, producing an effect that is simultaneously quaint and desperate.*

In all, more than seventy musicals were released in 1930, a large proportion of them producing dismal artistic and commercial results. Even *So Long Letty,* with that glorious rowdy Charlotte Greenwood, barely broke even after being released late in 1929. Like most of his songwriting brethren, Oscar Hammerstein II had gone west in 1929, only to see the favorable environment for musicals disappear virtually overnight. "[1930 was] the year they had so many bad musicals that theaters hung out signs saying NO MUSIC IN THIS PICTURE as a lure to get people inside," he said in 1943. "So the party was over and we all came home."

MGM released one of the exceptions to the run of disasters with *They Learned About Women,* a baseball musical starring the great vaudevillians Gus Van and Joe Schenck (not to be confused with the producer Joe Schenck) that's a clear precursor of Gene Kelly's *Take Me Out to the Ballgame.* Van and Schenck were a bouncy pair of middle-aged Sunshine Boys, and the film—about a vaudeville act that plays pro baseball all summer long—captures their faded but pleasant gusto. "She's so crooked they'll have to bury her in a trombone," exclaims Gus Van at one point, and the Jewish monologuist Benny Rubin has a routine where he asks, "Why does that candle remind you of seven days?"

"Because it's a wick long."

* It was about the time of *Good News* that the studios devised cue marks for the ends of reels, to help projectionists make smooth changeovers. "In the future, and until further notice, all changeover signals will be visual," said the small print on the bottom of the *Good News* cue sheet. "These signals appear at the end of the reel in the form of a round, black spot appearing steady in the upper right hand corner of the screen during four consecutive frames. On a very dark screen or fadeout, the spot has a white line around it. The signal is fashioned so that it is clearly visible if watched for, but not particularly noticeable to an audience. Two sets of these signals appear on the end of each reel. The FIRST SET is the signal to start the motor of the incoming machine, and the SECOND SET is the signal to cut over picture and sound . . ." When MGM said "until further notice," they probably didn't think they were referring to the next seventy years, for cue marks have remained the norm to the present day.

The string of musical disasters grew so alarming that the studios panicked; most musical films in production were unceremoniously shorn of their production numbers — Douglas Fairbanks's *Reaching for the Moon*, and Warners' *Fifty Million Frenchmen*, among others. For several years, musicals became an endangered species; only Ernst Lubitsch continued with the production of his boudoir operettas, until Astaire and Rogers and Warners' *42nd Street* brought the form roaring back to life.

If the genre began with *The Jazz Singer*, musicals took three years to wear out their welcome; but for the boomlet of 70mm wide-screen releases, nobody ever came to the door. For perhaps the only time in film history, the studios were actually ahead of the public. Fox's *The Big Trail* (in Grandeur) was a commercial failure, as were Warners' *A Soldier's Plaything* (in Vitascope) and King Vidor's MGM film *Billy the Kid* (in Realife, amassing a loss of $119,000).*

The extra expense of large-format film was hardly matched by any extra revenue, mostly because exhibitors obstinately refused to invest in new hardware so soon after the conversion to sound. By the end of the year, fewer than twenty theaters had been equipped for 63mm, 65mm, or 70mm projection. The handwriting was on the wall by mid-1930, when Adolph Zukor, speaking on behalf of the Producers Association of America, said that it "would be folly to bring out the wide film and place additional burdens on the exhibitors. I can assure you that the producers of America have decided to delay the advent of the wide film until such time as it is necessary again to provide an attraction to the public."

That took slightly more than twenty years, when 20th Century–Fox's CinemaScope, an old invention in a new wrapping, started

---

* All that would be preserved from the commercial rubble of *The Big Trail* was the starring debut of a young, astonishingly handsome John Wayne. As the Fox publicity put it, "A handsome youth weighing 200 pounds and all bone and muscle, a smile that is worth a million, a marvelous speaking voice, a fearless rider, a fine natural actor and he has everything the femmes want in their leading man. Less than two years ago, Wayne was playing football at the University of Southern California. Watch this boy go, for it would be well to remember that [director] Raoul Walsh has brought to stardom more unknowns than any man in the industry. This is his biggest bet."

another revolution, albeit one far less cataclysmic than sound. The 70mm Mitchell cameras that had been in storage were brought out of mothballs, retooled, and turned into Todd-AO, MGM's Camera 65, Super Panavision 70, and the rest of the wide-screen processes that followed in the wake of CinemaScope.

Also doing a fast fade were the foreign-language films embarked on with such optimism late in 1929. "One thing that the American filmmakers didn't realize," commented Edward Dmytryk, "was that there are many, many dialects in Spanish. We'd have one actor from Spain and one from Mexico and one from Argentina . . . So when the pictures were released the Mexicans didn't like it because of the [Argentinians], the Argentinians didn't like it because of the Mexican[s]."

The moguls had made an essential mistake, imagining that stars were less important than the movie, when the entire history of Hollywood instructed them that the reverse was the case. Few French wanted to be Germans, few Italians wanted to be British, yet every man wanted to be Gary Cooper, every woman Marlene Dietrich.

Only Spanish versions released in the American Southwest ever produced sizable revenues. Besides the resistance of the audience, the economics were dicey; each foreign-language film produced cost between $30,000 and $40,000 above and beyond the cost of the original production, compared with the $3,500 it cost to dub a picture. MGM called off the production of foreign-language versions in April 1932, Paramount shortly thereafter.

❑ ❑ ❑

Howard Hughes premiered *Hell's Angels* in May at Grauman's Chinese Theater. Robert E. Sherwood wrote that "with his four million dollars, Mr. Hughes acquired about five cents' worth of plot, approximately thirty-eight cents' worth of acting, and a huge amount of dialogue, the total value of which may be estimated by the following specimen. Boy: 'What do you think of my new uniform?' Girl: 'Oh, it's ripping!' Boy: (nervously) 'Where?' " *Hell's Angels* was a financial disaster, grossing $1.6 million domestically, with another million coming in from foreign markets. Hughes's personal loss on the picture was in the vicinity of $1 million. He could afford it, for the Hughes Tool Company was making profits of about $2 million a year. Dazzled by the glamour of Hollywood and its beautiful women, an undaunted Hughes promptly put five more pictures into production.

❏ ❏ ❏

John Gilbert was the most obvious casualty of sound, but there were many others. In fact, actors were not necessarily the only victims, or even the most tragic. Some writers made the transition — Anita Loos, Bess Meredyth, C. Gardner Sullivan, Frances Marion, and Lenore Coffee, among others — but they were mostly skilled at story construction, not dialogue.

"The executives were terrified of a new word, 'dialogue,' " recalled Casey Robinson, who was writing titles at First National when sound hit. "And if you hadn't written a play, you couldn't possibly write dialogue. And I had never written a play." Robinson would recover and become famous for his scripts for Bette Davis. Other writers, however, found sound an impenetrable wall.

After supervising, editing, and titling *Sunrise, Four Sons, Ben-Hur, Seventh Heaven, The River, The Loves of Carmen,* and *Cameo Kirby,* Katherine Hilliker and H. H. Caldwell found to their mounting consternation that they couldn't get a job. They logged their last stint at a studio with eight months at Fox ending in August 1929, earning $5,000 a month. For the next three years, they struggled. In October 1931, Caldwell was back in New York, while his wife persisted in trying to get screen work.

One of their few nibbles involved Sol Lesser, who offered them $1,500 for a complete shooting script of *Peck's Bad Boy.* "If I'd had two hundred in the bank I'd have walked out on him," Hilliker wrote her husband. She didn't have two hundred in the bank, so she took the deal. "I can't help a glow of relief at knowing that at least you can get your hair cut and you won't have to take [their son] Harry out of school for lack of carfare. I really almost went mad last week. In all the years of my life I can remember no such terrible grief and worry."

The problem was the inevitable question: What have they done in talkies? The prejudice was frankly stated by, among others, Richard Schayer, head of Universal's scenario department, who told Hilliker that he'd love to hire them but that "the difficulty would be in selling

Junior [Laemmle], who has the usual peculiar ideas about ladies and gentlemen of the Silent Era."

By January 1932, Hilliker was selling off her paintings to keep going. Old friends were called: Frank Borzage, Josef von Sternberg, men for whom they had done valuable work. They were cordial but impersonal, as if unemployment might be catching. "How does one get a lighthouse to keep?" wrote a frantic Hilliker.

A $500-a-week job with the independent World Wide Pictures lasted only two months. Hilliker finally bailed out of Hollywood and left for New York, where she and her husband wrote a couple of plays, one of which, *Little Stranger*, was produced in London. In April 1936, she went on the payroll of the Works Projects Administration for the next four years, earning about $2,400 a year. It seems not to have been enough as there are records of small loans they obtained from the Authors' League Fund.

□ □ □

Audiences quickly grew tired of Al Jolson. *Say It With Songs*, released in August 1929, grossed more than $2 million on an investment of $470,000, in spite of the fact that it was an atrocious film. The first half hour has no music at all, just Jolson's over-the-top emoting in a male version of *Stella Dallas* by Darryl Zanuck. Jolson plays a radio singer who goes to prison and achieves redemption by singing ("Violets can do it / Why can't you?") to hardened convicts.

Say It With Songs must have turned off multitudes, for Jolson's next picture, *Mammy*, grossed only $947,000 on a cost of almost $800,000, followed by the out-and-out disaster *Big Boy*, which Jolson played entirely in blackface. *Big Boy* grossed $498,000, some $76,000 less than it cost. Warners also saw Marilyn Miller's appeal quickly dissipate. *Sunny*, her follow-up to *Sally*, grossed only $690,000 on a cost of $745,000. After one more equally unsuccessful picture, Miller left Hollywood and never came back before her premature death in 1936.

For the industry in general, however, 1930 would prove to be an enormously profitable year; Paramount earned $18 million in profits, the highest in their history up until that time. Yet, Sam Katz, head of the theater division, had made a prescient remark in 1927: "We can lose enough money on our theaters to sink [Paramount]." The next year, the spread of the Depression reduced Paramount's profits to $6 million. In 1932, the company lost a staggering $21 million. The entire motion picture industry went into a steep business decline that would culminate in Warners and MGM cutting salaries, and Paramount, severely overextended by its theater chain, actually going bankrupt.

❑ ❑ ❑

In December 1931, William Fox's Tri-Ergon patents were adjudged legal and the American patents were issued. Fox immediately filed suit against ERPI, RCA, Paramount, RKO, and everybody else in the motion picture business for violating his patents. He excluded only the Fox studio, for he had assigned his Tri-Ergon license to them as part of his agreement with the studio.

For the second time, William Fox was attempting to enforce a private monopoly of the entire talking-picture business. As a combination of self-justification and spin control, Fox cooperated with the muckraking journalist Upton Sinclair on a biography, the theme of which was that Fox had been robbed of his company by an unholy alliance of the movie companies, Wall Street, and Washington. Throughout, both Sinclair and Fox seemed blissfully unaware that Fox had actually been beaten at his own game, that by attempting to buy Loew's/MGM, he had been every bit as guilty of attempted monopoly as AT&T.

In March 1932, William Fox announced that he would not reenter films, preferring to concentrate on his health and his golf. When reporters asked if he retained any interest in the activities of the Fox company, he indicated by sign language that, on that subject at least, he was deaf and dumb.

The government soon charged that Fox had "manipulated as he saw fit" the stock of his companies and had "utilized the corporation for his own enrichment..." Nine days after the government filed suit asking damages of more than $5 million, the Fox Film Corporation filed suit asking for between $10 and $15 million for Fox's misfeasance, malfeasance, and nonfeasance. Fox Film Corporation also asked that the contracts between Fox and the company be set aside, including the annual salary of $500,000, and that the Tri-Ergon patents be remanded to the company.

Save for the government's intervention, Fox might have been able to outlast his opponents, but with the Attorney General's office arrayed against him, capitulation was not a matter of if, but when. There was a temporary reprieve when, in October 1934, the Supreme Court decided that the Fox patents were in fact legal. Fox danced a jig on the ornate rug in his office at the Roxy Theater and exulted, "Now I've got the sonsabitches by the balls, and don't think I won't twist them." And once again he overreached.

He sent fourteen thousand letters to exhibitors and published ads in the trade papers warning the entire world that any projection of a sound movie in America was a violation of his patents. Attorneys for the opposing side used the letter as documentary evidence that Fox was coercing the competition and attempting to restrain trade. They asked the Supreme Court to reconsider their original decision. On March 14, 1935, the Supreme Court, realizing that their earlier decision, while observing the strict letter of the law, had essentially handed over the entire motion picture industry to one man, reversed themselves, and decided that the same patents that had been valid in October were no longer valid.

Now Fox was trapped, finally and irrevocably. In June 1936, he declared bankruptcy, listing $100 in assets and $9,935,261 in liabilities. Then, Fox attempted to bribe the federal judge handling his case, paying $12,500 to a bagman. He was found guilty of conspiracy to bribe, obstruction of justice, and fraud. He spent a year and a day in prison. Shortly before his death on May 8, 1952, he turned to his niece and suddenly exclaimed, "Don't ever marry a gentile. Someday he will turn on you and call you a 'dirty Jew.'" In the mind of William Fox, the collapse of his empire, perhaps even the stock-market crash itself, had all been an immaculately orchestrated plot by gentile corporation heads and bankers.

❏ ❏ ❏

The bedraggled remnants of Murnau's *City Girl* finally appeared for public inspection in February 1930. The film ran only seventy minutes, was about 50 percent sound, and met with a response that was 100 percent negative. "*City Girl* two years ago was on Fox schedule as a potential two-buck topper," said *Variety*. "It was Murnau's last for Fox . . . and was to have been an epic of the wheat fields. In its release state it represents a weak, slow theme, with little action of the conventional kind worked into a finis obviously reshot." *Harrison's Reports* said that "it is not very entertaining. Nor will it be inspiring. The first half of the picture is silent. The sound of the talking part has been recorded fairly well."

Yet, in one of film history's few fortuitous flukes, it is the released part-sound version that has been lost, and something approaching Murnau's original silent version that has survived. It's not a definitive Murnau film — it lacks the textural density, the precise rhythm of his other work; as historian David Shepard says, it represents a compromised version of the original silent, "before everybody threw up their hands and walked away." It's also two full reels longer than the hopelessly compromised sound version. (The last few reels follow the suggestions of Katherine Hilliker and H. H. Caldwell fairly closely, which explains their credit for "Editing and Titling.")

If *Sunrise* is a symphony, *City Girl* is a chamber piece, a film of a few simple settings and some carefully observed byplay. The characterizations are archetypal — innocent country boy, hardened but decent city girl, harsh rural patriarch — and the theme is Murnau's very own: two lost souls finding redemption as they rediscover their love despite, or because of, dire circumstances.

Murnau works in that striking image that so impressed him on his first trip to America — legions of disembodied legs striding by the window of a below-ground restaurant — and, in one short scene, he masterfully creates an aura of urban loneliness that would do justice to Edward Hopper: the girl's small, bare apartment; an elevated train passing by the window; flashing neon lights in the distance; her careful tending of a bedraggled plant.

But, once the couple leave the city and go to his farm in the country, except for a few grace notes — Murnau's camera flows through the wheat fields like wind — we are in the land of obvious compromise. Murnau — or, more likely, the multitudes looking over his shoulder — spends too much time away from the lovers. In *Sunrise*, everything is seen through the eyes of George O'Brien and Janet Gaynor. Here, the viewpoint is more objective, the climax rushed, and the film lurches into patchy melodrama. What Lotte Eisner called "the soft modeling" of Murnau's luminous lighting is present, but the all-important rhythm and sense of environment is, especially in the second half, disrupted.

City Girl was a financial disaster and a creative disappointment. Well before it was released, Murnau had renounced Fox, and all of Hollywood.

❑ ❑ ❑

MGM's contretemps with Lon Chaney finally ended when the company backed down; the contract Chaney signed on January 23, 1930, gave him his $50,000 bonus, as well as an equal amount if and when the studio picked up the next of his yearly options.

Production of *The Unholy Three,* a remake of one of Chaney's biggest silent hits (with dialogue courtesy of the blundering J. C. Nugent), began on April 1 and finished on April 24. But Chaney's health was failing; although it doesn't particularly show in the finished film, there were days he could barely struggle through his scenes, and he looks far older than his actual age of forty-seven. On July 10, MGM again took him off salary because he was unable to work. On August 26, 1930, Lon Chaney died of cancer.

The next day, Louis B. Mayer issued a statement to all the employees of MGM: "To honor the memory of our beloved friend Lon Chaney, whose untimely passing has been a severe blow to us all, this studio will observe a period of silence tomorrow, Thursday, at three o'clock. At this time, the remains are to be lowered to their final resting place and in respect to our departed co-worker everyone at the studio is requested to maintain complete silence at his post between signals of the siren."

A few weeks later, Mayer was in deep consultation with studio lawyers to see if MGM had any legal recourse to recover Chaney's $50,000 bonus. The attorneys regretfully informed Mayer that the money belonged to Chaney's estate.

❑ ❑ ❑

Paramount began a series of films featuring William Powell as the insufferable Philo Vance. *The Benson Murder Case,* released in April, soon devolves into a standard old-dark-house murder-mystery à la *The Bat,* complete with notably inauthentic thunder effects, but it opens with a smashing montage of the stock market crash: a buzzing of surrealistic crowd noises, melting numerals, towers of coins falling, and rapid cutting in the best Russian manner. *The Benson Murder Case* starts with a bang and never bangs so loudly again, but such films constituted tentative baby-steps toward a complete melding of sound and the basic storytelling aspects of silent film.

Paramount continued its experimental bracketing of film directors with stage directors well into 1932. Although George Cukor had come from New York, he became one of the more adept practitioners of sound's new wave. When he codirected *The Royal Family of Broadway* at the Astoria studio, Cukor and cameraman George Folsey wanted to get the effect of the camera tracking and rising at the same time. What they wanted could be easily achieved by a camera crane, but the Astoria studio didn't have one. Somebody came up with the idea of renting a large forklift and converting it into a camera platform.

"Going up and down was fine," remembered assistant director Arthur Jacobson, "but it couldn't go forward or back or sideways, except by manpower. We had about twenty men pushing it, and we got the shot." Even at Astoria, camera movement was back.

The pure engineers that had ruled the studios for the first eighteen months of sound were quickly shunted aside, for even the moguls realized that in a contest between technical brilliance or dramatic brilliance, moviemakers had to go with the actors every time.

What Edward Bernds would call "a kind of cinematic peace treaty" became the rule at the studios; the soundman tried to keep his mike shadow out of the cameraman's composition, and the cameraman tried to light the set so that the mike could be placed in a reasonably good position.

King Vidor had a long, mostly successful career in sound films, although one of incremental artistic decline. His private life remained one of intellectual and erotic curiosity. In 1932, Eleanor Boardman sued him for divorce, naming script girl Betty Hill as co-respondent. After a bitter custody battle over his and Boardman's child, Vidor married Hill, although that marriage too ended in steely estrangement. Vidor ended his days with Colleen Moore, the delightful actress of the silent era whose career did not survive sound.

In some private way, Vidor seems to have known that his talent was particularly suited to silent films, and he would cling to memories of the days when he had created his finest achievements. In 1937, he told an interviewer that a few days before, a manicurist had said to him, "Oh, are you the man who made *The Crowd*? I'll never forget the scene where the boy comes out and tries to shush the fire engines passing by as his baby is dying! It was so beautiful!"

"That was in 1928," said Vidor. "And yesterday, on the set, someone remembered John Gilbert's love scene — in a boat drifting under low, sweeping trees — from *Bardelys the Magnificent*. Just a flash in an otherwise ordinary movie, but it hasn't been forgotten."

If the audience didn't forget, neither did Vidor; he spent years wrangling with MGM over his percentages of *The Crowd* and *Hallelujah*. As of August 1981, he had received $69,385 from his deferred salary for *Hallelujah*, which meant that his idealism in pledging his salary to get the film made had cost him $31,000.

The studios continued to make up special prints with sound on disc for theaters equipped only for disc sound (5,042 of them, according to a May 1931 *Motion Picture Herald*). These tended to be the smaller or rural houses, but the cumulative income derived from those theaters was considerable and could not be ignored.*

For a time, studios even continued to service unwired theaters

---

* Some small theaters took years to be able to afford sound at all. The Gem Theater in St. Paris, Ohio, population 1,200, didn't have sound until March of 1931 — the premiere attraction was *The King of Jazz*. The rural theater managed to keep admission prices at 10 cents and 25 cents in spite of the cost of the equipment. "We are trying to please our local community and create home town prosperity for everyone," read an ad in the local paper. "Help to boost St. Paris and keep the street lights burning."

Even then, "volume fluctuated wildly . . . as personnel tried to learn how to operate the equipment," reported one resident. In addition, once a week the Gem would shut down the projectors and air *Amos and Andy* over the speaker system, for it was far more popular than most of the movies being shown.

By January 1932, the job of wiring theaters for sound was essentially over. According to *Film Daily*'s *Film Year Book 1933*, covering the year 1932, 14,405 of the nation's 18,553 theaters were wired. Silent houses that had closed totaled 4,128; sound houses that had closed totaled 1,925, with a disproportionate percentage of those in northern industrial states devastated by the Depression.

with silent versions of talking pictures. Frank Capra's charming, vivacious 1930 picture *Ladies of Leisure* survives in both sound and silent versions. The silent version runs eighty-five minutes compared to the talkie's ninety-seven. Since titles tend to get to the dramatic point of a scene faster than dialogue, which is often about character as much as plot, the silent version moves faster. The silent version's speed is also accentuated by its occasional lopping off of the first or last part of a scene that plays out full-length in the talkie; it isn't missed at all in the silent version. The silent film also occasionally uses different takes from the sound version.

Although the silent spares the audience the gauche line-readings of the crude, lumbering Ralph Graves, the film's key sequence works better in sound. Capra crosscuts between Graves and Barbara Stanwyck going to bed in different parts of the same apartment, building up suspense as to which of them will relent and go to the other. The natural sound effects — rain on the window, the creak of the door opening — accent the sexual tension far more than music — or even silence — ever could.

❑ ❑ ❑

As for Warner Bros., its asset base had grown from slightly more than $5 million in 1925 to $230 million by 1930, a 4,600 percent increase in five years. Harry had bought the First National studio in Burbank, where the studio remains to this day, as well as the Stanley Warner chain of theaters, a couple of music publishing companies, and a production outfit for Broadway plays. The studio continued recording on disc until well into 1931 and films such as *The Public Enemy*, and didn't switch over to releasing sound on film until 1932. Almost immediately, the pace of Warner Bros. pictures began to pick up.

Personally, Harry and Jack were now comfortably ensconced as members in good standing of Hollywood's *nouveau riche:* big bank accounts, new houses (Jack's in Beverly Hills, Harry's in Westchester County, New York). In a rare moment of self-appraisal, the self-effacing Albert Warner would say, "We've made millions. But that doesn't bring Sam back."

In the middle of 1930, Warners released a cheerfully self-aggrandizing short called *An Intimate Dinner in Celebration of War-*

ner Bros. Silver Jubilee, with Otis Skinner as Mr. W. B. Pictures and Beryl Mercer as Mrs. W. B. Pictures presiding over a *faux* banquet. "It hardly seems twenty-five years since I led you to the altar," Skinner intones. The star of the picture is Little Miss Vitaphone, a toddling horror who introduces a succession of Warner Bros. stars (Loretta Young, Douglas Fairbanks Jr., Edward G. Robinson, and Joan Blondell) and some of the premier musical talents then working on the lot (Jerome Kern, Rodgers and Hart, Otto Harbach, Oscar Hammerstein II, and Marilyn Miller).

The absence of some stars, who were presumably insulated from such degrading personal appearances, is explained by a line: "I supposed you're wondering why John Barrymore, George Arliss, and Richard Barthelmess aren't here." Whereupon some palpably phony telegrams of good wishes from the presumably on-location stars are flashed on the screen. Otis Skinner ends the moribund festivities by proclaiming, "Here's hoping that twenty-five years from now we'll be able to celebrate Warner Bros. Golden Anniversary!"

While all this self-congratulation was going on, Harry's three-year quest to wrest Sam's daughter, Lita, from her mother finally succeeded. Lina Basquette's career, despite a couple of costarring jobs opposite major stars like Richard Barthelmess and Adolphe Menjou, and the lead in *The Godless Girl,* had obstinately refused to take off. Plus her fiancé was cameraman J. Peverell Marley, who didn't like children.

Basquette settled her interest in Sam's estate and gave up guardianship of her daughter for a $40,000 life insurance policy, his Minerva car, complete with a chauffeur who doubled as a Warner spy, a $100,000 trust fund, and a $300,000 trust for the little girl. Erratic and fun-loving, Lina Basquette blew a lot of the money on bad stocks and bonds, while the interest from the $100,000 — about $85 a week — just about covered expenses. On March 19, 1930, Harry and his wife Rea became legal guardians of Lita Basquette Warner. Lina Basquette would see her daughter precisely twice in the next twenty years.

"I believe the main reason Harry wanted me with his family," said Lita Warner over sixty years later, "was so I would be brought up as a Warner. He didn't want my mother to get [Sam's] money, but neither did he want to deprive me . . . With Lina I would've had a wild life. It wouldn't have been the greatest thing to have been brought up by her."

After selling what amounted to 20 percent of Warner Bros. for something less than a penny on the dollar, Lina Basquette's starring career ended with the coming of sound. She went on to marry six more times, eventually reestablish contact with her daughter, live in a West Virginia condo, and become one of the nation's leading judges of dog shows, specializing in Great Danes.

"Today," she said in 1993, "I've outlived 'em all. And I've become closer and closer to my daughter. In the end, I've conquered all."

And then, Lina Basquette summed up her life and varied careers by confiding, "In my whole life, nothing has been as satisfying to me as purebred dogs." She died in 1994.

❑ ❑ ❑

In July 1932, Jack and Harry's long-simmmering resentment of the squeeze play AT&T executed when it coerced Warners into relinquishing its exclusive license for talking motion pictures finally exploded. Warners filed a suit against AT&T, Western Electric, and ERPI. The previous year Warners had charged that ERPI owed them $50 million from royalties on sales of disc recordings. The new lawsuit went even further, charging that AT&T, Western Electric, and ERPI had sought to monopolize the business of furnishing recording and reproducing equipment and had, in effect, committed the mortal sin of excluding Warners from both the monopoly and the profits. Warners also asked the court to force ERPI to drop their compulsory weekly service fee from each theater and to stop leasing their equipment to theaters and begin selling it outright. (In 1928, ERPI had been charging an average of $60 per theater per week; by 1932, the figure had been lowered to $20.)

Under Hoover's Justice Department, AT&T might have had a fighting chance; under Roosevelt's, none. AT&T got out of the movie business in 1934, after racking up earnings of $21,314,000 strictly from sound film, or about a 15.5-percent return on investment, most of which derived from the windfall profits of wiring and installing sound equipment.

❑ ❑ ❑

F. W. Murnau was sick of Hollywood; indeed, he seemed to be sick of the entire industrial process of filmmaking. He bought a yacht, christened it the *Bali,* and sailed for Tahiti in May 1929 to make an independent film from a story by Robert Flaherty. After Murnau and Flaherty arrived, their backers defaulted on the production loan. Murnau decided to finance the production himself, out of his savings from the Fox contract.

Production began in January 1930 on the island of Bora Bora, with a crew that consisted of cameraman Floyd Crosby and a native assistant, using one camera and two or three reflectors. The film's story evolved from an anecdote involving a native boy and girl whose love brings down a curse from a holy man, who implacably pursues them as they vainly attempt to flee the islands.

Production stretched on for a leisurely nine months; Murnau was stalling, luxuriating in his environment. In a letter to his mother, he wrote, "When I think I shall have to leave all this I already suffer all the agony of going. I am bewitched by this place. I have been here a year and I don't want to be anywhere else. The thought of cities and all those people is repulsive to me. I want to be alone, or with a few rare people ... [but] I am never 'at home' anywhere ... not in any country nor in any house nor with anybody."

Back in Los Angeles, Murnau spent the rest of his savings to pay for Hugo Riesenfeld's score. *Tabu* had cost him slightly more than $150,000. Although the trade papers noted that Paramount, which picked up the distribution, was offering him a contract—Lubitsch, von Sternberg, and Murnau at the same studio!—he was already planning to return to Tahiti as quickly as possible. His career had clearly become of secondary importance, for this rigid aesthete had discovered the joys of going native.

"And then his homosexuality cost him his life," recalled Peter Viertel. "He fell in love with this Tahitian boy, and he allowed him to drive his car. The boy didn't have a license or anything."

On March 10, 1931, at 6:30 P.M., while the object of his affections was driving along the Pacific Coast Highway twenty miles north of Santa Barbara, he swerved to avoid hitting a truck. Murnau's rented Packard went off the road, rolled twice, and landed bottom up. Murnau suffered a fractured skull, punctured lungs, and other internal injuries. He died the next morning at Santa Barbara College Hospital.

Tabu opened a week later, playing for twelve weeks in New York. Other locations had less successful runs. The world gross was $472,000, but after Paramount deducted $200,000 for distribution costs, Murnau's advance, and print and advertising costs, Murnau's estate was left with just $141,000 — some $13,000 less than he spent.

Tabu shows Murnau moving with his characteristic pathological intensity toward pure cinema: meaning melding with movement, a cinema of beauty and ideas, of the harmony of bodies and the rhythm of space.

Forty years after he photographed the movie, Floyd Crosby went back to Tahiti, showing his wife where some of the scenes had been shot. An old man became hysterical with joy when he saw Crosby. He had been one of the dancers in the film, and he told Crosby that, occasionally, *Tabu* would be shown in Tahiti and everyone would go to see Grandma and Grandpa. The audience would cry because everyone was now dead. Except on the screen, in the radiant silver light, in that gentle tropical night . . .

❑ ❑ ❑

After the rough ride of the first eighteen months, where sound had been a bulbous carbuncle, an unwieldy technical accretion, it now, in some psychic sense, provided film with a sense of completeness. Silent film had made a virtue out of its limitations, as any art must, but for the audience, there could be no going back.

A Peter Arno cartoon in *The New Yorker* poked fun at the few remaining purists: a down-on-his-luck actor is panhandling at a premiere. "Say, ccc-can you sss-spare me a fff-fiver 'till this ttt-talkie th-thing blows over?"

Although Warner Bros. and William Fox had hit precisely the right psychological moment for sound, the clock was speeding up, and even watershed films like *The Jazz Singer* belonged to the past. In 1931, Warners tried a reissue of the Jolson film at the Warner Theater in New York. The film was pulled after only three days.

For the twenty-fifth anniversary of talkies Jack Warner embarked on a lavish remake featuring the exceedingly odd cast of Danny Thomas and Peggy Lee, directed by a past-his-prime Michael Curtiz.

The film failed, as did an even more pointless Neil Diamond remake in 1980, which was sufficiently bizarre to attain semilegendary status.

The Warner boys had left Youngstown far behind, and they meant to keep it that way. The last time any of them came back home was in November 1935, when Benjamin Warner died and Harry arrived to make the funeral arrangements. He was terse and reticent, and the Ohio Hotel had to put on an extra telephone operator to handle the volume of calls that came for him during his twenty-four hours in town.

The last time Jack Warner Jr. saw Al Jolson was at the Hillcrest Country Club shortly before Jolson died in 1950. "Say hello to your father for me, that son of a bitch," Jolson said in farewell. Jack and Harry ran the studio together until 1956, when Jack organized the sale of their shares, then, in a sweetheart deal, bought his shares back for what he had been paid. He at last had what he wanted: full and complete control, without having to answer to anybody. Harry Warner died in 1958. Soon afterward, Jack fired his son from Warner Bros. The two men saw each other only a few more times.

In his old age, Jack Warner developed a glamorized memory of the beginnings of Warner Bros. He thought about Sam and Harry, Barrymore and Jolson, the way old soldiers talk about war: not mud and death, but drinking and women and winning. In 1966, Jack was asked by a reporter which single film had given him the most satisfaction in his career.

"*The Jazz Singer,*" he replied. In his Century City office at the end of his career, there was a wall of photos, a chronicle of the history of Hollywood as we know it. In the center was a framed trade-paper ad for *The Jazz Singer,* providing a sense of the importance of the film to the man, and the man to the industry.

Jack Warner died in 1978. He left millions to his wife and daughter, $200,000 to his only son. "It's one of those things," said Jack Junior. "You drive down the freeway and a truck's coming right at you. And you think, 'This is unjust!' Too damn bad. That's life."

As an old man himself, Jack Junior would say, "I should have gone into the law, but I listened to my father. 'You want a lawyer?' he'd say. 'You *hire* a lawyer. I got a floor of them in New York. Lawyers just screw things up.'

"Trying to figure out my father is a waste of time; there are too many labyrinths, and when you get to the center of it, it just isn't worth it." A gentle, warm man, Jack Warner Jr. died in 1995.

◻ ◻ ◻

Chief Vitaphone engineer Stanley Watkins returned to England in 1929, wired the stages at Gaumont, worked with Herbert Wilcox, then went to studios in Paris and Nice to wire them for sound. His devotion to the cause cost him his first marriage, but the second one lasted. In essence, the entire first generation of American and European soundmen were trained by Stanley Watkins.

In 1936, he went back to work for Bell Labs in America, developing improved hearing aids. He retired in 1948 and, for the last time, went back to England because it was cheaper to live there on his pension. In the early 1960s, he wrote down his reminiscences of his life and work. Regarding talking pictures, he concluded that "[although] change was inevitable, I'm not sure that my conscience is altogether satisfied with my having had a finger in the pie." He died in London in February 1976, at the age of eighty-eight. His life is marked by tens of thousands of talking pictures and a plaque in the West Norwood Cemetery that reads: IN LOVING MEMORY OF STANLEY S. A. WATKINS, TALKIES PIONEER.

◻ ◻ ◻

The primary technical innovation of synchronized sound was followed by dozens of improvements, foremost among them the lessening of background noise that, with a badly recorded or processed sound track, sounded like there was a waterfall just out of the frame.

Western Electric devised their "noiseless recording" early in the 1930s. "Noiseless recording" involved nothing more than darkening the emulsion of the sound track so that less light, hence background noise, leaked through to the soundhead. It was a clever idea, but truly clean, clear sound recording would not really come about until 1950, when the studios moved from recording sound on film to recording sound on tape, then dubbing onto film.

By 1929, Lee De Forest was essentially broke from the expenses of the unsuccessful Phonofilms and the legal bills from his litigation. Except for the fact that his attorney, Sam Darby Jr., was a good friend and continued to litigate, De Forest would probably have ended a pauper.

In 1931, De Forest won his battles for patent infringement. The U.S. District Judge declared that De Forest owned and held exclusive patents dealing with sound recording and reproduction. De Forest was awarded a measly $60,000. Restraining orders were issued, but several companies continued manufacturing and distributing sound equipment in defiance of court orders.

De Forest figured that it might be a better idea to utilize his reasserted patent rights by returning to production rather than by engaging in another drawn-out legal battle for reparations, a decision that made his court victory an increasingly hollow one. Soon after his court victory, he was lured into forming a company called General Talking Pictures, a holding company for the De Forest patents. But the needed infusion of capital never came, and De Forest resumed work on new inventions. By the time of his death in 1961, De Forest had amassed over three hundred patents, including one, issued in 1948, for color television.

CHAPTER 2

Beyond the legal maneuvering and the obvious aesthetic alterations, it quickly became apparent that sound had subtly altered the internal chemistry of the industrial process of filmmaking. Because the early sound equipment was fairly cumbersome, and location work was an arduous process, the studios were firm in their determination to centralize production on the back lot. As a result, process photography became far more important than it had been in the silent days, where it had mostly been used for special-effects scenes.

Sound made location work comparatively rare, except for outdoor films like westerns. "We tried to confine everything we could to the studio," said MGM's Joe Cohn. "It was cheaper. You went on location, you had to pay for people's food and board and transportation. And you had to contend with the problems of sound; you couldn't very well say to a city like Los Angeles, 'Don't make any noise.' "

Likewise, the moviegoing experience itself was subtly altered. Food, previously a rarity in movie theaters, began to appear. Selling food had always been associated with low-rent burlesque shows and the like, from which companies like Loew's and Balaban & Katz had striven to keep a distance. "High-class" movie theaters only allowed patrons to bring in candy that they had bought at the store that was often adjacent to the theater.

But with the Depression came the realization that a simple stand manned by a high school student could produce hundreds of dollars of pure profit even in a bad week. Even if the viewer was distracted by noisy foods like popcorn or the rustling of candy wrappers, a movie's sound track would keep the viewer from getting lost. By 1936, sales of food in movie theaters would top $10 million.

❑ ❑ ❑

Over the years, many people would blame talkies for the death of vaudeville, but George Burns thought that was an erroneous assumption. "What killed vaudeville wasn't talkies but radio. Show biz started coming to your house, so you didn't have to go out. Radio killed the dumb [silent] acts. Swayne's Rats and Cats, all those acts. They didn't talk so they didn't work on radio. Actually, until I met Gracie, I was a dumb act."

Really?

"No. I lie a lot."

In secondary markets, vaudeville gave up the ghost slowly. Circuit acts died out by the mid 1930s, but local acts were still offered in towns like Syracuse, and in the winter of 1935–36, on Saturday evenings, that theater did better business than any other there. "People," remembered Gilbert Bahn, the son of the editor of *The Film Daily*, "were so economically depressed by the Great Depression that they wanted all of the entertainment they could get out of one theater [ticket], and, bad as the acts were, they were live and colorful and noisy in a drab, subdued world. I remember that in those days the dime stores' candy counters sold sorghum and sassafras and wintergreen candies, and those have long since passed from favor, but they sufficed then, and I look back on vaudeville in an equivalent sense, as 'make-do' entertainment (for grown-ups, that is)."

After making a few pictures in England, Esther Ralston was called back to Paramount. The star dressing-room was long gone, as was the $3,500-a-week salary. One day, Ralston was on the way to the commissary when she saw Gary Cooper, her leading man in several silent pictures, now the biggest star on the lot.

"If he snubs me now, it would break my heart," thought Ralston. She kept her head down and kept walking, then heard a cowboy whoop. Cooper leaped over the hedge by the water fountain and hugged her. "Esther, you were gonna pass me by!"

"I was afraid it was going to be the other way around, Gary," said Ralston.

Ralston went over to MGM, where Louis B. Mayer attempted to recruit her as his mistress. "The suggestion wasn't delicate. The last premiere Mayer took me to . . . Mayer kept pawing me and I asked him not to do that.

"We'd come in my car, and I had noticed Randy Scott with his date when we'd come in. I was going to get Johnny, my chauffeur, when Randy asked if I'd had any trouble. I wasn't taking any chances, so I asked if he'd mind getting in the car with us. When my car came up and Mayer saw Randy and his date in the car, he was so furious.

"The next morning I was called in to see Mr. Mayer. 'You think you're pretty smart, don't you? Well, you sing your songs and see where you get. I'll blackball you in every major studio in this town!' From that time, people I'd thought were my friends passed me on the street."

After stints as an agent and a salesgirl, with a few last acting jobs, Esther Ralston retired to a trailer park in Ventura, California. At the age of ninety-one, just a few months before her death in 1994, she was still merry and bright. "I've had all that Hollywood stuff," she said. "The big home, the town car, the chauffeur, and the maids. To be here in this little place, I'm part of a family, you know. I'm helped out by the Motion Picture Home. They call me every once in a while to see if I'd like to come there, and I tell them not yet. I don't want to hurt their feelings, but . . .

"I was never that good an actress. I was sincere, but I don't think I ever stopped any traffic as an actress. Although I did think that in *The Case of Lena Smith* I did well, but von Sternberg was so clear and coherent in his direction. I loved his directing; I practically worshiped him. But the rest? Light comedy and personality.

"I'm very grateful to have had as interesting a career as I did have. If I had to do it over again, I'd try to manage my own money. And I wouldn't marry the men I married. But I don't have any bitterness. I don't hate anybody or even dislike anybody. Mayer? I dislike what he did, not him. I've found that no matter what you go through, someday you look back and laugh about it. Well, these are my laughing years."

❑ ❑ ❑

Sound-on-film pioneer Theodore Case took his money and lived lavishly in the town of Auburn, New York, occasionally dabbling in his laboratory. Even during the depths of the Depression, the Case household was notable for the profusion of parties and events that took place. He died in 1944. In 1952, the Cayuga Museum, the site of Case's old laboratory, burned many of Case's surviving experimental films. Among the films destroyed were shorts featuring Beatrice Lillie, Gallagher and Sheean, Gertrude Lawrence, and many miscellaneous tests, with tantalizing labels like "De Forest negatives" and "De Forest experiment."

Had the experimental reels been preserved, they might well have indicated with some specificity just which refinements of sound on film were De Forest's and which were Case and Sponable's. De Forest's name is invariably featured in the standard encyclopedias of film, but you will look in vain for the names of Theodore Case and Earl Sponable.

❑ ❑ ❑

By the mid-1930s, early talkies seemed particularly graceless hybrids, and many of the negatives were burned long before the television era. The metal stampers that provided the separate sound masters were junked for scrap. With time, the sound and film components of hundreds of features and shorts inevitably became separated from each other; Warner Bros. reported master recordings missing as early as 1931. Historians thus have had to extrapolate theories and opinions from an extremely small sample of surviving films. With time, film archivists have assembled a reasonable collection of the picture elements for many films of the Vitaphone era, but the sound discs are considerably harder to come by.

Although MGM's corporate caution forbade them being in the forefront of the changeover to sound, they always took good care of their library. In the mid-1970s, the sound discs that had been stored in a room above the sound department were carefully removed and put on film, then married to their visual counterparts. All the discs had been used, and some films had two or three sets of discs. Sound engineer Scott Perry married about twenty films to their tracks, titles like *Wild Orchids, Show People, Spite Marriage, White Shadows in the South Seas, The Wind, Where East Is East, Broadway Melody,* and so on.

Other than those few titles transferred by specific order of Jack Warner (*The Jazz Singer, Lights of New York,* etc.), Warner Bros. let the rest of their Vitaphone library languish. The studio collection of Vitaphone discs was fragmentary, partially because of pilfering; the sound discs for *Glorious Betsy* (1927) survived, except for the discs for the two talking sequences. Other gaps in the historical record were the result of basic vandalism: it's reported that rock musicians working on the scoring stage of the Burbank studio would serve pizzas on Vitaphone records and would occasionally use the shellac discs as Frisbees during session breaks.

In 1987, Robert Gitt, of the UCLA Film and Television Archive, and Leith Adams, archivist of the Warner Bros. collection at the University of Southern California, embarked on an expedition through the dim recesses of the studio in search of El Dorado.

Years before, Adams had seen racks of large records behind a projection screen on a scoring stage, but, as they retraced his earlier steps, they found nothing. Bewailing the situation to Chris Chigaridas, a director of postproduction sound, they were interrupted by his query: "Did you check the *other* scoring stage?" Next to the room they had already searched was an identical space. There, behind another projection screen, they found a dusty wooden cabinet holding 2,500 Vitaphone discs, most of them never played.

A worldwide cross-referencing search of archives ultimately enabled about twenty features and 140 short subjects to be recombined with their sound tracks from this one cache alone. As the films were restored and put into circulation, they gradually began to dispel old myths as absurd as the story of John Gilbert's fluty tenor, or the completely fabricated story of Sam Taylor's seizure of an "Additional Dialogue" writing credit for *The Taming of the Shrew.*

For years, the history books had reported that Warners star May McAvoy had seen her career disappear because of a lisp. "I'm thick and tired of thuch thilly antics!" was the way she supposedly read a line in 1928's *The Terror.* Although McAvoy had retired from movies in 1929 to get married, it was widely assumed it was a tactical retreat in the face of a speech impediment, despite McAvoy's angry denials.

While the quoted line was more or less correct, Gitt's restoration of the sound discs clearly revealed that McAvoy had no speech impediment whatever; any lisping detected in 1928 was due to a bad tube in an amplifier, or, even more likely, a worn disc.

□ □ □

Although recording sound on disc was obsolete by 1932, more than sixty years later it came charging back, bigger and — finally — better than ever. The system known as DTS (Digital Theater Sound) provided for off-the-shelf, mass-produced CD drives to be adapted so that CDs with the film sound-track encoded on them could run in interlock with the projector. The cost of the basic playback unit was in the vicinity of $2,500, although various bells and whistles could raise the price to between $6,000 and $10,000. Installation took only about two hours.

The CDs were shipped in a special plastic reel that fit side by side with the 35mm print in a standard industry shipping case. (Films of ninety minutes or less fit on one CD; more than that takes two.) The resulting sound was noticeably richer and fuller than conventional optical sound, without the trebly harshness of much Dolby sound.

Working against DTS was the fact that it was a dual system, a spinning disc in interlock with the projector, the same idea as the first sound-on-film experiments a full hundred years earlier. However, the addition of a time code on the film itself that corresponded to the correct sound for that frame meant that synchronization was a given rather than hit-or-miss as with the Vitaphone system. Splices were no problem, and, because of the digital format the sound track didn't accumulate scratches and pops as the print became worn. In addition, DTS encoding was placed on prints with conventional optical sound-tracks, providing a backup in case the CD system failed to operate.

The film industry has traditionally been loath to invest in technical research and development — no major cinematic innovation of the century, not sound, color, 3-D, or wide-screen, was developed in-house at a movie studio — so nobody embraced digital sound. At the beginning of 1993, there were no digital theaters equipped for disc sound in the United States; by the fourth quarter, there were over a thousand, largely because of the highly effective use of the process in Steven Spielberg's *Jurassic Park,* which led Universal Studios to adopt DTS as its favored high-end sound system. In mid-1996, Digital Theater Systems was installed in more than six thousand theaters worldwide.

By 1997, it seemed as though Stan Watkins, John Otterson, and Sam and Harry Warner might have had the right idea all along, just the wrong technology.

Jolson—and sound—triumphant.

Epilogue

So Hollywood was nudged, however unwillingly, into its corporate and creative future. Victims retired, victors took their place. In the early 1930s, the deco designs of Hans Dreier and Van Nest Polglase replaced the stuffy English furniture that was *de rigueur* at most studios in the silent days; short, stylish hair was adopted by women stars. The industry had been turned upside down, but had righted itself with considerable dispatch.

The fact that sound wasn't accepted until thirty years after it was first (roughly) devised was due in great part to factors both sociological and human: the immaculate presentation of silent films, and the reactionary attitudes of producers and exhibitors. Then there were two secondary technical factors: amplification (had that been available, talkies might have arrived in the 1900s) and electrical recording (acoustic recording lacked the necessary clarity).

Sound gave us the artistry of Astaire, the shattering screech of Kane's cockatoo, the wrenching anguish of Brando's "I coulda been a contender." It gave movies a more comprehensive form and smoothed out their dramatic flow. But the transition to sound was no gentle grafting, but a brutal, crude transplantation. As a result, many of cinema's roots withered and died, and much native strength was lost. The culture of Hollywood itself grew harsher, more Darwinian.

"The fun, easy, relaxed days of the motion picture were over the minute dialogue came in," asserted Charles "Buddy" Rogers. "Not only did the director want the dialogue his way, but the dialogue director, the soundman—we had to cope with about six or seven different technicians, and it was quite different."

William deMille, who had arrived in town in September 1914, observed the precipitous alteration in the landscape and didn't much like what he saw. "Within two years," he wrote, "our little old Hollywood was gone and in its place stood a fair, new city, talking a new language, having different manners and customs, a more terrifying city full of strange faces, less friendly, more businesslike, twice as populous — and much more cruel."

Directors who began in silent films maintained a loyalty to the art form they had fallen in love with. Indeed, some great directors made their best movies with sound — Lubitsch and Ford, among others. Sound also made possible a whole new breed of director — directors of character and performance like Cukor, Sturges, and Wilder — whereas the silent cinema had offered only an occasional, comparable talent like William deMille.

Although Clarence Brown went on to direct for nearly a quarter century after sound, and made such superb films as *National Velvet* and *The Yearling,* to the end of his life he remained a partisan of silent film. "I think that silent pictures were more of an art than talkies ever have been. No matter how you manage it, talkies have dialogue and dialogue belongs to the stage; too many people let the dialogue do their thinking for them, do the plot exposition for them, do everything for them. Silents were . . . subtler, I guess.

"In [the silent film] *A Woman of Affairs,* which I made after *Flesh and the Devil,* there's a scene involving an emerald ring that Garbo wears. [John] Gilbert makes a comment about it and she says, 'I would only take it off for the man I love.' Later, they have a love scene on the couch that I shot in close-up. The camera pans from their faces, across her shoulder, down her arm to her hand, just as the ring slips off her finger. Now, once your premise is established, basically via words, the resolution is entirely visual."

"The thing that made me so sad, really," said the writer and critic Cedric Belfrage, "was that the international language was over. This was really a thing which nobody seemed to notice very much, but after all, the human species had lived on the face of the globe for a number of years and they had never had a language in which they could all speak to each other, which could be shown everywhere, and which everyone could understand. We just blew it up. And it was really rather sad."

❏ ❏ ❏

Two final vignettes of lost days in the sunshine:

One of the army of New York writers recruited for the talkies was Joseph L. Mankiewicz. He recalled "coming out of the Brown Derby on Vine one afternoon with Bob Cobb, Joe Schenck . . . and Norma Talmadge. [A] gang of autograph hunters descended on Norma, who was a little liquefied. She told them, 'Get away, you little bastards. I don't need you anymore.' That to me was the definitive end of silent pictures."

The sound equipment for United Artists was installed about half-way through production of Douglas Fairbanks's *The Iron Mask* (a film that ends with the middle-aged but still blithe and vital D'Artagnan being stabbed in the back). Laurence Irving, one of the film's art directors, noticed the changed atmosphere. The open-air stages were being enclosed, and the *al fresco* atmosphere, where guests and onlookers were welcome, was being radically transformed into a monastic, closely guarded environment where only those absolutely necessary to production were admitted.

"The propmen and the electricians, everybody were all cheerful, bronzed Californians," remembered Irving. "The studios were brightly lit, and whenever a scene was played a nice little orchestra played to encourage the actors to get into the right mood. And then gradually there appeared these pale, harassed charges from almost outer space, who were of course the minions of the Western Electric Company who were installing the first sound-stage.

"Douglas came to my room one day and said, 'Let's go down and have a look at the soundstage.' We walked down and the doors of the big studios were open, and instead of seeing a nice bright place where everybody was extremely happy working, it was a ghastly sort of cave hung with blankets, no lights, the whole of the floor covered with serpentine wires and cables, and then these menacing microphones . . .

"As he took this in, Douglas laid his hand on my arm, as he often did when he spoke to me, and he said, 'Laurence, the romance of motion picture making ends here.' "

Acknowledgments

The initial idea for *The Speed of Sound* was Chris Stager's, but the execution would have been impossible without the steadfast help of a wide variety of people on two continents. Foremost among them are the dedicatees, who opened their files and interviews gathered over the past thirty years in order to make this book as comprehensive as possible. Collectively, Kevin Brownlow and David Gill have always served as my inspiration and scholarly role models; individually, they and their partner Patrick Stanbury are my friends.

Jeff Heise, my strong right arm, once again functioned as my research assistant; as always, I couldn't do it without him.

Scott MacQueen showed enormous generosity — not always a prominent quality of writers — when he lent me research material and photos from his own groundbreaking articles on our mutual subject. John Andrew Gallagher did the same when he gave me relevant material from his forthcoming biography of Tay Garnett. Douglas Gomery helpfully cleared up a few inconsistencies, and UCLA's Bob Gitt, without whom so much film scholarship would be a matter of conjecture rather than opinion, arranged screenings, talked with me, and kept me from too many blunders.

No less important was Barbara Witemeyer, the daughter of Stanley Watkins, who shared with me her late father's unpublished memoirs as well as her own interview with his first wife, and gave me permission to quote from them. Also contributing valuable material were Miles Kreuger and Jack Hurd.

For research materials: the noble crew at The Vitaphone Project, especially Ron Hutchinson and John Newton; at the AT&T Archives in New Jersey, Sheldon Hochheiser arranged for me to examine the pertinent files, and Elizabeth Colmant guided me through them; Ned Comstock at the USC Cinema-Television Library was his usual steadfast self, and several times surprised me with delightful CARE packages in the mail; at Brigham Young University in Provo, Utah, the estimable James D'Arc gave me free rein to wander in the overwhelming Cecil B. DeMille Archives; at the Museum of Modern Art, Charles Silver was immensely helpful and supportive; Peter Jones, of the Case Museum in Auburn, New York, opened the files of the gifted, creative Theodore Case for me.

Interviews: the late William Bakewell, Mary Ellin Barrett, the late Lina Basquette, dear Edward Bernds, the late Clarence Brown, the amazing late George Burns, the equally amazing Gaylord Carter, Frank Coghlan, the late Joseph J. Cohn, Douglas Fairbanks Jr., Samuel Goldwyn Jr., the late Henry Hathaway, the late James Wong Howe, Irving "Buster" Libott, Darcy O'Brien, Donald O'Connor, Anita Page, the late Esther Ralston, Charles "Buddy" Rogers, Alvin Sloan, Cass Warner Sperling, the late Karl Struss, Peter Viertel, the late Jack Warner Jr., and the late Joseph Youngerman.

As always, Dennis and Amy Heller-Doros saved my life a half-dozen times and bolstered my morale weekly. They didn't stop there, funneling films and material through the front lines. David Stenn contributed several valuable hints about research material. Old friend David Pierce consistently supplied immensely valuable financial information that provided the foundation for much theorizing. Kent Jones, from Cappa Productions, made an enormous difference, far more than he knew. Blessings on all of them.

Russell Merritt not only introduced me to Venice, he gave me a guided tour. Besides that, he has served as a loyal friend, sounding board, and supplier of data available nowhere else. Next to the introduction to Venice, this is minor, but it mattered nonetheless. Paolo Cherchi Usai, of the George Eastman House and the Giornate del Cinema Muto in Pordenone, Italy, leaped to help me when I needed him.

A wide variety of correspondents shared their memories of the early sound era and gave my history an immediacy I tried to communicate to the reader. A deep bow to the selfless generosity of the following: William Bowers, William Brower, Bernard R. DeRemer, Grace W. Ely, Richard Erwin, Albert Green, Viola Hardy, Bruce

ACKNOWLEDGMENTS

Hoover, Carolyn Irwin, Jere (Mrs. Eric) Knight, Maybelle Lacey, Helen Laidlaw, Franklin Raiter, Alvin Sloan, and Debbie Swanbach.

At *The Palm Beach Post,* Jan Tuckwood, Eddie Sears, Tom Giuffrida, Tom O'Hara, and Larry Aydlette remind me daily why I'm proud to work there. Their patience and interest has made this book, and much else, possible.

Howard and Amy Green, and Mike and Linda Connelly provided me with lodging in Los Angeles during my research trips. Howard also supplied me with some very rare films from the 1926–1930 period. As a result of such prodigious displays of selflessness, they are all being considered for canonization.

My wife, Lynn Kalber, who has been with me through five books and shows no sign of weakening, once again soothed my more feverish paranoias. She continues to provide me with the nurturing, love, and security every writer seeks and few find. I love you, Lynn.

At Simon & Schuster, Chuck Adams remains the ideal editor: questioning, suggesting, gently leading. And, he actually knows movies. (Now, Chuck, right away, before something interrupts you, go see Jeanne Eagels in *The Letter.*) Virginia Clark did her usual painstaking copy edit, on which I rely.

Scott Eyman

Hollywood — New York — London — Warren — Provo — Pordenone — Fort Lauderdale
January 1993 – October 1996

Bibliography

Adamson, Joe. *Groucho, Harpo, Chico and Sometimes Zeppo.* New York: Simon and Schuster, 1973.

Allvine, Glendon. *The Greatest Fox of Them All.* New York: Lyle Stuart, 1969.

Amory, Cleveland, and Frederic Bradlee, ed. *Vanity Fair.* New York: Bonanza Books, 1960.

Anderson, John Murray, as told to Hugh Abercrombie Anderson. *Out Without My Rubbers.* Library Publishers, 1954.

Arce, Hector. *Groucho.* New York: G. P. Putnam's Sons, 1979.

Arliss, George. *My Ten Years in the Studios.* Boston: Little, Brown, 1940.

Astor, Mary. *A Life on Film.* New York: Delacorte Press, 1971.

Atkins, Irene. *Arthur Jacobson: An Oral History.* Metuchen, N.J.: Scarecrow Press/Director's Guild of America, 1991.

Balaban, Carrie. *Continuous Performance: The Story of A. J. Balaban.* New York: A. J. Balaban Foundation, 1964.

Baldwin, Neil. *Edison: Inventing the Century.* New York: Hyperion, 1995.

Balio, Tino, ed. *The American Film Industry.* Madison: University of Wisconsin Press, 1976.

———. *United Artists.* Madison: University of Wisconsin Press, 1976.

Bandy, Mary Lea, ed. *The Dawn of Sound.* New York: The Museum of Modern Art, 1989.

Barrymore, Lionel. *We Barrymores.* New York: Appleton-Century-Crofts, 1951.

Basquette, Lina. *Lina: DeMille's Godless Girl.* Fairfax, Va.: Denlinger's Publishers, 1990.

Baxter, John. *King Vidor.* New York: Monarch Press, 1976.

Baxter, Peter, ed. *Sternberg.* London: British Film Institute, 1980.

Behlmer, Rudy, ed. *Inside Warner Bros.* New York: Viking, 1985.

———, ed. *Memo from David O. Selznick.* New York: Viking, 1972.

Bellamy, Madge. *A Darling of the Twenties.* Vestal, N.Y.: The Vestal Press, 1989.

Bellamy, Ralph. *When the Smoke Hit the Fan.* Garden City, N.Y.: Doubleday, 1979.

Berg, A. Scott. *Goldwyn.* New York: Alfred A. Knopf, 1989.

Bernstein, Matthew. *Walter Wanger: Hollywood Independent.* Berkeley: University of California Press, 1994.

Blake, Michael. *Lon Chaney: The Man Behind the Thousand Faces.* Vestal, N.Y.: The Vestal Press, 1993.

Brown, Bernard. *Talking Pictures.* London: Pitman & Sons, 1933.

Brown, Gene, ed. *The New York Times Encyclopedia of Film, 1896–1928.* New York: Times Books, 1984.

———, ed. *The New York Times Encyclopedia of Film, 1929–1936.* New York: Times Books, 1984.

Brown, Royal S. *Overtones and Undertones.* Berkeley: University of California Press, 1994.

Brownlow, Kevin. *The Parade's Gone By.* New York: Alfred A. Knopf, 1968.

Cahn, William. *Harold Lloyd's World of Comedy.* New York: Duell, Sloan and Pearce, 1964.

Cameron, Evan William, ed. *Sound and the Cinema.* Pleasantville, N.Y.: Redgrave Publishing Co., 1980.

Capra, Frank. *The Name Above the Title.* New York: Macmillan, 1971.

Carey, Gary. *All the Stars in Heaven.* New York: E. P. Dutton, 1981.

Carr, Robert E., and R. M. Hayes. *Wide-Screen Movies.* Jefferson, N.C.: McFarland and Co., 1988.

Carriere, Jean-Claude. *The Secret Language of Film.* New York: Pantheon Books, 1994.

Carringer, Robert L., ed. *The Jazz Singer.* Madison: University of Wisconsin Press, 1979.

Case, Frank. *Tales of a Wayward Inn.* New York: Frederick A. Stokes Co., 1938.

Coghlan, Frank, Jr. *They Still Call Me Junior.* Jefferson, N.C.: McFarland and Co., 1993.

Cohn, Lawrence. *Movietone Presents the 20th Century.* New York: St. Martin's Press, 1976.

Colman, Juliet Benita. *Ronald Colman: A Very Private Person.* New York: William Morrow, 1975.

Curtis, James. *James Whale.* Metuchen, N.J.: Scarecrow Press, 1982.

Dale, Rodney, and Rebecca Weaver. *Home Entertainment.* New York: Oxford University Press, 1993.

Dardis, Tom. *Harold Lloyd: The Man on the Clock.* New York: Viking, 1983.

Davies, Marion. *The Times We Had.* Edited by Pamela Pfau and Kenneth S. Marx. Indianapolis: Bobbs-Merrill, 1975.

Davis, Ronald L. *The Glamour Factory.* Dallas: Southern Methodist University Press, 1993.

De Long, Thomas A. *Pops: Paul Whiteman, King of Jazz.* Piscataway, N.J.: New Century Publishing, 1983.

DeMille, Cecil B. *Autobiography.* Englewood Cliffs, N.J.: Prentice-Hall, 1959.

deMille, William C. *Hollywood Saga.* New York: E. P. Dutton, 1939.

Deutelbaum, Marshall, *"Image" on the Art and Evolution of the Film.* New York: Dover Publications, 1979.

Dmytryk, Edward. *It's a Hell of a Life But Not a Bad Living.* New York: Times Books, 1978.

Dowd, Nancy, and David Shepard. *King Vidor.* Metuchen, N.J.: Scarecrow Press, 1988.

Drew, William S. *Speaking of Silents.* Vestal, N.Y.: The Vestal Press, 1989.

Durgnat, Raymond, and Scott Simmon. *King Vidor, American.* Berkeley: University of California Press, 1988.

Edwards, Anne. *The DeMilles.* New York: Harry N. Abrams, 1988.

Eels, George. *Hedda and Louella.* New York: G. P. Putnam's Sons, 1972.

Eisner, Lotte. *Murnau.* Berkeley: University of California Press, 1973.

Ellwood, David, and Rob Kroes, eds. *Hollywood in Europe.* Amsterdam: VU University Press, 1994.

Everson, William K. *American Silent Film.* New York: Oxford University Press, 1978.

Eyman, Scott. *Ernst Lubitsch: Laughter in Paradise.* New York: Simon & Schuster, 1993.

———. *Five American Cinematographers.* Metuchen, N.J.: Scarecrow Press, 1987.

———. *Mary Pickford: America's Sweetheart.* New York: Donald I. Fine Inc., 1990.

Fielding, Raymond. *A Technological History of Motion Pictures.* Berkeley: University of California Press, 1983.

Finler, Joel. *The Hollywood Story.* New York: Crown, 1988.

Finstad, Suzanne. *Heir Not Apparent.* Dallas: Texas Monthly Press, 1984.

Flamini, Roland. *Thalberg.* New York: Crown, 1994.

Francisco, Charles. *Gentleman: The William Powell Story.* New York: St. Martin's Press, 1985.

Freedland, Michael. *The Warner Brothers.* New York: St. Martin's Press, 1983.

Gabler, Neal. *An Empire of Their Own.* New York: Crown, 1988.

Garcon, François. *Gaumont: A Century of French Cinema.* New York: Harry N. Abrams, 1994.

Geduld, Harry M. *The Birth of the Talkies.* Bloomington: Indiana University Press, 1975.

Geist, Kenneth L. *Pictures Will Talk.* New York: Charles Scribner's Sons, 1978.

Goldman, Herbert G. *Jolson: The Legend Comes to Life.* New York: Oxford University Press, 1988.

Gomery, Douglas. *The Hollywood Studio System.* New York: St. Martin's Press, 1986.

——. *Shared Pleasures.* Madison: University of Wisconsin Press, 1992.

Guiles, Fred Lawrence. *Marion Davies.* New York: McGraw-Hill, 1972.

Gussow, Mel. *Don't Say Yes Until I'm Finished Talking.* Garden City, N.Y.: Doubleday, 1971.

Haines, Richard W. *Technicolor Movies.* Jefferson, N.C.: McFarland and Co., 1993.

Hall, Ben M. *The Best Remaining Seats.* New York: Bramhall House, 1961.

Hampton, Benjamin B. *History of the American Film Industry.* 1931. Reprint, New York: Dover, 1970.

Hardy, Phil. *Raoul Walsh.* Edinburgh: Edinburgh Film Festival, 1974.

Harris, Marlys J. *The Zanucks of Hollywood.* New York: Crown, 1989.

Haskin, Byron, with Joe Adamson. *Byron Haskin.* Metuchen, N.J.: Scarecrow Press/Director's Guild of America, 1984.

Haver, Ronald. *David O. Selznick's Hollywood.* New York: Alfred A. Knopf, 1980.

Hays, Will H. *See and Hear.* New York: Motion Picture Producers and Distributors of America, Inc., 1929.

Herzog, Peter, and Romano Tozzi. *Lya De Putti: Loving Life and Not Fearing Death.* New York: Corvin Publishing, 1993.

Higashi, Sumiko. *Cecil B. DeMille and American Culture.* Berkeley: University of California Press, 1994.

Higham, Charles. *Hollywood Cameramen.* Bloomington: Indiana University Press, 1970.

——. *Merchant of Dreams.* New York: Donald I. Fine, 1993.

——. *Warner Brothers.* New York: Charles Scribner's Sons, 1975.

Hoberman, J. *42nd Street.* London: British Film Institute, 1993.

Horowitz, Joseph. *Understanding Toscanini.* New York: Alfred A. Knopf, 1987.

Izod, John. *Hollywood and the Box Office, 1895–1986.* London: Macmillan Press, 1988.

Janis, Elsie. *So Far, So Good.* New York: E. P. Dutton, 1932.

Jenkins, Henry. *What Made Pistachio Nuts?* New York: Columbia University Press, 1992.

Jessel, George. *So Help Me.* Cleveland: World Publishing, 1943.

Jewell, Richard B. *A History of RKO Radio Pictures, Incorporated.* Ph.D. diss., 1978.

Jewell, Richard B., and Vernon Harbin. *The RKO Story.* New York: Crown, 1982.

Jobes, Gertrude. *Motion Picture Empire.* Hamden, Conn.: Archon Books, 1966.

Johnson, Nora. *Flashback.* Garden City, N.Y.: Doubleday, 1979.

Kalmus, Herbert, with Eleanore King Kalmus. *Mr. Technicolor.* Absecon, N.J.: MagicImage, 1993.

Karr, Kathleen, ed. *The American Film Heritage.* Washington: Acropolis Books, 1972.

Kennedy, Joseph P., ed. *The Story of the Films.* Chicago and New York: A. W. Shaw Co., 1927.

Kenner, Hugh. *Chuck Jones.* Berkeley: University of California Press, 1994.

Kiesling, Barrett C. *Talking Pictures.* New York: Johnson Publishing Co., 1937.

Kobal, John. *People Will Talk.* New York: Alfred A. Knopf, 1985.

Koszarski, Richard. *The Astoria Studio and Its Fabulous Films.* New York: Dover, 1983.

———. *Hollywood Directors, 1914–1940.* New York: Oxford University Press, 1976.

———. *The Man You Love to Hate.* New York: Oxford University Press, 1983.

Lambert, Gavin. *Norma Shearer.* New York: Alfred A. Knopf, 1990.

———. *On Cukor.* New York: Capricorn Books, 1973.

Lasky, Jesse L., with Don Weldon. *I Blow My Own Horn.* Garden City, N.Y.: Doubleday, 1957.

LeRoy, Mervyn, as told to Dick Kleiner. *Mervyn LeRoy: Take One.* New York: Hawthorn Books, 1974.

Lescarboura, Austin C. *Behind the Motion Picture Screen.* New York: Scientific American Publishing Company, 1921.

Levy, Emanuel. *George Cukor: Master of Elegance.* New York: William Morrow, 1994.

Lewis, David. *The Creative Producer.* Edited by James Curtis. Metuchen, N.J.: Scarecrow Press, 1993.

Lloyd, Ann, ed. *The Brave and the Bloodthirsty.* London: Orbis Publishing, 1984.

Lloyd, Harold, with Wesley Stout. *An American Comedy.* New York: Longman's, Green and Co., 1928. (Also 1971 reprint.)

Love, Bessie. *From Hollywood With Love.* London: Elm Tree Books, 1977.

Loy, Myrna, with James Kotsilibas-Davis. *Being and Becoming.* New York: Alfred A. Knopf, 1987.

MacCann, Richard Dyer. *The First Tycoons.* Metuchen, N.J.: Scarecrow Press, 1987.

MacGowan, Kenneth. *Behind the Screen.* New York: Delacorte Press, 1965.

Madsen, Axel. *William Wyler.* New York: Thomas Crowell, 1973.

Maltin, Leonard. *The Art of the Cinematographer.* New York: Dover, 1978.

Marill, Alvin H. *Samuel Goldwyn Presents.* South Brunswick, N.J.: A. S. Barnes, 1976.

Marx, Arthur. *Goldwyn.* New York: Norton, 1976.

Marx, Groucho, with Richard Anobile. *The Marx Bros. Scrapbook.* New York: Darien House, 1973.

Marx, Harpo, with Rowland Barber. *Harpo Speaks.* New York: Bernard Geis, 1961.

Marx, Samuel. *Mayer and Thalberg*. New York: Random House, 1975.

Mast, Gerald. *The Comic Mind*. Chicago: University of Chicago Press, 1979.

———. *A Short History of the Movies*. 4th ed. New York: Macmillan, 1986.

McCoy, Tim, with Ronald McCoy. *Tim McCoy Remembers the West*. Garden City, N.Y.: Doubleday, 1977.

McGilligan, Pat, ed. *Backstory*. Berkeley: University of California Press, 1986.

Menjou, Adolphe, with M. M. Musselman. *It Took Nine Tailors*. New York: Whittlesey House, 1948.

Meryman, Richard. *Mank*. New York: William Morrow, 1978.

Miller, Patsy Ruth. *My Hollywood: When Both of Us Were Young*. Atlantic City, N.J.: O'Raghailligh Ltd., 1988.

Milne, Tom. *Mamoulian*. Bloomington: Indiana University Press, 1969.

Moore, Colleen. *Silent Star*. Garden City, N.Y.: Doubleday, 1968.

Mordden, Ethan. *The Hollywood Musical*. New York: St. Martin's Press, 1981.

Nugent, J. C. *It's a Great Life*. New York: The Dial Press, 1940.

O'Leary, Liam. *Rex Ingram*. Dublin: The Academy Press, 1980.

Paris, Barry. *Garbo*. New York: Alfred A. Knopf, 1994.

———. *Louise Brooks*. New York: Alfred A. Knopf, 1989.

Parish, James Robert, and Michael Pitts. *Film Directors: A Guide to Their American Films*. Metuchen, N.J.: Scarecrow Press, 1974.

Payne, Robert. *The Great Garbo*. New York: Praeger, 1976.

Peters, Margot. *The House of Barrymore*. New York: Alfred A. Knopf, 1990.

Powell, Michael. *A Life in Movies*. New York: Alfred A. Knopf, 1987.

Pratt, George C. *Spellbound in Darkness*. Greenwich, Conn.: New York Graphic Society, 1973.

Ralston, Esther. *Someday We'll Laugh*. Metuchen, N.J.: Scarecrow Press, 1985.

Rathbun, John B. *Motion Picture Making and Exhibiting*. Chicago: Charles C. Thompson Co., 1914.

Ringgold, Gene, and DeWitt Bodeen. *The Films of Cecil B. DeMille*. New York: Cadillac Publishing, 1969.

Riva, Maria. *Marlene Dietrich*. New York: Alfred A. Knopf, 1993.

Robinson, David. *Chaplin: His Life and Art*. New York: McGraw-Hill, 1985.

Robinson, Edward G., with Leonard Spigelgass. *All My Yesterdays*. New York: Hawthorn Books, 1973.

Rosenberg, Bernard, and Harry Silverstein. *The Real Tinsel*. New York: Macmillan, 1970.

Sarris, Andrew. *The Films of Josef von Sternberg*. New York: Museum of Modern Art, 1966.

Schickel, Richard. *D. W. Griffith: An American Life*. New York: Simon and Schuster, 1984.

Seldes, Gilbert. *An Hour with the Movies and the Talkies*. Philadelphia: Lippincott, 1929.

Sennett, Ted. *Hollywood Musicals*. New York: Harry N. Abrams, 1981.

Shorris, Sylvia, and Marion Abbott Bundy. *Talking Pictures*. New York: The New Press, 1994.

Silke, James R. *Here's Looking at You, Kid*. Boston: Little, Brown, 1976.

Sinclair, Upton. *Upton Sinclair Presents William Fox*. Los Angeles: Sinclair, 1933.

Skal, David J. *The Monster Show: A Cultural History of Horror*. New York: Norton, 1993.

Sklar, Robert. *Film: An International History of the Medium*. New York: Harry N. Abrams, 1993.

———. *Movie-Made America*. 2nd ed. New York: Vintage Books, 1994.

Skretvedt, Randy. *Laurel and Hardy: The Magic Behind the Movies*. Beverly Hills: Moonstone Press, 1987.

Slide, Anthony. *Encyclopedia of Vaudeville*. Westport, Conn.: Greenwood Press, 1984.

———, ed. *The Picture Dancing on the Screen*. Vestal, N.Y.: The Vestal Press, 1988.

———. *Selected Film Criticism, 1921–1930*. Metuchen, N.J.: Scarecrow Press, 1982.

Sperling, Cass Warner, with Cork Millner and Jack Warner Jr. *Hollywood Be Thy Name*. Rocklin, Ca.: Prima Publishing, 1994.

Steen, Mike. *Hollywood Speaks*. New York: G. P. Putnam's Sons, 1974.

Stempel, Tom. *Framework*. New York: Continuum, 1988.

Stenn, David. *Clara Bow: Runnin' Wild*. New York: Doubleday, 1988.

Sterling, Anna Kate. *Cinematographers on the Art and Craft of Cinematography*. Metuchen, N.J.: Scarecrow Press, 1987.

Sterling, Bryan, and Frances Sterling. *Will Rogers in Hollywood*. New York: Crown Publishers, 1984.

Swindell, Larry. *Spencer Tracy*. New York: World Publishing, 1969.

Taves, Brian. *Robert Florey*. Metuchen, N.J.: Scarecrow Press, 1987.

Thomas, Bob. *Clown Prince of Hollywood*. New York: McGraw-Hill, 1990.

———. *Thalberg*. Garden City, N.Y.: Doubleday, 1969.

Thomas, Tony. *Howard Hughes in Hollywood*. Secaucus, N.J.: Citadel Press, 1985.

Thompson, Frank T. *William A. Wellman*. Metuchen, N.J.: Scarecrow Press, 1983.

Thrasher, Frederic M., ed. *Okay for Sound!* New York: Duell, Sloan and Pearce, 1946.

Turner, George E., ed. *The Cinema of Adventure, Romance & Terror*. Hollywood: The ASC Press, 1989.

Tuska, Jon. *The Filming of the West*. Garden City, N.Y.: Doubleday, 1976.

Usai, Paolo Cherchi, and Lorenzo Codelli, eds. *The DeMille Legacy*. Pordenone: Le Giornate del Cinema Muto, 1991.

Vidor, King. *King Vidor on Filmmaking*. New York: David McKay, 1972.

———. *A Tree Is a Tree*. New York: Harcourt, Brace and Co., 1952.

Viertel, Salka. *The Kindness of Strangers*. New York: Holt, Rinehart & Winston, 1969.

von Sternberg, Josef. *Fun in a Chinese Laundry*. New York: Macmillan, 1965.

Wagner, Paul, *I Just Can't See Daylight*... In *Fitzgerald/Hemingway Annual, 1970*. Edited by Matthew J. Bruccoli. Columbia: University of South Carolina Press, 1970.

Wagner, Walter. *You Must Remember This*. New York: G. P. Putnam's Sons, 1975.

Walker, Alexander. *Garbo*. New York: Macmillan, 1980.

——. *The Shattered Silents*. New York: William Morrow, 1979.

——. *Stardom*. New York: Stein and Day, 1970.

Walker, Joseph, with Juanita Walker. *The Light on Her Face*. Hollywood: The ASC Press, 1984.

Wallis, Hal, with Charles Higham. *Starmaker*. New York: Macmillan, 1980.

Walsh, Raoul. *Each Man in His Time*. New York: Farrar, Straus and Giroux, 1974.

Warner, Jack. *My First Hundred Years in Hollywood*. New York: Random House, 1964.

Wood, Leslie. *The Romance of the Movies*. London: Heinemann, 1937.

Yagoda, Ben. *Will Rogers*. New York: Alfred A. Knopf, 1993.

Ziegfeld, Richard, and Paulette Ziegfeld. *The Ziegfeld Touch*. New York: Harry N. Abrams, 1993.

Zukor, Adolph, with Dale Kramer. *The Public Is Never Wrong*. New York: G. P. Putnam's Sons, 1953.

Also consulted were the *Film Daily* Yearbooks for 1926–1932.

Index